THE OTHER SIDE OF THE POPUL

GARETH WILLIAMS

The Other Side of the Popular

NEOLIBERALISM AND SUBALTERNITY

IN LATIN AMERICA

Duke University Press   *Durham & London*   2002

In loving memory of Eldred Williams

After so much effort I have lost the train of reason,

of names, and all my stories are unravelling. I bleed, lie a lot.

Now, barely warmed by a glass of wine, I wonder—in what

state of collapse will I have to outlast the harshness of winter?

—DIAMELA ELTIT, *Sacred Cow*

I believe that utopianism lies not in intentions, however

praiseworthy, but in the articulation of language. The utopian

question is a simple one: what possibilities today lie beyond

reality?—CARLOS MONSIVÁIS, *Mexican Postcards*

CONTENTS

ACKNOWLEDGMENTS

The ideas for this book emerged over a period of years and are the result of my sustained dialogue and discussion with a number of people who share the practical concerns and theoretical interests represented in these pages. I thank all of these people for their remarkable intelligence and loyal friendship and support over the last six or seven years. Since this book would never have been formulated (much less completed) without them, I would like to think that they will be able to recognize their fundamental contributions to its completion. If, for any reason, they cannot, the fault lies fully in my hands and I apologize sincerely.

First and foremost I express my indebtedness and gratitude to Alberto Moreiras whose long-standing friendship and unflagging commitment to open, honest dialogue and debate have been exemplary. Alongside him I would also like to acknowledge a number of people who, over the years, and through sometimes quite intense discussions and e-mail exchanges, have left their indelible mark on the conceptual development of this book. They are Jon Beasley-Murray, John Beverley, John Kraniauskas, Horacio Legrás, Brett Levinson, Cristina Moreiras Menor, Ileana Rodríguez, Teresa Vilarós, and George Yúdice. In similar fashion I would also like to extend my thanks and enormous appreciation to the following people for their valued friendship, sustained dialogue, and support: Marco Dorfsman, Lori Hopkins, Guillermo Irizarry, Daniel James, Anne Lambright, Ramonita Marcano Ogando, Celio Pichardo, Nelly Richard, and Willy Thayer.

A few added words of appreciation are necessary. I would like to thank Ann Wightman for her intelligence, integrity, and support at all times. Without the commitment and guidance of Reynolds Smith at Duke University Press this book might never have seen the light of day. I would also like to acknowledge Paz Errázuriz for giving me permission to include a number of her photographs in the book's final chapter.

To my parents, Shirl and Ed, my family, and my long-standing friendships in the United Kingdom I offer my unmeasureable indebtedness. Somehow or other (though I'm not sure what its mechanisms actually are) this book originates in, yet displaces, the relation between Thatcherism and the Liverpool of the early to mid-1980s. The Falklands/Malvinas war, the battle against the miners, the Toxteth riots, mass unemployment, and migration southward or abroad in search of employment are all traces of things that have not yet been erased for me and these pages bear witness to the persistence of their specters. Finally, this book is dedicated to the ones I love: Cristina, Carlos, and Elena with my thanks for putting up with so much.

Acknowledgments

INTRODUCTION

In this book I examine the uneven, incomplete, and ongoing passage from national to postnational cultural and political paradigms in Latin America, with the understanding that postnational does not signify the final demise of the nation but, rather, its profound and far-reaching redefinition and restructuration in the face of increasingly transnational realities. The analyses included in this volume draw specifically on literature, film, popular culture, and theoretical reflection on the relation between modern Latin American national histories and postmodern state and culture formations. This interdisciplinary approach to contemporary social, political, and cultural processes allows me to discuss the complexity of some of the distinct periods of transition that, over the course of the last three decades, have risen to the fore of intellectual, popular, and governmental concerns in, for example, Mexico, Central America (El Salvador), the Andes (Peru), the Southern Cone (Argentina and Chile), and the United States.

This volume is a meditation on the distinct terms, conditions, and limits (as well as on the profound differences generated from within and as a result) of Latin America's continued and often violent insertion into late capitalism and its increasingly global networks of accumulation. However, the book also raises the question of the thinkability of that order, together with reflection's relation to social change, in what are generally hailed to be postrevolutionary times. It is an evaluation of inherited conceptual and representational systems, and of their limits and usefulness (or lack thereof), when thinking through the conditions of the current historical transition *away from* the national revolutionary period and *into* the passage toward global accumulation.

A few words here are necessary regarding, first, the overall structure of the book and, second, its title. Following this I will give a preliminary overview of the issues and themes presented in each chapter.

As already noted, this book includes specific evaluations of the passage from national to transnational realities in direct reference to Mexico, Peru, El Salvador, Argentina, and Chile. It also includes brief analyses of Venezuelan, Ecuadorian, and Bolivian culture and state formations, together with a chapter dealing with the ways in which recent Latin

American cultural production (*testimonio,* for example) has been read and appropriated in the United States. As a result of presenting and thinking through the enormous cultural and political complexities underlying Latin America's different passages toward transnationalism, I will not provide myself (or the reader, for that matter) with the false sense of comfort that derives from the establishment of a single unitary model of analysis, from the forceful imposition of a privileged method of interpretation, or from the consolidation of an exclusive geographical or cultural ground from which to think about current transnational realities. This is not to say, of course, that there are no lines of cultural or interpretative continuity within the book. There are very specific and concrete relations between chapters and between the analyses contained therein, which point to the notion of subalternity as a privileged category and critical perspective from which to grapple with the complexities of current cultural and political configurations in Latin America.

In the passage from modernity to postmodernity the grounds and frontiers of Latin American regional and national cultures, traditions, and patrimonies are being opened up and transformed with an intensity and depth that have probably never been seen or experienced before. As a result, the relatively recent integration of national economies into the new world order raises a series of questions regarding modernization, modernity, postmodernity, and pluralism in contemporary Latin America. Recent phenomena—for example, mass migration; the newly established friendship between George W. Bush and Vicente Fox; the recent decision of the Republican and Democratic parties to provide presidential radio addresses and rebuttals in both English and Spanish; the formal and informal "dollarization" of Latin American national economies from Cuba to Argentina; and the emergence of an informal yet highly organized barter economy for the exchange of goods and services throughout Argentina, Chile, Bolivia, and elsewhere (a decidedly premodern form of social organization that is nevertheless coordinated through the Internet)—are obvious indications that something is happening to the grounds and frontiers of Latin American nations. Something is happening to the underlying telos of nationhood and of national identity formations, and the shifts that I consider in these pages appear to be exhausting the value of unitary models of analysis, of singular interpretative structures, and of specific methodological or disciplinary approaches to contemporary Latin American realities and forms of cultural production.

In contrast to such approaches, and as a result of having taken very seriously Richard Beardsworth's important and yet quite simple reminder that "a thinker with a method has already decided *how* to proceed, is unable to give him or herself up to the matter of thought in hand, is a functionary of the criteria which structure his or her conceptual gestures" (4), in this volume I have chosen to write on the limits of (and as a means of questioning) functionary or masterful conceptual and disciplinary approaches. After all, these are times in which there is no longer a single master discourse capable of mapping out a new path for our understanding of self, society, or, for that matter, the world. As a result, my work should be read as a hybrid and inherently incomplete accumulation of distinct processes of approximation toward the contemporary. I am less interested in the possibility of providing an all-encompassing explanation for, or of promising the revelation of a singular truth in regard to, recent Latin American cultural and social histories than I am in advancing discussion on the ways in which distinct histories, realities, and representations can be evaluated at the current time in cultural and political terms. It is for this reason that the book is not designed to lay claim to a specific or unique conclusion or final omniscient vision of the present. If I were to presume such a possibility—an interpretative or conceptual resolution or completeness of sorts—then the book would be grounded implicitly in the silent affirmation of foundational notions such as historical transcendence, development, or homogeneity.

In contrast, this volume calls attention to the fact that if there is a cultural politics that is in tune with the times it has to be grounded in the interruption or suspension of all forms of foundationalism. In particular, it has to be anchored in the interruption of those critical paradigms that strived to consolidate the historical formation of the nation along with its concomitant cultural nationalisms. Contemporary thought, in this sense, can only resonate from within the ruins of modern history's foundational narratives.

It is for this reason that I argue that the Gramscian notion of subalternity—a category that has been taken up and reworked in recent years by, among others, the members of the South Asian Subaltern Studies Group as well as the members of the former Latin American Subaltern Studies Group—can provide a fundamental yet nonfoundational and nondevelopmentalist critical perspective from which to examine the cultural production of the last thirty years in Latin America. It is also for this very reason that this volume has been structured (indeed, can probably only be read) as a collage or patchwork of interconnected fragments, instances, or flashes designed to shed light on distinct cultural and social specificities, as well as on a number of theoretical questions relating to subalternity that strive to think through the heterogeneity of, and the disparities between, Latin America's current social orders, dominant discourses, and subaltern responses. In this sense, the overall structure of the book uncovers a fragmentary point of view that undermines any critical investment in omniscience, homogeneity, or disciplinary mastery.

With this in mind, what is to be understood by my title: *The Other Side of the Popular*? This act of naming signifies on two distinct yet intimately related levels. The first is historical; the second is theoretical and calls attention to the hegemony/subalternity relation.

In a recent essay Horacio Legrás made the following important observation regarding the history of national development in Latin America:

> The universal development of capitalism shapes the identity of modern Latin America; but simultaneously a developmentalist historical model is unable to account for the many principles of alterity confronting the modernizing paradigm. Those alternative forms of organization are, in most cases, referred to as pre-capitalist, feudal, residual or simply recalcitrantly local. The developmentalist paradigm relied on the nation as the all powerful form through which the discourse of modernization, linear development and the obliteration of any nonmodern form was to be instrumented in the region. (92)

As Legrás notes, and as the numerous cultural histories of the twentieth century demonstrate, the universal development of capitalism in Latin America was largely predicated on the formation of the modern nation-state. However, the formation of the modern nation-state in Latin America (dating roughly from the decades immediately preceding and following the Great Depression through to the debt crisis and the economic collapse of the 1980s) was for the most part predicated on the active integration and institutionalization of the notion of the people—of the common populace, or the popular/subaltern sectors of society—as the originary ground from which to consider the contours of national history, national identity formations, and national modernization. From the monumental, all-inclusive public art of Diego Rivera, José Clemente Orozco, and David Siqueiros in postrevolutionary Mexico to Andean literary *indigenismo;* from the so-called New Man of postrevolutionary Cuba to the poetics of Sandinismo in the Nicaragua of the 1970s and 1980s, what appeared to be at stake in the shaping of modern Latin America was the incorporation, representation, and institutionalization of the individual as *homo nationalis* at the same time as he (but rarely she) was to be instituted also as *homo economicus* and *homo politicus* (Balibar, "Nation" 93). The idea of the people and, along with it, the concept of the popular, came to be construed as a potentially hegemonic formation designed to suture the totality of the nation's demographic and cultural differences to the formation and expansion of the nation-state.

In this sense, the terms of state capitalist (and, of course, socialist) hegemony came to be predicated on the people's ability to reproduce itself continually as a national community, as a single-willed "national-popular" community, and therefore as a constituted synthesis of multiple racial, ethnic, regional, and cultural (but rarely gendered) identities negotiated from within, and reflected directly through, the nation-state's relation to regional and national territory, as well as to the promise of national capitalist development. For this reason the production and institutionalization of the people—of *homo nationalis*—came to be negotiated (often violently) from within populist—that is, integration-oriented—state configurations that were considered by social elites to be *the* condition of possibility for the articulation of positive equivalences between diverse populations. Popular integration was deemed to be fundamental for the consolidation of state hegemony, for the formation of disciplined national industrial labor forces (for *homo laborans*), for capitalist/socialist development, for the successful nationalization of society and, ultimately, for the end to Latin America's socioeconomic and cultural backwardness. However, although populist integration-oriented policies allowed for the inclusion of the people into civil society, for the most part they kept the ideological state apparatuses firmly in the grasp of the oligarchic classes.

As the work of Ernesto Laclau and Chantal Mouffe has clearly demonstrated, the articulation of positive equivalences between heterogeneous populations and divergent social sectors (for example, the state's articulation of the nation as a people and of the people as a national community defined by and through the state in Latin America) always constitutes itself in relation to something beyond or outside the social field defined by the production of positive equivalences themselves. Hence, in Latin America the populist nation-state forged its normative identities and languages against supposedly nonnormative (for example, non-Spanish-speaking or non-Hispanic) identities, as a means of constituting the grounds and limits of its own hegemonic field. As can be seen, for example, in postrevolutionary Mexico's promotion of the mestizo as *the* identity of the nation, or in Rafael Leónidas Trujillo's promotion of the Dominican Republic's hispanic heritage as *the* privileged ground on which to forge national culture (in direct opposition, of course, to the perceived threat posed by Haiti's Africanness), populist integration-oriented hegemony forges common geographies, histories, identities, and destinies.

As the history of capitalist development in Latin America demonstrates, however, hegemony also constitutes the grounds of subalternity. It actively forges the terrain on which subaltern/nonnational populations, social groupings, or imaginaries are integrated into the nation as exceptions, as examples of forms of membership in the nation that are included without inclusion. Populist hegemony either condemns subalternity to absolute exclusion, or it introduces it into the social field as a subordinate and potentially negative condition that nevertheless upholds and guarantees the constitution of the hegemonic. Populist state hegemony therefore creates the conditions of its own potential "unworking" as it consolidates itself through specific relations to its negative outsides. It imposes itself from above as a constitutive rule or natural social law that is always in relation to, in the name of, and against those potentially disruptive outsides that exceed it or that exist on its outer margins (that is, simultaneously within and without it). Either through its total exclusion or through its integration into hegemony as its negative and subordinate partner, subalternity becomes hegemony's real or potential site of suspension or breakdown. Subalternity therefore corresponds to "a principle of external negativity" (Legrás 88) that is always capable of interrupting or unworking hegemonic social or conceptual systems. Indeed, as Horacio Legrás observes, the historical failure of the Latin American nation-state lies in its failure to grant the condition of citizen to all its inhabitants. In his words, "While the nation-state [proclaimed] its commitment to inclusive politics, the reality [was] everywhere a matter of sheer exclusion" (92). Indeed, "part of this 'failure' [was due to] the success of popular sectors to resist some forms of citizenship promoted by local elites and international powers" (92).

As a result of the persistent failure of the Latin American nation-states to integrate all their inhabitants as citizens with equal rights, equal protection, and equal representation, the category of the people very often came to be articulated from within popular sectors in direct opposition to the power bloc that had created the conditions for its initial emergence, organization, and institutionalization. Originally required and represented as desirable by the modern nation-state system (as the popular origin of national history, identity, and development), the national-popular very often articulated alternative ways of imagining the nation and its internal economic and cultural realities. As a result, by the late 1960s the nation-state became increasingly entrenched in militarized national security policies designed to keep the lid on social tensions and on the increasing possibility of popular insurrection and revolution.

The nation-state's need to produce the people as a national community capable of forging state hegemony, and thereby of consolidating the universal history of capitalist development in Latin America, largely paved the way for the people/power bloc antagonisms (Laclau, "Towards") that fueled the revolutionary period of post–World War II Latin America. As a result of the gradual intensification in national people/power bloc antagonisms that characterized much of the second half of the twentieth century (dating roughly from the consolidation of cold war conditions in 1948 to the economic crises of the 1980s), by the late 1960s the threat or possibility of revolution became the dominant horizon for Latin American subaltern and intellectual sectors, as well as for the nation-states themselves. As Alberto Moreiras indicates:

> The Latin American national security state made politics turn around the issue of revolution, in the sense that it was understood as a national revolution. Cultural workers of all shades in the political spectrum were forced to confront the revolutionary question, since that was, it was thought, what ultimately regulated their relationship to the state. The perception of culture was therefore heavily determined by national politics, although national politics was understood, according to individual political positions, through the prism of class and interclass alliances around the primary revolutionary possibility. ("Aura" 193)

Needless to say, the profound economic and sociocultural transformations of the last thirty years, together with the recent emergence of the so-called neoliberal order, denote a radical shift and a fundamental weakening in the foundations of the modern nation-state. These recent phenomena also pose serious challenges to the idea of popular national integration—to the idea of *hòmo nationalis*—as either a reality denoting actual institutional inclusion and representation, or, for that matter, as a viable working concept in the present.

At least since the 1980s the national revolutionary question or possibility has entered a period characterized by profound practical and theoretical crisis. The modernizing drive of the national-popular period of development—the nation-state's drive to both forge and control the contours of *homo nationalis,* in other words—has been, and is still in the process of becoming, eclipsed. With this in mind, the title of this volume insinuates that the contemporary orders of Latin America (now generically termed the neoliberal order) signify the demise of the people as a constituted force visible exclusively in its relation to and through the nation-state, its discretely bordered territories, and its forging of national social and cultural hegemonies.

Quite literally, transnationalization and the insertion of Latin American nations into global networks has ungrounded the nation-state and, alongside it, the transformational potential of the national-popular. It has brought the nation-state and the national-popular (Gramsci's "nation-people") to their economic, institutional, and conceptual knees. Therefore, through increasing transnationalization we are living the historical "other side" of the national-popular; the (collapsed/collapsing) side of the people; the national-popular in its state of exhaustion and redistribution across regional and national frontiers.

As already indicated, "the other side of the popular" refers not just to the demise of the national modernizing paradigm and of the fabrication and integration of the people as the foundational ground for national capitalist and cultural development, it also refers in theoretical terms to the hegemony/subalternity relation. Under what are now post–cold war conditions the proliferation of nonnational social movements and postnational capital and demographic flows attests to the increasing exhaustion of previously hegemonic national models, cultural forms, and critical languages. The emergence of these nonnational movements and postnational flows bears witness to a marked decline in the way sociopolitical and cultural praxis can be articulated from within exclusively national horizons. As a result, previous forms of epistemological and political mediation between the state, culture, and cultural workers now seem to have succumbed to a certain historical limit of functionality and thinkability. Quite simply, the underlying telos for social mediation and for sustained reflection on the politics of culture in Latin America—namely, the developmentalist modernization of the nation-state and its relation to historical forms of "people production"—has shifted so profoundly in recent years that contemporary thought can only fulfill itself in relation to the conceptual ruins and fragments that it now inherits from its multiple national-popular pasts.

Needless to say, the weakening of a certain telos from which to think does not indicate the end of reflection. On the contrary, it demands it. Hence, in the following chapters I trace the contours of a finitude—of a certain historical, epistemological, and political limit—that seems to have emerged from within, and as a result of, the failure of previously hegemonic forms of social thought and of cultural mediation. Thus in this volume I think through the nature of neoliberalism as the peculiar disclosure of a finitude at which national cultural histories continue, and yet appear to exhaust themselves from within the very performance of their cultural continuities (that is, from within their day-to-day business).

In this sense, I examine the emergence in recent years of the neoliberal order as the coming into being of a historical, epistemological, cultural, and political limit at which the social imperatives and conceptual systems of the past reveal themselves as still here and, indeed, still as imperatives. But they do so precisely by uncovering themselves as inheritances and imperatives that are no longer viable as such—that is, as they used to be. In the current order of global accumulation it is becoming increasingly obvious that words such as "nation," "the people," "development," or "national culture" can no longer mean what they used to mean in Latin America. They can no longer have the same conceptual value that they had before the advent of global capitalism, before the integration of Latin American economies into transnational configurations, before the demise of "actually existing socialism," and before the emergence of the new world order. Indeed, I would hazard to say that this is the case precisely because the underlying philosophical, political, cultural, and economic presuppositions that defined their meaning and that brought them into the field of social reproduction after the emergence of the Latin American nation-states in the nineteenth century have, for all intents and purposes, succumbed to the nihilisms that grounded them for decades.

The question, then, is how to think about the politics of culture in Latin America when the terrain for the forging of national sociocultural hegemonies and/or counterhegemonies—or, for that matter, the underlying terrain from which the history of modern Latin American thought itself emerged—has shifted so radically and so profoundly in recent years. Is there a way of thinking of and engaging recent cultural production and processes of state re-formation that can account not just for the historical transition to transnationalism but also for the possible definition of future political communities and commonalities? How, in other words, do we articulate a theoretically grounded reflection on what remains after, and perhaps exceeds, the uneven and incomplete histories of national development in Latin America as well as those of an even more uneven and incomplete transnationalism? If we understand Latin America's current transnational regimes of accumulation as the effect of a seismic shift in the production of meaning and of sense production themselves—as the effect of a historical transformation in what Jean-Luc Nancy has called "the sense of the world" in his book by that title—then one of the many challenges for contemporary thought is that of indicating a common ground or measure from which to think the parameters of a possible future cultural politics.

As mentioned earlier, in this book I argue that the notion of subalternity can provide us with an important critical perspective from which to examine the cultural production in Latin America, as well as the social, economic, and cultural transformations that have occurred there in the last thirty years.

As Ranajit Guha noted in his preface to *Selected Subaltern Studies* (and as John Beverley has discussed more recently [*Subalternity*]), the term "subaltern" can be defined as "a name for the general attribute of subordination . . . whether this is expressed in terms of class, caste, age, gender and office or in any other way" (35). However, in her introduction to the same volume, Gayatri Spivak supplements Guha's essentially historical-materialist approach to the subaltern by articulating a definition that, I believe, has potentially profound and far-reaching effects for theoretical and philosophical reflection as a whole. In Spivak's formulation "the subaltern is necessarily the absolute limit of the place where history is narrativized into logic" (16). For Spivak, then, subalternity is not just the material/social effect of the ways in which hegemony guarantees subordination. It is also, as she says, the ground for "a theory of reading in the strongest possible general sense" (4). Subalternity points to the site in both the social field and in the philosophical/epistemological realms at which the displacement from hegemonic to nonhegemonic sign systems may occur. Therefore, for Spivak the category of subalternity upholds the possibility of disrupting hegemonic chains of signification and of re-linking them in perhaps new nonhegemonic ways. As such, subalternity promises a displacement of the function of hegemonic sign systems and upholds "the name of reading as active transaction between past and future" (5). It suggests the possibility of reading culture in relation to a new theoretical telos, the intimations of which can be glimpsed from within the suspension or interruption of hegemony's logics and sociocultural horizons. This labor of disruption, Spivak suggests, is subalternity's philosophical and political potentiality. It is its relation to the future and to the possible generation of alternative critical narratives.

In this volume I understand the category of subalternity in the terms articulated by both Guha and Spivak. I consider it to be the often violent subject-effect of national and postnational processes of social subordination, but also as the epistemological limit at which the nonhegemonic announces the limits of hegemonic thought and of hegemony thinking. In my use of the term, then, there is no resolution in the relation between Guha's and Spivak's definitions. There is no privileging of one definition over the other. I merely approach the question of subalternity as a site of practical and theoretical tension between the historical-materialist and the philosophical-deconstructive. As a result, I read subalternity as the trace of a political telos within the sociopolitical and epistemological fields and therefore within and on the limits of our current conceptual systems, at which hegemonic (and, in the case of Latin America, that means predominantly developmentalist) reflection is confronted and destabilized by the emergence of its own limit of thinkability.

Subalternity is therefore the name for the multifarious points of excess within the national and postnational histories of Latin American developmentalism. It is the limit at which hegemonic narratives and dominant modes of social and intellectual (re)production encounter their points of radical unworkability. As a result it brings hegemonic thought (and in Latin America this invariably means hegemonic Creole thought) face to face with imminent ruin. And by doing this it keeps alive the demand for reflection and for a sustained politics of culture.

In this volume, then, subalternity stands not just as a specific dispossessed individual or downtrodden and marginalized collective subjectivity, but as the site within any given social field (be it regional, national, or postnational) at which the very relation between hegemony and hegemony's exclusions—its constitutive outsides, in other words—interrupts the natural(ized) logics and representations that underlie hegemony's ability to reproduce itself in institutional and epistemological terms. The notion of subalternity promises to interrupt, for example, hegemony's ability to hegemonize. It suspends Creole hegemony's ability to represent itself and reproduce itself as hegemonic, as the single producer of common geographies, common histories, and common destinies in both national and postnational times.

In this sense, subalternity constitutes the possibility of, and yet promises to destabilize, hegemony's often neocolonial expansion of its universalizing social logics. It is the disclosure of a relation between hegemony and its outsides that obliges a consideration of its own relation to practical and theoretical excess. It obliges us to commit to a thought of relationality and of potential finitude. It is therefore the promise of a radical interruption within any given hegemonic conceptual system, for it undoes the naturalized constitution of that system and thereby establishes the demand for other relations between critical reason and its cultural objects. As a result, it marks the promise of a negative telos at which the politics of culture both stops, as such, and simultaneously begins (perhaps otherwise). Subalternity, then, is a limit to constituted power that is potentially constitutive of alternative forms of thinking, reading, and acting.

At this point I would like to give a brief discussion of the chapters that comprise this book. As already noted, my work is both an examination of the emergence of the neoliberal social order in Latin America and an evaluation of the ways in which to think about it in cultural and political terms. It is an analysis of the failure of the modern nation to come to its own, as well as an examination of modernization's sustained historical unevenness and incompletion. As such, this volume is a discussion of notions such as transculturation, hybridity, and identitarian difference, but it is also a reflection on the limits of their attendant cultural and critical narratives, on the limits of their disciplinary models of figuration, and on what I view as being the demand to reevaluate them at the current time.

I have already characterized the overall structure of the book as a collage or patchwork of interconnected instances, or flashes, disclosing a fragmentary perspective designed to undermine critical investments in omniscience, mastery, completion, or transcendence. With this in mind, I have divided the book into three distinct yet interrelated sections. The first section, titled "Closure," examines some of the limits characterizing three of the dominant discourses within contemporary reflection on Latin America. Chapter 1 examines transculturation and its ideological position within the wider field of the nation-state and national culture formation in twentieth-century Latin America. Chapter 2 traces the North's intellectual investments in the notion of the subaltern, together with the way that category has emerged in recent years as a cultural, political, and epistemological response to the overall crisis of the nation-state, national developmentalism, and the people/power bloc antagonisms that fueled the civil conflicts of the cold war years. Finally, chapter 3 analyzes the intimate and uncomfortable relationship between the notion of cultural hybridity (which rose to the fore of critical concerns in the 1990s) and neoliberal discourses of the marketplace, consumption, and citizenship in contemporary Mexico.

Through my critique of the notion, ideology, and writing of transculturation, in chapter 1 I analyze the limits of the underlying structures and codes of cultural and political legitimation—the hegemonic and hegemonizing paradigms—that dominated the uneven formation of Latin American national modernities and some of their respective cultural and literary traditions. I posit, not uncontroversially perhaps, that in spite of its investment in the notion of cultural difference the thought of transculturation was for the most part predicated on the possibility of fixing the notion of peoplehood (and therefore of national identity) within state-generated narratives of common histories and shared collective destinies. I offer, then, a traditional reconstruction of genesis that nevertheless calls attention to the limits of its own construction by positioning the thought of transculturation as the symptom, or cultural effect, of wider drives and desires of the state for capitalist modernization.

In chapter 1 I question the term "transculturation" by reading it not just as a space of popular or subaltern self-definition (which is how it appeared in Angel Rama's groundbreaking *Transculturación narrativa en América Latina,* for example) but rather (and more problematically, I think) as a thought of development, of hegemony, and of the state. In other words, I examine the notion of transculturation in order to historicize its relation to what could be called the more conservative structures of populism. In doing this, I also shed light on the fine line between the construction and negotiation of plurality in Latin America and the sustained Creole demand for hegemony.

In chapter 2 I continue my discussion by examining the initial conditions of emergence of a counterhegemonic thought of difference in the North American academy. This critical discourse surfaced in the 1980s as a response to the crisis of national development, of state discourses of popular integration, of the national-popular, and of the national revolutionary configurations of the South. In this chapter I call attention to the limits of, and the uncomfortable lines of continuity between, the crisis of the integrative national-popular model and the emergence of an identity-based politics of subaltern difference as a political and cultural alternative in the North. Through my discussion of the Latin American Subaltern Studies Group's founding statement, together with the analysis of a number of intellectual interventions dating from the first half of the 1990s, I shed light on the epistemological, ideological, and geopolitical constraints of northern intellectual interventions (my own included) that are grounded in the recuperation and representation of the notion of peoplehood and of common subaltern identities and agencies negotiated from within the hegemonic structures of the postmodern U.S. academy.

In chapter 3 I shift the terrain of critique from a predominantly northern model of political and cultural engagement—from the emergence of subaltern expressivity such as *testimonio,* for example—toward the notion of cultural hybridity and the work of Néstor García Canclini. In this chapter I read cultural hybridity together with García Canclini's concomitant forays into questions of consumption and citizenship as direct and important responses to the eclipse of the nation-state as *the* defining structure for the forging of collective cultural and political destinies in Latin America.

Néstor García Canclini's ideas on citizenship and consumption are an important attempt to redefine the notion of civil society along with the possibility of cultural democratization after the exhaustion of state-led national capitalism and its modernizing paradigms. However, in García Canclini's formulations there is a very fine line between the postmodern democratization of culture and the depoliticized dynamics of transnational market management. Indeed, as I argue in this chapter this is a limit that remains to be thought through. As a result, we see that García Canclini's notions of cultural hybridity, consumption, and citizenship implicitly uphold transnational market forces as a new potential universal and as the single most enabling force through which to express peripheral individual and collective desires and needs. However, these same categories fail to conceive of the possibility of a thought other than that which is always already structured and fabricated by, and from within, the managerial logics of neoliberal market forces themselves. In this sense, García Canclini's notion of cultural hybridity is to postmodernity what transculturation was to the modern (national-popular) history of capitalism: namely, the promise of a common cultural ground on which developmentalist paradigms can still be expanded, consolidated, and guaranteed (in other words, rendered hegemonic).

The second section of this volume, titled "Intermezzo . . . Hear Say Yes," marks a point of transition within the book in which my analysis opens up to the relationship between language (and, in particular, literary practice) and the postnational world. By offering a reading of Ricardo Piglia's 1992 novel *La ciudad ausente* (The absent city) I examine the possibility of hearing an affirmation (that is to say, the "yes" of a "common grammar of experience," as Piglia puts it) elaborated through literature and through its specific engagements with the limits of the nation and of national cultural history.

La ciudad ausente establishes explicit relations with the figure of Macedonio Fernández and with James Joyce's *Finnegans Wake*. In doing this it suggests the possibility of a future narrative of collective experience—the promise of a coming *polis*—that remains at all times unconstituted within the narrative itself, yet always imaginable from within the deconstructive and constitutive force and circulation of language itself. In this chapter, then, I read *La ciudad ausente* as an opening up of reflection to the demands (the intimations, the "hear-says") of a future political topos—a future relation to the production of language and to the relation between language and world—that remains on the other side of, and that interrupts or suspends, national history's constituted cultural and social hegemonies. I therefore read the absence signaled in the title of Piglia's novel as an absence that nevertheless signifies in ghostly fashion (at least if we lend it an ear). As my reading of the novel demonstrates, it is a call (from the future) for new ways of articulating and thinking history and the relation between self, society, and the world that positions itself firmly on, and as, the "absolute limit of the place where history is narrativized into logic" (Spivak, "Subaltern" 16).

The question, of course, is how to hear the sounds of that limit and how to make them make sense. In my evaluation of the novel, the absence announced by Piglia's absent city is precisely the same absence that the notion of the other side of the popular reserves for the future: namely, the possibility of a constitutive critical/political reflection grounded in an order and a language *other* than that of the hegemonic/counterhegemonic. As a result, in this chapter I forward the term "posthegemony" as the promising articulation of an *other* (subaltern) telos for reflection and for the critical evaluation of postnational commonalities.

The third section of the book, titled "Perhaps," provides three readings of contemporary Latin American culture that reveal the haunting force of the posthegemonic. This final section of the book opens in direct reference to El Salvador. Through an analysis of Jeffrey Paige's *Coffee and Power,* Manlio Argueta's novel *One Day of Life* (*Un día de vida*), and Mark Danner's journalistic/archeological essay *The Massacre at El Mozote,* I examine the ways in which the sacred embodiment of the Catholic national-popular was thought through and narrativized in the 1980s, as well as the ways in which the militarized nation-state —and the infamous Atlacatl Batallion in particular—responded to the force of that messianic popular corpus through ceremonial sacrificial bloodletting.

My analysis of the representational and performative systems underlining the Salvadoran people/power bloc antagonism of the 1980s allows me to go one step further and think through the exhaustion of that hegemonic/counterhegemonic struggle for the nation-state. By examining transnationalization as the distribution southward of the North's security and economic agendas and as the movement northward of the South's subaltern masses, I then evaluate the passage to postnational cultural and social configurations as a harrowing tremor in the nation's structures and experiences of collective being and belonging. The grounds of this tremor are discussed in relation to a part-*testimonio* of a female Salvadoran "gangbanger"—the daughter of ex-*guerrilleros* now living in South Central Los Angeles—who is an active member of the notorious Eighteenth Street Gang. My analysis of this subaltern part-narrative allows me to consider the difficulties of thinking about the transition from the struggle for hegemony (and for specifically national imaginaries) to the emergence of a posthegemonic migrant imaginary in the North.

Chapter 5 therefore traces the historical transition from the incarnation of the national people/power bloc antagonism in the 1980s to its exhaustion in the 1990s as a result of liberal democracy, hemispheric economic integration, and subaltern displacement. I evaluate the integration of the nation and its peoples into postnational security and economic agendas. And, finally, I think through the complexities that arise as a result of the establishment of South Central Los Angeles as a new (trans)national habitus and cultural threshold at which the nation is inevitably restructured and reimagined (now, however, from beyond the confines of national territory).

In chapter 6 I continue my discussion of the posthegemonic world. I focus on the hegemony/subalternity relation, with particular reference to the mass internal migration from the Andes highlands to the Peruvian coast in the last two decades. In so doing I grapple with the relation between the social violence that characterized the Peru of the 1980s and the neoliberal advent of *fujimorismo* in the 1990s.

Chapter 6 centers on specific evaluations of Mario Vargas Llosa's *La utopía arcaica* (The archaic utopia) and its relation to the exhaustion of literary *indigenismo* in Peru; on Vargas Llosa's novel *Death in the Andes* (*Lituma en los Andes*) and the underlying tensions that this narrative establishes with figures such as José Carlos Mariátegui, Domingo Faustino Sarmiento, and Friedrich Nietzsche; on Francisco Lombardi's internationally acclaimed film *Bajo la piel* (Beneath the skin) and its treatment of social violence, *indigenista* knowledge, and the uses and disadvantages of that knowledge for the consolidation of a post–Shining Path hegemonic order; and on recent sociological readings of *cholaje* (referring to the increasing urbanization of the indigenous masses) and of the challenges that this phenomenon presents to neoliberal reflection on governmentality, governability, and the possible forging of cultural, political, and economic hegemonies in contemporary Peru. Furthermore, these readings are generated in an attempt to come to terms with the complexities of a *chola* (that is, a specifically gendered and culturally hybrid) uprising that occurred in Lima's shantytowns on the eve of Peru's so-called integration into transnational (dominated by the International Monetary Fund) financial configurations.

In this chapter I view neoliberal hegemonization in Peru as predicated on the casting off and consequent "disappearing" of the nation's subaltern insurrectional histories. However, neoliberalism's active and sys-

The Other Side of the Popular

tematic whitewashing of recent history—its powerful investment in historical revisionism, in other words—cannot account fully for the notion of *cholaje*, which remains radically undefinable and unthinkable from within liberal/developmentalist conceptual systems. As a result, *cholaje* sustains the possibility of a semiotic rupture within the foundational discourses of both national and neoliberal hegemony in Peru. As Homi Bhabha would say, *cholaje* is the embodiment of "a shifting boundary that alienates the frontiers of the modern nation" (164). It challenges and undermines the signifying boundaries of hegemonic and counterhegemonic thought by exposing that thought to a negative point of cultural, political, and epistemological interruption. As such, *cholaje* and the hybrid (Andean-urban) social imaginaries that it generates trace a posthegemonic cultural topos that remains always on the limit of the current order's operative whitewashing of past heterogeneities, differences, and negativities. In this sense *cholaje* (and gendered *cholaje* in particular) signals the "absolute limit of the place where [liberal/developmentalist] history is narrativized into logic" (Spivak, "Subaltern" 16). It signifies the place of a posthegemonic "hear-say," the potentiality of which still (and perhaps always) remains to be thought through.

This volume ends with a direct reference to democratic Chile, with an examination of the relation between neoliberal historical revisionism and the idea of community. After an initial discussion of the notion of "perhaps," which names and lends structure to the final section of this book, I (like Nelly Richard before me) proceed to analyze Tomás Moulian's best-seller *Chile actual* (Present-day Chile), alongside and in contrast to the narrative and photographs that comprise Diamela Eltit and Paz Errázuriz's remarkable book *El infarto del alma* (The heart attack of the soul).

In *Chile actual* Tomás Moulian discusses the nation's peaceful transition to liberal democracy in the late 1980s and early 1990s as an institutional ceremony orchestrated by the political and economic elites. As Moulian notes, the passage from dictatorship to democracy was carried out with the specific intention of performing the signs and images of institutional consensus, of systematically whitewashing the violence and injustices of Chile's recent past, and of thereby guaranteeing (against all possible protest) the hegemony of a democratic order born directly out of, and fully dependent for its existence on, the paternalistic good will of General Augusto Pinochet's military regime.

However, in spite of the fact that Moulian challenges the grounds of the hegemonic democratic order by uncovering it as an operative whitewash of the past—as a performative exercise in the production of historical amnesia—his book does not account for any outsides to the cultural and institutional logics that it exposes and critiques. At one point in the narrative Moulian discusses the new democratic government's famous and widely discussed decision to transport an iceberg across the Atlantic Ocean as the centerpiece for Chile's national marquee at the 1992 World Trade Fair in Seville, Spain. The iceberg was intended to be the central symbol of the new (and officially sanitized) image of the New Chile and of its new democratic place in the economic new world order. In this particular section of *Chile actual* Moulian calls attention to the persistence of the nation's negative histories, experiences, and affects. For example, he makes a point of highlighting the blood, screams, and groans of the tortured; the suffering and nostalgia of the exiled; and the long-standing misery of those fired from their jobs for political reasons and left unemployed for years, and the like. Moulian notes that these collective histories, affects, and "hear-says" do exist (that they are "there"), but, as he observes, they are actively excluded from the smooth, clean, and translucent surfaces of the iceberg. However, the histories and affects that Moulian calls attention to in this section are, within the development of his narrative itself, very quickly set aside in favor of returning to his description of operational whitewash. As such, *Chile actual* calls attention to the existence of certain spaces of experiential, discursive, and affective negativity—communitarian zones that could potentially interrupt the smooth mechanisms of the democratic/capitalist amnesia machine—but the book does not seem to be able to avail itself of a critical language that could bring such histories into the field of signification. Rather, it disavows them quite rapidly in order to continue its (on the other hand, very convincing) examination of the positive history of operational whitewash in Chile. Thus the book implicitly upholds the logics of its object of critique. It fails to displace operational whitewash—the dominant institutional sign system of the New Chile—and disavows the possibility of a reading that could be characterized as an active transaction between past and future (Spivak, "Subaltern" 5). The result, of course, is that operational whitewash is implicitly hegemonized from within the very critique of hegemony formation itself.

In contrast, Diamela Eltit and Paz Errázuriz's collective work *El infarto del alma* offers a forceful alternative to Moulian's hegemonizing critique of hegemony, for this is a book that uncovers the kind of communitarian negative spaces that Moulian's text needs to displace in order for it to achieve completion. *El infarto del alma* challenges the possibility of any hegemonic or hegemonizing critical intervention, appropriation, or displacement because it suspends the exercise, force, or imposition of critical reason. It disallows all possible attempts at critical mastery. And by doing so it demands that we reevaluate the relation between critical reason and the posthegemonic subaltern spaces that it strives to think through, negotiate, understand, and thereby appropriate.

El infarto del alma constructs itself on, and as, a limit between textual and photographic representations—a limit conjoining two complimentary, intertwined, yet distinct symbolic bodies—that strives to expose critical reason to the phenomenal proliferation of communities of mad lovers that remain confined within the walls of the Putaendo insane asylum, located on the outskirts of Santiago de Chile. Through my discussion of Eltit and Errázuriz's book—an analysis that is itself repeatedly suspended by the inclusion of Errázuriz's black-and-white portraits of Putaendo's abject and inarticulate communities—I offer as a conclusion a discussion of negative community—"the community of those who have no community," as Georges Bataille called it; the "unavowable community," as Maurice Blanchot named it; or the "inoperative" ("unworked") community, as Jean-Luc Nancy preferred to call it. In this discussion, negative community is viewed as a potential condition of possibility for new constitutive relations between institutionalized thought, theoretical reflection, and the subaltern/posthegemonic specters of the neoliberal social order.

As I argue in this final chapter (indeed, as I argue throughout the second half of the book) the notion of the negative community uncovers forms of commonality that reside on the limit, and as the limit, of the place where history is narrativized into logic (Spivak, "Subaltern" 16). The negative community exposes institutional critical reason—reason's masterful quest to reproduce itself as reason and therefore as hegemonic —to its own point of suspension. In doing this it demands a relation with the Other and with otherness that is itself potentially Other: other than what we have had in the past, beyond what we have in the hegemonic discourses of the present, and, therefore, potentially constitutive of alternative critical pathways. As such, any critical investment in the negative community is an investment in the articulation of future relations and future narratives, because engaging the negative community upholds the task of reading, of thinking, and, indeed, of articulating critical language as an active and committed transaction between the past and the future.

With this transaction in mind, the exposure of thought to the community of those who have no community—its exposure to the scattered communitarian works that suspend the state-related, hegemonic, and profoundly developmentalist idea of the community as a constituted communion between national subjects actively engaged in producing and sharing transparent and fully intelligible territories, common identities, common values, or common destinies—demands that theoretical reflection on the notion of political community open itself up to the potentially constitutive force of the finitude of hegemony, development, and, indeed, intelligibility.

Within the context of Latin America—a context in which the intellectual sectors have for the most part defined themselves as a republic of letters profoundly invested in consolidating and expanding the relation between critical reason, the developmentalist historical model, and the fabrication of cultural and state hegemonies—this constitutive force presupposes a need to reevaluate the nature and purpose of intellectual practice itself. As Paz Errázuriz's portraits of mad lovers clearly illustrate, the notion of the negative community obliges that we expose ourselves, that we expose our thought, and that our thought *be* the active exposure of itself, to the haunting promise of hegemony's and of counter-hegemony's other side. After all, that is where the horizon for interruptive (non- or posthegemonic) cultural, social, and theoretical narratives—indeed, the constitutive potentiality of the future itself—always resides.

Closure

1

The State of Things Passed

Transculturation as National-Popular

Master Language

> There is no more potent tool for rupture than the reconstruction of
> genesis: by bringing back into view the conflicts and confrontations
> of the early beginnings and therefore all the discarded possibilities, it
> retrieves the possibility that things could have been (and still could be)
> otherwise. — Pierre Bourdieu, "Rethinking the State"

I suggested in the introduction, in very preliminary fashion, some of
the ways in which the underlying telos of the nation appears to have
shifted in recent years in Latin America. This historical transformation, which is not a single process of evolution but an accumulation of
distinct and uneven processes of transition toward so-called globalization, has come about as a result of the neoliberal restructuring of the
nation-state together with the emergence of the transnational marketplace as a new and dominant force throughout Latin America. As Néstor
García Canclini observed in recent years, Latin American contemporaneity is a consequence of the radical fragmentation of modernity's
national scripts. Indeed, as García Canclini puts it, the disappearance of
the national script "means that the great narratives no longer exist that
used to order and hierarchize the periods of the patrimony and the flora
of cultured and popular works in which societies and classes recognized
each other and consecrated their virtues" (*Hybrid* 243–44).

Before evaluating the complexities of the contemporary political and
cultural imagination in Latin America, and before considering the tensions underlying the contexts and horizons of today's cultural politics, I
propose to examine in this chapter the contours of what is surely one of
Latin American modernity's foundational, or great, narratives. As such
I evaluate the notion of transculturation as an *intellectual desire* firmly

rooted within modern processes of nation-state and national culture for-mation in Latin America.

The realities of transculturation are, of course, one of the many direct effects of colonial contact. The idea of transculturation, however, per-tains very much to modern social organization. Indeed, and as I suggest in the pages that follow, transculturation is not just a name for the anthro-pological phenomenon of cultural miscegenation between dominant and dominated cultures. It assumes a fundamental legitimating function in-side the nation-state, as well as in the relation between the state and the popular/elite cultural spheres. It establishes the fictive relation between the state and the notion of the people that constitutes collectivities as par-ticular represented populations that are (supposedly) naturally inserted into the specific mechanisms and calculations of the nation's constituted power structures and truth regimes.

It is through the idea of transculturation—and, in particular, in the relation between this idea and the "hegemonization" of populist, integra-tion-oriented social policies in the twentieth century—that social elites first began to imagine disparate subaltern social agents as fully integrated into national space and into the supposedly singular body of the nation. In general terms, nineteenth-century models of cultural and political modernization had been negotiated on the grounds of a persistent and often violent struggle between the importation of essentially European models of civilization (the nation, for example), and the recalcitrant backwardness of so-called American or subaltern forms of barbarism. By the turn of the century, however, such models, which generally be-came synonymous with the idea of modernization through elimination, extermination, and violent coercion of the "barbaric" masses by oligar-chic local and national elites, entered into a period of profound crisis (Euclides da Cunha's account of the Canudos campaign in *Rebellion in the Backlands* is, of course, a paradigmatic document in this regard). The gradual yet almost simultaneous hegemonization of ideas such as popu-lar integration into the nation-state (that is, the emergence of specific social policies designed to suture the people to the modernizing designs of the nation-state) and, of course, transculturation, appear to mark, in one way or another, a fundamental response to that crisis of legitimacy in nineteenth-century models of nation formation.

Needless to say, the term "transculturation" was first coined in 1940 by the Cuban anthropologist Fernando Ortiz, even though its realities both predate and transcend his signature. In *Cuban Counterpoint* Ortiz defined transculturation as a name for "the different phases of the pro-cess of transition from one culture to another . . . [entailing] vital change

The Other Side of the Popular

... at tempos varying from gradual to sudden" (98–99). In particular, he notes, transculturation accounts for the syncretism of the national cultural economy as well as for the most violent clashes of colonial history:

> In Cuba the terms Ciboney, Taino, Spaniard, Jew, English, French, Anglo-American, Negro, Yucatec, Chinese, and Creole do not mean merely the different elements that go into the make-up of the Cuban nation, as expressed by their different indications of origin. Each of these has come to mean in addition the synthetic and historic appellation of one of the various economies and cultures that have existed in Cuba successively and even simultaneously, at times giving rise to the most terrible clashes. We have only to recall that described by Bartolomé de las Casas as the "destruction of the Indies". (99)

In more recent years, Gustavo Pérez Firmat has provided us with the following important observation regarding Ortiz's use of the term: "More than a comprehensive rubric for the sum or result of culture contact, transculturation is the name for the collision of cultures, for that interval between deculturation and neoculturation that defines a vernacular culture in its formative phase. Although at one point Ortiz states that transculturation names the 'synthesis' of cultures . . . , the word properly designates the fermentation and turmoil that *precedes* synthesis" (23). As such, and as George Yúdice has noted, transculturation is "a dynamic whereby different cultural matrices impact reciprocally — though not from equal positions — on each other, not to produce a single syncretic culture but rather a heterogenous ensemble" ("We" 209).

Transculturation is therefore an important signifier denoting, and accounting for, the presence of Latin American hybrid cultural and social forms dating from colonial times through to the present day. However, the idea of transculturation has a thornier side to it that, I believe, requires further evaluation. Pérez Firmat has observed that transculturation signals a collision of cultures that produces the underlying ground for a colonized "vernacular culture in its formative phase" (23). As he observes, it therefore "designates the fermentation and turmoil that *precedes* synthesis" (23). Transculturation is thus always a question of the relation between order and instability; between constituted and constitutive powers; between the production of cultural difference and the potential subsumption of difference by, for example, colonialism's or modernity's deployments of institutional power. In this formulation, then, transculturation is the name for a profoundly ambivalent period of turmoil and of potential transition toward a social order that, through the achievement of synthesis, can put an effective end to the cultural upheaval of transculturation itself. As Ortiz had previously indicated, and as is cited above, transculturation is grounded in both the traumatic negativity of colonial or neocolonial violence and subordination, as well as in the utopic promise of cultural synthesis, resolution, and stability. As such, it is linked fundamentally to the historical meaning through time—and, in particular, through the time of peripheral capital—of the grounds and terms of social stabilization and of modernization themselves. Transculturation and the cultural heterogeneity that it produces can either establish the conditions for cultural or socioeconomic development, or it can be the greatest impediment to cultural and institutional modernization. It can either suture the people to the mechanisms and calculations of power, or it can produce cultural rationales and practices that resist appropriation by the state. It can either be the underlying telos for the fabrication of cultural and social hegemonies, or it can denote the anarchic instability of a world of signification beyond hegemony; the chaos of subaltern "worldings" that cannot be incorporated into hegemony's systems of signification. It can either produce the grounds for communication, or it can produce complete incommunication between diverse social sectors.

With this in mind, transculturation, understood as the fermentation, turmoil, and ambivalence that precedes synthesis, immediately positions the idea as part of a national evolutionary path toward potential social stability, synthesis, and order. As such, transculturation, understood as a persistently and recalcitrantly violent collision between, for example, distinct modes of production or conflicting thresholds of social, historical, and cultural consistency, is systematically set aside in favor of what Fernando Coronil has called "a trope of the liberal imagination with deep roots in Latin American fiction: a fruitful marriage, compromise and fusion, rather than conflict or transformation" (xiv). This rendering of the notion, in which transculturation as collision is subsumed by transculturation as an evolutionary stage on the way to national synthesis, therefore situates transculturation firmly within the critical horizons of liberal reformist nationalism, in which heterogeneity is considered to be the cultural essence of both the people and the nation, and therefore the foundational ground for notions such as development or modernization.

Indeed, the relation between transculturation and potential cultural synthesis has been the dominant underlying (and, we should add, somewhat tamed) ground for the idea of transculturation since its inception, as well as for the tradition of transculturation thinking as a whole since Ortiz. In *Cuban Counterpoint* Ortiz expresses transculturation as a permanent dialogue between mutually exclusive and often contradictory

The Other Side of the Popular

forms, values, and cultural/economic products. This dialogic form—this permanent and productive circulation of differences—is nevertheless capable of affirming a national unity that is constituted, as Coronil observes, by "making the productive relations established under colonialism the basis of Cuban culture" (xiv). As such, Ortiz actively (and quite ingeniously) displaces transculturation as a violent collision of cultures—as a negative, in other words—and replaces it with a positive dialogical form that is capable of forging the contours of Cuban and Latin American modernity after independence.

In similar fashion, Peruvian novelist and anthropologist José María Arguedas positioned transculturation firmly within the horizons of national (capitalist) modernization and its discourses of cultural integration and development. In his foundational anthropological research on processes of *mestizaje* in the Mantaro Valley, Arguedas was quite categorical about the value of the idea of transculturation and of its fundamental relation to wider state (and, in particular, economic) processes. Thus, in his essay *Formación de una cultura nacional indoamericana* (9–27) Arguedas indicates the intimate relation between transculturation, geographic and ethnic social integration, and capitalist production. However, within this narrative the term transculturation could also go by the name of acculturation or even of subsumption, for the ground from which Indian transculturation is negotiated is at all times the Creole/mestizo understanding of the relation between the land and the capitalist mode of production:

> As soon as the Indian, as a result of particular circumstances, manages to understand this [economic] aspect of western culture, as soon as he arms himself with it, he proceeds as we do. He becomes mestizo and transforms himself into a positive factor of economic production. His whole cultural structure readjusts, thereby attaining a completely new ground, a new axis. By transforming not one of "the superficial elements of his culture" but its very foundation, the confusion that we observe in his culture begins to present itself to us as ordered, clear, and logical. That is, his *conduct begins to identify itself with ours.* And all of this by becoming an individual who really participates in our culture! This is a complete conversion in which, naturally, some ancient elements will still exercise influence as mere signs of a personality that, for the most part, will be moved by incentives, *by ideals,* similar to our own. This is the case of the former Indians of the Mantaro Valley, in Jauja, Concepción, and Huancayo provinces, which is the first case of mass transculturation that I have examined in the initial pages of the current study. (26; translation mine)

The State of Things Passed

As with Ortiz before him, in Arguedas's research in the Mantaro Valley transculturation signifies social reconciliation between previously disconnected social sectors. But it signifies more than reconciliation. Through transculturation the subordinate classes are able to inscribe themselves within the socioeconomic and cultural horizons of the dominant social system. As such, transculturation promises to provide the grounds for economic and cultural integration between the highlands and the coast. Successful transculturation therefore promises not just capitalist modernization but becomes something like a bottom-up integration of the subaltern into the socioeconomic horizons of hegemony, as a result of which the social terrain of national capitalist development can be consolidated and expanded.

Of course, Arguedas's encounter with the chaotic, unmanageable, and therefore presumably unsuccessful transcultural processes of the port of Chimbote (as narrated in *El zorro de arriba y el zorro de abajo*) would ultimately lead to his suicide in 1969. At the same time, however, his work highlighted the delicate balance between transculturation as the grounds of modern social organization and transculturation as the grounds of cultural anarchy or the economic subsumption of labor to capital. In this sense, transculturation always appears to produce the following choice: integration and development (that is, capitalist hegemony) or hegemony's potential interruption.

In his important treatment of the relation between transculturation and the work of José María Arguedas, Angel Rama opted once again to interpret transculturation as a particular relation to national hegemonic formations. Given Arguedas's integration-based approach to transculturation in *Formación* it is hardly surprising that Angel Rama should classify the Peruvian novelist's life and work in almost mythically paradigmatic terms. After all, as the Uruguayan critic noted in *Transculturación narrativa en América Latina*, in Arguedas "a white man considers himself to be Indian in order to undermine the culture of domination from within, thereby incorporating indigenous culture" into national society (205; translation mine).

Certainly, in this path-breaking evaluation of José María Arguedas's life and work the underlying telos of Angel Rama's reading of narrative transculturation is also that of capitalist modernization and its relations to the forging of social and cultural hegemonies. Indeed, this is something that John Beverley has indicated in his important discussion of transculturation and its relation to the historical nexus between the lettered intelligentsia and the advance of capitalist modernity in twentieth-century Latin America. In direct reference to both Ortiz and Rama, but in which exactly the same could also be said of Arguedas's approach to the idea of transculturation in his aforementioned evaluation of *mestizaje,* Beverley observes that

> transculturation functions as a teleology, not without marks of violence and loss, but *necessary* in the last instance for the formation of the modern nation-state and a national (or continental) identity that would be something other than the sum of its parts, since the original identities are sublated in the process of transculturation itself. . . . For Rama, transculturation is above all an instrument for achieving Latin American cultural and economic modernity in the face of the obstacles to that modernity created by colonial and then neocolonial forms of dependency. (*Subalternity* 45)

As a result, Beverley concludes, "the idea of transculturation expresses in both Ortiz and Rama a *fantasy* of class, gender, and racial reconciliation (in, respectively, liberal and social-democratic forms)" (47).

In this chapter I intend to contribute to the discussion on the relation between transculturation and nation-state formation by examining the historical relation between transculturation, developmentalist populism, and the forging of the notion of the people and its relation to the intensification of social antagonisms in the second half of the twentieth century. By tracing a number of the historical, social, and cultural scenarios that underlie and inform the relationship within modern Latin America between transculturation and, for example, social engineering and the so-called unity of a collectivity (Jameson, *Political* 291); between transculturation and the elite's drive for the establishment of national languages, literatures, and cultural patrimonies; between transculturation and Creole political organization; or between transculturation and the development of intellectual discourses on modernization, I propose a reading of this category as a foundational institutionalizing language—as a grand narrative of modern integration—within the formation of social, cultural, economic, and intellectual hegemonies in Latin America.

TRANSCULTURATION, POPULISM, AND
FICTIVE ETHNICITY

My observations thus far suggest, in somewhat preliminary fashion, that there is an important difference between transculturation as an anthropological by-product of colonial or postcolonial histories and transculturation as an idea designed to make modernity make sense and reproduce itself as a particular kind of social order. In his discussion of Angel Rama's reading of José María Arguedas, Alberto Moreiras establishes a fundamental distinction between the anthropological formalities of transculturation and the implementation of the thought of transculturation as "an active, self-conscious cultural combination that is a tool for aesthetic or critical production" (*Exhaustion* 185). Moreiras examines the limits of transculturation when it is taken out of the realm of the everyday—out of the immediate or the purely anthropological—and put in the service of cultural or political reflection and therefore also in the service of the future. Critical and aesthetic transculturation such as that of Angel Rama, Moreiras indicates, "is not simply a response to modernization, understood as an "external influence"; but it is necessarily also a critical relationship to modernization. Literary transculturation is oriented transculturation . . . an *engaged* representation" (*Exhaustion* 186). Moreiras continues his critique of the thought of transculturation in the following terms:

> Although Rama is quite aware of the difference between literary and anthropological transculturation, transculturation for him is still something "to be accomplished" rather than something that simply happens. In that sense he thought of Arguedas's work as "a reduced model for transculturation, where one could show and prove the eventuality of its actualization, so that if it was possible in literature it was also possible in the rest of the culture" (Rama, "Arguedas" 15). All of this of course depends upon Rama's notion of transculturation as necessarily "successful" transculturation, that is, a transculturation where the dominated culture is able to register or inscribe itself into the dominant. That an inscription into the dominant culture as such may be considered to constitute a success (and the noninscription therefore a failure) implies a strong ideological positioning concerning transculturation as an everyday anthropological phenomenon: in fact, it ultimately implies the acceptance of modernization as ideological truth and world destiny. (*Exhaustion* 188).

In other words, if we momentarily distance ourselves from transculturation's culturalist content—from the positive assertion of its so-called everyday dynamics and circulations—and insert it into the historical framework of nation-state formation in modern Latin America; if we distinguish between transculturation as a heterogeneous cultural ensemble and transculturation as a desire and an intellectual discourse; and if we do this as a means of viewing the thought of transculturation in relation to the formation of institutional structures, political identities, state apparatuses, and intellectual interventions into the public sphere (in relation to

The Other Side of the Popular

the notion of hegemony, in other words), then in transculturation we encounter not only popular forms of self-expression and differential modes of collective self-definition but also an immensely powerful ideological machinery of which popular expressions of difference are often merely little more than an effect.

What are the limits between these two domains, in which one affirms transculturation as social transformation from below while the other affirms it as a means of converting the notion of collective life into shared, commonly recognized, and fully institutionalized forms of subject formation? By reflecting on the presence and agency of transculturation as a powerful social and intellectual discourse of collective subjection and subjectivation—as a discourse of peoplehood production that is intimately related to the state's drive for social nationalization, or to the state's attempts to mobilize populations and classes as a fundamental basis for political support and for nation building—we can approach transculturation not merely as a positive culturalism but, more problematically, as a privileged discourse in the consolidation and often violent expansion of the Creole state's hegemony over national territories, populations, and classes.

Of particular significance in this approach are the ways in which intellectual discourses and representations have, in one way or another, intersected with, contested, and/or perpetuated the hegemonic discourses of capitalist modernization. Within this overall framework, the purpose of my discussion in these pages is to suggest a means of tracing a particular critical path, a partial history of tranculturation's interventions and intersections in certain sociocultural spheres and milieus, in order to review, revise, and rethink the category of transculturation itself as well as its problematic location within the national-populist phase of Latin American modernization.

Of course, such a line of reflection can scarcely pretend to be all-inclusive or representative of all Latin American social spaces, or of all the complexities contained therein. As such, the following reflection should be read as a self-conscious fragment that is nevertheless capable of grappling with, and of shedding some light on, the complexities of social nationalization and of peoplehood fabrication during the populist phase of development in Latin America. Needless to say, there will always be exceptions to, and absences within, my argument. The challenge, however, is to weave those exceptions and absences into a critical discourse that is as uncannily continuous as that which I present and evaluate in these pages.

Without doubt, transculturation emerges as an idea and as a critical concern at a time in which Latin America's elites were striving to renegotiate the terms by which to integrate the peasantry, working class, and middle sectors into national polities that would be capable of harmonizing the interests of capital and labor and of advancing into a future no longer characterized by cultural and socioeconomic backwardness. By the turn of the century, the outbreak of the First World War, the opening of the Panama Canal, the beginnings of migration from the countryside to the cities, and increased industrialization in the years immediately preceding and following the stock market crash of 1929, Latin American national economies were striving to establish the means by which to transcend, once and for all, the perpetually delayed nationalization of the Latin American social space, the historical failure of neocolonial ideologies and economies of state formation and of national socialization, and the failure of the postindependence nation to come to its own.

Throughout the twentieth century the desire for popular incorporation and integration—the state's desire for the deliberative mobilization of the people as a means of restructuring its own frameworks of legitimacy—has shaped the course of Latin America's incomplete and uneven projects of social modernization. The phenomenon of transculturation, then, should be framed within the context of the state's desires for popular incorporation, legalization, and control. After all, while the history of Latin American modernization and industrialization has very often been little more than a reminder of the persistent inequality of relations between town and countryside, between Creole and indigenous or black, between male and female, between metropolis and periphery, or between educated and uneducated, transculturation (understood as Ortiz, Arguedas, and Rama understand it—that is, as the successful inscription of a subordinate culture into the workings of domination) promises a common cultural framework of meaning and of understanding that is potentially capable of neutralizing age-old (colonial or neocolonial) antagonisms and contradictions.

It is not by chance, then, that this understanding of the power and force of transculturation—as the initial threshold of a future mestizo synthesis—should coincide with the advent of populism as a privileged form of social organization. Transculturation emerges in Ortiz, Arguedas, and Rama as a means of overcoming historical heterogeneity and incommunication in exactly the same way developmental populism (which came to the fore in the years immediately preceding and following the Great Depression) strived to transcend, neutralize, and depoliticize the potential violence of the people/power bloc antagonisms grounded in class contradiction.[1] As we will see, populism and transculturation emerge as simultaneous and intertwined cultural and political forces within the nation-state's ongoing attempt to consolidate hegemony in the twentieth century.

Populism (which I discuss further as my argument advances) refers to the sociopolitical phenomenon of vertical, Creole-led integration and incorporation of the masses into national social processes. Invariably born from within the crisis of the liberal patrimonial state in Latin America, populist phenomena—be they mass movements, multiclass political parties, syndicalism, charismatic bonapartism, economic nationalism, developmentalism, reformism, populist democracy, or populist dictatorship—were directly linked to profound transformations in the political, social, and economic relations of production of society. They always emerged, for example, within times of profound economic or institutional crisis that threatened to weaken, and perhaps even to destroy, the oligarchic state. As Octavio Ianni has indicated, populist phenomena in the 1920s and 1930s were invariably rooted in urban social processes, as if the city and the country (in profound contradiction and conflict since colonial times) suddenly needed to enter into a relationship of dialogue and mutual accommodation in order to facilitate the state's incorporation, domestication, and modernization of its peripheries. Populism, then, was designed historically to incorporate the peasantry into urban developmentalist projects and to transform the salaried urban worker into a citizen of the nation. Thus, populism strived to inaugurate a new kind of social arrangement between civil society and the state; between city and country; between Creole and indigenous, black, or mestizo; and ultimately between civilization and barbarism, as a result of which social antagonisms and their histories could be transcended through the top-down generation of the category of national peoplehood.

Within this overall horizon, then, populism invariably became associated with the hegemony of industrialization over agriculture and mining (in the words of José Carlos Mariátegui, "Neither the bourgeoisie nor the proletariat can conceive of a civilization that is not based on industry. There are some who predict the decay of the city, but there is no one who predicts the decline of industry. No one denies the power of industry" ["Seven" 178]). Indeed, as Ianni indicates, with the advent of populist social arrangements throughout Latin America (in particular in the years following the First World War and the Russian Revolution through to the period following the Second World War) industrialization came to stand exclusively for economic development as the sole indicator of social well-being for the working classes. Meanwhile, of course, the agricultural and mining sectors came to be viewed as the primary causes of social, economic, and cultural backwardness.

Thus the general view emerged from within Latin America's populisms that countries that exported primary materials and imported manufactured goods could not be economically emancipated because they were incapable of making autonomous decisions regarding their own basic economic problems, desires, or needs. Populism, then, emerged from within the elite's postindependence awareness of economic dependency, as a discourse of cultural nationalism and of national (supposedly nondependent) capitalist development. As such, populism grounded itself in the need to fabricate populations—collective popular identities—that were capable of transforming and of overcoming their peripheral histories and subaltern identities in order to build autonomous identitarian formalities and nondependent forms of capitalist modernization.[2]

In this sense, what appears to be at stake in both developmentalist populism and in the discourse of transculturation is their ability to produce and articulate the people as an effective means of transcending the neocolonial oligarchic state apparatus and of integrating the disenfranchised sectors into modern (national) socioeconomic configurations. (Having said this, of course, integration processes were actually generally negotiated without seriously disrupting or restructuring neocolonial systems of patronage and privilege).

The purpose of national peoplehood production—which, as already mentioned, is probably *the* foundational ground for the articulation of populist social integration is, in the words of Etienne Balibar, "to make the people produce itself continually as national community. Or again, it is to produce the effect of unity by virtue of which the people will appear, in everyone's eyes, 'as a people', that is, as the basis and origin of political power" ("Nation" 93–94). If, as Balibar indicates, the production of peoplehood is to formulate national identity as the origin of political life, then the emergence and consolidation of both developmentalist populism and transculturation as foundational and almost simultaneous points of discursive reference in Latin American modernity must be linked to the crisis of the dominant ideological discourses of postindependence liberalism; to the socioeconomic crises that wrought the reformation of the national oligarchies around the time of the Great Depression; to the elite's desire for the expansion of the state's ability to intervene across any given national territory; as well as to the stately demand to produce representational models of unity—desired fields of cultural articulation and of collective interpellation—that, in one way or another, could anticipate and promote the constitution of specific and supposedly natural nationalized individuals, cultural types, or models of citizenship.

As Ruth and David Collier point out in *Shaping the Political Arena,* in the first decades of the twentieth century the relationship between the state and labor changed fundamentally. Prior to that time oligarchic state policies toward labor had depended invariably on direct and often violent interventions into the public sphere by the police or the armed forces (6). However, they argue that during a well-defined period in each country this relationship was altered as the political dominance of older oligarchic groups diminished. Newer modernizing elites, whose general goal was to overcome potential political antagonisms by harmonizing the interests of labor with those of capital, initiated processes of institutionalization, mobilization, and mass incorporation that were designed to redistribute the exclusionary logics that had perpetuated civilization versus barbarism and the traditional elite's dualistic notions of nationhood, which had dominated the liberal order of the nineteenth century as well as the first decades of the twentieth century.[3]

As Antonio Cornejo Polar notes in *Escribir en el aire* in specific reference to the Andean region, it was hardly by chance that in the first decades of the twentieth century writers as ideologically distinct as Alcides Arguedas (*Pueblo enfermo*), Franz Tamayo (*Creación de la pedagogía nacional*), Pío Jaramillo Alvarado (*El indio ecuatoriano*), Luis E. Valcárcel (*Tempestad en los Andes*), and José Carlos Mariátegui (*Siete ensayos de interpretación de la realidad peruana*) should all engage in far-reaching analyses of geographic, ethnic, and linguistic disarticulation stemming from the inherited contradictions and antagonisms of the postcolonial nation-states. What all these writers had in common—what they were all writing in response to in spite of their obvious differences—was the demand to transcend historically rooted fragmentation in order to forge new national social subjects and political identities from which modernizing processes could consequently be renegotiated.[4]

The challenge for Latin America's nationalizing (populist) elites was always how to transcend historical fragmentation and incommunication between divergent social sectors in such a way as to consolidate a sense of national unity that could define the limits of a totalized sense of social coexistence. In this sense, perhaps it would not be erroneous to suggest that Latin America's nationalizing elites were deeply invested (without knowing it, of course) in the notion of fictive ethnicity and in its relation to the suturing of the notion of the people to the projects and designs of capitalist modernization. As Etienne Balibar indicates, fictive ethnicity is

> an intentionally complex expression in which the term fiction . . . should not be taken in the sense of a pure and simple illusion without historical effects, but must, on the contrary, be understood by analogy with the *persona ficta* of the juridical tradition in the sense of an institutional effect, a "fabrication". No nation possesses an ethnic base naturally, but as social formations are nationalized, the populations included within them, divided up among them or dominated by them are ethnicized—that is, represented in the past or in the future *as if* they formed a natural community, possessing of itself an identity of origins, culture and interests which transcends individuals and social conditions. Fictive ethnicity is not purely and simply identical with the *ideal nation* which is the object of patriotism, but it is indispensable to it, for, without it, the nation would appear precisely only as an idea or an arbitrary abstraction: patriotism's appeal would be addressed to no one. It is fictive ethnicity which makes it possible for the expression of a pre-existing unity to be seen in the state, and continually to measure the state against its "historic mission" in the service of the nation and, as a consequence, to idealize politics. By constituting the people as a fictively ethnic unity against the background of a universalistic representation which attributes to each individual one—and only one—ethnic identity and which thus divides up the whole of humanity between different ethnic groups corresponding potentially to so many nations, national ideology does much more than justify the strategies employed by the state to control populations. It inscribes their demands in advance in a sense of belonging in the double sense of the term—both what it is that makes one belong to oneself and also what makes one belong to other fellow human beings. Which means that one can be interpellated, as an individual, *in the name of* the collectivity whose name one bears. The naturalization of belonging and the sublimation of the ideal nation are two aspects of the same process. ("Nation" 96)

Indeed, it is through populism's repeated attempts to convey an image of national community, and therefore through the modernizing elite's attempts to convey the nation as a utopic commonality thought and negotiated from above, that language and race (as "the most natural of origins" of identity [96]) become foundational protagonists in the construction of the people as a recognizably autonomous group and as the embodiment of the ideal (national) community.

In Balibar's formulation, both language and race "express the idea that the national character . . . is immanent in the people. But both offer a means of transcending actual individuals and political relations. They constitute two ways of rooting historical populations in a fact of 'nature' (the diversity of languages and the diversity of races appearing predestined) but also two ways of giving a meaning to their continued existence, of transcending its contingency" (96–97). National fictive ethnicity, then, negotiated and imposed from within the state's naturalization of linguistic and ethnic heterogeneity, preconditions the construction and representation of what Pierre Bourdieu has called the nation's theoretical unification through the state ("Rethinking" 7).[5]

Obviously, within this framework the function of language and, in particular, the function of literature and of the lettered intellectual has been to produce and promote common cultural frameworks of reference (nationally functional forms of cultural translation, representation, and institutionalization) between language groups, classes, regions, and ethnicities. As such, economic modernizing processes have actively institutionalized symbolic processes — literature, the visual arts, radio, cinema — into the state's deployments of power and of hegemonic reproduction.

Needless to say, we would do well to examine such processes in further depth in order to trace the tenuous frontiers between the idea of transculturation as an explanatory model of the ways in which subordinate cultures effect change on dominant ones through contact (in other words, as a path toward the democratization of modern culture) and transculturation as a fundamental element in the state's subsumption of cultural difference to socioeconomic and cultural modernization. In the partial genealogy that follows I establish my own transcultural cartography — my own uneven and differential representation of some of modernity's cultural and institutional settings — in the interest, quite simply, of calling attention to the foundational nexus between the phenomenon and idea of transculturation and the dominant languages and repertoires of national populism and of modern nation-state formation in twentieth-century Latin America.

TRANSCULTURAL FRAGMENTS

One of the most fascinating modern fabrications of transcultural national fictive ethnicity can be seen in Acción Democrática's promotion of the ideology of racial democracy and of *café con leche* society in Venezuela. The years following the death of the dictator Juan Vincente Gómez witnessed the marked decline of the agrarian oligarchy, the expansion of the bourgeoisie, and the increasing organization of a nascent working class. General Eleazar López Contrera (1936–1941) formulated the first state plan of development, which was later continued, along with certain democratic openings and a revision of the petroleum laws, by the regime of General Isaias Medina Angarita (1941–1945) (Hellinger 39). As Winthrop Wright explains, as a result of these openings Acción Democrática came into existence under the leadership of a number of dedicated *café con leche* activists from the nation's middle class: "Inspired by the Peruvian Víctor Raúl Haya de la Torre's multiclass Alianza Popular Revolucionaria Americana (APRA) party, the leaders of AD [Acción Democrática] soon formed an alliance with the *pardo* and black masses. In so doing they adopted the myth of racial democracy as their party's official position on race" (10–11). According to Mariano Picón Salas these events marked the beginnings of the future for Venezuela. He wrote: "The twentieth century began in Venezuela only with the demise of the Gómez dictatorship" (quoted in Britto García 240; translation mine). It is hardly coincidental, then, that the events spanning from the 1930s through to the first Acción Democrática government in 1947 should coincide with the emergence of a group of cultural nationalist writers attempting to awaken an interest in topics related to Venezuela's African heritage. From Ramón Díaz Sánchez's "Cam, ensayo sobre el negro" (1933) and Juan Pablo Sojo's *Nochebuena negra* (written in 1930, but published in 1943 along with Díaz Sánchez's *Mene*) through to the writings of Juan Liscano and Carlos Siso we witness a concerted effort to represent, for the first time, the integration of ethno-African groups into national life and literary culture.

Yet, as Wright notes, for Liscano, Siso, Sojo, and others, a whitening of the race—the postindependence de-Africanization of Venezuelan blacks—served a particularly useful purpose within the modernizing processes because they "viewed miscegenation as both a whitening and a strengthening process," and "advocated the continued assimilation of blacks into a whiter race, a process they readily traced back to the colonial period" (119). Acción Democrática's cultural nationalism— its active promotion of racial miscegenation as a prerequisite for social mobility and as a protective against national backwardness—obviously echoes the racial determinism of Rómulo Gallegos's novels *Doña Bárbara* (1929) and *Pobre negro* (1937). Founder of the anti-Gómez publication *Alborada* in 1909, yet later collaborator and even director of the pro-Gómez *Actualidades* between 1920 and 1921, Gallegos, in *Una posición en la vida,* stated that Venezuela was composed of "amorphous multitudes of hybrid origin formed by the *still incomplete fusion* of diverse ethnic elements in which atavisms and remnants of all races remain in struggle"

The Other Side of the Popular

(quoted in Britto García 142–43; translation and emphasis mine). On this ground, he adds, "it is useless to want to build anything solid or stable" (142–43). The Creole intellectual classes, meanwhile, were portrayed by Gallegos not in their incompletion but as "the fruit of selection, the product of a culture that is always superior to that of its environment, and sometimes of its time" (144).

Indeed, within this same text and within the same vein of Creole intellectual paternalism, Gallegos proposed that the national intellectual should act in one of two ways: "from the position of power, and in more or less authoritarian terms as in Germany, or from below, and with the use of propaganda and exemplarity as in England" (144). Gallegos, writer/intellectual and president of the Republic under the populist Acción Democrática banner in 1947 must surely have been inspired by the fusion-effect of both modes of intellectual intervention, because Acción Democrática's populist *café con leche* social engineering was always negotiated from above yet as if from below, almost as if the liberal elite's vision of Venezuelan cultural nationalism were itself the fusion effect of German and British authoritarian/populist intellectual practices.

Modern thought in Latin America invariably occupies and reproduces a tenuous epistemological and political border that allows for the promise of a decolonizing thought yet does so through the redistribution of neocolonial power and authority. Thus Acción Democrática's attempt to fabricate national peoplehood as an ethnicized effect of institutionalization—as a transcultural national fictive ethnicity in other words— provides us with a foundation from which to broaden our critical horizon and to reevaluate, for example, Andean *indigenismo*'s quest for new literary languages and national subjectivities both preceding and following the economic crisis of 1929.

In such processes José María Arguedas's search for the "quechuanization" of Spanish as a new norm for national Peruvian cultural production, or the incorporation of Jorge Icaza's Quichua inferences as an avant-garde renovation of Ecuadorian oligarchic literature and expression, become not wholly devoid of neocolonial resonances themselves. For as Arguedas's suicide in 1969 so forcefully reveals, there is a very fine line between the fabrication of common cultural frameworks and the naturalization of de-Indianizing processes presented by dominant forces as preconditions for the building of the modern nation. Obviously, writers as enormously diverse as César Vallejo (*El tungsteno*), Alcides Arguedas (*Pueblo enfermo*), Ciro Alegría (*El mundo es ancho y ajeno*), Jorge Icaza (*Huasipungo*), José María Arguedas (*Canto kechwa; Yawar fiesta; Los ríos profundos; Todas las sangres; El zorro de arriba y el zorro de abajo*), José Carlos Mariátegui (*Siete ensayos de interpretación de la realidad peruana*), Franz Tamayo (*Creación de la pedagogía nacional*), Pío Jaramillo (*El indio ecuatoriano*), Uriel García (*El nuevo indio*), Armando Chirveches (*La casa solariega*), and Tristan Marof (*La justicia del inca; La verdad socialista en Bolivia*) can all be positioned, in one way or another, along this fine line of modern neocolonial redistribution.[6] For all these works are invested in the development of the category of the nation and of a national peoplehood—in the fabrication of a national institutionalized "we" grounded in common cultural frameworks and languages—as the privileged site of postcolonial historical transcendence. Yet, as Antonio Cornejo Polar seems to suggest in *Escribir en el aire*, his important reading of Andean heterogeneity, precisely because these writers remain firmly rooted in the maintenance of national thought—in the upholding of the nation as the exclusive horizon for modernization; in national peoplehood as the primary interpretative code by which the present and future can be rendered intelligible; and, ultimately, in fictive ethnicity as the outside of colonial social relations—their work is inevitably fraught with the potential perpetuation of subalternity, and hence with the tension of colonialism's imminent reinscriptions and sustained exclusions. Cornejo Polar states:

> In the complex and difficult process that leads to the definition of national identity, a political and intellectual operation emerges that remains in the charge of the social elites: to produce an image of the Indian, both for society and for the Indian himself, as the embodiment of that identity (either as its prophet or as its somewhat less than natural representative). Within this order of things national identity requires the conversion of an exclusive "we"—in which only the elites, their allies, together with their self-image, interests, and desires, fit comfortably—into a widely inclusive, almost ontological, "we". The true protagonists (who are never actually consulted in this matter) are obliged to insert themselves into this process. On the way, they lose parts of their condition and mutate in order to gain access to the newly adopted ground, which is now declared sacrosant from within the ideological maneuvers of its promoters. (186; translation mine)

In this important critique of, for example, the political and epistemological function of the intellectual in Andean nationalizing processes, Cornejo points to the exclusions that underlie and constitute the contours of transcultural fictive ethnicity as a nation-building discourse. Without doubt the logics of such processes were not fabricated overnight, and it is to the construction of their genealogy that we must now turn.

In 1915 the poet José Gálvez presented his treatise on the future of national culture, *Posibilidad de una genuina literatura nacional*, in which he revindicated mestizo literature as the essence and destiny of Peruvian letters. Writing on the threshold of both Augusto Leguía's authoritarian (prepopulist) *oncenio* (1919–1930) and of the post–World War I mobilizations that first brought Víctor Haya de la Torre into the political arena after his participation in the struggle for the establishment of the eight-hour workday and for the regulation of subsistence prices (struggles that in turn led to the formation in 1919 of the most important labor organization in Peruvian history, the Regional Workers' Federation of Peru), Gálvez's intervention advanced discussion of the debates of the Generation of 1900 regarding the means of forging national culture, character, and peoplehood after the disastrous consequences of the War of the Pacific (1879–1883).

By 1920, of course, the Generation of 1900 had already established the two major currents of modern Peruvian thought (Arguedas, *Formación* 189). The decades following the War of the Pacific had revealed the increasing illegitimacy of oligarchical state processes. Manuel González Prada (the "least Peruvian" of literary figures according to the Generation of 1900 hispanist Ventura García Calderón [quoted in Mariátegui, *Seven* 204]) had played an instrumental role in calling for the regeneration of the country (passing from positivist to anarchist positions during the course of his career), and his presence was fundamental to Haya de la Torre's mobilization of the masses in the early 1920s.[7]

The oligarchy's persistent crisis of hegemony after the War of the Pacific (a crisis that had always given legitimacy to González Prada's calls for social and cultural regeneration) merely intensified after the opening of the Panama Canal in 1914, for while this event facilitated the growth of an export economy to Europe during the years of the First World War it also signaled the beginnings of an increasing concentration of Peru's dependency on external markets. Profound transformations resulting from the gradual growth of the export economy and the broadening of tax revenues slowly contributed to the establishment of new elites within the urban finance sector, as well as significant changes in urban social structures and demographic processes as a result of the beginnings of massive migration from the sierras to the coast (between 1920 and 1931, for example, Lima's population increased 68 percent as a result of predominantly Indian migration [see

Stein, 51]). This phenomenon would contribute inevitably to the gradual development and organization of an industrial labor force, to the increased "Indianization" of Lima, to the greater bureaucratization of the state, and, under Leguía, to the attempted "westernization" of the Indian hinterlands through the construction of road systems (as represented later, of course, in José María Arguedas's *Yawar fiesta*).[8] Within this overarching framework of oligarchic crisis, gradual economic expansion, and interclass/interregional miscegenation (during which Lima's Creole elites began to enter into increasing daily contact with the largely ignorant Indian masses), José de la Riva Agüero and Víctor A. Belaúnde emerged as the intellectual founders of *hispanismo*, which, Arguedas wrote, recognized the human value of the Catholic mestizo as a potential promoter of hispanic values and of the Spanish tradition in Peruvian national society and its culture.[9]

In 1905 Riva Agüero, in *Carácter de la literatura del Perú independiente* (a work profoundly influenced by Menéndez Pelayo), argued that *hispanismo* affirmed the superiority of hispanic culture over serrano culture and valorized the indigenous world exclusively to the extent that it could be transformed and modernized through processes of *mestizaje*. To this degree, there was always a marked correlation between *hispanismo* and the pedagogical underpinnings of Sarmiento's discourse on civilization.[10]

In contrast to the hispanists, Julio C. Tello strived to construct the intellectual foundations for the analysis of the origins of indigenous culture. However, although firmly located in what could be considered the *indigenista* camp, Tello remained limited in his affirmations because he failed to position himself beyond Creole idealizations of *mestizaje* as a possible modernizing corrective to indigenous backwardness. According to Arguedas, Tello strived to insert Indian folklore and dance into the developmentalist logics of Creole modernization by transforming his objects of analysis into aesthetically pleasing objects for Creole consumption: "Tello . . . overlooks the real Indian. He admires his folklore but, upon forming a group of dancers from his native Huarochirí, proceeds to dress them in costumes inspired by archeological motifs which were 'stylized' and created by him, to the complete exclusion of the typical dress of the Huarochirí people" (*Formación* 191; translation mine). Thus, as far as Arguedas was concerned, in Tello's *indigenismo* the Indian signified once again only to the extent that dominant classes could maintain their civilizing mission of indigenist identity fabrication.[11]

Obviously, then, by 1920 José Gálvez, in *Posibilidad de una genuina literatura nacional*, was not alone in his celebration of miscegenation as

The Other Side of the Popular

a fusion effect from which to negotiate a genuinely national experience of Peruvian culture and development. Indeed, the second decade of the century revealed a marked investment, both in Lima's Creole intellectual circles as well as among the provincial intellectual elites, in the recuperation and dissemination of the figure of the indigenous—of Indian popular tradition, dress, and folklore—as a means of redefining national cultural paradigms after the loss of prestige that had been inflicted on the ruling elites by Chile's victory of 1883 in the War of the Pacific.

Worthy of note in this process is the fact that this early labor of national cultural renovation and indigenous restitution coincided with the inclusion on the national scene of new provincial cultural workers. For the first time in Peru, intellectuals from the provincial social elites of Trujillo, Puno, Cuzco, and Arequipa began to intervene and redefine Lima's debates on Peruvian peoplehood, national character, and national culture. Thus Luis Valcárcel (who stated "the essential Peru, the invariable Peru was always and can only ever be Indian . . . Peru is Indian!" [112; translation mine]) stood out as one of the founding members of the Escuela Cuzqueña and of the Cuzco-based Grupo Resurgimiento.

Indeed, as can also be seen in what would later come to be called the tradition of the *novela de la tierra* (and, in particular, in José Eustasio Rivera's *La vorágine*, Ricardo Güiraldes's *Don Segundo Sombra*, and Rómulo Gallegos's *Doña Bárbara*), the incorporation and dissemination of regional modes and mores testifies to one of the most lasting facets of Latin American cultural nationalism: namely, the fusion effect's drive to inscribe, translate, and domesticate the nation's outsides—its negative or noncontemporaneous foundations—into totalizing modes of representation and self-constitution. Moreover, in a similar fashion as in Peru and Venezuela the advent of populist mobilizations in Ecuador in the 1930s led to the increasing nationalization of provincial identities, ethnicities, languages, and representational forms. In this sense Jorge Icaza's Creole renovation of Andean literary language in novels such as *Huasipungo* (published in 1934, the first year of Velasco Ibarra's first populist presidency—from a total of five administrations between 1934 and 1972), encounters its regional correlative in the Grupo de Guayaquil's concern for the representation of coastal *negros, cholos,* and *montuvios*.[12]

Peru's nascent indigenism, however, was by far the most powerful cultural machinery for presenting, negotiating, and governing the symbolic terms of national unity and of universal cultural difference in the Andes. Even before the integration-oriented period of the 1920s (that is, as early as 1912–1918) Abraham Valdelomar had produced a number of pseudo-indigenous modernist poems. In the art world—and just a few years before the institutionalization of the Escuela de Bellas Artes in Lima, which would later produce such painters as José Sabagal, Julia Codesido, Camilo Blas, and Carlos Quíspez Asín (Sánchez 34)—Augusto Aguirre Morales had offered up *La injusticia de Huayna Cápac;* César Vallejo, a recent arrival to the capital from Trujillo, had praised indigenous culture in his *Sonetos imperiales,* which he later inserted into *Los heraldos negros* (1919); Percy Gibson mixed mestizo and semi-Indian traditions in his *Sonetos Arequipeños;* Enrique López Albújar edited his *Cuentos andinos* (1920); and Felipe Cossio del Pomar published *La pintura en el Cusco* (1921) (Sánchez 8). And in 1920, five years after Gálvez edited his *Posibilidad de una genuina literatura nacional,* Luis Alberto Sánchez presented his own thesis, *Nosotros,* which dealt with the possible fabrication of a nationalized culture and community. In this work he defends the notion of a "totalist Peruvianism" achievable through the integration and harmonization of the nation's conflicting heritages and the cultural geographies that they implied. Sánchez, then, advocated the active construction of a totalizing fictive ethnicity grounded firmly in top-down transculturation. Indeed, all indigenism came to be born in one way or another—as more or less indigenist or more or less mestizo—from the tensions emerging from within differential visions of transcultural fictive ethnicity, at a moment of crisis in which the need to somehow nationalize the nation (to "Peruvianize Peru," as Mariátegui puts it) reigned supreme (though often for different reasons) among the intellectual classes and the nascent modernizing urban bourgeoisie.

Yet the specters of neocolonialism always haunt indigenism's quest for national fictive ethnicity. For example, while a number of the provincial indigenistas such as Luis Valcárcel proclaimed the need to Peruvianize Peru by fabricating prehispanic identities as foundations for the establishment of the modern nation and of national culture, his *Tempestad en los Andes* reveals the irresolvably neocolonial resonances of such projects. Valcárcel's restoration of the prehispanic (a restitution that would later resonate in Pablo Neruda's romantic evocation of the dead in "Las alturas de Macchu Picchu") uncovers the intellectual's desire to erase, sometimes apparently at will, all vestiges of colonialism—and ultimately all vestiges of society's contemporary modes of production—from the arena of national fictive ethnicity production. But so forceful is the location of the ideal nation in the prehispanic—so powerful and simplistic the fabrication of the identity of national origins, along with their supposed ability to transcend all individuals and actually existing social conditions—that the very desire for nationhood on such terms merely inscribes the Indian as a Creole fantasy of cultural redemption and of

The Other Side of the Popular

ethnic purity. In this sense, the cultural mechanisms by which the integration, representation, and institutionalization of backward populations were often negotiated ultimately served to realign the status quo of colonial epistemologies, even when they represented themselves explicitly as dissident voices within the formulation of national culture.

In this regard let us not forget the fundamental role played by the institutionalization of literature, of the *indigenista* intelligentsia, and of indigenist knowledge within the state's drive for the consolidation of a national ideology and therefore within its drive for the expression of the people as a preexisting popular unity visible within, and as, the construction of the state itself. For example, it is hardly by chance that in 1938 Jorge Basadre's *Literatura Inca* should become the inaugural volume of the Biblioteca de Cultura Peruana (an institution directed, incidentally, by the old *hispanista* Ventura García Calderón [Cornejo Polar, *La formacion* 121]). In similar fashion José María Arguedas, who in 1950 announced that Spanish was the legitimate mode of expression for the Peruvian Andean world, became one of the founders of the Instituto de Estudios Peruanos, which to this day is one of the major state organs for the institutionalized representation and dissemination of knowledge and research on indigenous cultures in the Andean region.

However, the integration of a national fictive ethnicity into state-related power/knowledge configurations was by no means a uniform phenomenon within the Andean region. The cultural history of populism and of popular (Indian) institutional integration differed considerably in Bolivia, for example, when compared to the Peruvian or even the Ecuadorian experiences. This is largely due to the fact that given the economic, ethnic, geographical, historical, and demographic particularities of the region, the populist era in Bolivia lent itself more explicitly to the redistribution of oligarchic Creole control over the state. This was done by maintaining the rhetoric of a national Indian citizenry while essentially upholding, through the incorporation of the rural peasantry into state enterprises, neocolonial social divisions and the hierarchies associated with them. In other words, Bolivia's period of populist incorporation was designed to neutralize threatening popular appeals for transformation and inclusion, and to control from within the revolutionary state all attempts at redefining common aspirations.

As in Peru (though considerably later) the revolutionary nationalism of the Bolivian uprising of 1952 was rooted in the outcome of the War of the Pacific. Unlike its neighbor, however, the events of 1952 were grounded specifically in the loss of Bolivia's territorial access to the ocean after Chile's victory. For this reason (and, once again, in contrast to

Peru and Ecuador) Bolivia was unable to take economic advantage of the opening of the Panama Canal in 1914. As such, it could not create a dynamic export economy capable of creating new class alliances and new principles of social organization.

The economic crash of 1929 revealed a severe deterioration in Bolivia's already waning position in the international tin and silver markets and accentuated the increasing dependency of the national elite on external forces. The Great Depression reduced both prices and demand for tin to such an extent that the oligarchic order, which was built almost exclusively around this industry, finally strived to divert attention away from its deadlocked internal politics and international economic standing by attempting to obtain access to the Atlantic through the Río de la Plata system. This, of course, intensified skirmishes in the Chaco region and ultimately led to the slaughter of the Chaco War (1932–1935). The Chaco fiasco led to the almost complete delegitimization of oligarchic institutionality and its liberal ideology, and produced a populist "indianist" military takeover that later would provide the foundations for the increasingly radicalized working-class movement that in 1952 filled the ranks of Paz Estenssoro's Movimiento Nacionalista Revolucionario (MNR) (see Antezana; Halperín Donghi). In this sense, a book such as Augusto Céspedes's *Sangre de mestizos* (1936) can be seen as a symbolic rendering of the originary social violence from which the collective desires and rhetoric of cultural nationalism and of the Bolivian national-popular would later emerge.

Although the 1952 revolution transformed the basis of political power by tinkering with the semicolonial feudalism of the previous order—conferring the vote for the first time on the illiterate indigenous majority and making the miners the foremost armed power in the nation (at least for a time)—the creation of monumental state enterprises such as COMIBOL (Corporación Minera de Bolivia) did little more than incorporate the indigenous working class into the economic structures of an exclusively Creole-led state capitalism that remained rooted in the perpetuation of neocolonial exclusion and privilege. In this sense, the Bolivian literary traditions of mining narrative and *testimonio*—often glorifying the popular in almost a celebration of collective sacrifice and suffering—critique the rhetoric of a transformational Bolivian fictive ethnicity that nevertheless reinscribed traditional exclusions and reinstitutionalized the colonial division of labor, power, and ethnicity.[13]

While the Bolivian revolutionary state became the single largest producer in the nation, its self-proclaimed historic mission in the service of national capitalism spoke considerably more to the failure of national-popular fictive ethnicity as the origin of political, economic, and cultural life. After all, although opening up a space for the urbanization of the peasantry and for the airing of popular aspirations, the revolution's idealization of politics and of the state's ability to forge a national-popular culture remained at all times heavily structured by Creole aspirations and modes of institutionalization, and even more heavily subsidized by the Creole elite's dependency on the U.S. cold war government of Dwight D. Eisenhower. By 1958, just six years after the revolution, one third of the Bolivian state's budget was paid directly from U.S. funds, while this peculiar brand of national capitalism/culturalism became increasingly dependent on IMF aid programs (Klein 238). Indeed, by the early 1960s, and in the wake of the Cuban revolution and of Kennedy's Alliance for Progress, Paz Estenssoro had begun to rearm the national army as a means of controlling potential popular uprisings and of "preventing communist subversion," while the United States now had direct access to the Bolivian command structure with most officers in the armed forces trained in the United States (244).

Through Bolivia one can see one of the great dilemmas of Latin America's modernizing quest for (transcultural) national fictive ethnicity: that the state's attempted consolidation and expansion of hegemony over national territories, populations, and classes—its naturalization of national belonging and its sublimation of the ideal nation through transcultural ethnic processes negotiated from within a dependent and always uneven capitalist order—inserted Latin America into the international arena of the cold war and the global struggle against communism. It located popular revolution as the ultimate threat and defining horizon of intellectual thought and political experience, and intensified the state's production of "enemies within," as a means by which to control and neutralize populations and subjectivities—both integrated fictive ethnicities and their subaltern leftovers—that the state had previously organized and unleashed onto (or that it had merely excluded from) the national public sphere.

The fictive ethnicity of the national-popular, in other words, inscribed itself as the reassertion and perpetuation of popular control and/or exclusion. Therefore, Creole-led attempts to transcend colonial history through the neutralization, idealization, and depoliticization of class and ethnic antagonisms—with transcultural fictive ethnicity as its primary goal, trope, and/or rhetorical foundation—merely tended toward the redistribution of neocolonial divisions of labor and of institutional power.

Needless to say, pedagogy, education, and the university (both popular and elite) became fundamental institutional spaces within the state's promotion of the ideology of national progress, popular incorporation, and transculturation. Indeed, the university came to play a primary political role in the institutionalization, integration, and crisis of developmentalist populism throughout Latin America. A case in point is, once again, Peru. The university reforms of 1919—initiated and promoted from within the Universidad de San Marcos's Facultad de Letras [Mariátegui, *Seven* 104])—alongside Haya de la Torre's establishment in March 1920 of the Universidad Popular González Prada, together indicated pedagogy as a transformational practice of modern citizenship formation, popular empowerment, and integration. The Universidad Popular also came to provide a fundamental means of strengthening Alianza Popular Revolucionara Americana's (APRA) contacts with labor and the student movement throughout the 1920s, and even became the organizational and educational base for the party's political infrastructure during the 1930s and 1940s. For the Universidad Popular was, in effect, a space from within which to negotiate and promote an institutionalized fictive ethnicity capable of transcending what Mariátegui identified as the elite's persistent inability to overcome Peru's "dualism of race, language, and sentiment, born of the invasion and conquest of indigenous Peru by a foreign race that has not managed to merge with the Indian race, or eliminate it, or absorb it" (*Seven* 164).[14]

By the early 1930s the need for state integration and education in Peru was becoming increasingly urgent as Lima's population boomed from 150,000 inhabitants in 1900 to 376,000 in 1931. Within this context Steve Stein's description of Haya de la Torre's institutionalization of popular redemption and of pedagogic de-Indianization gives us particular insight into the location of popular pedagogy in APRA's forging of the urban social sphere:

> The schools operated three nights weekly in Lima and twice weekly in Vitarte from approximately 9 to 11 P.M. The curriculum placed a heavy emphasis on practicability with classes on hygiene, anatomy, arithmetic, grammar, and geography. Morality campaigns were also a salient feature of the education in the Universidad Popular . . . the workers and professors joined in a common effort to eradicate alcoholism and to curb disease. The educational functions of these schools

also extended to proceedings outside of the classroom. The Universidades Populares organized regularly scheduled sporting events, hikes into the countryside, and special musical programs. Medical school students . . . established popular clinics [where they] diagnosed illnesses and prescribed remedies. . . . Men who conducted the major unions in this period and who would direct labor in the 1930s and 1940s shared a common experience in the classrooms of Haya's schools. (140)

Obviously, then, the Universidad Popular became a privileged arena within the Peruvian populist infrastructure because it was a perfect site for the inculcation of nationalist mestizo ideology and for the fabrication of a fictive ethnicity born of institutional acculturation, Christian morality, the privileging of western medical science and hygiene, grammatical Spanish, civic (mestizo) consciousness and good citizenship, as well as a sense of urban belonging grounded in the collective benefits of industrial progress and development.

Thus APRA's ideology of the transcultural fusion effect, negotiated at least in part from within the integrationist university reforms that swept Latin America after the Córdoba Reforms of Yrigoyenist Argentina in 1918, was ultimately designed to transcend the exclusivist colonial pedagogies that had been reproduced under the postindependence liberal order. It was intended to provide the basis for the formation, incorporation, and reproduction of an effectively integrated (and therefore de-Indianized, mestizo, or transcultural) national workforce, and was deemed to be fundamental for the recruiting of local, regional, and ethnic talents that were thought to be necessary for the modernizing projects of the social elites. It provided for greater flexibility and mobility within the limitations imposed by national class, interregional, and interethnic structures, and fabricated a national sense of cultural, linguistic, and social consensus. Finally, it institutionalized a new citizenry capable of consolidating and perpetuating dominant ideologies, of contributing to them and, if necessary, of transcending them.

It must be noted, however, that Mariátegui staked out a distinctive position within such processes. In his essay on public education, written in the same year in which he split from Haya by favoring the establishment of the Peruvian Communist Party, Mariátegui had stated that "the problem of Indian illiteracy goes beyond the pedagogical sphere. It becomes increasingly evident that to teach a man to read and write is not to educate him. Primary school does not redeem the Indian morally and socially. The first real step toward his redemption must be to free him from serfdom" (*Seven* 122). Whereas Haya de la Torre's promotion of the Universidad Popular largely echoed Vasconcelos's faith in the mestizo as the promise of a new secular culture (locating miscegenation as the ultimate prerequisite for social mobility and for protection against collective backwardness) Mariátegui rejected the conceptual horizons of a Creole faith in transculturation's ability to harmonize antagonisms and to resolve what he viewed as being *the* great national dilemma: the land.

Mariátegui, then, chose to counter Vasconcelos's ethnic utopianism by stating that "*Mestizaje* has produced a complex species rather than a solution of the dualism of Spaniard and Indian" (287). In contrast to Vasconcelos and Haya de la Torre, Mariátegui viewed the privileging and positioning of the mestizo as the secular subjectivity and social agent of the future as little more than a preventive revolution of mass containment and control, rather than as a transformational articulation of forces positioned outside or against Creole domination and its history of economic exploitation. For Mariátegui, then, social transformation negotiated through pedagogy and capitalist modernization represented a principle of neocolonial social engineering that simply failed to erase class conflict and ultimately perpetuated Creole modernity as the reinscription and redistribution throughout the modernizing social sphere of hispanic colonization (see Moraña, *Literatura* 46). Thus in a remarkable section of "El proceso de la literatura," in which Mariátegui's ideas themselves reproduce many of the neocolonial racist categories of his day, the founder of Peruvian marxism evaluates *mestizaje* in its relation to industrialization and capitalist developmentalism as a social phenomenon capable of naturalizing the subsumption of ethnicized labor to Creole capital:

> In existing socio-economic conditions, *mestizaje* produces not only a new human and ethnic type but a new social type. The blurring of that type by a confused combination of races does not in itself imply any inferiority and may even presage, in certain ideal mixtures, the characteristics of the cosmic race. However, because of a murky predominance of negative sediments, the undefined or hybrid nature of the social type manifests itself in a sordid and unhealthy stagnation. Chinese and negro admixtures have almost always had a destructive and aberrant effect on this mestizaje. Neither European nor Indian tradition is perpetuated in the mestizo; they sterilize each other. In an urban, industrial, and dynamic environment, the mestizo rapidly catches up with the white man and assimilates Western culture together with its customs, motivations, and consequences. Usually he does not grasp the complex beliefs, myths, and feelings that under-

lie the material and intellectual creations of the European or white civilization; but the mechanics and discipline of the latter automatically impose its habits and ideas on him. When he comes in contact with a mechanized civilization that is amazingly equipped to dominate nature, he finds the idea of progress, for example, irresistible. But this process of assimilation and incorporation is quickly accomplished only within a vigorous industrial culture. (*Seven* 281–82)

Mariátegui challenged Vasconcelos's and Haya's insistence on tamed (state-promoted) transculturation as the kernel of national culture's self-constitution, and questioned their privileging of the mestizo as the primary social subject in the establishment of common cultural, institutional, and linguistic frameworks. Yet, as this passage affirms, Mariátegui did not position himself beyond or outside the constitution of community as a fictively ethnic unity measured exclusively in terms of universalist representation. Indeed, it is precisely by upholding national belonging as monumental singularity and as the exclusive precondition for emancipatory thought that Mariátegui ultimately reinscribed the demands and limits of fictive ethnicity, the violence of its conceptual determinations, and the specters of exclusion that he intended to counter.

Of course, at this point it should be noted that the incorporation of the literary intelligentsia into populist or protopopulist nation-state formations was by no means a uniform phenomenon throughout Latin America. As we have seen, in the cases of Peru, Venezuela, Ecuador, and, to a lesser extent, Bolivia, national fictive ethnicity was negotiated and promoted actively from within literary, intellectual, and university circles, either in conjunction with, or at least in light of, popular aspirations and new forms of vertical-led organization and mobilization.

This active incorporation of the intellectual into the definition of national political organization and culture contrasts radically with the cultural history of other regions. In Argentina, for example, populist nation formation and its labor of translation between language groups, classes, and ethnicities required very little cooperation from the traditional literary sectors. Indeed, Peronism's processes of state incorporation ultimately bypassed the liberal ideology of the Argentine intelligentsia. Thus under Perón the political influence of even sympathetic intellectuals such as Raul Scalabrini Ortiz, Arturo Jauretche, or Luis Dellapiane was limited (James 268). As Silvia Sigal puts it:

The advent of Peronism constituted, without doubt, a cultural mutation—understood in the broad sense of the term—in Argentine history. However, its imprint on the production of cultural goods is not immediately self-evident. In the area of high culture Peronism lacked specific strategies and, in the case of cultural conflict, could not even produce an ideology capable of deciding for either silence or active promotion. Characterized by an anti-intellectualism even more pronounced than that of other forms of populism, its cultural politics were essentially limited to direct or indirect authoritarian gestures. Its decision not to share control of mass communication systems (radio, cinema, the press) made this evident. The alternative between books and sandals did not merely owe its success to the socialist leader who popularized it. Rather, its roots went back to the fact that the majority of intellectuals belonged to the liberal tradition, which led them to open opposition to virtually everything that Peronism embodied. (45; translation mine. See also Sebreli, 242–44)

Peronism's historical mission in the area of national citizenship formation, then, did not need the institutionalized literary intelligentsia for the construction and representation of Peronist peoplehood, and it adopted cultural models and forms other than those informed by the liberal literary tradition. The *década infame*, of course, had brought the anti-working-class repression of the Uriburu regime, the death of Yrigoyen in 1933, and the increasing heterodoxy of intellectual and literary life in Argentina (Macedonio Fernández and Roberto Arlt, of course, stand out as examples of such heterodoxy at this time). As David Viñas indicates (Literatura 185–86), novels such as Atilio Cattáneo's *Entre rejas* (1933) or Alcides Greca's *Tras el alambrado de Martín García* (1934) attest to an increasingly militant rejection of orthodox forms and cultural norms in the years following the overthrow of Yrigoyen. Furthermore, the emergence during the *década infame* of publications such as *Metrópolis* (1931–32) and *Columna* (1937), or the Popular Front style of *Conducta* (1938–43), bears witness to a generalized move away from the cultural patrimony of Leopoldo Lugones and Ricardo Rojas in an attempt to further define the contours of an intellectual Left that had emerged alongside, and in response to, the increasing radicalization of the Yrigoyenist popular sectors.

In June 1943, however, the military intervention that would later bring Perón to power put an end to any meaningful or long-standing articulation between the literary intelligentsia and the popular sectors (at least during the initial period of classic Peronism, from 1945 to 1955). In contrast, Peronism chose to affirm national commonality by means of popular radio, commercial cinema, music (the tango), and theater; through popular cultural forms that could easily uphold and disseminate the image of Peronism (and of the Plaza de Mayo as the symbolic center of the times) as the return of Sarmiento's rural barbarians finally washing their feet in the fountains of the capital's liberal and conservative civilization (Leónidas Lamborghini, quoted in Ciria 277). Thus, in terms of the articulation of cultural forms other than those popular modes officially sanctioned by the regime, pro-Peronist literary culture represented little more than "a moment of creative vacuousness" (Juan Carlos Portantiero, quoted in Ciria 263).[15]

As was the case with Haya de la Torre, Acción Democrática, Velasco Ibarra, and, later, Paz Estenssoro, Perón's explicit goals were to achieve development and class harmony without explosive social conflict; to promote national integration and a certain redistribution of wealth; and to advance an interventionist role for the state as supreme arbiter between capital and labor. For such goals, however (and unlike other populist articulations), Perón did not need the intellectual classes, for time itself was transforming the knowledges required to implement industrialized modernity and modern national subjectivities in Argentina.

By the time Perón came to power the technological innovations of the 1920s and 1930s in Argentina had produced a boom in the development of technical forms of knowledge production and, in particular, in those forms of knowledge that correspond to what Beatriz Sarlo has called the *saberes del pobre* (knowledges of the poor). By the turn of the century massive European immigration had still not produced a significant level of citizenship in Argentina (in 1895 only 0.16 percent of immigrants had been naturalized, and by 1914 only 1.4 percent of immigrants were naturalized Argentine citizens [Madsen and Snow 37]). Against such threatening traces of heterogeneity and the concept of non-*argentinidad,* education in the first decades of the century had become a privileged arena for the production of a patriotic citizenry built on the neutralization of difference, on the active promotion of the teaching of Spanish, national history, and national geography, and on an almost obsessive official reverence for the inculcation of national symbols and ceremonies. It is at this time, of course, that Leopoldo Lugones and Ricardo Rojas begin their reflection on the dangers of immigration and the need for the fabrication of a specifically national literary culture. But the 1920s and 1930s marked a significant reorganization in the hierarchies of knowledge production within the Argentine social sphere (Dussel and Pineau 112). The emergence in the 1930s of state organizations such as SIPCE (State System of Centralized Public Instruction) and of the Popular Education Societies, including their popular libraries, neighborhood organizations, adult education groups, and so forth, paved the way for a moment of profound social transformation in which *saber* (knowledge) gave way to *saber hacer* (know-how) and to the new social hegemony of the civil and industrial engineer as a privileged figure in the advancement of national modernization, progress, and development. What Perón managed to do was to envision a specifically Peronist ideological state apparatus constructed by channeling the new "knowledges of the poor" into the workings of the state union and pedagogic machinery; by disarticulating and delegitimizing liberal intellectual discourse against the state; and by "Peronizing" university faculty and administrative positions. By 1950, in fact, such maneuvers had led to open and stubborn opposition to Perón from the liberal Facultad de Letras y Filosofía as well as from the more conservative Catholic-nationalist Facultad de Derecho at the Universidad de Buenos Aires (Mangone and Warley 27–40).

Meanwhile, the formation of the Peronist ideological state apparatus continued by leaps and bounds. Between 1945 and 1955 the number of registered students in the school of engineering at the Universidad de Buenos Aires doubled (Dussel and Pineau 157). In 1948 the Universidad Obrera Nacional, grounded in a regionalist model of applied, technical, and vocational knowledge production was established, signaling a new attempt at articulating national pedagogical norms with the economic and political spheres of civil society. Indeed, such was the success of the Universidad Obrera Nacional in its ability to establish and fortify relations between labor, the pedagogical institutions, and the state that it even survived the anti-Peronist backlash of the 1950s and became fully integrated into the developmentalist discourses of Peronism's opposition under Arturo Frondizi.

Thus, in contrast to other local and national cultural traditions of the region, Argentine populism did not actively promote literature as a privileged space from within which to make the people reproduce itself as national community and institutional effect. This is not to say, however, that Peronism did not promote social and racial miscegenation as the precondition of social mobility and progress. In the case of Argentine populism, fictive ethnicity did not have to draw on the fabrication and institutionalized translation, through literature, of utopian *mestizaje* as a necessary prerequisite for national progress and development. What had become an active process of state-sanctioned literary transculturation in other areas—that is, what had become a quest for a modernized civil society grounded in ethnic miscegenation as the promise of linguistic, cultural, and economic modernization—in Argentina took on a different hue, simply because the "African problem" or the "Indian problem" could not be lived to the same level of intensity.

This is not to say, however, that transcultural fictive ethnicity was not

The Other Side of the Popular

a fundamental component in the arsenal of Argentine national integration. If we understand fictive ethnicity as the formation of populations represented "*as if* they formed a natural community, possessing of itself an identity of origins, culture and interests which transcends individuals and social conditions . . . which makes it possible for the expression of a preexisting unity to be seen in the state" (Balibar, "Nation" 96), then we can identify within Peronism the active and foundational fabrication of a phantom transculturation that was designed to promote a specifically Peronist vision of working-class social contamination, miscegenation, heresy, transformation, and state formation.

Indeed, it is through the dissemination of the specter of transculturation (once again, through the image of Sarmiento's rural barbarians washing their feet in the fountains of the liberal and conservative urban center) that the Peronist working class came to identify itself as a preexisting unity in the state. It could even be said that Perón construed his body as the point of convergence for a transregional (country/city) fusion effect, capable of transcending the rift in the history of national development that had been inflicted on the working class by the Great Depression and the antilabor repression of the *década infame*. By presenting himself as the absolute locus of mediation and translation between distinct regions, past movements and periods of popular mobilization, and what were perceived to be the needs and aspirations of the immediate present, Perón was able to take advantage of the weakness and in-fighting of the socialists and communists in order to conjure up the ethnicized specters of Yrigoyenism and of the initial moments of labor migration and organization in Argentina under Unión Cívica Radical. This allowed him to fabricate the image of a future form of citizenship that was to be constructed exclusively by the working class's ability to (through him) intervene in, mediate, and influence state processes.

To a considerable degree Perón's phantom transculturation fabricated a peculiarly Peronist form of popular affect, which provided a common framework of meaning to the emergence of the working class as the historical and institutionalized contamination of the landed oligarchy's dualist social structures. As Daniel James notes in *Resistance and Integration*, Perón systematically transformed the discursive *habitus* of the worker in Argentine society by questioning "social assumptions concerning social relationships, forms of deference and largely tacit understandings about the 'natural order of things'. . . . In this sense Peronism's power ultimately lay in its capacity to give utterance to what had until then been internalised, lived as private experience" (30). Moreover, this articulation of Argentine working-class peoplehood was achieved by conjuring up the image of a powerful social force of miscegenation and contamination that would ultimately undermine the symbolic authority and pretensions of the national elites. As James suggests, Perón was deeply invested in the discourse of transculturation, which he conjured up regularly in order to fabricate the people as an organized and institutionalized Peronist worker-citizenry, a new fictive ethnicity:

> *Negro* in general usage referred to inhabitants from the interior of the country and often had clear ethnic, pejorative, connotations. The traditional elite had disrespectfully referred to Yrigoyen's supporters as *los negreros radicales*. With the mass influx of internal migrants to the industry of Buenos Aires in the 1930s the word was commonly used as synonymous with manual workers and the *negrada* was used as a generic equivalent of proletariat. . . . The use of *negrada* as a synonym for the proletariat of the 1930s thus had a strong social symbolism which was at the root of its use by anti-Peronist forces. *La negrada de Perón, las cabecitas negras,* were frequent terms of derision used by Perón's political opponents from the mid 1940s on. Their incorporation into the language of Peronism conferred on them a new status. The fact that *la negrada* found expression and affirmation in this public discourse meant that a range of experiences normally associated with the term . . . could now be spoken and enter into the realm of public discourse, social concern and hence political action. (31–32)

Without going so far as to say that Perón's phantom transculturation was solely responsible for the Peronization of the social sphere, it would probably be safe to say that it did construct a particular fictive ethnicity affect—a working-class transcultural affective investment—that contributed enormously to the organization and incorporation of workers into the processes of nationalist modernization, industrialization, and development of the state. Indeed the effects of Perón's insistence on the heretical character of his fictive ethnicity, which emerged hand-in-hand with his systematic and often violent neutralization and delegitimization of the Communist and Socialist parties, were enormous (though by no means absolute). Although in 1943 the vast majority of the industrial proletariat was outside effective union organization, by 1948 "the rate of unionisation had risen to 30.5% of the wage earning population, and in 1954 it had reached 42.5%. In the majority of manufacturing industries the rate was between 50% and 70%. Between 1946 and 1951 total union membership increased from 520,000 members to 2,334,000" (James 9–10).

Peronist transculturation, then, provided the means by which Perón himself could locate whole sectors of the working class and its system of identifications within the framework of a new national citizenry. Once again in the words of Daniel James: "In an important sense the working class was constituted by Perón; its self-identification as a social and political force within national society was, in part at least, constructed by Peronist political discourse which offered workers viable solutions for their problems and a credible vision of Argentine society and their role within it. This was evidently a complex process, involving for some workers a *re*-constitution of their sense of identity and political loyalty as they abandoned established allegiances and identities" (38).

Peronist transculturation touched a nerve within the Argentine working class and unleashed upon society a particular vision of citizenship, organization, and transformational potential, which, while emerging from within the elite's desire for the harmonization of relations between capital and labor, nevertheless threatened the historical status quo with what would later be called the ugly specter of communist subversion. If, as James indicates, "much of the Peronist state's efforts between 1946 and its demise in 1955 can be viewed as an attempt to institutionalise and control the heretical challenge it had unleashed in the earlier period and to absorb this challenge within a new state-sponsored orthodoxy" (34), then it would not be far from the truth to suggest that the years between Perón's overthrow (1955) and the emergence of the military's Process of National Reorganization (1976–1983) mark the violent intensification of the struggle between cultural nationalism's conservative orthodoxy and its increasingly radical and heretical impulses. The years between 1955 and 1976 signal an intensification in the struggle over the terms of societal order and its representations that takes us in general literary terms from Rodolfo Walsh's *Operación masacre* in 1964 and Osvaldo Lamborghini's "El fiord" in 1969 through to the unresolvable fragmentation of the nation form, of the notion of collective social organization, and of history's signifying processes that characterize many of the narratives that emerged in the late 1970s and 1980s in response to the military Proceso.[16]

FICTIVE ETHNICITY, THE PEOPLE, AND
THE QUESTION OF SECURITY

The partial genealogies and fragmented histories related in these pages have served to trace and uncover the foundational nexus between the nation-state, the mobilization of the subaltern masses, and the forging of the notion of the people as a transcultural national fictive ethnicity in modern Latin America. The functional trinity of land (the establishment of new relations between city and country, between center and periphery), a determinate order (the expansion of the nation-state, as opposed to other forms of organizational power, over national territory), and people (the active fabrication and integration of the subaltern population as the grounds of transcultural national identity and as the origin of national political and cultural life) constitutes the grounds for the organizational power of accumulation on a national scale. Of course, this is not to say that this process was ever truly functional. The persistence of feudal and neocolonial relations of production throughout Latin American modernity attests to the unevenness and incompletion of these processes. However, there can be little doubt that the aforementioned functional trinity (the land–order–people nexus) is the ideal telos on which the notion of nationhood was forged in a number of Latin American regions and in a number of specifically populist social configurations.

As seen earlier in my discussion of Fernando Ortiz, José María Arguedas, and Angel Rama, and as witnessed in my reading of the historical relation between populist social processes and transculturation in, for example, Venezuela, Bolivia, Peru, and Argentina, transculturation is generally considered to be a faithful explicative for the insertion and integration of the dominated masses into the sociopolitical, economic, and cultural horizons of the social elites. Through this process of mutual contact and collision the terms of domination do certainly shift. However, even though the terms of domination generally shift in favor of popular interests, it would be difficult to disagree with a writer such as John Beverley who suggests that such processes are the direct effect of a hegemonic fantasy of class, gender, and racial reconciliation that is foundational to the necessary neutralization of persistent class contradictions (*Subalternity* 47). In the same vein, it would be equally difficult to disagree with Alberto Moreiras when he notes that the thought of transculturation generally implies the acceptance of modernization as ideological truth and as world destiny (*Exhaustion* 188).

But the history of the relation between populism, the state's forging of transcultural fictive ethnicities, and capitalist modernization cannot end there. After all, it was precisely this relation, and the multiple histories that attest to its functionality, that came to create the conditions for Latin America's experience of, for example, the cold war. Indeed, it is precisely at this point that we can begin to trace the ways in which Latin America's official discourses of transculturation production—the nation-state's uneven attempts at constituting and consolidating national community as a universal and stable transcultural fictive ethnicity—intersected with transnational cold war configurations (such as the U.S.-

backed National Security Doctrine) and ultimately preconditioned the formation of transcultural (and transcontinental) knowledge production within pedagogic institutions in both Europe and the United States.

A point of departure in this regard is, once again, Peronism. As is the case in all cultural nationalist movements, Peronism was grounded in the promotion of the elite fantasy of a harmonizing arbiter state, standing above and mediating between class antagonisms, as the nation's single most effective promoter of class collaboration, modernization, and industrialization. As Steve Stein indicates in his analysis of Peru, however, such harmonizing (and neutralizing) models of social organization "posited the necessity not only of a more effectual state apparatus but also one sufficiently enlarged and strengthened so as to extend itself into wider areas of national concern while vigorously keeping the lid on possible internal conflict" (174). By the late 1950s Perón's anti-Peronist successor, Frondizi, intensified the state's drive (already mobilized and unleashed on civil society under Perón) to keep the lid on internal social agents. But Frondizi's developmentalist state remained incapable, and perhaps even uninterested in the possibility, of mediating the social antagonisms that (thanks in part to the international context of the Cuban revolution and increasing anticommunist cold war pressures) would prove to be the underlying ground for the imminent radicalization of cultural and political life in Argentina. In other words, during the years of Peronist resistance it appeared to be too late to fully pacify the forces of the Peronist working classes.

Positioning himself within the longstanding tradition of Argentine economic nationalism of which Perón was just one example, Frondizi had first criticized Perón in 1955 for making trade contracts with Standard Oil. By early 1958, however, Frondizi was contradicting his previous economic nationalist stance by promoting increased petroleum production and a controlled injection of foreign capital as a possible means of supporting capital accumulation in certain desired areas (James 107–8). Yet the chronic balance-of-payments crisis of late 1958 in Argentina marked a new round of union unrest and political repression that was accompanied by the insertion of the IMF into national socioeconomic processes. The IMF stabilization plan, which was viewed by many as the final capitulation of economic nationalism to foreign capital, had disastrous consequences for the working class, with real wages dropping 20 percent between 1958 and 1959 (110).

As in the case of Bolivia's national revolution and of APRA's constant accommodations to the interests of foreign capital, this event also made Argentine economic and cultural nationalism a decidedly international

geopolitical affair. Thus the internal contradictions of domestic industrialization and national populist organization and control in times of
anticommunist developmentalism (the cold war) paved the way for the
intensification of social antagonisms that would ultimately feed into, and
fuel, the struggle and turmoil of the 1960s, the increasing legitimization
of the state's forces of law and order, the 1969 Cordobazo, the disastrous
consequences of the return of Perón in June 1973, the even more disastrous consequences of Isabel Perón's presidency, and finally the military
regimes of 1976 through 1983.

With the end of the Second World War, the advent of the cold war,
and direct U.S. involvement in the overthrow of democracy (of Acción
Democrática) in Venezuela in 1948 and in Guatemala in 1954, Latin
America's always incomplete populist mobilizations—its multifarious
quests for the consolidation of national identity as the cultural and political vehicle by which to counter socioeconomic backwardness—intertwined and conflicted with U.S. foreign policy's anticommunist modernization theory. This policy had surged to the fore of hemispheric
relations after the Bretton Woods agreements of 1944, the establishment
of the Organization of American States in 1948, and the United Nations'
promotion of the Comisión Económica para América Latina (CEPAL)
in the same year. During the Truman administration economic aid and
the funding of development programs emerged briefly as fundamental components of the cold war crusade against communism in Latin
America. But this would soon be displaced by the military component of
development. Thus, under Eisenhower almost $400 million flowed into
Latin America—in particular into the armies of Brazil, Colombia, Chile,
and Peru—as a means of guarding against potential communist upheaval
(Berger 68).

It was a commonly held belief in the metropolitan nations after the
Second World War that the capitalist development of the so-called Third
World was essential (along with the exportation of North American
values and institutional processes) for the success of the global struggle
against underdevelopment, social disorder, and potential communist
revolution. It was not by chance, then, that the radical formulations of
intellectuals such as Paul Sweezy and Paul Baran, who provided the theoretical foundations of what would later become Latin American dependency theory (that is, the idea that the expansion of monopoly capitalism
and of the world market actually produces an increasingly dependent
"backwardness" in Latin America) were diluted from within the United
Nations Comisión Económica para América Latina (CEPAL) through "a
relatively conservative version of dependency theory, in the context of a

shift to an import-substitution industrialization policy in Latin America"
(Berger 108).

Thus, as a result of the United Nations' attempts to neutralize critical evaluations of the capitalist world system, import-substitution became the hegemonic developmentalist discourse in the United States in the years following the Second World War. However, the inability of import-substitution to address historically grounded social inequities was soon revealed, and it led instead to a new emphasis on the military as the privileged custodians of the law and order that was deemed to be desirable for anticommunist progress and development throughout Latin America. Within the context of cold war anticommunism and the advent of the import-substitution model promoted by CEPAL (in which Creole national-populist development came to be structured through Keynesian state-led economic policy, injections of foreign capital, industrialization, the protection of internal markets, and the economic integration of national populations) populism proved to be one of the privileged yet most problematic means of negotiating the legitimacy of the patrimonial state.

Needless to say, then, CEPAL's promotion of exclusively orthodox (that is, nonsocialist and noncommunist) popular integration, together with its international legitimization of the state's active economic role in society, created its own monsters. Massive insertions of foreign capital into local processes of national industrialization, state formation, and peoplehood construction threatened the legitimacy of patrimonial states grounded in the rhetoric of economic nationalism and undermined the interests of foreign capital as national fictive ethnicity production became increasingly challenged and channeled by mass anti-imperialist sentiment.

However, it is really only after fictive ethnicity's radicalization under the banner of the Cuban revolution's New Man (the fabrication and imposition of a revolutionary, national, and anti-imperialist subject committed to workers and peasants who was considered to be self-sacrificing and of high moral principles) that we witness the full flowering of both the ideology of the national-popular, as well as that of developmentalism's attempts to keep the international lid on impending social antagonism.[17]

In the years immediately following the Cuban revolution the Kennedy administration's Alliance for Progress was born. As Mark Berger informs us in this regard: "At the center of the Alliance for Progress was a decade-long program of land and economic reform which was going to cost 100 billion dollars and [was] aimed at bringing about an annual growth rate of at least 2.5 per cent. It also sought to achieve greater productivity in the agricultural sector, eradicate illiteracy, stimulate trade diversification, generate improvements in housing and bring about improved income distribution in the region" (88). But hemispheric liberal developmentalism within the context of local elite privilege and historic impunity (now working hand in hand with cold war anticommunism) soon revealed its limitations as a coherent alternative form of social organization and of popular representation. As such, liberal developmentalism soon turned to military-led forms of modernization as the armed forces gradually came to be viewed by Washington and its allies as a stabilizing factor in the face of popular unrest and as the only force in society with the administrative and technical skills necessary to directly facilitate capitalist modernization. Once again, Berger's words are decisive:

> The Alliance for Progress was a failure. Its central unstated goal was the protection of North American investments in Latin America at the same time as many of the Alliance's reforms endangered those investments. Trade diversification threatened the US-based transnationals' monopoly in primary agricultural products and mineral extraction. Any significant land reform also threatened the interests of the still largely land-based ruling elites in Latin America. This contradiction was apparent in the way that Kennedy's reformist rhetoric went hand in hand with Washington's ever-deepening commitment to military and police aid and counterinsurgency to quash peasant-based rebellions in the region. From the very beginning, US-based transnationals and the landed oligarchies attempted to preserve the status quo and prevent any meaningful change. There were sixteen military coups within eight years of the launch of the Alliance for Progress. By the late 1960s, high rates of economic growth in many Latin American countries had been achieved. However, high growth rates had served primarily to increase social inequality, while the middle class moved to side with the ruling political and socio-economic elite as politics, instead of evolving towards democracy, moved ever further towards authoritarianism and military dictatorship. Already by the time of Kennedy's assassination, the reformist element in the Alliance had been sidelined in favour of a more straightforward approach of military and economic aid to any regime which was committed to the status quo. . . . Increasingly, military officers in Latin America . . . were represented as the vanguard of secular modernization and industrialization. Military modernization theory soon became a subdiscipline of North American area studies, as influential members of the Kennedy administration, such as Walt Whitman Rostow, emphasized the need to cultivate members of the Third World officer class. Policy-oriented academics,

such as Lucien Pye, Edward Shils, and Samuel Huntington put forward a new view of military elites as the key to both order and development. (88–90)

Thus, cold war demands to keep the lid on the popular effects of what had been, in the first place, the elite's drive for universal (transcultural) fictive ethnicity—synonymous, of course, with the hegemonization of the nation-state as a total ideology—uncover the origins of the Southern Cone military regimes of the 1970s, the low-intensity warfare of the Central American civil wars of the 1980s, and Latin America's institutionalization in the North as an object of political and epistemological concern after the initial successes of the Cuban revolution.

Moreover, we also should remember that it is from within the horizons of the Alliance for Progress that the Latin American "boom" novel, together with its aesthetic models of magical realism and of the marvellous real, became gradually incorporated into North American and European liberal pedagogical networks as the privileged form, technique, and imagination of Latin America's singularity, backwardness, and potential cultural modernization. The boom novel was soon understood to be Latin American literature's universalizing moment. It quickly became a living monument to the positive influence of Euro/North American literary modernism (Faulkner, Proust, James, Woolf, Kafka, Breton, Dos Passos, etc.) on the socioeconomically backward yet culturally affluent capitalist peripheries.[18] Euro/North American high culture, when consumed and reworked by a small, select group of exceptional (male) writers, very quickly came to constitute a peripheral great books tradition that was quickly (and, I think, correctly) deemed to be comparable to that of the First World. Grounded in the assimilation and resignification by the periphery of the center's models and modes of cultural representation, the boom (by its very existence) became something akin to a faithful explicative (when viewed, of course, purely from within the ideological lens of modernization) of the ways in which subordinate cultures can systematically insert themselves into, and transform, dominant ones through contact. It was emblematic of the productive gains that could be made as a result of the successful suturing of transculturation to capitalist modernization.

Writers as strikingly cosmopolitan and transcultural as Fuentes, Vargas Llosa, Cortázar, García Márquez, Cabrera Infante, Donoso, and so forth became the superstars of developmentalism's increasingly international labor of translation, representation, and institutionalization between geopolitical spheres (Latin America/Europe/the United States).

Thus the calculated and orchestrated presence and promotion of the boom writers within the institutional circuits of the First World can almost be read as an aesthetic overcompensation for Latin American development's persistent inability to mediate adequately between language groups, classes, genders, and ethnicities (that is, between its centers and peripheries). In other words, the boom—the dazzling technical prowess of Latin America's monumental national allegories—can be read not just as Latin America's moment of symbolic universalization, but also (and perhaps more astutely) as a last-ditch attempt to breathe symbolic-aesthetic life into the persistent inability of modernity (and fictive ethnicity, the nation-state, and the national-popular) to come to its own. The boom, in this sense, would be the writing of modernity's and of the nation-state's recalcitrant state of crisis, rather than that of its felicitous moment of symbolic universalization.

As the result of the persistent crisis of hegemony in the South (that is, the persistent failure of the nation to come to its own), an anxious Richard Nixon sent Nelson A. Rockefeller to Latin America in 1969 to meet with heads of state and military leaders. However, Rockefeller failed to gain access to Peru where, in a show of customary nationalist bravado, Juan Velasco Alvarado's populist military regime had nationalized North American oil interests. Rockefeller's trips to Chile and Venezuela, meanwhile, had been canceled before he even came close. The conclusions of Rockefeller's report called attention to the need for military modernization in order to curb what was quickly proving to be a dangerous period of popular mobilization in Latin America: "Without some framework for order," he wrote, "no progress can be achieved" because the military was "the essential force for constructive social change" (quoted in Berger 104).

Of course, Rockefeller's framework for order and for constructive social change—the means, in other words, by which to counter the negative effects of the functional trinity between land, order, and the people —emerged just a few years later as National Security Doctrine (the U.S.-inspired notion that the cold war was a military and moral crusade against the international spread of communism). Needless to say, it was this doctrine that provided the ideological and practical framework for the military interventions and dictatorial regimes of the 1970s and 1980s in Chile, Argentina, and Uruguay; for the Central American civil wars of the late 1970s and 1980s in Nicaragua, El Salvador, and Guatemala; for the Peruvian state's war against the Shining Path in the Andean highlands in the 1980s; and for the economic restructuration that these

regimes and conflicts invariably supported and/or installed as their ideological legacies for future generations.

Indeed, it is precisely here, in the violent and bloody transition away
from economic nationalism, and away from the hegemonic articulations
of the national-popular (and therefore toward the contemporary realities
that emerge as a result of national capitalism's crisis in the early 1980s),
that we encounter the problematic nature of one of Latin America's most
powerful great narratives and most faithful and trustworthy explicatives
of sociocultural (re)production in the twentieth century. Now that we
are obliged to confront the effects of the "lost decade" (the final and
often violent erosion of the national-popular and of its ideologies of economic nationalism; the emergence of the transnational marketplace as
the privileged site of mediation between peoples, classes, genders, ethnicities, neighborhoods, etc.; the structural adjustments of the nation-state
and the realignment of the political map through geo-economic arrangements such as the North American Free Trade Agreement (NAFTA) and
Mercosur; the advent of economic deregulation, flexible labor, mass migration, and the burgeoning informal sector), we would do well to reevaluate the notion of transculturation and reflect further on the extent
to which its differential fusion effects are, or have been, a faithful explicative of the ways in which subordinate cultures systematically transform
dominant ones through contact.

In the purely skeletal cultural and institutional histories presented
here, official discourses of transculturation (that is, discourses of ordered
or tamed transculturation rather than those of radical heterogeneities
capable of interrupting or suspending capitalist development's dominant discourses) have been fabricated almost exclusively as a means
of constructing a universalistic "we"; an institutionalized national fictive ethnicity negotiated from within the neocolonial elites, which has
remained throughout the history of Latin American modernity "without specific content or aim, without a common good *other than* abstract
universal representation or pluralism" (Brown 57). Within this framework the critical and artistic discourse of transculturation—which without doubt is one of the most important points of reference in the intellectual's and in the state's forging of collective social identity in modern
Latin America—emerges as something akin to a Borgesian play of mirrors. In this subtle game of inversion and reversal, capitalist modernization's dominant categories (transcultural fictive ethnicity, for example)
enter into intellectual critique as a means of accounting for the contours
of popular agency in the face of a dominant culture and social system.

However, the ghostly truth of this agency (also known as transcultura-tion) is located in the continual dislocations, realignments, and persis-tently violent determinations of elite notions of developmentalism and of the nation-state's quest for hegemonic universalization. Thus, as Alberto Moreiras maintains:

> Transculturation—that is, the macroprocess of translation by means of which elements of one culture are naturalized in another culture, although not without undergoing some changes during the process— of course insists on conciliation, conjunction, and dialectical unifica-tion of the global cultural field. It is a productive model, but it is also a model that must work and even feed on the systematic erasure of what does not fit into it. . . . Transculturation is a war machine, feed-ing on cultural difference, whose principal function is the reduction of the possibility of radical cultural heterogeneity. Transculturation is a part of the ideology of cultural productionism, indeed a systemic part of a Western metaphysics of production, which still retains a strong colonizing grip on the cultural field. (*Exhaustion* 195–96)

In this sense, populist/culturalist transculturation—our unflinching faith in transculturation as a positive assertion of individual/group iden-tity or of counterhegemonic difference, or as an impediment to the com-plete assimilation of subaltern classes and identities into dominant power structures, hegemonic state configurations, and neocolonial forms of representation—is something like an occlusion or an in-built obstruction that, nevertheless, has shaped the analytical course and cause of Latin American state and culture formation, and of Latin Americanist critical discourse, in the twentieth century. Perhaps it could be said that it marks one of those not so rare instances "in which the effects of choices made by the state have so completely impressed themselves in reality and in minds that possibilities initially discarded have become totally unthink-able" (Bourdieu, "Rethinking" 2).

But perhaps it is only now—after the demise of the national-popular —that we can suggest that transculturation is precisely the state's symp-tom: the discursive product of a patrimonial language of mastery that always needs to be re-represented as Other (and in the case of mod-ern Latin America, as national-popular). Of course, if this is the case then the thought of transculturation is a historical phenomenon of neo-colonial redistribution that, in Freudian terms, represses its object—neo-colonialism, noncontemporaneity, the division of labor, civilization ver-sus barbarism—yet simultaneously reveals it in displaced form as an affirmation of national-popular culture, and as a means of neutralizing

The Other Side of the Popular

and naturalizing labor-capital antagonisms through the fabrication of the people.

As such, the affirmation of transculturation as a national or continental identitarian essence does not provide us with a site from which to counter colonialism's spectral and often violent reemergence onto the political landscapes of the capitalist social order. It merely redistributes ethnic divisions in an attempt to somehow save the meaning and order of historical order and foreclose the possibility of a radical break with the genealogies of domination and of their social organization. In this sense, transculturation is (at least to the extent that it has been generated in relation to populism) not so much the telos for a popular heterogeneity capable of opening up the social field to alternative repertoires of thought, experience, and practice, but rather it is a fundamental path into the uneven subsumption of subalternity to the dominant horizons of capitalist modernization.

In this regard, we would probably do well to heed Alejo Carpentier's call, in the final passages of his *Los pasos perdidos,* for a return to reflection, because the restructuring of the nation-state that has resulted from fictive ethnicity's collapse in recent years, along with the expansion of the transnational marketplace as a major constitutive principle of social organization throughout contemporary Latin America, are the ultimate confirmation that "today Sisyphus' vacation came to an end" (279; translation mine).

As Stuart Hall suggests in reference to the capitalist world system's erosion of the nation-state—in reference, that is, to the expansion in recent years of global economic structures; to the emergence of economic, migrant, and communications networks interacting across traditional borders; to the establishment of new supranational structures of control and domination, and therefore to the social order of neoliberalism—"through the erosion and instability of the nation-state, of the self-sufficiency of national economies and consequently, of national identities as points of reference, there has simultaneously been a fragmentation and erosion of collective social identity" (44). In this chapter I have traced the modern thought of transculturation and of the national-popular as a thought devoted to, partaking of, and invested in the orchestration and construction of the nation-state, the forging of national identity, and the constitution and reproduction throughout the social and cultural fields of their relations of force.

Thus transculturation, as the means by which subordinate cultures systematically transform dominant ones through contact, uncovers itself as a particular relation to the notion of hegemony. However, it does so not so much as a critique of the notion on the grounds of its exclusions but as an affirmation of its modernizing function. As a reflection on the possibility of protouniversal unification—of unification under the banner of national-popular difference—the thought of transculturation, as shown in the skeletal histories that I have traced in this chapter, strives to establish an immanent relationship between the construction of national hegemony and the individual in such a way that national transcultural fictive ethnicity uncovers identitarian flexibility as the precondition for successfully negotiating and mediating between the social languages, functions, and differential positions adherent within national territory.

The thought of transculturation is, in this sense, a discourse invested in the state's fabrication of common principles of vision. However, this is a critical, aesthetic, and institutional discourse that strives to displace the fact that transcultural national fictive ethnicity—the utopic formation of the nation-state and of national culture through the transcendent articulation of the people as a people—always leaves the logics of development themselves untouched. As such, it is a thought of development, of hegemony, and of the state that incorporates and affirms the popular, the people, or the masses, but does so always and exclusively as a subordinate position within the articulation and construction of the national cultural market. In this sense the thought of transculturation, as it has been construed throughout modernity, is about as hegemonic as it is counterhegemonic, to the extent that it tends to bolster the illusion that Creole hegemony is both hegemonic and national-popular. Thus the intellectual maneuvers and repertoires pertaining to the thought of transculturation—to a thought of transculturation invested in the expansion and deepening of sustained social intelligibility—take their full meaning, as Bourdieu would say, "not only as theoretical contributions to the knowledge of the state but also as political strategies aimed at imposing a particular vision of the state, a vision in agreement with the interests and values associated with the particular position of those who produce them in the bureaucratic universe" ("Rethinking" 3). The thought of transculturation, then, promises "a faithful explicative of the ways in which subordinate cultures systematically transform dominant ones through contact" (Rowe and Schelling 205). But, it remains just that: a promise that nevertheless provides no rupture with the thought of domination itself.

Having said this, however, recent transformations in the capitalist world system have uncovered the limits of such hegemonizing intellectual/state projects, for we have crossed a decisive historical threshold in intellectual/state/culture (and therefore in power/knowledge) relations that makes a positive return to transculturation and to its thought of hegemony fabrication almost a restaging of Creole developmentalist utopias; a neohegemonic discourse at a time in which, as Etienne Balibar informs us, new conditions that directly challenge the notion and possibility of hegemony and of national peoplehood production prevail. According to Balibar:

> The geographic and geo-political pattern of the world has been subjected to considerable modifications. The very term "globalization" still reminds us of a process in which it was the "center" (in fact made of rival powers) which was incorporating successive "peripheries" and outer regions (Wallerstein's "external arenas") within the limits of its domination. This process took the form of subjecting states and societies, importing goods and men, exploiting manpower and natural resources, exporting languages, techniques, and institutions (ultimately: the nation-state itself). What strikes us now is the "backfire" effect of this process. It is not the suppression of domination and economic inequalities (perhaps it could be said that the polarization of wealth and misery, power and dependency, has reached unprecedented levels), but the multiplication of centers, forming a network rather than a "core" area. And it is the reverse movement which projects elements of the former periphery into the "central" societies. ("Ambiguous" 51–52)

The thought of transculturation, the thought of national fictive ethnicity, and the underlying dynamics recounted in these pages can no longer provide models for the community-producing and/or thought-producing processes of the present or of the future. They are the state of things passed (which is not to say that they are obsolete as objects of reflection, merely that they cannot be engaged with obsolete critical tools). But no other subsistent ground for intellectual engagement has yet taken the place of the cultural and political thought of the nation-state or of the national-popular, for in neoliberal/postnational times it appears that we are merely living the experience of the continual fragmentation and redistribution of the nation-state's previously hegemonic and contested signifying processes. As such, we must wonder whether the conditions for such a new telos for reflection are actually present in the current neoliberal social order and, consequently, in the contemporary reorganization of knowledge.

In the chapters that follow I hazard to say that these conditions both are and are not simultaneously. This peculiar limit to our current conceptual systems requires that in order to keep alive the promise of political and cultural thought—and, alongside it, in order to keep alive a notion of radical heterogeneity—we should perhaps subject the state and the thought of the state, and therefore the social foundations of the contemporary order, to the work of *hyperbolic doubt:* that is, to an interrogation of relations of power that is governed by a critical insistence not on the possibility of reinscribing, recuperating, or reforging preexisting social hegemonies, but rather on the possibility of thinking about those realms within the social field that have tended historically to "unwork" the mechanisms and calculations of hegemonic power and reproduction.[19]

As will be shown in the following chapters, those realms of thought and practice tend to belong to the notion of subalternity. Subalternity, on the other hand, is the negative site on the outer margins of the thought of (counter)hegemony (hegemony's negative foundation or point of finitude and of radical breakdown) that fractures its naturalizing symbolizations in order to erupt onto the field of signification as "the absolute limit of the place where history is narrativized into logic" (Spivak, "Subaltern" 16). This limit, and the experience of finitude that it promises, inaugurates not the stabilization of heterogeneity—not the positive articulation of social signifiers around state-related or controled processes of transculturation—but the emergence of radical heterogeneity as a persistent demand for a political and cultural thought that is grounded in the disjuncture and fragmentation that lies on the other side of hegemony and on the other side of hegemony's traditions and cultural histories.

The Other Side of the Popular

2

Intellectual Populism and
the Geopolitical Structure of Knowledge

> Ideology . . . is not just a matter of what I think about a situation; it is
> somehow inscribed in that situation itself. It is no good me reminding
> myself that I am opposed to racism as I sit down on a park bench
> marked "Whites Only"; by the act of sitting on it, I have supported
> and perpetuated racist ideology. The ideology, so to speak, is in the
> bench, not in my head. — Terry Eagleton, *Ideology*

The previous chapter examined the notion of transculturation in its relation to the formation of the modern nation-state and to the national-
popular period of development in Latin America. As a result of these
relations, the idea of transculturation was seen as largely predicated on
the fixing of the notion of peoplehood within narratives of national interests and common concerns of the state. As John Beverley ("Theses"
308) has observed, hegemonic nationalist discourse in twentieth-century
Latin America was designed generally to suture the gaps and discontinuities within the corpus of the so-called national people rather than
to allow heterogeneity and multiplicity to function as the real grounds
and origins of national political life. Heterogeneity, in other words, was
celebrated to the extent that it did not disturb the nation-state's promotion of normative national identities. As described in the last chapter, the
state's unifying projects, which were carried out invariably in the name of
cultural heterogeneity and of economic integration simultaneously, were
designed in such a way as to expand the interests of recently emerging
elites who were intent on incorporating nationalist rhetoric — a rhetoric
of universal transculturation or hybridity, as Beverley puts it — in order
to secure hegemony.

However, the cycle of national liberation struggles that followed the
Cuban revolution, the intensification of cold war antagonisms, the emergence of military dictatorships as guardians of elite interests in the face

of increasing popular destabilization during the 1960s and 1970s in the Southern Cone, the Central American wars of the 1980s, the failure of import-substitution industrialization, and the ultimate eclipse of the national-popular Left (including, of course, the electoral defeat of the Sandinistas in 1990) bear witness to the ways in which the struggle over the stabilization of the category of the people, and over its organization through narratives of universal historical destiny, have now produced what Néstor García Canclini has referred to as the eclipse of Latin America's national scripts and grand narratives (*Hybrid* 243–44).

The contemporary crisis in modern ideologies of national community, national identity, and national political organization has brought about such enormous rifts in populism's foundational discourses that it appears that we must now confront the fact that Latin American postcolonial social hegemonies have always been at best fragmented and at worst illusory, or perhaps just so incomplete and contested that the idea of hegemony itself in Latin America has been about as productive as it has been limited. Counterhegemony, meanwhile, appears to have always been just as varied, as contingent, and perhaps as illusory as its counterpart.

Without doubt, the emergence (predominantly in the U.S. academy) of subaltern forms of expressivity such as that of the Latin American *testimonio* in the 1980s is symptomatic of this permanent state of crisis in the forging of national social and cultural hegemonies in Latin America. This predominantly northern phenomenon (with, of course, Rigoberta Menchú as its figurehead) coincided with a time of enormous upheaval in the capitalist world economy and in the organization of international power/knowledge relations as a whole. In particular, *testimonio* (a cultural form that has been around for years in Latin America, of course) was suddenly incorporated as a valued object of analysis at quite a precise point in the reorganization of the political conjuncture within the United States, as well as within the history of intellectual production in the metropolitan countries in general. As such, the emergence of the notion of the subaltern, along with the rapid canonization of *testimonio* in the U.S. academy, is, in one way or another, a direct response not only to the crisis of national (transcultural) fictive ethnicity throughout Latin America, but also to the shifting grounds of political and economic life in the years following the defeat of U.S. military forces in Vietnam.

Even though there was no way of knowing it at the time, when in 1983 *Me llamo Rigoberta Menchú y así me nació la conciencia* was first published the so-called revolutionary period—which had begun after the Second World War and had included the Bolivian revolution, the Arbenz government in Guatemala, the Cuban revolution, Popular Unity and the Chilean Road to Socialism, the Sandinista revolution, and the emergence of insurgent movements in Guatemala and El Salvador—was actually drawing to a close. As it turned out, the decisive turning point had come in 1973 with the defeat of Salvador Allende's Popular Unity at the hands of the Chilean military and with the shock to the world economic order that transpired as a result of the international oil crisis.

Tulio Halperín Donghi traces the economic upheaval of the early 1970s in Latin America and the United States in the following terms:

> Reformist and revolutionary impulses had not disappeared by the end of the 1960s, but after 1970 changes in the international context created a substantially new situation in Latin America. . . . The world economic order changed rapidly after 1970. The end of the long postwar economic boom in the capitalist core came clearly into sight by 1971, when U.S. president Richard Nixon suspended the parity of the dollar (that is, its convertibility for a fixed amount of gold, established by the Bretton Woods Accords of 1944) in an attempt to adapt to his country's loss of absolute economic predominance over other industrial powers. (338)

However, Halperín Donghi continues, it was the oil shock of 1973 that brought a sudden and dramatic corrective to a global economic order in which, since the end of the Second World War, the most advanced nations had grown more rapidly in industrial output than in production of the food and raw materials they consumed:

> The adoption of new production limits by OPEC led to a sudden jump in oil prices that caused inflation in the world's heavily industrialized economies and slowed their expansion. . . . The relative position of the world's major powers was affected by the new facts of international economic life. . . . All of the most developed capitalist countries had to deal with dangerous levels of inflation in the late 1970s. In 1978, U.S. financial managers tried to curb inflation by imposing a drastic increase in interest rates. The measure reduced earnings and increased unemployment but failed utterly to halt inflation. The second oil shock in 1979 reinforced the inflationary trend and made combating it a priority for governments all over the industrialized world. (339–40)

The economic policies implemented by the industrial core countries in their efforts to defeat inflation greatly reduced the flow of loans to Latin America. These policies also made repayment of preexisting loans increasingly difficult to negotiate. This situation only worsened in the early 1980s when successive budget deficits in the United States led to massive and sustained borrowing, which absorbed much of the investment capital that had been available on the international market (Halperín Donghi 340). Meanwhile, the new prioritization of anti-inflationary measures in the core countries of the capitalist world system coincided with a radical shift in power relations, as the Anglo-Saxon countries "witnessed the rise to governmental power of the most reactionary ideologues, Reagan and Thatcher[,] movements for racial and social justice in the United States were beaten back, and the defeat of the miner's strike in Britain put an end to labour militancy there for years to come" (Ahmad 191). As a result of this ideological shift in power relations, "conservative administrations like those in Great Britain and (beginning a bit later) the United States turned the anti-inflation campaign into an assault on the social welfare programs that had proliferated during the postwar boom, and even governments far more committed to maintaining a welfare state, such as the socialist administrations of France and Spain, saw a need for retrenchment in that regard" (Halperín Donghi 340).[1]

In the relation between the global inflationary cycle, which was initiated by the international oil crisis of 1973, and the ideological shift in power relations that followed we witness the underlying political and economic conditions that helped to delegitimize the Keynesian-Fordist economic model of development. This relation created the grounds for the restructuring of international production processes as well as for that of their political and institutional frameworks; the disorganization of previously functional patterns of socialization such as those offered by the frontiers of the nation and by the geographic specificity of the nation-state; the deregulation, decentralization, and privatization of the economic sphere; the emergence within the core countries of global trade liberalization as a fundamental principle of foreign policy; the increasingly international division of labor; and the erosion of redistributive measures that had previously been guaranteed through business-labor negotiations regulated by the nation-state. In Kenneth Surin's words:

> This latest phase of capitalist development has been "theorized" under a variety of now familiar labels (by Ernest Mandel, Immanuel Wallerstein, David Harvey, Toni Negri, the members of the regulation school, and others): "late capitalism", "advanced capitalism", "disorganized capitalism", "globalized capitalism", "post-Fordism", and so on. The transition to this phase has been marked in a number of registers: the creation of an international division of labor, the rise of an international debt economy, the modulation of capital into the struc-

The Other Side of the Popular

tures of transnational corporations, the introduction of flexible manufacturing systems and labor processes, the growth of decentralized and
informal economies, the exponential growth . . . of standardized markets and patterns of consumption, the development of complex secu-
rities and credit systems, the inauguration of a new semiotics of value,
and so forth. (1185)[2]

From the outset, the success or failure of the most advanced nation's
anti-inflationary maneuvers in the 1970s and early 1980s depended on
the ability of the industrialized nations to overcome political resistance
in the zones in which capitalist expansion was taking place, or in which
it could take place in the future. The result was the vehement revival
in the early 1980s of the language of 1950s-style anticommunism under
Ronald Reagan, together with the newly emergent language of free trade
across national frontiers as the basic ground for democracy. As such,
the notion of free trade became equated with freedom as a whole, to
the exclusion of all possible alternative interpretations. As far as U.S.
economic and foreign policy were concerned, both of these languages
were absolutely necessary for the opening up of markets to capitalist expansion and to the further integration of cheap labor into an increasingly transnational market system. Thus "the Reagan victory of 1980
put the right wing of the Republican party in the White House, banished
human rights to rhetorical obscurity, and returned anti-insurgency and
the struggle against communism to top priority in U.S. foreign policy"
(Halperín Donghi 342).[3]

Furthermore, the language of anticommunism under Reagan very
quickly became a language dominated by the notion of morality. As
Michael Hardt and Antonio Negri observe in reference to the 1980s, the
increased insertion of the state into daily life in the United States became
increasingly justified by shifting the onus of political discourse onto the
realm of Christian morality:

> Much of the rhetoric of the Reagan and Bush administrations posed
> the contemporary crisis not principally as an economic crisis or even
> a crisis of law and order but a crisis of values, of national direction,
> of the moral fabric. The intervention of the State, then, was increas-
> ingly conceived as an instrument for not only the economic welfare but
> also the moral welfare of the citizenry. Areas such as women's produc-
> tive capacities, drug use, religious practices, family values, and sexual
> orientation became more and more important as sites for direct State
> involvement. The country needed moral leadership and moral educa-
> tion. (243)

But moral leadership and moral education after the oil crisis were by no means limited to the sphere of U.S. domestic policy. Rather, they were a decidedly international affair. In the early 1980s U.S. foreign policy and the crusade against hemispheric communism quickly became subject to the claims of conservative morality. On April 15, 1983—the same year in which *Me llamo Rigoberta Menchú* was first published, and just sixteen months after the cover-up of a military massacre of hundreds of peasants in El Salvador, which was carried out by the U.S.-trained and equipped Atlacatl Battalion—U.S. Secretary of State George Schultz declared in reference to the insurgent Frente Farabundo Martí para la Liberación Nacional (FMLN) in El Salvador that "there are many reasons for us to care about what happens in Central America. One is strategic, and we better remember it. ... . But an equal reason is moral. How can we, in the name of human rights, abandon our neighbors to a brutal, military takeover by a totalitarian minority?" (4). Indeed, twelve days after Secretary Schultz delivered this speech, President Reagan, in a joint session of Congress, shared similar moral insights into the intricacies of Central American foreign policy: "The national security of all the Americas is at stake in Central America. . . . We have a vital interest, a moral duty, and a solemn responsibility. This is not a partisan issue. It is a question of meeting our moral responsibility to ourselves, our friends, and our posterity. It is a duty that falls on all of us—the President, the Congress, and the people. We must perform it together. Who among us would wish to bear responsibility for failing to meet our shared obligation?" ("Central America" 5). Approximately three months later, on July 18, 1983, in a speech titled "Saving Freedom in Central America" delivered before representatives of the International Longshoremen's Association, Reagan extended his call for national and transnational moral unity by inscribing his mission firmly within the Pan Americanist agendas that had prevailed in the U.S. foreign policy of the 1930s (see Berger 227). Here he claimed a civilizing role for the United States capable of negotiating a hemispheric universalization of northern history, religion, and economic development:

> You know, I was down in that area on a trip. I met with the heads of states of Central and South America. And I pointed something out to them that very often we tend to forget. This Western Hemisphere is unique. We are, as I said before, 30 countries down there, 3 here on the northern continent, but we all are Americans. We cross the line into another country; it is still North and South and Central America. And we haven't gotten together the way we should. We don't know enough about that area. And we need to do more. Can you imagine what a

power for good in the world these two continents, linked by the isthmus of Central America—we worship from North Pole to South Pole the same God, we have the same heritage of coming here as pioneers to these virtually undiscovered continents. And what a power for good we could be with all the resources available to these continents if we help them in achieving what we have achieved here in this land in freedom, in economic progress, in standard of living. ("Saving" 3)

In the struggle against Central American insurgency Reagan almost assumes the mantle of Christopher Columbus as he charts, deciphers, understands, reinvents, and reproduces his own privately discovered geopolitical gold mine of Christian goodness and accumulation. By doing this he positions Central America as a utopic space that signifies historically only to the extent that it can be the mirror image of northern models of capitalist freedom, progress, homogeneity, knowability, unity, and goodness.

At the other end of the U.S. political spectrum, however, *testimonio* came to be considered a powerful subaltern expressivity and ideological counterweight in the mid-1980s, because as a genre it challenged Reaganism's claims to universal representation by upholding the marginal histories and multiple and heterogeneous identities repressed by historically constituted dominant epistemologies and institutional configurations. As such, *testimonio* afforded intellectuals the opportunity to disseminate discursive kernels of resistance to Reaganism's reworking of Depression-era pan-Americanism in the early to mid-1980s.

Within the transition to neoliberal models of development and domination, *testimonio* promised alternative forms of expression and of subaltern/intellectual agency. In *Against Literature* John Beverley notes that *testimonio* was thought to represent "the possibility of regional, national, and/or transnational coalitions of radicalized intellectuals and professionals with subaltern classes or social groups," for this was a form of subaltern expression that, within the very structures of its textual composition, promised the possibility of "a form of a global 'alliance politics' of the left" (90).[4]

In a later essay, Beverley situates *testimonio* within the reorganization of the political atmosphere in the United States and abroad in the years leading up to the fall of the Berlin Wall in 1989 and up to the defeat of the Sandinistas in the Nicaraguan elections of the following year:

> Testimonio began as an adjunct to armed liberation struggle in Latin America and elsewhere in the Third World in the sixties. But its canonization was tied even more, perhaps, to the military, political, and

economic force of counterrevolution in the years after 1973. It was the Real, the voice of the body in pain, of the disappeared, of the losers in the rush to marketize, that demystified the false utopian discourse of neoliberalism, its claims to have finally reconciled history and society. At the same time, testimonio relativized the moral liberal or even progressive claim of the high-culture writers and artists of the boom to speak for the majority of Latin Americans. It marked a new site of discursive authority, which challenged the authority of the "great writer" to establish the reality principle of Latin American culture and development.

Testimonio was intimately linked to international solidarity networks in support of revolutionary movements or struggles around human rights, apartheid, democratization; but it was also a way of testing the contradictions and limits of revolutionary and reformist projects still structured in part around elite assumptions about the role of cultural vanguards. Detached from these contexts, it loses its special aesthetic and ideological power, and runs the risk of becoming a new form of *costumbrismo,* the Spanish term for "local color" writing. ("Real" 281)[5]

In other words, the history of the emergence and institutionalization of *testimonio* as a specific response to the hegemonic crisis of national fictive ethnicity and of national political organization in general is anything but disinterested. As Beverley indicates, "the reception of *testimonio* today is bound up with the globalization of both capitalist exploitation and the new forms of resistance to it, and thus traverses directly that center of information retrieval and knowledge production which is the university" (*Against* 90).[6] *Testimonio,* in other words, and in particular the canonization of the genre within metropolitan power/knowledge configurations, is intimately tied to broader questions of how to read culture in times dominated by a crisis of hegemonic models; a crisis that has wrought fundamental shifts in the grounds of fictive ethnicity, in the idea of social integration, and, indeed, in the category of the nation itself as the privileged terrain and exclusive horizon from within which to produce critical reason as a whole.[7]

The founding statement of the Latin American Subaltern Studies Group formulates the cultural, political, and institutional challenges facing contemporary intellectual practice in the following terms:

> The present dismantling of authoritarian regimes in Latin America, the end of communism and the consequent displacement of revolutionary projects, the processes of redemocratization, and the new dynamics created by the effects of the mass media and transnational eco-

nomic arrangements: these are all developments that call for new ways of thinking and acting politically. The redefinition of Latin American political and cultural space in recent years has, in turn, impelled scholars of the region to revise established and previously functional epistemologies in the social sciences and humanities. (110)

As I suggested at the end of the last chapter in reference to the work of Etienne Balibar, and as the founding statement of the Latin American Subaltern Studies Group upholds, we have crossed a decisive historical threshold in power/knowledge relations as the result of far-reaching modifications in the geographic and geopolitical patterns of the world.

As already noted, during the Keynesian-Fordist model of (national) development the center (or rather the core industrial powers that assumed economic and political centrality as leaders of the First and Second worlds) incorporated successive peripheries and outer regions (the so-called Third World nations, or Immanuel Wallerstein's "external arenas") into their respective spheres of influence. Since the beginning of the 1980s, however, we have been experiencing the "backfire" effect of this system, in which "the process of globalization progressively makes it impossible to organize hegemony (purely) within the national framework, or requires . . . that it take post-national or trans-national forms" (Balibar, "Ambiguous" 71). The order of accumulation that has emerged over the course of the last three decades circulates power relations through an endless multiplication of (no longer necessarily national) centers and border-crossing networks. It does this in such a way that traditional relations of power and mediation between culture and state configurations have been transformed forever. As stated by William Rowe and Vivian Schelling: "The vast increase in channels of communication which flow across cultural boundaries has the effect of dismantling old forms of marginalization and domination and making new forms of democratization and cultural multiplicity imaginable" (1).

Although dependency theory, for example, testified to the ways in which national peripheries were tied to central nations as second best, and therefore as spatially fixed imitations or mirror cultures within the modern capitalist world system, recent transnational modifications in the geographic and geopolitical pattern of the world reconfigure historical relations of dependency and redistribute previously fixed notions of local, regional, and national location in their relation to the dynamics of a new and increasingly postnational global economy. Needless to say, such transformations oblige that we somehow give new meaning—a new critical language—to the repertoires and maneuvers of cultural transference, contact, and exchange at the current time. Once again, in the words of the Latin American Subaltern Studies Group's founding statement:

> There is a new sense that both cultural and political dynamics have begun to function in a global context that problematizes the center-periphery model of dependency theory as well as the strategies of economic nationalism that follow from it. . . . The rapid development and spread of information technology is the defining technological feature of this phase, permitting, among other things, the circulation of texts and cultural practices from areas of the formerly colonial world in new, global circuits of information retrieval and exchange (the publication, subsequent reception, and current centrality in the U.S. multiculturalism debate of Rigoberta Menchú's testimonio, is one small, but significant, example of the new ways in which cultural objects are created and circulate). (116)

Aijaz Ahmad upholds this line of investigation as he calls attention to the increasingly decentralized hierarchies and dispersed relations of domination and subordination that characterize contemporary realities:

> The capitalist world today is not divided into monolithic oppositions: white/non-white, industrialized/non-industrialized. Rather its chief characteristics in the present phase are (1) that it is a hierarchically structured global system in which locations of particular countries are determined, in the final analysis, by the strengths and/or weaknesses of their economies; and (2) the system itself is undergoing a new phase of vast global restructuring. . . . In other words, the tendential law of global accumulation functions not towards greater homogenization or similarity of location in zones of backward capitalism, but towards greater differentiation among its various national units. . . . Conversely, *advanced* capital has now reached a level of global self-organization where conflicts between its national units cannot be settled through warfare because supranational interpenetrations of its national capitals are now such that the nation-state has ceased to be the discrete site for the reproduction of *advanced* capital, which must now survive as a global system or not at all. (311–13)

As such, in order to reproduce itself capital must now extend its logic of command over the entire (or almost entire) domain of productive relations. It must extend itself throughout the articulation of local, regional, national, and transnational forms of institutionality and of cultural belonging. Needless to say, this process of extension is never even or complete and it very rarely guarantees complete subsumption. However, it does suggest that the idea of the nation-state (even the idea of the former

The Other Side of the Popular

peripheral nation-states, many of which viewed their role largely as a defense against the potential ravages of metropolitan capital) has mutated. Nation-states around the globe now view themselves in a relation of reciprocity with capital, rather than as a last line of defense. As such, and as Kenneth Surin has observed, "the absolute spatial division between exploiters and exploited posited by a more conventional Marxism has effectively been eliminated—the exploiters are everywhere and so are the exploited" (1188).[8]

Indeed, these are developments that call for new ways of thinking and acting politically. The question, of course, is how to think about contemporary relations without simply reinscribing the residual categories and methodologies of the past; without, for example, fixing once again the notion of peoplehood firmly within state-related narratives of national interests, national normative identities, and national common concerns negotiated from within the immediate interests of the national elites.

If, as Aijaz Ahmad suggests, the nation-state has ceased to be the privileged site for the reproduction of advanced capital and culture; and if, as the Latin American Subaltern Studies Group's founding statement indicates, cultural and political dynamics have begun to function in a global context that undermines the center-periphery model of dependency theory as well as the strategies of economic nationalism that structured it; and if, as Kenneth Surin notes, the absolute spatial division between exploiters and exploited has waned in the current phase of development, then perhaps we can no longer think exclusively from within the stable boundaries of national culture. Perhaps we can only think along lines of varying intensities. These lines might occasionally indicate to us that there is still antagonism between radically divergent political subjectivities or locations. However, they might remind us rather more of the weakening of stable boundaries and divergent political locations as a whole. The events of September 11, 2001 in New York and Washington, D.C. are surely a reminder of that fact.

This challenge to contemporary reflection suggests that as soon as we think that subalternity, for example, is inscribed in a predetermined identity or in a location grounded in the notion of place fixity—that is, in an almost inherent "belowness" in relation to a particular form of domination or hegemony—we might have missed the point of subalternity's relation to contemporary patterns of organization. The subject that is subaltern in one moment or under one set of conditions produces subalternity in others in other circumstances and conditions. It might even be that, with the apparent demise of national fictive ethnicity, any evaluation of subalternity that remains governed by a fixed or grounded notion of the subject—for example, by the workings of an intersubjective social bond of recognition articulated between already given subjects (Americans, Mexicans, Bolivians, Latinos, etc.)—might just be overlooking the fact that community, for example, is perhaps more than ever an experience grounded not merely in the production of internal bonds of intersubjective communal recognition, but in the exposure of all such internal bonds to their external limits. Rigoberta Menchú's complex and often contradictory construction of political subjectivity in her *testimonio* is, at least in part, living testimony to the workings of communal exposure and to the destabilizing force of transculturation negotiated from below.

It is from within the shifting geographies and changing geopolitical configurations of the last two decades that the founding statement of the Latin American Subaltern Studies Group emerges.[9] This statement is a call for new forms of intellectual engagement after the collapse of the national-popular in Latin America, together with its "problematization of the center-periphery model of dependency theory" (116). Ultimately, what is at stake in the group's call for self-interrogation is the intellectual's ability to negotiate the new limits, the new borders, and the new possibilities of the global cultural economy: to engage in discourses of critical exchange between North and South that do not reproduce neocolonial epistemologies and historical forms of intellectual paternalism.

Obviously, as an increasingly internationalized, yet predominantly U.S.-based, Latin American cultural studies paradigm becomes more and more implicated in the redefinition of North-South relations, it is imperative that we address the ways in which subaltern cultural production can be chronicled alongside, rather than beneath, northern intellectual production itself. It would seem that in order to do this we would have to inquire into contemporary forms of intellectual engagement so that we might be able to imagine the possibility of modifying discourses that remain complicit with the current languages of global capitalist accumulation. Peter Hitchcock advances this discussion with the following questions:

> What strategies might obtain to disable the continued reproduction of the logic of Western cultural critique that fosters the "othering" of the so-called "Third World Subject"? Does the rise of cultural studies in the American academy foreshadow the dissolution of the Subjected Other or the next round of a neo-colonialist project that advocates "know thy global neighbors" the better to exploit them[?] . . . How do theories and theoreticians resist the "inevitability" that "thinking global" is the next chapter in the Western will-to-hegemony? (11)[10]

The Other Side of the Popular

The central question raised by both Hitchcock and the Latin American Subaltern Studies Group's founding statement is how to conceptualize and re-represent the subaltern without reverting to fetishistic or exploitative forms of discursive practice. Of course, within this process we should question the positional implications of the subaltern's increasing presence in the United States as a cultural studies growth industry, in which money and institutional resources are thrown at academic research and in which Latin American subaltern cultural production becomes increasingly intertwined in the North's drive for information retrieval and knowledge dissemination on a global scale.

My purpose in this chapter is to advance the conviction of the Latin American Subaltern Studies Group that we have crossed a decisive historical threshold in power/knowledge relations that challenges the secure boundaries of the nation and of the center-periphery model of dependency theory. I contribute to the ongoing debates surrounding current paradigm shifts and disciplinary configurations in order to call attention to the problematic gaps and fissures that underlie relations of exchange between Latin American subaltern cultural production and metropolitan forms of intervention after the crisis of the national-popular. This is not to say that my own interest is to establish a position that is outside or against the possibility of a Latin American subaltern studies in neoliberal times. Nor, I might add, is my intention to engage in what Nancy Scheper-Hughes has called an obsessive and self-reflexive hermeneutics in which the self, and not the Other, becomes the subject of academic inquiry (*Death* 28). What is at stake in my analysis, as it is in the founding statement of the Latin American Subaltern Studies Group, and, indeed, in the corpus of criticism on *testimonio* that emerged in the mid-1980s in the United States, is not only how to conceptualize and represent the Latin American subaltern but, equally, how to represent ourselves—our own intellectual positionality or northern situational consciousness—after the exhaustion of the so-called revolutionary era in Latin America. As such, it should be understood that I consider my own work to be deeply enmeshed in the questions I evaluate here. Indeed, the whole of this book is (always already) caught up in the terms and horizons of my critique in this chapter.

As the founding statement of the Latin American Subaltern Studies Group indicates, with the growing presence over the last fifteen years or so of subaltern cultural production such as *testimonio* in metropolitan critical practices, previously functional boundaries between identity and difference, or between inside and outside, have become far less discreet than they might ever have seemed. This is so not just because

Rigoberta Menchú's *testimonio* circulates throughout the metropolitan countries (mediated, of course, by the ghostly presence of Elizabeth Burgos Debray), but because geopolitical relations of power inevitably impact on critical discourses on Rigoberta Menchú that emerge from within the metropolitan academy. As a result, recourse to neatly delineated categories or discreetly oppositional positionalities—critical gestures or repertoires grounded in categories such as inside versus outside, identity and difference, or center and periphery—become enormously problematic.

Having said this, however, the erosion of national fictive ethnicity and the ongoing fatigue of notions such as national identity, national culture, national tradition, and national capitalism have done little to erode the attraction of center-periphery models that originated in theoretical models of national dependency and that we have inherited from the periods of industrialized nation formation and their subsequent cold war logics.

The goal of the Latin American Subaltern Studies Group as expressed in its founding statement is to recuperate the figure of the subaltern in order to highlight and to advance discussion on the contemporary crisis of national models and cultural forms. By examining historically constituted constructions of subalternity the group proposes restoring disciplinary presence to those cultural languages that have challenged or unworked the hegemony of Latin America's national cultural elites. The purpose of the group, then, is to challenge those supposedly elitist forms of conceptualization that have silenced Latin American subalternity within Latin America's histories of nation formation.

However, further consideration of the founding statement uncovers the problems arising when intellectuals place subalternity immediately on the side of redemption by positing the subaltern as an external and inaccessible site of pilgrimage: "We need to access the vast (and mobile) array of the masses—peasants, proletarians, the informal and formal sectors, the sub- and under-employed, vendors, those outside or at the margin of the money economy, lumpens and ex-lumpens of all sorts, children, the growing numbers of the homeless. . . . Clearly, it is a question not only of new ways of looking at the subaltern . . . but also of building new relations between ourselves and those human contemporaries whom we posit as objects of study" (121). In the interests of building new relations between a "them" to be accessed and a noncoincident "we" that needs to access, the Latin American subaltern is implicitly located by the group—in the very elaboration of its critical language—as the peripheral example and positional site of the historically obliterated subject. In this sense, the statement's examination of the Latin American subaltern is achieved through the affirmation of a center-periphery/identity-difference model, in which the periphery is accessed by the center and converted as such into an object of contemporary counterhegemonic knowledge production and theoretical practice. This may be viewed as splitting academic hairs but, given the complexity of recent modifications in the geopolitical and geographic pattern of the world, it could be said that such a treatment of subaltern cultural production is inherently flawed on account of its tendency to maintain monumental conceptual boundaries between the peripheral places of production and difference (Latin America) and the centralized places of self-identity and theorization (North America).

The statement maintains a conscious and apparently necessary disjuncture between inside and outside locations by imposing on Latin American subaltern production the exigencies of a modern center-periphery binary. In this mechanism, the subaltern comes to be a homogeneous and totalizing resistance to the metropolitan center. Yet recurrence to a critical model grounded explicitly or implicitly in the center-periphery/identity-difference duality inevitably establishes truth regimes that reveal as much about the imposition of Latin Americanist knowledge management as they do about the effective properties of the object of study itself. After all, in its very implementation and practice the center-periphery model must first pass through a foundational process by which it assumes the preexistence of inherently oppositional sites. It then needs to integrate them into a transcultural relationality that is governed implicitly by analytical integration, continuity, connectedness, and structural harmony (a Latin American form of orientalism, in other words).[11]

On adopting such a model we render Latin American subalternity abstract (peripheral to the center in which we position ourselves), yet we act as if within our appropriative practice we were not in fact allegorizing or fetishizing the concrete in such a way as to reify heterogeneity, thereby making it more representable and therefore more controllable. In short, we act as if Latin American subalternity were not, in the very practice of cultural exchange, inevitably subsumed by discursive commodification; as if the object actually realized itself as something other than a redemptive exchange-value within northern critical practices.[12]

Within the geopolitical production of knowledge, recurrence to center-periphery models isolates the object, encoding its cultural paradigms within a specific position defined as a single place within an objective set of global relations. These relations correspond to a belief—or a need to believe—in the singularity of, for example, cultural identities and collective practices constructed around socially predefined differences. In the active implementation of center-periphery thinking, then, it very often becomes the act of positioning itself that defines the site of what the intellectual may call subaltern resistance or ideological struggle. As such, subaltern expressivities such as *testimonio* are considered, more often than not, to be resistant not because they *practice* difference but, rather, because they just *are* difference.

By systematically positioning Latin America as periphery the northern university locates subalternity as an identitarian "is" always already in relation and opposition to metropolis; the center. This, of course, positions and maintains the subaltern both as the monumental outside of metropolis and as a fundamental means by which the center critiques itself and defines the parameters of its own institutional struggles. Such conceptual logic is extremely problematic for the thought of subalternity, since blind recourse to center-periphery models, to "us" accessing "them" (or to "us" being accessed by "them"), betrays an underlying critical desire for a unified totality, or perhaps even an implicit critical hyperconformity to the institutional logic of transnational capitalism masked as essentialist resistance.

By defining transnational cultural relations through the workings of an unreflexive center-periphery duality, redemptive gestures of solidarity become extremely problematic. If we position the subaltern as a periphery to be accessed by its centered intellectual, then subalternity succumbs to an essentialized exotopic position that precludes the possibility of difference as either a subaltern or intellectual practice. Rather, the subaltern is valued as an identity, an "is," and is dragged into the field of critical discourse by an act of abstraction that remains the organizing support and guarantor of the center's discourses of knowledge appropriation.

The Latin American Subaltern Studies Group's founding statement calls for the redefinition of intellectual practices as a means of restoring disciplinary presence to the nonelite. The underlying paradox here is that in order to question elite symbolic forms the group would have to divert attention away from writing while, of course, always dwelling within its structures. This paradox first comes to light in the group's reference to the work of Ranajit Guha as fundamental to their own counterhegemonic reading of subaltern agency: "Reading this [official, elite] historiography 'in reverse' . . . to recover the cultural and political specificity of peasant insurrections has, for Guha, two components: identifying the logic of the distortions in the representation of the subaltern in official or elite culture; and uncovering the social semiotics of the strategies and cultural practices of peasant insurgencies themselves"

The Other Side of the Popular

(111). Having said this, however, in the founding statement the process of self-interrogation that is implicit in Guha's first component—namely, the necessary deconstruction of symbolic "distortions in the representation of the subaltern in official or elite culture"—is bypassed when the group (somewhat paradoxically, yet consciously) declares its admiration for Guha's work and simultaneously its aversion to intellectual self-interrogation: "Retaining a focus on the intelligentsia and on its characteristic intellectual practices—centered on the cultivation of writing, science, and the like—leaves us in the space of historiographic prejudice and 'not-seeing' . . . ; where Said and Retamar envision a new type of intellectual as the protagonist of decolonization, the, admittedly paradoxical, intent of Subaltern Studies is precisely to displace the centrality of intellectuals and intellectual 'culture' in social history" (120). The founding statement appears to be working toward its own demise by erasing the "I" in the I/Other dichotomy. This antipositionality implies an essentialist utopian politics that, by actively abstaining from self-representation, refuses to take into account the ideological ground of intellectual appropriation that makes re-representation of the subaltern possible in the first place.

By effectively stepping around metropolitan institutional forms of knowledge production, and by directly accessing the Latin American subaltern (since it is considered that "retaining a focus . . . on the cultivation of writing, science, and the like—leaves us in the space of historiographic prejudice and 'not-seeing' " [120]), the founding statement appears to unmask an underlying desire to not have to attend to the mechanics of representation that precondition all cultural exchange. Rather, it seems that the statement's proposed re-presentations of the subaltern are the result of an underlying desire to portray the intellectual as a transparent nonagent (no longer subject to the mechanics of "the centrality of intellectuals and intellectual 'culture' in social history" [120]). The statement effectively rejects intellectual centrality, yet actively occupies a center from which to access the periphery. Thus, it seems to rely on a form of critical engagement in which the intellectual presides over subalternity yet refuses to address intellectual production itself.[13]

The dilemma raised by the statement's disavowal of self-representation is that this disavowal is staged in order to represent the intellectual as an agent that is so powerful that he or she can disclaim the exercise of power itself. Thus it appears that it is only by assuming the exigencies of self-sacrifice—the active erasure of the "I" in the I/Other dichotomy—that the subaltern can be recognized and restored to a position of historical agency. Curiously, this desire to invoke subaltern restoration obliges us to acknowledge the presence of an unresolvable tension in the language of the statement: it is only through intellectual practice that the subaltern can be restituted, and it is equally only through intellectual demise that the subaltern can be restituted. Here, it would seem, we are on the brink of a performative or spectacular mode of redemptive discourse. However, the prerequisite for its successful elaboration involves misrecognizing or overlooking the agency of intellectual/disciplinary fantasy.[14]

Indeed, we glimpse what could be considered to be a constitutive moment of symptomatic fantasy when, toward the end of the statement, and having already declared that "we need to access the vast (and mobile) array of the masses—peasants, proletarians, the informal and formal sectors, the sub- and under-employed, vendors, those outside or at the margin of the money economy, lumpens and ex-lumpens of all sorts, children, the growing numbers of the homeless" (121), the group then concludes its statement with the following observation: "Clearly, it is a question not only of new ways of looking at the subaltern . . . but also of building new relations between ourselves and those human contemporaries whom we posit as objects of study. Rigoberta Menchú's injunction at the end of her famous testimonio is perhaps relevant in this regard: 'I'm still keeping secret what I think no-one should know. Not even anthropologists or intellectuals, no matter how many books they have, can find out all our secrets' " (121). At this point, the statement appears to demand intellectual prohibition and self-exclusion from the reproduction of transnational power relations. In the interests of "building new relations" between "us" and "them" they desire to access the "vast . . . array of the masses," yet recognize that they may be masses who do not necessarily see the benefits of being accessed. The statement thus proposes displacing hierarchy-producing intellectual endeavor by accessing subalterns who reject paternalistic critical gestures because, like Menchú, they fully recognize and defend themselves against the hierarchies built into the production of transnational knowledge and transcultural exchanges of value.

Needless to say, such logics have contributed enormously to some of the most important evaluations of subaltern cultural production in recent years. In particular, they have structured debate around the question of Menchú's "secrets," those famously guarded distances of her *testimonio* that, in Doris Sommer's opinion, form "the most noteworthy and instructive feature of her book" ("No Secrets" 130). By repeatedly claiming the existence of unknowable Maya-Quiché secrets in her *testimonio*, Menchú uncovers her desire to project her story as an articulation of

The Other Side of the Popular

loss for metropolitan interpretation. Her *testimonio* presents itself as an afterlife of hermeneutic expenditure, in which the site of the ethnographer (Burgos Debray) and of her readership can only assume their value through the positive assumption of the power to lose power, and, as Jon Beasley-Murray reminds us, through their ability to mourn that loss as the precondition for the establishment of a transnational "politics of respect" ("Thinking" 127) . The spectacularly untranslatable surplus that Menchú indicates to us in the form of untold secrets exposes her *testimonio*—what she does say—almost as the guarantee of herself, rather than the ethnographer or the reader, as primary translator and establisher of the law of transcultural exchange. By talking, Menchú promises the gift of revelation. Yet the positive property of the gift that she gives for consumption is the loss that guarantees the partial dereliction of metropolitan intellectual expenditure, together with the eclipse of the knowledge machine into which she is appropriated and to which she surrenders herself.

In Doris Sommer's complex interpretation of the *testimonio* the secrets expose the unspeakable site of cultural difference through which Menchú can once and for all "put one over" on western political and epistemological formations. After all, in the spectacle of constant nonrevelation the metropolitan thinking/teaching machine, as Gayatri Spivak calls it, is at least partially dismantled. It cannot fully consume the whole text. It is denied the chance to accord appropriation with the status of an absolute law in the postcolonial contact zone. As such, it is the unthinkability of meaning in the secret's supplementarity, and the apparent transgression of the value of western signification in the obsessive nonrevelation of spoken silences that, in Sommer's interpretation, maintains and upholds the negativity of the *testimonio,* thereby making it resistant to Euro/North American hermeneutic paradigms and neocolonial forms of appropriation. As Sommer indicates: "It is the degree of our foreignness, our cultural difference that would make her secrets incomprehensible to the outsider" ("Resisting" 417). The secrets, then, are the placeholders of a peripheral identitarian difference by means of which "our" centrist identity is maintained at a safe distance.

Indeed, as Sommer notes, it is only through the intellectual's affirmation of hermeneutic incompetence, and therefore through the exhaustion of a certain kind of critical practice grounded in explicit appropriation, that a transnational coalitional politics of respect can be forged: "There is no good reason for filling in the distance that testimonials safeguard through secrets with either veiled theoretical disdain or sentimental identification. Instead, their distance can be read as a lesson in the condition of possibility for coalitional politics. It is similar to learning that respect is the condition of possibility for the kind of love that takes care not to simply appropriate its object" ("No Secrets" 157).

Having said this, however, a certain dilemma does arise when we locate difference—and therefore the philosophical notion of negativity—within the enunciation of subaltern secrets. By assuming the power to lose power the metropolitan intellectual does achieve an ethical position by affirming the death of metropolitan hermeneutic mastery. But we have to recognize that such a position is itself inherently masterful, since it renegotiates signification exclusively from within the north's ability to lose power. Thus the secrets, as a locus grounded in the negativity of identitarian difference, can never really be negative, for as "a *lesson* in the condition of possibility for coalitional politics" (Sommer, "No Secrets" 157; emphasis mine) they can only ever be a tamed allegory of difference.

In other words, and as Derrida informs us in his reading of Hegel and Bataille, there is no actual labor of the negative (and therefore, we might add, no grounds for coalitional politics other than those of the imaginary) without the active revelation and enactment of negativity qua negativity. The textual secrets are an abstraction of negativity, and it is only by being an abstraction that they can actually signify through the continuity of a chain of signifiers (a text). Thus they elide the negativity of difference and promise the pedagogical means by which the reader can reinvest in hegemony or counterhegemony after the demise of the national-popular.

However, negative difference is only so to the extent that it labors to signify itself as such. It is always a practice, then, rather than the representation of an identitarian "is." In other words, it is a dynamic of actual crisis production within meaning, rather than a placeholder of identity or a locus of (in this case) nonenunciation that nevertheless brings forth both the meaning of the subaltern subject as well as that of her or his metropolitan counterpart. In order to really be the site of subaltern negativity the secrets would have to signify actively the actual end of thought's ability to think the subject, rather than allegorizing the possibility of transsubjective recognition and imaginary mutual empowerment. Moreover, if the secrets failed to instigate this dynamic of active crisis production—a radical point of no return for the thought of the subject, in other words—then they would fall inevitably under the rubric of a coalitional politics of respect grounded in the metropolitan "theoretical fiction" (Spivak, "Subaltern" 7) not of positive equivalences between subject positions, but of equivalences constructed on the maintenance of absolute difference and therefore, once again, of absolute identity.

In this sense, and as Jon Beasley-Murray suggests, in such herme-neutic mechanisms we are engaged in a form of *inverted populism* that cannot imagine an outside to the thought of populist hegemony (and identity) construction itself. For Beasley-Murray, the only difference be-tween traditional populism and this new form is that "whereas traditional populism articulates a set of otherwise disparate elements against an op-posed term to construct a fuller, common identity (paradigmatically the 'people' against the 'power bloc' as in Ernesto Laclau's analysis of popu-lism), this inverted populism unites the diverse positions of those who consume *testimonio,* but only to *empty* their common identity in an invi-tation to loss and mourning" ("Thinking" 127–28). As such, there is a very fine line between the conceptual complexities of inverted populism (Sommer's interpretation of the secrets) and those (traditionally popu-list) modes of knowledge production that reproduce hegemony for the always already hegemonic.

An example of the latter can be seen in *Against Literature* when John Beverley quotes Allen Carey-Webb's reasons for incorporating *I, Rigo-berta Menchú* into a world literature course:

> [*Rigoberta Menchú*] is one of the most moving books I have ever read. It is the kind of book I feel I must pass on, that I must urge fellow teachers to use in their classes. . . . My students were immediately sympathetic to Menchú's story and were anxious to know more, to involve themselves. They asked questions about culture and history, about their own position in the world, and about the purposes and methods of education. Many saw in the society of the Guatemalan Indian attractive features they found lacking in their own lives, strong family relationships, community solidarity, an intimate relationship with nature, commitment to others and to one's beliefs. (91)

Rigoberta Menchú and the Maya-Quiché carry the load of a single social, global function; becoming the means by which metropolis can reflect on itself and define its own areas of struggle and political en-gagement. Thus the Latin American subaltern becomes everything the United States lacks and craves in order for it to think about itself and to formulate the terms of northern reader empowerment (Beasley-Murray, "Thinking" 127). Rigoberta Menchú is therefore obliged to become an unsuspecting participant in the transference of discursive property rights, victim of a relation of cultural exchange between an outside made Other (Menchú and the Maya-Quiché) that, nevertheless, permits an inside (U.S. networks of knowledge production) to define the parame-ters of its own dilemmas and institutional struggles, even though voice is articulated within that transcultural exchange as a redemptive site of resistance.

Latin American subaltern expression faces the threat of becoming systematically domesticated by an implicit faith in the authenticity of discrete subject positions (the center-periphery/identity-difference binary). This in turn permits the intellectual to locate the resistant identitarian authenticity of the Other. Subaltern counterdiscourse, then, is symptomatically made Other in its exchange with northern institutionality, and such unquestioning inclusion can become almost a means of reminding the dominant classes of what it was necessary to lose in order to attain their position of transnational dominance ("strong family relationships, community solidarity, an intimate relationship with nature, commitment to others and to one's beliefs" [91]). Indeed, it is precisely in the misrecognition of internally vertical political matrices, and in the recognition of having lost something on the long, hard road to hegemony, that U.S. enjoyment of the subaltern constructs itself: colonial history and systemic exploitation are transformed into a positive reminder to the hegemonic of their own possible identitarian myth of origins.[15]

My purpose thus far has been to trace the underlying problems of intellectual practice after the hegemonic crisis of national fictive ethnicity in Latin America. As a result of this crisis we are now undergoing a shift in the relation between the thought of subalternity and the question of subalternity per se. I have strived to uncover the limits of certain intellectual practices that are engaged in identifying the subaltern as an identitarian ground on which to construct counterhegemonic articulations, empowerments, and new coalitions after the exhaustion of the national-popular. In the pages that follow I extend this analysis by examining a number of critical interventions that construct themselves, as does the work of Doris Sommer, in light of the geopolitical structure of knowledge. Recognition of the geopolitical structure of knowledge adds new twists to our ability to formulate a concept of subalternity or an adequate model of figuration for transnational/post–national-popular times. In the remainder of this chapter I examine three such examples of the politics of geopolitical thought—focusing primarily on the recent work of Walter Mignolo, Nancy Scheper-Hughes, and Ruth Behar—in order to advance discussion on the limits of subaltern recuperation and on the geopolitics of contemporary reflection.

Walter Mignolo's *The Darker Side of the Renaissance* attempts to expose the orientalist presuppositions of the colonial project in the Americas, while simultaneously striving to reveal and unravel its historically silenced cultural and epistemological shadows. It positions itself, in other words, as a postcolonialist examination of the means by which subaltern knowledges can be effectively de-orientalized in such a way as to actively interrupt the foundations of the western episteme and its neocolonial relations of power.[16] However, there is an internal limit to such an intellectual practice which, when left unaddressed, comes back to haunt and to challenge the de-orientalist investments of the postcolonial intellectual who is engaged in bringing the dark side back into the realm of cultural and political reflection. As we will see, that internal limit to postcolonial de-orientalism lies, at least in part, in the geopolitics of representation itself.

In *The Darker Side of the Renaissance* Mignolo points out that he eschews the notion of representation as the practice of an individual—a postcolonial intellectual—engaged in "the delegation of responsibility from a larger group to one person or to a smaller number of 'representatives' " (332). In contrast to what would be an overly blatant exercise of epistemological and political authority over the subaltern object of analysis, the author notes that "representation is a notion I have tried to avoid as much as possible in my argument" (331). Instead, he proposes an alternative model of figuration and suggests moving further toward the idea of enactment in order to focus on the subaltern locus of enunciation, rather than on the idea of the subaltern as the effect of a particular metropolitan labor of representation and recuperation. This is certainly a suggestive critical gesture since it strives to displace the self-evident power relations that are inherent in knowledge's geopolitical processes of signification. But enactment inevitably leaves the material problem of representation (understood as previously stated) untouched, because it tends to return us to relations of *absolute* representation in which, as Ernesto Laclau puts it, "the total transparency between the representative and the represented means the extinction of the relationship of representation." He continues:

> Representation presupposes the presence of someone in a place from which they are actually absent. It is therefore a *fictio iuris*. But this is precisely where the difficulties begin, as the terrain on which representation takes place is different from that on which the identity of the person represented is constituted. In this sense, representation cannot simply be the transmission belt of a will that has already been constituted, but must involve the construction of something new. There is thus a double process: on the one hand, to exist as such, a representation cannot operate completely behind the back of a person represented; and on the other, to be a representation at all requires the ar-

ticulation of something new which is not just provided by the identity of what is being represented. ("New" 38)

In other words, enactment tends to elide the inherent opacity of the representational process by striving to uphold relations in which the representative and the represented constitute the same and single will in two different places. But the elision of opacity inevitably returns us—via the institutional locus of enunciation of the U.S. university—to the question of the role of the postcolonial or subalternist intellectual who positions the subaltern as an allegorical locus of enunciation from within a transnational knowledge machine that is increasingly administered by the commodifying (and allegorizing?) logics of corporate capitalism. Such a return of expenditure is probably inevitable, and perhaps Mignolo cannot be taken to task on this account. But the inevitability of our return to this institutional locus of enunciation raises another question regarding postcolonial investments in the recuperation of the western episteme's silent or silenced zones, as well as in the consequent destabilization of that epistemic edifice. For in order to *truly* de-orientalize (that is, in order to truly destabilize or even collapse the orientalist, and, therefore, the neocolonial production of knowledge), orientalist knowledge must be erased from within the belly of the beast of western knowledge production itself, so to speak. Yet since this is, at least in part, a question of writing and representation, in order to be erased effectively orientalism must always *show* itself to be erased, or at least would have to be erased as a kind of self-revelation of erasure within representation. As such, in order to de-orientalize metropolitan knowledge formations for once and for all, those dominant formations would have to die as such. Yet, once again, since it is always a question of writing it could only ever die while actively bearing witness to its demise, and therefore simultaneously to its presence and persistence, within the field of signification. The construction of a post-orientalist knowledge, of a subaltern knowledge somehow beyond orientalism and therefore beyond the western episteme, would have to entail self-conscious strategies designed to interrupt western self-consciousness, or, at least, strategies of production that eschew production in the very instance in which they produce the demise of the orientalist reproduction of the subaltern Other. In this sense, the means by which de-orientalism could organize itself as non-orientalist meaning within the production of meaning would require a labor of representation, or of enactment, that is so radically grounded in negativity that it would unwork dominant systems of signification.

Subalternist thought, in other words, would emerge as a thought

The Other Side of the Popular

that embodies, at every step of its development, both its conditions of possibility and its conditions of impossibility, always in the interest of "persistently transforming conditions of impossibility into possibility" (Spivak, "Subaltern" 9). Subalternity would come to be thought through a model of figuration that remains in permanent conflict with thought itself: that is, a model with the subaltern positioned figuratively as a structural issue within the historical development and expansion of western power/knowledge relations rather than as a sovereign placeholder of identity to be recuperated and restituted to the realm of signification. As such, subaltern history and agency would be produced through a conflictive "dissimulation of discontinuity" (31) within thought and within power/knowledge relations. It would signify the potential to empty out the ways in which meaning and the power/knowledge configurations that structure the production of knowledge, and that precondition the establishment of social hegemonies and institutionalities, can be reproduced. The subaltern, in other words, would be that point in history, in power, and in knowledge—and therefore in critical language—that disallows and interrupts the continuity of the illusions of seamlessness of history, power, and knowledge.

Indeed, this is an area of discussion that has also been taken up by Nancy Scheper-Hughes in her introduction to *Death without Weeping*. Here Scheper-Hughes probes, from within the strategic space of cultural translation, the de-orientalized limits of an academic practice that she calls "good-enough" ethnography. This is an ethnography that, though empirical, need not be empiricist, since "it need not entail a philosophical commitment to Enlightenment notions of reason and truth" (23). She states her case as follows:

> The history of Western philosophy, thought, and science has been characterized by a "refusal of engagement" with the other or, worse, by an "indifference" to the other—to alterity, to difference, to polyvocality, all of which are leveled out or pummeled into a form compatible with a discourse that promotes the Western project. And so the "Enlightenment", with its universal and absolute notions of truth and reason, may be seen as a grand pretext for exploitation and violence and for the expansion of Western culture ("our ideas", "our truths"). (23–24)

Scheper-Hughes posits that cultural studies as a field of academic practice can tarry with de-orientalism, and, by flaunting its necessarily flawed and biased strategies of translation and incorporation it can "disrupt expected roles and statuses in the spirit of the carnavelsco, the carnivalesque," in order to "exchange gifts based on our labors and so finally subvert the law that puts our work at the service of the machine in the scientific, academic factory" (25).[17]

One book that is deeply invested in this possibility is Ruth Behar's *Translated Woman*. In this text, however, the notion of "gift giving" is not without its problems. *Translated Woman* is a text grounded in gift giving that challenges all discreet positional categories or neatly delineated sites of knowledge production such as those of informant and ethnographer, center and periphery, or identity and difference. However, in the end the book returns to, and reinscribes, the strategies that it strives to challenge.

In Esperanza's/Behar's life story, metropolitan strategies of exchange are continually, and almost obsessively, re-presented, and sometimes even subverted, by a cultural translation that translates little more than the conditions of its own construction. The object of translation is as much the process of translation itself as it is the ethnographic subject —Esperanza—whose words are always already translated into the language of metropolitan cultural capital: English. Thus it is a subaltern life story (a kind of part-*testimonio*) that informs us that it forbids any privileged site of transparency, systematically claiming to render ethnographic univocity impossible, while perhaps remaining one of the most univocal ethnographic texts of recent years. There is, in this sense, no constructivist translation of an original or authentic subject within the text, and therefore no investment in the revelation of an identitarian subaltern locus of enunciation (even though the book is continuously positioning Esperanza as a revealed subaltern identity). After all, within the text itself Esperanza is always already translated and therefore erased as a placeholder of authentic identity. Indeed, as we've already stated, the original object of Behar's ethnographic impulse is often not the words of her *comadre* but the ethnographic drive and disciplinary will-to-power/knowledge, mediated explicitly within the text by institutional funding apparatuses and university tenure committees that produce translated objects of analysis for consumption and appropriation by metropolitan academic institutions.

For Behar this production of ethnographic translation—its disciplinary and institutional drive to restitute "voice to the voiceless" (in English?)—reveals and widens the cracks and fissures of its own practical strategies by flaunting and carrying them to their limit of acceptability. It is a text that upholds identity yet constantly puts one over on notions of positional singularity and disciplinary appropriation, since it labors to carry the historical and hegemonic logics of epistemic object accumulation almost to a point of no return.

Having said this, however, in the end the book returns to the economy of identity and difference in spectacular fashion. Although it could be said that the wealth of *Translated Woman* lies in its power to expose and nullify the reproduction of the Other, it also performs that same economy. In its final pages the book enacts an economy of exchange grounded in the potlatch, in "an interplay of voluntary allowances that counts on reciprocity and organizes a social network articulated by the 'obligation to give'" (de Certeau 27). The final gesture of the text, however, implements the "obligation to give" almost as a means of reinscribing the passive homogeneity of center-periphery/identity-difference configurations.

Behar evokes the economy of the gift in an attempt to restitute Esperanza's words to her in book form, thereby fulfilling a demand for repaying the debt of ethnographic translation by symbolically returning control over the production of knowledge to the subaltern: "July-August 1993. By December of 1992 I had the book. I held it in my hands. Smiled along with the picture of my comadre and I giggling on the back cover. Opened the book. Closed it. Taught it. Peddled it. And all the time I was wondering: what will my comadre think when she sees the book? Finally I placed it in her hands. She kept it for a few days. Showed it to her customers in San Luis. Listened as I read passages to her from it" (342). Needless to say, in a profit economy the politics of the gift is, as de Certeau and Scheper-Hughes claim, a transgressive act, because "it appears as an excess (a waste), a challenge (a rejection of profit), or a crime (an attack on property)" (de Certeau 27). In Behar's text, then, it could be considered to be the representation of a diversionary practice that subverts the law that puts disciplinary labor exclusively at the service of northern institutional domestication. The re-presentation of such a gesture in *Translated Woman*, it seems, marks an attempt by the metropolitan intellectual to undermine, or at least to represent the undermining of, the economic logics of appropriation, consumption, and conservation that govern transcultural exchange with the subaltern. It uncovers a gesture that achieves its signifying value by having the act of acquisition assume the positive property of loss: a final gesture of a text that constantly claims that it is putting one over on the established order on its own turf.

Yet *Translated Woman* is a gift refused: "Then she gave the book back to me. 'I already know my *historia*,' she said. 'And besides, this is in English. My children can't read it.' I insisted she keep the book as a souvenir. 'No comadre, you take it back. Sell it. So it won't be sitting there'" (342). The subaltern renders metropolitan ethnographic labor (in English) valueless on the other side of the border. In this sense the debt owed to the translated subaltern (Esperanza) by the metropolitan ethnographic restitutor (Behar) is a debt that can never be discharged. The northern intellectual's labor is declared insolvent, bankrupt on the other side, because in her final act the "native informant" defies the ethnographer's restitutive gift giving. Behar's *comadre* is represented as authoring herself within the book by rejecting the authority of the metropolitan author and her cultural capital. But it is this subaltern rejection of gift giving that guarantees the inevitable return of cultural capital—the book—to metropolis.

But there is another question, for the final gesture of the text strives to absolve the metropolitan ethnographer from the sin of intellectual expenditure and appropriation. *Translated Woman* declares itself a form of academic expenditure that is unproductive, of no end or utility beyond itself, since the translation is declared by its very object of investigation to be of no restitutive or economic value in the transnational cultural economy. Thus it calls attention to itself as a limit to the economic logics of transnational subsumption, fully representing and flaunting its own inevitable commodification and consumption on this (U.S.) side of the border, while upholding difference as a subaltern limit to consumption and to a profit economy on the other side of the border.

Thus the final suggestion, or desire, of the book is that the Mexican subaltern be so authentically Other that she not indulge in either vanity or the logics of commodity fetishism. In this implicit implementation, once again, of absolute difference, and therefore once again of absolute identity, the book fails to think the border itself and merely positions the other side of the border as the placeholder and final truth of identitarian, economic, linguistic, and cultural difference. Despite its claims to the contrary, then, *Translated Woman* provides no displacement of the logics of identity/difference, and therefore merely initiates a process that returns knowledge to the monumental domain of the already-centered center of power production: the North.

Translated Woman, in this sense, uncovers the current tensions that ground the concept of subalternity in post–national-popular times. On the one hand, it promises the formulation of an antihumanist and antipositivist strategy designed to bring to crisis the center-periphery/identity-difference model of reflection, along with the formalities of hegemonic ethnography and identitarian notions of subaltern sovereignty. Furthermore, the book is quite successful in these endeavors. On the other hand, however, the book reproduces all the strategies that it strives to unwork.

Translated Woman is caught (as probably we all are) in the relation between traditional populism and inverted populism (Beasley-Murray "Thinking"). It is therefore an allegory of the current predicament of geopolitical and geocultural reflection as a whole. Moreover, as an allegory that is true to its own underlying tensions it can offer no alternative pathway to the predicament that it interrogates and embodies.

Without doubt, the conditions for the traditional populist articulation of peoplehood—understood as the overarching interpellation of the people against the power bloc—appear to be lacking in contemporary conditions. With this in mind, the possibility of thinking about subalternity seems to belong to a structure of experience and of reflection that most likely lies beyond the Marxian-Hegelian pattern of growing antagonism between symmetric forces, and probably beyond the possibility of conceptualizing an overarching interpellation of the people within the geographically specific site of the nation-state. What, then, to do?

In *Negative Dialectics* Theodor Adorno makes the following statement regarding the production of theoretical reflection: "The object of theory is not something immediate, of which theory might carry home a replica. Knowledge has not, like the state police, a rogue's gallery of its objects. Rather it conceives them as it conveys them" (206). If this is the case, then our ability to move beyond "the perception that relations between dominant and subaltern are necessarily mournful distance, on the one hand, or that populist hegemony must be built upon an educational model on the other" (Beasley-Murray, "Thinking" 128)—a situation in which mournful distance and the pedagogical model of populist hegemony both articulate discourses of origin and end, and of identity and difference as placeholders of the truth of the subject—depends very much on our ability to convey "a tactic and a way of dealing with the world, hence a habitus, understood in a general fashion, that determines both being and action" (Conley 630); a style of composition that would be capable of moving beyond center-periphery/identity-difference formalities in order to forge the possibility of really inaugurating "new ways of thinking and acting politically" (Latin American Subaltern Studies Group 110). This, of course, is easier said than done.

Dipesh Chakrabarty has noted that "the subaltern . . . is not the empirical peasant or tribal in any straightforward sense that a populist programme of history-writing may want to imagine. The figure of the subaltern is necessarily mediated by problems of representation [and] one might say that 'subaltern' is what fractures from within the signs that tell of the insertion of the historian (as a speaking subject) into the global narratives of capital" ("Marx" 15). If this is the case, then the project of writing subaltern history and, analogously, that of writing culture and cultural politics from within that critical perspective must, as Gyan Prakash observes, "fall short of its aims. But this does not mean that subaltern histories cannot be written. If subalternity is defined by a certain 'lack', it is also construed as intractable, resistant to complete appropriation by the dominant system" (287).

Both subalternity and the thought of subalternity appear to reside on the limits of representation. Both, in their own way, are a confrontation with the "absolute limit of the place where history is narrativized into logic" (Spivak, "Subaltern" 16) and, we might add, of the place where logics are narrativized into histories. As such, subalternity is not necessarily an "is" to be immediately retrieved and recuperated for signification. Rather, it is a question of the conditions of possibility and impossibility of critical reason and of the latter's relation to domination. A thought of subalternity, then, requires a discontinuous conceptual and political matrix that strains against itself, that remains incompatible and at all times in debate with its own procedures and proceedings and that therefore remains in a permanent state of confrontation with its own forces of subjectivation. It is a "folded thought: thought which no longer consists in unravelling, in connection, in representative subsumption, in the determination or convocation of ends" (Nancy, "Deleuzian" 109–10). It consists, rather, in the uncovering of particular cracks or fissures in the edifice of critical reason. These fissures desuture, destabilize, or interrupt the geopolitical power/knowledge edifice that upholds dominant narratives of, for example, the subject, identity, development, or progress.

In "On Producing the Concept of a Global Culture" Kenneth Surin makes the following observation:

> Every culture generates for itself its own "thinkability" (and concomitantly its own "unthinkability" as the obverse of this "thinkability"), and its concepts are constitutive of that "thinkability". Another way of making this point would be to say that a culture has to secrete its myriad expressivities precisely in order to be what it is and that its concepts . . . are the thematizations or representations of these expressivities. Or, more generally, the concepts of a culture are its expressivities rendered in the form of that culture's "thinkability". (1183)

In particular relation to the notion of subalternity, expressivities (concepts/representations) render subalternity thinkable. However, within this thinkability the subaltern announces an aberrant disequilibrium of

The Other Side of the Popular

signification that destabilizes the illusory seamlessness of hegemonic thought, politics, and culture. This is, let's say, the creative and hard-core enactment of subalternity's singularity, which nevertheless has nothing to do with going back to the subject, and therefore nothing to do with going back to identity-difference/center-periphery modalities. Whether the conditions of possibility of such a reflection are actually conceivable can only be evaluated through my attempts to trace, destabilize, and perhaps even interrupt the grounds of hegemony and of hegemony thinking. In the meantime, however, it would probably be safe to say that subalternity, as "a trace of that which eludes the dominant discourse" (Prakash 288), is precisely what "remains irreducible to any deconstruction, what remains undeconstructible as the possibility itself of deconstruction . . . a certain experience of the emancipatory promise . . . perhaps even the formality of a structural messianism, a messianism without religion, even a messianic without messianism, an idea of justice—which we distinguish from law or right and even from human rights—and an idea of democracy—which we distinguish from its current concept and from its determined predicates today" (Derrida, *Specters* 59).

3

Formalities of Consumption and Citizenship in the Age of Cultural Hybridity

> In the shift from national mono-identities to global multiculturality I wonder whether fundamentalism now attempts to survive in the form of Latin-Americanism. —Néstor García Canclini, *Consumidores y ciudadanos* (translation mine)

> The State is no longer defensible, not even with irony.
> —Michael Hardt and Antonio Negri, *Labor of Dionysus*

In the previous chapter I evaluated the emergence of the category of subalternity in Latin American literary/cultural studies in the United States as a result of the crisis of national fictive ethnicity in the 1980s and 1990s. I also examined some of the limits that appear to characterize that emergence, as well as a number of the epistemological and political problems that accompany the recuperation and representation of notions such as subalternity, identity, or the people from within the postmodern U.S. academy. As already noted, my own engagement with such notions in these pages is firmly rooted in the problematic dynamics underlined in the previous chapter. As such, I can offer no definitive alternative pathway, rather only the suggestion of new inflections and of differential nuances. In this chapter I extend the terms of my discussion on intellectual practice in increasingly transnational times by focusing attention on the notions of citizenship and consumption. In particular, I concentrate on the relation of these notions to postmodern cultural hybridity and contemporary forms of political and cultural mediation in Latin America.

As Mark Berger's book *Under Northern Eyes* so forcefully reveals (and, indeed, as already suggested in this volume at the end of chapter 1), the complex web of institutional and epistemological practices that emerged in the United States between the outbreak of the Spanish-American War and the fall of the Berlin Wall constructed not only the panorama of U.S. state formation and economic hegemonization throughout this century but also framed the socioeconomic, political, institutional, and ideological underpinnings of Latin America's fabrication as an object of knowledge in the United States and beyond.

It is through *Under Northern Eyes* that we witness the hemispheric implications of disciplinary construction. Furthermore, we can hardly evaluate the genesis of disciplinary configurations throughout the twentieth century without linking them, through a relation of causal interdependence, to the wider field of hemispheric power production, management, and containment. Thus Berger concludes his work in the following convincing terms:

> Since the early twentieth century, US foreign policy has flowed from a commitment to a powerful liberal teleology which understands history as progress towards liberal capitalist democracy. The practice of US foreign policy in Latin America has continued to be shaped by the idea that North American political and economic development provides both a measure and a model for the history of Latin America. . . . Despite the sometimes critical perspective of Latin American specialists, the liberal professional discourses on Latin America have also been shaped by these assumptions, and they have facilitated the practice of US foreign policy in Latin America. . . . The dominant professional discourses [in particular those of political scientists and international-relations specialists] have complemented US hegemony and played an important role in the ongoing efforts of the US imperial state to manage Latin America and in the more recent attempt to contain Central America. (231–32)

In Berger's account, then, the social sciences within U.S. Latin American area studies have consolidated their disciplinary hegemony through a relation of structural homology to the field of hemispheric economic power and contestation in general. Emerging around the fabrication of the Good Neighbor Policy, cold war development theory, the Cuban revolution, the Alliance for Progress, and the war against communism in Vietnam, by the late 1960s Latin American area studies had consolidated its position within the North American tertiary system.[1]

In other words, through Berger's detailed and documented history of disciplinary development and expansion it becomes obvious that Latin Americanist thought has been, and, indeed, still is, a thought of the state. As such, to try to think about Latin Americanism as a critical practice is to take the risk of taking over, or of being taken over by, another thought of the state. It is to risk applying to the discipline's processes categories of thought that are already desired and produced by the state, and that are perhaps even guaranteed by it. No doubt we must agree with Enrico Mario Santí when he points to the relation of structural homology between current disciplinary practices and the historical construction of the West's peripheries:

> Latinamericanism, like Orientalism, is never far from the collective notion that identifies Europe, and by extension the United States, as a superior culture in comparison with all other non-European peoples and cultures. Like the Orient, "Latin America" is there to be charted, deciphered, understood, remade, and ultimately controlled by Latin-americanists, that is, implicitly at least positionally superior Western Europeans who never lose the upper hand. What creates and preserves that "upper hand" is none other than Latinamericanism, the discourse that guarantees a representation of Latin America that satisfies those hierarchical requirements quite apart from whether it has anything to do with a real historical existence. (90)

However, we must also recognize that a de-orientalist critique of orientalism (a critique that requires the implicit maintenance of the category of the West), or the de-orientalist critique of Latin Americanism (a critique that requires the implicit maintenance of the category of the North) reveals the internal economy, ultimately, of a state-related thought of metropolis. Within contemporary critiques of unequal power relations there is always an inevitable return of the West or of the North's academic expenditure to its own categories of analysis and intervention, which are negotiated, mediated, legitimized, and guaranteed from within the U.S. multicultural university's astounding ability to appropriate other areas of the planet, and to simultaneously position itself as their moral super-ego.

As Pierre Bourdieu tells us, disciplinary production is but one of the many arenas for hegemony's insistent naturalizing processes. As he puts it, "one of the major powers of the state is to produce and impose (especially through the school system) categories of thought that we spontaneously apply to all things of the social world—including the state itself" ("Rethinking" 1). Of course, if this is the case then recent epistemological and political configurations such as the cultural studies paradigm are also potentially the naturalized effect of "the effects of choices made by the state" (2), in which the state has so completely impressed its effects into disciplinary reality and into the minds of its practitioners that "possibilities initially discarded have become totally unthinkable" (2).

It is foolhardy, in other words, to declare a position for oneself that is somehow untouched by, outside, or against this overarching field of epistemological and political naturalization. In spite of such inevitabilities, however, the astounding ability of mainstream cultural studies to constitute and reproduce identitarian difference as immediately oppositional or as always already political—its ability to produce a disciplinary machine that continually underwrites the constitution of identity as a resistance or a way out of the state; or the multiculturalist intellectual populism that construes minority cultural practices as totalizing ruptures with the thought of high culture—is always potentially state-oriented in its ramifications.

After all, perhaps the recent turn to cultural particularism and micro-identitarian difference is precisely what late capitalism desires and needs in order to naturalize the subsumption of difference to capital. Meanwhile, at the other end of the disciplinary spectrum the embattled guardians of the modernist literary tradition merely reproduce and redistribute a profoundly outdated preservationist desire to maintain, uphold, and perpetuate discourses of national cultural patrimony, folklore, linguistic purity, and canonical tradition, in the same way that neoliberal states desperately strive to maintain the illusion of cultural hegemony, historical continuity, and social cohesion by conjuring up the sacred national symbols of, for example, the flag or the national anthem.

Any examination of contemporary knowledge production, then, is at one and the same time a reflection on, and a product of, knowledge as a practice of the state. As Mark Berger has shown us, Latin Americanist thought has emerged in such a way that, as a cultural and political practice, it has always been the function of its own ultimate horizon: the nation-state and the interests of the hemispheric interstate system. Thus, by not engaging at all moments this foundational yet always opaque horizon of knowledge production we systematically sidestep knowledge's most intimate and historically grounded kernel of structuration.

In this chapter I posit that the passage from national-popular formations to transnational configurations such as NAFTA and Mercosur is transforming forever not only state/culture relations but also intellectual/state/culture relations. Recent shifts in the cultural and political terrain are effectively redistributing the terms, grounds, and goals of institutional knowledge production. With the advent of the cybercodes and flows of the new world information order previous forms of experience and of representation are being transfigured into increasingly technocratic institutional and intellectual structures. Moreover, transnational technology's astounding ability to disperse and to redistribute the grounds of capitalist hegemony directly affect the ways in which contemporary subjectivities can be evaluated from within current disciplinary configurations.

Mark Berger's book is without doubt an extremely valuable contribution to the analysis of the formation of state and disciplinary processes both before and during the cold war. But it is also a book that inscribes its implicit untimeliness, for it does not (cannot?) account for the systematic erosion—under the increasingly powerful repertoires of the capitalist world economy—of the cold war's comparatively homogeneous and monumental center-periphery positionalities. Thanks to Berger's work we can now reflect on the last four decades as the emergence of an immensely powerful (yet not completely homogeneous) disciplinary machinery superimposed on the local realities of its southern objects of analysis and appropriation.

Indeed, the North's cold war institutionalization of cultural difference and of economic underdevelopment in the South was something against which Latin American Latin Americanists, working in Latin America, were always extremely wary. Since its inception in the early 1960s under the auspices of the Alliance for Progress, the history of the Latin American Studies Association's International Congress is, at least in part, the history of Latin Americanists based in Latin America protesting (often justifiably) that U.S. paradigms and methodologies were very often far removed from the local engagements of intellectuals and critics in, say, Caracas, Lima, or Montevideo.

Having said this, however, the cultural nationalist formations that legitimized the basic terms of such critiques—critiques that portrayed northern paradigms and methodologies as imperialistic misreadings or misappropriations of *lo nuestro,* thereby positioning intellectual practice in the South as implicitly more authentic, more *nuestro,* the real thing— are now increasingly difficult to sustain as valid positions from which to critique the grounds of contemporary knowledge production. On the one hand, increasing transnationalization is restructuring and redistributing what used to be the North's obviously romanticized "Macondismo." On the other hand, this does not mean that we have overcome it forever. Although the new configuration provides the opportunity to challenge the wholesale appropriation and homogenization of profoundly heterogenous cultural traditions, or to deconstruct the North's not-so-naive sanctification of Latin America as a place of premodern passions, nature, purity, and exotic underdevelopment, the schema of power relations that emerges with transnationalization also signals a new era in which intellectuals based in Latin America are also becoming increasingly integrated into transnationalism's technocratic structures. In this sense, Latin American intellectuals run the risk (perhaps more than ever) of maintaining (or of having to maintain) painfully uncomfortable relationships to transnational structures of domination even though the everyday hardships of sustained intellectual practice in neoliberal Latin America testify rather more to the increasing subalternization of the intellectual classes and of pedagogical practice in general.[2]

In other words, in neoliberal times national frontiers and national traditions can no longer be upheld by Latin American intellectuals as pure distinctive markers denoting radically divergent interests and unrelated intellectual concerns between North and South. After all, if the passage toward postnational multiculturality announces anything, it announces the problematic repositioning of the Latin American intellectual not only in relation to the state, but also in relation to the restructuration of local cultural politics in face of transnational market forces and capital flows.

In Latin American modernity the conscientious lettered intellectual was positioned in the social sphere as a fundamental point of mediation between local civil society, the nation-state, and external forces, influences, and desires. Within increasingly transnational and market-dominated configurations and structures of public exchange, however, that internal labor of mediation is both diluted and transformed beyond recognition. With the erosion in recent years of national fictive ethnicity as a hegemonic discourse of state and culture formation throughout Latin America, the emergence of transnational market forces has transformed the underlying ground of the nation and, along with it, the very notion of public culture. As such, contemporary evaluations of civil society, for example, are inevitably the result of new relations between the technocratic neoliberal state, the increasing omniscience of the ideology of the marketplace, multicultural or hybrid sociopolitical identities often marked by the traumatic nomadism of deregulated postmodern labor, and the myriad forms in which these social agents position themselves in face of the mass-media and culture industries. Obviously, such new circuits of mediation and of public exchange are the result of neoliberalism's decompression of the center as a fundamental modus operandi for relocating places, peoples, neighborhoods, regions, and nations within the complex restructuring of contemporary global accumulation (Harvey 297). As such, this is the new terrain on which we must now approach questions of individual and collective experience, citizenship, and civil society in Latin America.[3]

Latin Americanism is a fundamental arena for understanding the passage from Foucault's disciplinary society to the emergence of the period of concentration that Gilles Deleuze has termed the "society of control." This historical transformation—which has produced social configurations, cultural definitions, and assemblages of domination structured exclusively around the logics of the marketplace and the transnational division of labor—refers to the latest mutation of the capitalist system and to the crisis of metropolitan institutionality (not only that of the nation-state but also that of the university and its traditional objects and disciplinary practices). This transition toward Deleuze's almost intuitive notion of control has guaranteed the intensified erosion of what were always the uneven and inconstant paradigms of civil society and public culture in Latin America. As Deleuze notes, the postmodern erosion of historical forms of public culture has guaranteed the progressive and dispersed installation of new circuits of domination and control:

> Nineteenth century capitalism is a capitalism of concentration, for production and for property. It therefore erects the factory as a space of enclosure, the capitalist being the owner of the means of production but also, progressively, the owner of other spaces conceived through analogy (the worker's familial house, the school). As for markets, they are conquered sometimes by specialization, sometimes by colonization, sometimes by lowering the costs of production. But, in the present situation, capitalism is no longer involved in production, which it often relegates to the Third World. . . . It's a capitalism of higher-order production. It no longer buys raw materials and no longer sells the finished products: it buys the finished products or assembles parts. What it wants to sell is services and what it wants to buy is stocks. This is no longer a capitalism for production but for the product, which is to say, for being sold or marketed. Thus it is essentially dispersive, and the factory has given way to the corporation. The family, the school, the army, the factory are no longer the distinct analogical spaces that converge towards an owner—state or private power—but coded figures—deformable and transformable—of a single corporation that now has stockholders. . . . The operation of markets is now the instrument of social control and forms the impudent breed of our masters. Control is short-term and of rapid rates of turnover, but also continuous and without limit, while discipline was of long duration, infinite and discontinuous. (6)[4]

In contrast to the productive mechanisms of discipline—in contrast, in other words, to the nation's pedagogic apparatuses of social reproduction—the seemingly never-ending extension of postindustrial life in the "Los Angelesized" megacities of the South transforms Latin American modernity's models of fictive ethnicity production into an undefinable hybrid mix of discipline/control-based apparatuses. Meanwhile, undisciplined migrant populations attempt to eke out a meager existence in the maquiladoras and on the street corners of the intentionally disorganized, deregulated, and denationalized labor markets of the neoliberal order's informal economy. This produces a populace that is, on the one hand, subsumed by market forces, yet, on the other, embodies a potential for ungovernability that the neoliberal state constantly needs to control, manage, and, when necessary, dominate (though not necessarily incorporate, integrate, or educate as it strived to do during the populist phase of Latin American development).

Within the systemic ungroundedness of the postnational, then, abandoned and isolated people hang on (sometimes fanatically) to historically sedimented truths—local, regional, or even neighborhood identities—as if they were natural; or they elaborate ad hoc arrangements that serve as provisional refuge while searching for a meaningful future (Lechner, "*Por qué*" 65). Uncertainty, instability, and the degree of social control achieved through the intensification of so-called flexible labor practices, systemic social ungroundedness, and the sensation of meaningless transformation—of transformation intensified to such a degree that it is experienced almost as a hypostasis of the everyday—have produced a generalized climate of fear and disengagement that nevertheless lends structure to the international division of labor, and upholds the reign of the marketplace, the illusory withdrawal of the state, and consumption, as the dominant ideological realities and institutional practices of our times. As George Yúdice puts it:

> The shift to post-Fordism and other changes in the mode of production . . . correspond to a weakening of the articulation of national discourse and state apparatuses, particularly the disciplinary, "educational" ones. This does not mean that the state itself has been weakened; it has, rather, reconverted to accommodate new forms of organization and capital accumulation. Flexible accumulation, consumer culture, and the "new world information order" are produced or distributed (made to flow) globally, to occupy the space of the nation, but are no longer "motivated" by any essential connections to a state, as embodied, for example, in a "national-popular" formation. Their motivations are both infra- and supranational. We might say that, from the purview of the national proscenium, a posthegemonic situation holds. That is, the "compromise solution" that culture provided for Gramsci is not now one that pertains to the national level but to the local and transnational. Instead, the "culture-ideology of consumerism" serves to naturalize global capitalism everywhere. ("Civil" 4)[5]

Obviously, such transformations in the organization of power have enormous effects on our ability to examine both the institutional structures of rule as well as reflection's role within those structures. As Michael Hardt points out in his reading of Deleuze, the (incomplete) shift from discipline to the societies of control appears to challenge the notion of civil society as a privileged space for national citizenship formation and for active mediation between the interests of the people and the interests of the state. The underlying telos from within which to consider the relation between society and the state has shifted. The question, of course, is how to visualize that shift. As Hardt notes, Michel Foucault always implemented the diagram as a fundamental means of evoking in metaphorical terms the historical shifts in the assemblages of power. The panopticon, in this sense, was emblematic of the disciplinary societies because it functioned primarily in terms of positions, fixed points, and identities (36). How, though, to visualize the passage toward the societies of control? Hardt proposes the following schema:

> The Gramscian metaphor of a system of trenches that supported the war of position in civil society [has] been definitively surpassed by the contemporary techniques of warfare. Fixed positions have become a liability in an age of combat where monitoring, mobility, and speed have become the dominant characteristics. The Iraqi army certainly learned this lesson in the Gulf War. Iraqi soldiers were literally buried alive when their trenches were smoothed over by the U.S. war machine. The metaphorical space of the societies of control is perhaps best characterized by the shifting desert sands, where positions are continually swept away; or better, by the smooth surfaces of cyberspace, with its infinitely programmable flows of codes and information. (36)[6]

As such, Hardt adds, "The diagram of control . . . is not oriented toward position and identity, but rather toward mobility and anonymity. It functions on the basis of the 'whatever', the flexible and mobile performance of contingent identities, and thus its assemblages or institutions are elaborated primarily through repetition and the production of simulacra" (36).

Examples of the society of control's apparently empty, uninteresting, and banal "whatever" identities abound in the saturating imagery of the neoliberal marketplace. Few, however, are as suggestive as that of a recent commercial that appeared on U.S. television (and, therefore, probably around the globe). In an ad for a Citibank check card, an ad that is also a partial imitation of a Calvin Klein perfume commercial (and that is, therefore, an accumulation of images allegorizing ques-

The Other Side of the Popular

tions of ownership, property rights, identity, and the legal guarantee of consumption) Argentine supermodel Linda Evangelista appears floating freely through a series of black-and-white scenes filled with mirrors and perfume bottles. As her ungrounded body passes from image to image—apparently separated from any concrete context of social experience and any sense of the real, and perhaps little more than an abstract or even sublime corpus given over to the magical abolition of spatial and temporal differentiations—she repeatedly poses the quandary: "Identity, what is identity? . . . What is identity?" After having repeated the question four or five times, Evangelista (along with the viewer) is suddenly confronted (now in color) by a store cashier who is apparently annoyed by the fact that, while Evangelista muses over questions of identity and belonging, a line of potential consumers standing behind her are waiting their turn to participate in this identity quest as consumption ceremony. The cashier replies to the supermodel's dilemma: "Yes, Ms. Evangelista, identity. I need to see some identity before you can make a purchase!" "I don't *have* identity,'" replies Evangelista, both wistfully and tongue-in-cheek. Of course, if this pseudointellectual supermodel had possessed the Citibank card—which is concrete proof of her identity, of her eligibility to exercise her right as a citizen and to participate in the culture ideology of consumerism; the resolution and transcendence of all identity quests, the prime safeguard against potential rejection or marginalization in light of the demands of the marketplace, and also the guarantor of a particular free-floating ground from which to operate in the public domain—in other words, if she had acquired the card and had therefore assumed fully the relation of common immanence between identity and her creditline, she would not be confronting the potential angst and alienation of social rejection and marginalization that comes with not having access to the marketplace. The commercial, which empties out the meaning of intellectual inquiry in the face of market forces while poking fun at this very process, structures itself around the new religion of consumption and the threat of a potential fall from grace: not being able to make a purchase. This fall can only be avoided by acquiring the Citibank check card. The supermodel therefore reveals speculation on identity as useless abstraction while simultaneously presenting herself as an even more intensified form of abstraction: a lightly accented (foreign) and, therefore, singularized citizen of the capitalist world system, socialized thanks only to her acceptance of an absolute relation of immanence between selfhood—her name on a colorfully encrypted piece of plastic—and the transnational culture ideology of consumerism. Thanks to Linda Evangelista's free-floating disembodiment and its relation to the dissemination and perpetuation of identity/debt, Hardt's Foucauldian diagram of the society of control's metaphorical spacings can be supplemented by the representation of the experience of mobile and anonymous contingent identity, which is just another empty and uninteresting commodity for cosmopolitan life at the turn of the century.

All of this leads to a predicament that should be central to the concerns of contemporary thinkers both in the United States and beyond. If, as George Yúdice states, "societies may have reached a historical threshold in which it is no longer possible to think such ideals as citizenship and democracy in the absence of consumption" ("Civil" 20), then how do we formulate a sustained political response to the logics of control at a time dedicated almost exclusively to the erosion of national, regional, and local frontiers, to the tendential leveling of the transnational political terrain, and to the increasingly generalized penetration of the culture ideology of consumerism into everyday experience and practice? How can we think through such processes? Furthermore, to what extent do we, within our own processes of symbolization, merely reproduce and naturalize the neoliberal market/state's geo-economic configurations that are, increasingly, contemporary thought's invisible kernel of structuration?

In order to formulate a response, which, of course, will be little more than a further problematization of such matters, I examine the work of one of the most prominent and influential thinkers of public and urban culture in contemporary Latin America: Néstor García Canclini. In particular, I analyze García Canclini's rearticulation of civil society and of the popular in contemporary Mexico as they appear in *Consumidores y ciudadanos* (Consumers and citizens) and *Hybrid Cultures*.

In recent years the collapse of the national-popular as the defining vehicle for collective cultural and political articulation, the emergence of hybrid transnationalism as the ground for contemporary thought and social practice, the restructuring of state/culture relations through the dismantling of traditional local/national civil configurations, and the establishment of the informal economy as an increasingly privileged space of mediation between classes, genders, and ethnicities, have preconditioned the emergence of critical discourses dealing with the relation between citizenship and consumption as a potentially new arena for subject formation and collective agency. Within this new multicultural configuration such categories are thought to be capable of redefining the infrastructure of the neoliberal social sphere, and of rethinking civil society in the face of the unfettered expansion of market forces. As we will see, Néstor García Canclini's critical examination of the relationship between citizenship and consumption is an important response to

The Other Side of the Popular

the postmodern crisis of the nation-state and to the exhaustion of the national-popular in Latin America. It is also a valuable attempt to transcend the internal flaws, limits, and contradictions of a public sphere that is structured increasingly by micro group difference as a political and cultural category. García Canclini's work is therefore a critique of the universalizing pretensions of the modern Latin American state during the national-populist phase of development, as well as a response to the emergence of micro-identitarian subaltern injury as the apparent precondition for the elaboration of political action at the current time.

However, in order to arrive at the analysis of contemporary discourses of citizenship and collective agency through consumption, we should first take a step back and once again reflect on the logics of national fictive ethnicity. This will allow us to retrace in theoretical terms the genesis of subject, state, and culture formation that is still contemporary thought's problematic debt to, and inheritance from, the past. The genealogy that I propose as the necessary foundation from which to reflect on García Canclini's way of imagining a new civil society based on consumption, takes us from the heyday of state-promoted national and regional ethnic identities—in Mexico, for example, from the construction of the corporatist nation-state beginning with the presidency of Lázaro Cárdenas (1934-1940)—through to the postmodern crisis of the nation-state and the erosion in the 1980s of its previous projects of national socialization (aka the "Mexican miracle").

The genealogy that follows, then (a necessary digression that will nevertheless allow us to return to García Canclini and to his thought as a cultural and political practice after the eclipse of the nation-state and the demise of modernity's revolutionary configurations), is to be read alongside, and in tension with, the cold war crisis of national fictive ethnicity as it was portrayed in chapter 1, as well as alongside and in tension with the residual engagements of intellectual populism as discussed in chapter 2. The critical constellations presented in these three chapters are, in other words, the differential assemblages of a single horizon of epistemological and political inheritance—that of the collapse of national fictive ethnicity as a state-generated discourse of desire and universalization— viewed from within distinct yet intimately related theoretical and political moments, concerns, and epistemological positionalities and possibilities. The genealogy that follows, then, establishes a dialogue with the previous two chapters by advancing their respective arguments and limitations while opening up the possibility of an alternative realm of critical engagement with the contemporary.

As shown in chapter 1, throughout Latin America's uneven modernizing processes identitarian difference was articulated and negotiated predominantly as an object of desire from within, or at least in relation to, the universalizing projects of the Creole state and the always utopic coming-into-its-own of the nation-state. Having said this, however, popular identity was equally always viewed by the state as a force to be feared and controlled. Thus difference was invariably constructed and articulated through the state's constant, and inevitably failed, attempts to incorporate, integrate, and domesticate its national yet potentially unlawful or revolutionary outsides.[7]

Identitarian difference, then, was construed as national, popular, and cultural, while collective subject formation became negotiable exclusively through, and mediated from within, the image (the illusion) of the state as *the* subject and transcendental center of collective identification. Thus, the identitarian logics of the modern state in Mexico, for example, formulated themselves on the active generation of spatial metaphors such as place and region, from which peripheral subjects could then be fabricated, defined, controlled, ethnicized, and integrated into nation-state processes—or not, as the case may be. Having said this, however, the crisis of the national-popular subject-state in Mexico—a crisis that remains inexorably linked to the $170 billion that the country owes in foreign debt as a result of the economic collapse of the early 1980s (Marichal 25)—has now produced a proliferation in micro group politics that has surfaced as a result of the nation-state's perpetual inability to establish universal citizenship. This, of course, is precisely the social ground that underlies García Canclini's critical interventions. It is equally the ground that we should assume in order to reflect further on the role of intellectual practice in contemporary Latin America.

STATES OF IDENTITY AND INJURY: A GENEALOGY FOR
POTENTIAL CONSUMERS AND NONCITIZENS

In their seminal work Philip Corrigan and Derek Sayer present us with the great axiom of the state: the State states. Let me quote extensively from their representation of the modern state as the site for the formation and regulation of individual and collective identifications and identities:

> The arcane rituals of law, the formulae of royal assent to an Act of Parliament, visits of school inspectors, are all statements. They define, in great detail, acceptable forms and images of social activity and individual and collective identity; they regulate . . . much . . . of social life.

In this sense the "State" never stops talking. Out of the vast range of human social capacities—possible ways in which social life could be lived—state activities more or less forcibly "encourage" some whilst suppressing, marginalizing, eroding, undermining others. Schooling for instance comes to stand for education, policing for order, voting for political participation. Fundamental social classifications, like age and gender, are enshrined in law, embedded in institutions, routinized in administrative procedures and symbolized in rituals of state. Certain forms of activity are given the official seal of approval, others are situated beyond the pale. This has cumulative, and enormous, cultural consequences; consequences for how people identify . . . themselves and their "place" in the world. (3–4)

The constant production of statements frames or erases subject positions, defines and regulates individual and collective identities, and generates social spaces from which to mediate, recast, or perhaps even disarticulate the always illusory entity called the state itself. As such, the state under capital has always assumed a spatial syntax in order to produce and regulate the places of everyday life and labor. In these processes distinct forms of territory, social practice, community, and social intervention are continually imposed, renegotiated, and contested. The state as that which never stops talking, then, conjures up images of hegemony production that cannot be taken as unchallenged control.

For example, Jeffrey Rubin has argued convincingly that in reality the postrevolutionary Mexican state has never been a stable routinized entity gathering and negotiating power at the center among exclusively political actors. Rather, it has always been "a complex and changing center that coexists with and is constituted and embedded in the diversity of regional and cultural constructions evolving throughout Mexico since the 1930s" (86). Hence, he states, it must be taken as a constant transformation of social relations and of dominant belief systems. As Raymond Williams puts it in his reading of Gramsci, hegemony "has continually to be renewed, recreated, defended, and modified. It is also continually resisted, limited, altered, challenged by pressures not all its own" (quoted in Rubin 88). For Claudio Lomnitz Adler, of course, the state is necessarily both the producer and the retroactive product of an often geographically specific intersection between culture, economy, and politics. Without a doubt, then, Corrigan and Sayer's formulation of state processes complement these ideas which give us new insight into the complexity of local and national power formations. After all, the regional or the local that constitutes and/or opposes the universalizing pretensions of the nation-state (the always mythical transcendental subject-state of national populism) emerges as a complex web of relations of domination and subordination, rather than as a reified space "with discernible boundaries defined by this or that spatially hegemonic system" (Van Young 27).

The modern category of the nation was always intimately related to the native, and therefore to nature, to the extent that populations were viewed as being born into relationships that were typically settled in a single place (the etymological root of "nation" is, of course, *nascere*, to be born).[8] As can be seen in chapter 1, the cultural politics of populist integration that emerged around the time of the crash of the world capitalist system in 1929 and that lasted roughly up to the 1980s was predicated on what Jean Franco quite rightfully calls "certain common assumptions that are no longer generally accepted—organicist notions of society, the common identity of oppressed peoples, the notion of the writer as representative of an as yet unrealised collectivity" ("Latin" 269). Such common assumptions structured both sides of the political spectrum by positing nature and the native as the radical opposites, or antagonistic limits, to the nation and to the foundation of national fictive ethnicity. In the process the state drew up, universalized (or at least purported to universalize), and limited the collective archive of possible identifications and alliances. It did this by fabricating the notion of region as the radical outside to the modernizing machinery of the patrimonial Creole state. Thus it is that literary categories such as *criollismo, regionalismo, novela de la tierra, indigenismo,* the marvellous real, and magical realism all emerge over a period of roughly forty years as literary responses to, and as the cultural effects of, the continued postcolonial quest for state hegemony over the irrational cultural disorder of the regions and their unruly populations. Such literary formulations are, in other words, all responses to the persistent failure of state hegemony and to the perpetual neocolonial outsidedness—the exotopic place fixity—of the increasingly ethnicized people. As a compensation for the perpetuation of the outsidedness of the people, modernizing ideologies constructed and promoted regional and national identities exclusively in terms of the authentic, the natural, the ancestral, or the racial—all of which came to be little more than the Creole valorization and privileging of identities deemed to be precapitalist or premodern—as normalized representations of a Latin American essence that nevertheless needed to be domesticated, overcome, or erased in order for modernization to be implemented.[9] Before the demands of an always imminent modernity, and before the demands of national intelligentsia grounded invariably in the illusions of fortune-telling, the object of desire conjured up by the nation-state was precisely the popular culture that it desired to displace or delegitimize as a result of its very gestures of inclusion and sanctification (Ortiz 19).[10] Thus the state in modernity reformulated itself through the redemptive promotion of the popular, and of the region, as the original thresholds of a national identity that could be constructed on the propagation of sentimental localism. This, of course, remained for decades the conceptual ground of a Creole developmentalism that was, for the most part, anchored in the "necessary appropriation of alien wills" (Marx, *Grundrisse* 500–501) throughout the national space; in other words, in social processes that can also go by the name of internal colonialism or modernizing neocolonialism.

Therefore, in Latin American modernity nationhood articulated itself invariably through a circuit of state-sanctioned symbols designed to redeem regional identities from their lowly and often spiteful provincialisms. In the words of Carlos Monsiváis, in Mexico "regionalism [was] paraded as a strategy of compensation: local and regional identities were shining guides in the labyrinth of marginality; regional pride was the ultimately humorous variant of nationalism on the defensive" ("Just" 248). Thus the alcoves of ethnoidentitarian regionalism came to be evoked by the nation-state as the initial threshold of nation formation. The state, in other words, repeatedly portrayed, preserved, and disseminated illusory regional and national identities in order to conflate them with, and as, the preservation of the state itself (Martín Barbero 64).

Once again, the case of Mexico is particularly enlightening since, as Van Young tells us, the hegemonic rationales of postrevolutionary state discourse constructed themselves on very real social, economic, and cultural forms of disarticulation between center and periphery. In other words, modernization was constructed on the differences between a normative national identity and those regional subjectivities that, as a result of the recuperation and narrativization after the revolution of their local experiences and histories, contributed, paradoxically, to the formation of revolutionary national historiography in the first place (15). For Monsiváis such in-built disarticulations within the foundation and consolidation of the modern nation-state amounted to little more than "backwardness planned from the center" ("Just" 249). Thus, he notes, the statements of the postrevolutionary state persistently constituted the region as *the* site for identitarian, linguistic, and economic difference and negativity:

> Until very recently, to speak of Mexican regionalism was to refer almost exclusively to realities blurred by mythology . . . to mention

regionalism was most often to conjure up legends of the bewildered fringes and the feudal realities of backwardness. Regions: areas far removed from the impulse of progress, storehouses of raw materials (human talent included), minor ingredients of the Mexico City melting pot . . . any idea of regionalism was declared insufficient, unfortunate, impoverished (the height of localism). Thus, *regional* and *local* were categories opposed in principle to *national;* they were fragments adverse to integration. (247)

The region and its identities, then, were where the urban-metropolitan nation-state (as the sole promoter of capitalist progress and development) encountered its negative foundation, the ultimate limit at which the state could construct and nationalize itself. Moreover, the region was the generally undisciplined space within which negativity threatened the stability of the state's representations of desirable citizenship and collective belonging. Having said this, however, the fabrication of regional identities from within the urban realm also afforded the metropolitan national state a necessary point of departure from, and for, itself. It offered self-abandonment as a means of voyaging over and onto its others—onto the region as the privileged terrain of autochthonous difference (and of nonnational citizenship)—ultimately in order to return to itself, as well as to integrate those despised yet domesticated identities and cultural practices to their rightful place; back to the urban realm as the absolute locus of disciplinary progress, development, and institutionalization.[11]

The populist state, then, constituted the region and its place-fixed identities as the condition of possibility for its own continued self-representation and signification. Yet it was precisely this illusory act of self-constitution—the formation of a state of national identity grounded in the positive production and assimilation of necessarily peripheral noncitizens—that rendered difference as the modern state's greatest challenge. Distinctive national identity was, on the one hand, the nation-state's anti-imperial and antidependency desire, while, on the other hand, difference remained the antagonistic internal limit to the expansionist state's cultural-nationalist and capitalist syntax. In other words, in Latin American modernity the spatialized syntax of the nation-state construed the foundational, nostalgia-producing terrains of place and identity as the potential ferment of cultural nationalism and of the modern pedagogic state. However, it simultaneously represented these same ideas as a constant threat: as the potential placeholders of economic stagnation, underdevelopment, and national dissolution. In this sense,

The Other Side of the Popular

the state's spatial syntax empowered it in its spectacular quest for hegemonic "stateliness." But it also marked the limitation of a state that promoted communal interests that were always already unattainable in real
terms, since they were constructed on the maintenance of the region—
and therefore of negative identities and undisciplined forms of labor and
of public exchange—as emblems of a potentially antagonistic schism
underlying the dialectic between progress and stagnation, between boom
and bust.

In spite of the issues described above, however, the stifling experience of what Monsiváis calls "planned backwardness from the center"
began to change ostensibly in the 1970s in Mexico and elsewhere as a
result of demographic explosion, increasing urbanization and the emergence of mass society, the gradual transnationalization of symbolic markets and labor migrations, the increasing insertion of peripheral national
cultures and economies into global networks of symbolic production,
and the consolidation of a state-led move away from the defense of the
national-popular (which, of course, had traditionally defined and regulated the place of the intellectual in the national public sphere) in favor
of what Renato Ortiz calls the exportation of the Latin American "international popular."[12] As George Yúdice puts it, the advent of globalizing forces "transformed the traditional sentimental-educational terrain
of citizenship formation" forever ("Civil" 18). Indeed recent structural
transformations in the capitalist world economy have facilitated the erosion of economic nationalism, the downsizing and decentralization of the
nation-state, the deregulation of labor, and the increasing insertion of
private sector capital into the workings of the culture industries. As such,
with the advancement of new telecommunications systems (governed increasingly by homegrown transnational corporations such as Televisa in
Mexico and Rede Globo in Brazil), the circulation of mass-mediatized
images and storylines throughout the national space (and, of course,
abroad) has promoted the restructuring of the region, of regional cultures, of local identities, and of minority languages as domains no longer
defined as fixed peripheries located as the negative foundation of the
nation-state, or as organic obstacles to modernization. As García Canclini observes in *Hybrid Cultures:*

> Arriving at the 1990s, it is undeniable that Latin America has modern-
> ized, as a society and as a culture: symbolic modernism and socioeco-
> nomic modernization are no longer so divorced. The problem lies in
> modernization's having been produced in a different way from what
> we expected in earlier decades. In this second half of the century, mod-

ernization was not made so much by states as by private enterprise. The "socialization" or democratization of culture has been achieved by the culture industry—almost always in the hands of private corporations—more than by the cultural or political goodwill of the producers. There continues to be inequality in the appropriation of symbolic goods and in access to cultural innovation, but that inequality no longer takes the simple and polarized form we thought we would encounter when we were dividing every country into dominant or dominated, or the world into empires and dependent nations. (64-65)[13]

Perhaps it is not by chance, then, that such transformations in the capitalist world economy—which García Canclini equates with the "democratization of culture"—should come hand in hand with the renovation of identitarian categories of difference. As all (elite) hopes for social cohesion promoted from within the national-developmentalist state became systematically undermined during the "lost decade" of the 1980s, multicultural subjectivities grounded in the representation and reproduction of identitarian injury—identities whose bonds of collective attachment have been inexorably disarticulated or wounded by the homogenizing practices of the state of national identity or by the institutional effects of the transition to globalism—rose to the surface of the public sphere and of political practice in order to challenge and question the limits of Latin American development. The erosion and decline of the subject-state, of the state of identity, then, has ultimately produced what Ernesto Laclau has called "the death of the death of the subject; the re-emergence of the subject as a result of its own death; the proliferation of concrete finitudes whose limitations are the source of their strength; the realization that there can be subjects because the gap that the 'Subject' was supposed to bridge is unbridgeable" ("Universalism" 21).

Thus, the previously integration-oriented function of the political sphere has now lost its force as the organizing vortex of society, while micro or local identity—the development of identity now as a codification of injury, of powerlessness, and of collective exclusion as the affirmation of a particularly powerful source of commonality in neoliberal times—emerges and fills in the gap left behind by the restructuring of the nation-state, as a new frame of reference for any kind of political thought or practice in Latin America. As Norbert Lechner puts it, politics is not what it used to be because it has been destructured, informalized, and displaced as the center of social organization ("*Por qué*" 68). This has not only transformed the context within which politics can be conceived but has displaced the practice of politics itself as it, so to speak, disperses, downsizes, diversifies, and privatizes. Thus, as neoliberalism imposes

The Other Side of the Popular

itself as the dominant ideology of our times, particularist identity and the politics of differential subjectivity have become increasingly influential as forms of intervention on the capitalist peripheries. And this, it must be said, signals a curious hemispheric redistribution of the social logics that gave birth to the cultural politics of identity in the United States after the Civil Rights movement of the 1960s.

In his reflections on such phenomena Fredric Jameson has addressed the relationship between culture and the group libido by taking both as particularly connected to the emergence of consumerism in contemporary society. For Jameson identity conflict of an ethnic kind, for example, cannot be solved or resolved, but demands to be sublimated into a different form of struggle that can achieve some form of resolution. Class struggle, he states, offers the prototype of one such sublimation. But, he adds, the market and consumption are another kind of sublimation and this, in postmodern times, "has come to look equally as universal as the classless one, but perhaps owes its success predominantly to the specific circumstances of the postfeudal North American commonwealth, and the possibilities of social leveling that arose with the development of the mass media" (*Cultural* 275–76). Thus, as Jameson continues, we are faced with a particular demand when thinking about the theoretical and practical limits of a post subject-state marketplace conjuring up images of the politics of micro-identity: "We . . . need to take into account the possibility that the various politics of difference—the differences inherent in the various politics of 'group identity'—have been made possible only by the tendential leveling of social identity generated by consumer society; and to entertain the hypothesis that a cultural politics of difference becomes feasible itself only when the great and forbidding categories of classical Otherness have been substantially weakened by 'modernization'" (276).

Identity politics in the United States was born from the erosion in the boundary between public and private space; from within the advent of globalized telecommunications networks designed to deterritorialize the symbolic universe and to weaken decidedly premodern sensations such as belonging, rootedness, or place fixity. If this is the case, identity politics is both the product, and inevitably the perpetuation, of the logics of dispersal and fragmentation that gave birth to it, as social experience becomes increasingly characterized by privatization and a generalized retirement into the domain of the personal as the privileged sphere of social existence.[14]

Yet in the case of recent social movements in Mexico, for example, and of the Ejército Zapatista de Liberación Nacional (EZLN) in particular, micro-identity has been mobilized as an effective expression of local society and as a collective call for multicultural democratization in the face of the globalizing demands of the international market.[15] Such mobilizations are explicitly grounded in the representation of the idea of local community as a phantasm of former lives and of contemporary injuries. Thus, as Adolfo Gilly informs us, the initial communiqués of the EZLN included the following remarkable statement:

> The eldest of our people's elders spoke words that came from afar, from when our lives did not exist and our voices were silent. And truth walked in the words of the eldest of our people's elders. And we learned in the words of our elder's eldest that our people's long night of pain had come at the hands and words of the powerful. . . . But the truth that followed the steps of the eldest of the elder's words was not only of pain and death. In the words of the eldest of our elders there also came hope for our history. (*La Jornada*, February 22, 1994; quoted in Gilly 62; translation mine)[16]

Micro-identity—in this case profoundly and primordially ancestral in its strategic representations—is a final refuge from which globalization can be contested. Yet such statements uncover a particular dilemma when considering the reconceptualization of the public sphere, for this is obviously a politics grounded in the production and perpetuation of injury and wounds, in which, in the words of Wendy Brown,

> politicized identity emerges and obtains its unifying coherence through the politicization of *exclusion* from an ostensible universal, as a protest against exclusion: a protest premised on the fiction of the inclusive/universal community, a protest that thus reinstalls the humanist ideal—so far as it premises itself upon exclusion from it. Put the other way around, politicized identities generated out of liberal, disciplinary societies, insofar as they are premised on exclusion from a universal ideal, require that ideal, as well as their exclusion from it, for their own continuing existence as identities. (65)

Thus the representation of historical micro-patrimony, and of that patrimony as collective injury, extends stigma and exclusion as a necessary means of preserving and upholding the universalist categories of liberalism and of the nation-state. It thereby serves to affirm and perpetuate the immediacy of originary identitarian antagonisms rather than abolishing the notion of an identity grounded in exclusion. Once again Wendy Brown frames, in most poignant terms, the problematic agency of contemporary politicized micro-identity within the construction of public culture or civil society:

The Other Side of the Popular

In its emergence as a protest against marginalization or subordination, politicized identity . . . becomes attached to its own exclusion both because it is premised on this exclusion for its existence as identity and because the formation of identity as the site of exclusion, as exclusion, augments or "alters the direction of the suffering" entailed in subordination or marginalization by finding a site of blame for it. But in so doing, it installs pain over its unredeemed history in the very foundation of its political claim, in its demand for recognition as identity. In locating a site of blame for its powerlessness over its past—a past of injury, a past as a hurt will—and locating a "reason" for the "unendurable pain" of social powerlessness in the present, it converts this reasoning into an ethnicizing politics, a politics of recrimination that seeks to avenge the hurt even while it reaffirms it, discursively codifies it. Politicized identity thus enunciates itself, makes claims for itself, only by entrenching, restating, dramatizing, and inscribing its pain in politics; it can hold out no future—for itself or others—that triumphs over this pain. The loss of historical direction, and with it the loss of futurity characteristic of the late modern age, is thus homologically refigured in the structure of desire of the dominant political expression of the age: identity politics. (73–74)

Thus the emergence of identity politics after the crisis of the Latin American nation-state (of the state of identity, that is) might represent the only way of imagining cultural politics within neoliberal configurations (as the most effective way of sublimating historically constituted collective experience into negative thought and action), but its internal logics inevitably perpetuate and extend, rather than challenge, the persistence of the neoliberal market processes that gave rise to it in the first place. The fragmented particularism of politicized micro-identity, then, announces an inherently contradictory way of expressing collective democratizing desires in late capitalism, for its negativity is always "an effect of domination that reiterates impotence, a substitute for action, for power, for self-affirmation that reinscribes incapacity, powerlessness, and rejection" (Brown 69).[17]

OF CONSUMERS AND CITIZENS:
NÉSTOR GARCÍA CANCLINI AND THE FUNDAMENTALISM
OF NEOLIBERALISM

Toward the end of *Hybrid Cultures* Néstor García Canclini asks the following question: "In what, then, lies the novelty of postmodern decollection, deterritorialization, and hybridity?" (243). Perhaps we could suggest that his later work, *Consumidores y ciudadanos* (Consumers and citizens) is a response to this question, while simultaneously signaling an expansion and an extension of the critical issues first taken up in *Hybrid Cultures*. Indeed, it is with García Canclini's question in mind that we should return to George Yúdice's original observation that "societies may have reached a historical threshold in which it is no longer possible to think such ideals as citizenship and democracy in the absence of consumption" ("Civil" 20). After all, this historical threshold is precisely the response to García Canclini's question in *Hybrid Cultures* regarding the novelty of contemporary hybridity. Thus, a return to Yúdice's formulation allows us to reflect further on a critical project that has been formulated, at least in part, I believe, as a means of providing a modicum of social cohesion to those institutional infrastructures for political mediation and public exchange that have been eroded by recent transformations in the capitalist world system, by the undisciplined and apparently disorganized proliferation of informal social agents, and by the increasing practice of politics through the codification of particularist exclusion/inclusion.

In recent years Néstor García Canclini has emerged as one of the most prominent thinkers of public culture, civil society, and contemporary forms of community, as well as of the relation of those subjects to structural transformations in the order of post-Fordist capital accumulation. As we will see, his work upholds regional cultural affirmation and economic integration as a means of transforming late modernity's apparent loss of historical direction—its loss of a collective sense of futurity after the erosion of the national-popular—and as a means of establishing forms of social cohesion or collective order that are capable of reformulating democratic culture from within the snaking circuitry of NAFTA.

In *Consumidores y ciudadanos* García Canclini provides us, in the words of George Yúdice, with "the cultural adhesive for [Jorge] Castañeda's more economically conceived federal regionalism" ("Civil" 19). As Yúdice explains, in *Utopia Unarmed* Jorge Castañeda proposes a new "cross-cutting, longitudinal nationalism" (312), or "regional federalism," designed to negotiate economic integration into transnational circuitries. Such regional integration would guarantee, according to Castañeda, some kind of "intermediary solution between a largely unsustainable status quo and a highly harmful progression toward the dissolution of sovereignties and economic and social options for the developing nations" (313). "Conserving the nation-state as the prime area of economic activity," continues Castañeda, "appears impossible; joining one of the three large economic spheres of influence at a time of great flux and under conditions of gaping disparities and overwhelming weakness cannot be a desirable option, even if some resignedly accept it. Regional economic integration is a halfway house that possesses intrinsic merits and is preferable to existing alternatives. It can be either a lasting solution or a stepping-stone to a better world, when it arrives" (313). Thus (and, once again, mirroring Yúdice's argument) Castañeda's formulation of an alternative organization to contemporary globalism—that is, his formulation of a Latin American alternative to integration into one of the three large economic spheres of influence (United States, Europe, Japan)—is based on the development of institutional and economic infrastructures, which include the following:

> Compensatory financing funded by windfall profit taxes and duties, labor mobility, a common external tariff to protect sectors of industry and agriculture that are jointly considered strategic and worthy of support, subsidies and credit facilities in order to make them competitive, in a business-government alliance and industrial policy along East Asian lines, a social charter or its equivalent and an environmental charter that harmonize up, not down, and include financial provisions for the adoption of superior norms in one area or another, common subsidies, and expenditures for research and development, and dispute settlement mechanisms open to all interested parties and relevant issues. (317)[18]

Within this drive for regional affirmation and integration, but not for incorporation into the intrusive and "potentially damaging integration processes being proposed by the United States" (314), García Canclini "posits consumption as a 'means of thinking' that creates new ways of being citizens" (Yúdice, "Civil" 18). As George Yúdice highlights in his analysis of Canclini's approach to contemporary cultural politics:

> Traditional and even recent progressive thinking on the expansion of citizenship to the "popular" (or "subaltern") sectors is outdated, particularly insofar as it looks to the national frame as the proscenium of action and retains a "Gutenbergian" conception of how to negotiate the public sphere. García Canclini advocates rethinking politics in relation to consumption, although not in the accordance with the U.S. model. Globalization has transformed the traditional sentimental-educational terrain of citizenship formation. National patrimonies, folklore, and the high arts are losing viewers and users, or their functions have shifted. Consumption, then, has to be rethought in relation to the culture industries. In Latin America, though, this means confronting the problem of "Americanization." ("Civil" 18)

How, then, do we negotiate the restructuration of the public sphere and of the political field around the notion and practice of consumption? Furthermore, how do we do it in such a way as to not reinscribe and reproduce neoimperial logics such as those normally associated in the cultural field with "Americanization"?[19]

García Canclini states that he writes in order to imagine a Latin American cultural politics—what he terms a "postpolitics"—specific to the new negotiations, interactions, and conflicts that characterize multicultural civil society after the eclipse of the nation-state; after the demise of territorial (regional or place-specific) and monolinguistic conceptualizations of citizenship; and after the emergence of new communities formed not around the perpetuation of identitarian injury but around modes of symbolic consumption that overshadow productive processes normally associated with the macrosocial, the nation, or class interests. As he notes in *Consumidores y ciudadanos:* "Civil societies look increasingly less like national communities, understood as territorial, linguistic, and political communities. Rather, they emerge more as *communities of interpretive consumers;* that is, as groups of people sharing tastes and forms of reading certain goods (gastronomic, sporting, musical) that confer a shared identity upon them" (196).[20]

In this way, he says, we can see that "in the new generations, identities are organized not so much around historical-territorial symbols—those of the memory of the nation—but rather around Hollywood, Televisa, or Benetton" (33). Taking as his point of departure the dissolution of the national subject as the sole expression of the collective—a model of citizenship and belonging that was always, he says, negotiated from within totalizing identifications with land and ethnicity (from within the fictive ethnicities of the state of identity in other words)—García Canclini calls for a new conceptualization of politics. This politics presupposes a new formulation of multicultural democracy capable of reviving the idea of historical direction—of futurity—and of revitalizing the notion of the "state as the representative of the public interest, as arbiter and guarantor that collective needs for information, recreation, and innovation not be subordinated always to their commercial viability" (*Consumidores,* 162, 190).

The ultimate purpose of *Consumidores y ciudadanos,* then, is quite simply to recognize that the novelty of postmodern hybridity is essentially that of the market and of mass consumption. Of course, this immediately implies considering the ways in which to conceive of future forms of social cohesion and of possible models of citizenship. Future processes of democratization, García Canclini states, depend on the establishment of a politics of national and international pluricultural integration. The formation of an infrastructure for cultural and political integration could then work in defense of Latin American consumer's practices and tastes, all of which, he states, condition people's ability to exercise citizenship as a sense of commonality and belonging.

For García Canclini, then, what is required to transcend the formation of social identity as either monouniversal or as a particularist site of exclusion? What infrastructural formalities could democratize the public sphere in Latin America? As he puts it, "only the multiplication of actors can favor democratic cultural development and the representation of multiple identities. The new role of the states and of international organisms (UNESCO, OAS, . . . etc.) would consist in reconstructing the public space—to be understood as the multicultural collective—so that diverse agents (states, businesses, and independent groups) could negotiate agreements and develop public interests" (162–63).

García Canclini calls, then, for the end of politics as a proliferation of informal or self-regulated states of injury by suggesting constitutional and political reforms guaranteeing the rights of diverse groups. This includes promoting understanding and respect for differences in education and "traditional interactions," as well as facilitating the dissemination of information and knowledge from within the mass culture industries such as radio, TV, cinema, video, and interactive technology systems (160). Along with such policies, García Canclini continues, the state should promote the construction of a specifically Latin American cultural-media space by implementing the following procedures:

> (a) Forming Latin American common markets for books, magazines, cinema, TV, and video, along with concrete measures promoting distribution and the free circulation of cultural goods. . . .
> (b) Fixing minimum quotas in each of the countries of the region for movies, radio broadcasts, and other Latin American cultural goods. . . . The promotion of a Latin American market for cultural goods will be ineffective if it is not accompanied by measures protecting distribution and consumption.
> (c) Creating a Foundation for the Production and Distribution of Latin American Media, whose role would be to provide partial funding for cinema, TV, and video production, to coordinate state, business, and associative organisms, and to imagine new distributive channels. (160–61)

These regulating forces, García Canclini states, would be accompanied by the control of foreign capital and by the development of local and

regional radio and television as a means of promoting a politics of translocal recognition, which would help further the interests of democratic
cultural development and the positive representation of multiculturality
(162–63).

Obviously, such a vision suggests the architecture of a more demo-
cratically founded transnationalism, an attempt to overcome the center-
periphery/identity-difference binarisms of Monsiváis's "planned backwardness from the center," as well as a means of transcending identity
politics' perpetuation of exclusion by mobilizing a plurality of regional
styles, and perhaps even local modes of production, in order to negotiate the standardizing drives of late-capitalist corporatism. García Canclini, in other words, strives to overcome the radical exclusions that lie
at the heart of neoliberalism's social processes in Latin America by promoting a new institutional infrastructure and positive ground for local
sites of practice and intervention. Ultimately, he is attempting to overcome the exclusionary limits of state practices by eliminating the distinctive characters of regional and ethnic identity as the negative foundations for modern political thought and institutional intervention in Latin
America.

Thus, in García Canclini's formulation, what used to be the boundaries that divided and sometimes joined regional or local networks in
their relation to the nation-state are now surpassed by a new affirmation of translocal, transregional, and transnational relations anchored in
the equal representation and distribution of a hybrid multiculturality that
can now uphold the state as arbiter, guarantor, and protector of collective rights and cultural interests. García Canclini's vision, then, is that of
an explicitly constructivist program of postcrisis and of post–national-
popular social regulation and repair; an attempt to contain the cultural
and social effects of capital's transnationalized conquest of markets, territories, and populations and to limit its competitive pressures in order to
redistribute (in more regulated fashion) the effects of its hemispheric and
world-wide networks of accumulation. In other words, the current structure of accumulation is irrational and overly disorganized in its recent
swing toward so-called self-regulation. As such, more external regulation
is required.

But García Canclini's discourse also calls attention to its limits as a
sustainable politics—indeed, it calls attention to the sustainability of what
he calls "postpolitics" in general—for *Consumidores y ciudadanos*' proposed processes of democratization uncover a regulative cultural politics
designed to reterritorialize and redistribute what used to fall under the
rubric of *lo nuestro,* at a time in the history of market-based develop-

ment in which *lo nuestro* (in spite of Univisión's almost obsessive bombardment of the TV-viewing public with this vacuous nomenclature of collective belonging) is increasingly unsalvageable as a category of definition. In other words, García Canclini's postpolitical vision of cultural democratization appears to be rather more concerned with reconstituting and restabilizing the imaginary evenness of a cultural, commercial, and institutional playing field than it is with the imaginative projection of a postnational politics. It highlights, in other words, the extent to which counterhegemony can now be little more than an alternative discourse of, and path toward, capitalist hegemony.

García Canclini's discourse is, of course, the result of the repeated failure of the ideal of liberalism in Latin America. It is therefore the result of the repeated failure of the state as the embodiment of liberal universalism as universalism. If we view liberalism as "the tension between particularistic 'I's and a universal 'we' . . . sustainable as long as the constituent terms of the 'I' remain unpoliticized: indeed, as long as the 'I' itself remains unpoliticized on one hand, and the state (as the expression of the ideal of political universality) remains unpoliticized on the other" (Brown 56), then we can see that García Canclini constantly positions his discourse *after* the crisis of the nation-state and *after* the collapse of the (national-popular) ideal of forging the state as representative of universal interests. García Canclini, then, explicitly positions his critique as a means of transcending the state's homogenizing and universalizing pretensions. Furthermore, he does so in order to privilege the multiple particularities and differences of civil society's market-based multiculturality, yet he does this not just by upholding but by actively reinvesting in his object of critique—namely the universalizing management techniques of the market/state—as a sustainable ground for market-based reformation.

At this point, of course, we would do well to remember that it was liberal developmentalism's dependency on metropolitan capital that contributed to the crisis of the national-popular state in the first place. Although the economic and social policies of the Keynesian-Fordist model of development—of the national-popular model that, with many variations, rose to the fore in Latin America between the 1930s and 1970s—achieved widespread social mobility and economic integration (Vilas, "Neoliberal," 17), they could not represent or harmonize increasing divergence between capital and labor demands. Neither could they compete with changes in the capitalist world system that emerged after the Second World War.

Finally, bureaucratic authoritarianism and military dictatorship, coupled with the debt crisis of the early 1980s, delegitimized this state-led model of societal organization and development, and created the conditions for the current neoliberal model of market-based economic and social organization. In this sense the erosion of the geopolitical nation-state and of the Keynesian-Fordist model of development, and the transition toward a model in which transnational market forces and the insertion of subjects within those forces that supposedly produce democracy, remains the positive ground on which García Canclini construes the possibility of a postpolitics. And this is so in spite of the fact that, as George Yúdice puts it, "for García Canclini, as for Castañeda again, neoliberalism and privatization are not the answers; these just enable transnational corporations to gain greater control in Latin America" ("Civil" 18).

As is perhaps the case in all contemporary thought that is worth considering, there is a sense that García Canclini and the idea of regional federalism are always already caught up in their object of critique. García Canclini's response to the crisis of the postnational is to relegitimize the nation-state (under strictly postnational forms) by disseminating communitarian models that transpire exclusively within the regime of market forces. In this sense he gives capitalist hegemony what it wants. He rearticulates the liberal developmentalist ideology of historical direction and upholds the sustainable management of populations alongside the knowability and potential predictability of collective practices in times of increasing market-based control and consensus/crisis management.

Thus he forges a response to the failure in Latin America of the ideology of liberal universalism as universalism by reinstalling at its very center the idea of a managerial and market-based state as the potential provider of universal multicultural social cohesion and representation. Moreover, within this configuration the postmodern intellectual is positioned no longer as the imagination of the nation (the loss of which, of course, is not to be lamented), but, rather, as the state/market's broker in the management and administration of the increasingly postnational social sphere. In implicit yet apparently full synchronicity with the dominant discourses and structures of the contemporary socioeconomic and cultural order, García Canclini, in his attempt to, as he puts it, "defatalize the neoliberal paradigm and not confuse the necessary globalization of the economy and culture with U.S. hegemony" (128), upholds market forces and consumption as the new potential universals: as the single most enabling force by which to express peripheral individual and collective desires and needs.[21] Alberto Moreiras frames the argument in the following terms:

There is little in the logic of the statist social policies that we have noted under the name of regional federalism that will keep them from eventually being swallowed by global integration and made radically indistinguishable from neoliberal structural compensation. Even if, at the cultural level, those social policies did manage to control "the affective aspects of . . . identity formation" (Yúdice), it may well be because a degree of identity diversification, that is, a degree of difference production remains irreducibly essential for the global marketplace and its mechanisms of cultural consumption. Castañeda's "intermediate solution", in other words, would become just another structural part of the neoliberal order: the always surpassable limits upon which it will ceaselessly grow. (*Exhaustion* 66)

In other words, both García Canclini's and Castañeda's interventions are based implicitly on the forging of new forms of "responsibilized" freedom, in which freedom (both individual and collective) is only conceivable in its relation to political terrains that are always already determined by postnational market forces. But, as Moreiras has noted, this is precisely what the world structure of capitalist accumulation requires and depends on for its sustained hegemonic articulations.

Could we not suggest, then, that García Canclini's emphasis on the relation between citizenship and the circulation of cultural goods and images, together with his de-emphasis of late capitalism as a domain of power or even as a political economy of domination, ultimately maintain thought, social existence, and the freedom of expression purely within the realm of consumer identification, market-based choice, and the limits of neoliberal hegemonic thought? Furthermore, is it not for this reason that García Canclini's discursive system, which is intent on reformulating in positive terms the historical direction of peripheral development (while generally avoiding questions of recalcitrant subordination, exploitation, and subalternity), remains incapable of reflecting on its own constitutive outsides? It remains for the most part unwilling to think through the relation between market forces and "the constant antagonism between the shadow of opulence and the formalities of misery" (Monsiváis, *Mexican* 32) that guarantees long-term subalternity and its increasingly uncontainable social realities. Carlos Monsiváis calls attention to part of a national reality that cannot be accounted for in the relation between citizenship and consumption: "In Chiapas 15,000 people a year die of curable diseases; it boasts 90 percent of all cases of trachoma in the whole country . . . , 50 percent illiteracy, 34 percent of the communities have no electricity; there is one doctor per 1,500 people; the State's Penal Code punishes murder with six years of imprisonment and the stealing of a cow with eight" (143).

If we were to introduce the relation between consumption and citizenship—the democratization of culture negotiated through the culture ideology of consumerism—to the marxian critique of the social organization of labor, for example, then it would be unclear how citizenship through consumption could be reconciled with the systemic "disaggregation of vast portions of the working class into a mass of individuals competing with each other for survival" (Vilas, "Economic" 155). In other words, how could a consumption-based model of citizenship account for the sustained and increasing functionality of a postindustrial subaltern reserve army that scarcely has access to the means of consumption, never mind to the means of production? Here the words of Carlos Vilas are, once again, particularly poignant:

> All models of capital accumulation assume a given portion of "surplus population"—in other words, people who look for work, but don't find it. Since neoliberalism privileges the financial sector of the economy over the productive one, it presumes a much larger portion of surplus population than the Keynesian-Fordist model of the past. In this context, one can expect little of neoliberal social policy, regardless of its technical merits. Simply put, neoliberalism marginalizes and expels people at a greater rate than these programs can compensate. The case of Mexico is especially illustrative of the tension between the technical efficiency of a particular sectoral policy and the logic driving the overall economic model. While Pronasol, Salinas' poverty-alleviation program, succeeded in reducing the number of extremely poor Mexicans by 1.3 million between 1989 and 1992, the very same number of people lost jobs in the industrial sector of the economy between 1988 and 1992. . . . In Chile in 1970 . . . only 17% of households were poor; in 1989, after almost two decades of neoliberalism and dictatorship, poor households represented 38.1%. In 1995, the richest 20% of Chilean households earned 18 times the income of the poorest 20%. Chile, praised as a neoliberal success story, now has the fifth worst income distribution in the region. ("Neoliberal" 25)[22]

Surely what Vilas describes above is a challenge to the notions of civil society and of national hegemony as they have been formulated at least since the national-popular period of development in Latin America. If, in the words of Michael Hardt, "civil society . . . is central to a form of rule, or government, as Foucault says, that focuses, on the one hand, on the identity of the citizen and the processes of civilization and, on the other hand, on the organization of abstract labor" (40); and if, as Etienne

Balibar puts it, "class loyalties, especially *working class* loyalty, becomes a decisive pillar of national hegemony as soon as it is transformed into a particular 'culture' and a political 'opinion' or set of opinions *within* the political system, whose contribution to the national history or spirit is officially recognized in the (national) social state" ("Ambiguous" 73), then surely what Carlos Vilas describes is the erosion and exhaustion of the functional pillars of national hegemony and of a democratizing civil society in the transnational order. On the one hand, Vilas signals the eclipse of the state's drive to universalize particularities in order to represent them as the interests of the common (national) good. On the other, he testifies to the dissolution of civil society's primary function; that is, to channel, discipline, educate, and control labor through institutional modes of social mediation and representation.

If this is the case, and Vilas is testifying to an unstable and uncertain transition toward posthegemonic (Yúdice, "Civil" 4) and postcivil (Hardt 40) times, then perhaps it can be said that it is only when previously functional forms of democratization have been superseded by capital itself that citizenship and consumption (both notions grounded firmly in the workings of the culture ideology of consumerism) can be uncovered as a discourse of market-based developmentalism, repair, and potential rehegemonization.

Without a doubt, in *Consumidores y ciudadanos* we are faced with an examination of the cultural politics of neoliberalism that, while striving to transcend the failures of the past as well as the internal contradictions of politics in the present, remains strikingly similar to Wendy Brown's vision of the intellectual in relation to the postmodern state, as well as in relation to the contemporary erasure of capitalism as a political economy of domination, exploitation, and alienation. According to Brown,

> it is as if the terrible un-freedom and indignities attendant upon "actually existing socialisms" of the last half century persuaded . . . thinkers that free enterprise really is freer than the alternatives, that alienation is inherent in all labor, and that freedom, finally, is a matter of consumption, choice, and expression: an individual good rather than a social and political practice. Ironically, it is this conceptual move—and not the historical practices it claims to describe or decry—that succeeds in finally rendering Marxism as economism. Indeed, such apparent imperviousness to domination by capital—its mode of constructing and organizing social life and its specific form of subject production, combined with a preoccupation with goods and with private "liberty"—was precisely the nightmare forecast a quarter century ago by Herbert Marcuse in *One-Dimensional Man*. (13–14)

One is left wondering, then, whether *Consumidores y ciudadanos*—and, in particular, its fundamental formulation that it is no longer possible to think about and construct such ideals as citizenship and democracy in the absence of consumption—is itself a postnational rite of institution, an axiom in which Latin Americanism under neoliberalism produces marketable (and therefore always already hegemonic) categories of thought that are produced and guaranteed by neoliberal geoeconomic circuits themselves. After all, as Bourdieu states, it is always in the realm of symbolic production that the grip of the state (and, we must add, of the market) is felt most powerfully ("Rethinking" 1).

The dilemma facing us is that as we experience and trace the historical transformations by which subaltern subjectivities and their representations are now constituted, how are we to think through, or to overcome, the epistemological and political obstacles that condition our practice as contemporary intellectuals? In the choice between what García Canclini calls the "fundamentalism of Latin Americanism" (the romantic "Macondismo" of the North) and the terms and categories of his own reformist (neohegemonic) practice of social repair (a labor of Latin Americanist power brokering from within the forces of the geo-economic market/state), we can see the extent to which Deleuze and Guattari were right when they stated that "thought as such is already in conformity with a model that it borrows from the State apparatus, and which defines for it goals and paths, conduits, channels, organs, an entire *organon*" ("Thousand" 373). After all, in both García Canclini and Castañeda thought props itself up with the promise of a positive state form (the market) that extends itself throughout their formulations.

The question, however, is whether there is a way of not "speaking the established languages of politics, of 'playing the game' according to its well known rules, but of collectively breaking through the limits of public communication by means of a new language" that is somehow "always already beyond any simple or 'absolute' unity, therefore a source of conflicts forever" (Balibar, "Ambiguous," 72). To not do this is to risk finding oneself always already positioned as a naturalized effect of the effects of choices made by the neoliberal state and market. Ultimately, it is to repeat and redistribute the dominant discourses of knowledge and of population management that remain particular to what Deleuze has called "the impudent breed of our masters" in times of market-based social control.

To not recognize this might lead us to the conclusion that fundamentalism survives solely in the guise of Latin Americanism's supposed "Macondismo." But such a critical position would only lead us to mis-

The Other Side of the Popular

recognize the fact that the dominant fundamentalism of our times is *neo-liberalismo,* and its transnational insistence on consumption as the basic grounds for citizenship.

In the end, however, Latin Americanist desire for the construction of market-based social repair and cultural cohesion—for citizenship and democracy conceived from *within* the structurally hegemonic terms of the culture ideology of consumerism—flounders in its attempts to confront, and to think through, the processes of becoming outside to hegemony that condition the subaltern realities of what Marx called "the consumer needs of a society in which the great majority are always poor and must remain always poor" (*Capital* v. 2, 391). If we understand subalternity as an outside that both constitutes the social terrain of hegemony and yet, at the same time, fractures hegemony's ability to represent itself as universal—if we take it to be a spectral apparition on the limits of hegemony that reminds us that, like national wealth before it, postnational wealth "is, once again, by its very nature, identical with misery of the people" (Marx, *Capital* 845–46)—then we may have reached a historical threshold in which it is no longer possible to think about such ideals as citizenship and democracy (indeed, politics itself) in the absence of reflection on misery, and on its relation to the truth regimes of the neoliberal geo-economic state and marketplace.[23] Can one think about the cultural politics of the present without thinking about that potentially interruptive negativity that exists within yet exceeds, haunts, and fractures the thought of hegemony and of hegemonic social reproduction in neoliberal times?

With such a historical threshold in mind, perhaps we would do well to underline David Lloyd and Paul Thomas's view that "the recent demise of communism and of the decline of prior forms of labor struggle and institution at the present moment betoken less a moment of collapse for the left than a moment of opportunity for the transformation of conceptions of practice" (29). Lloyd and Thomas continue their reflection in the following terms: "In contemporary capitalism, the increasing fluidity of social spaces, and therefore of the definition of what constitutes the properly political, combined with the corresponding emergence of social movements which redefine both the practice and the objects of cultural, political and social struggle, offers the possibility of new formations of culture and intellectual work and the dissolution of a hegemonic cultural state" (29–30).

As already established in this chapter, citizenship affirmed exclusively through the assemblages of consumption and regulation fails to conceive of the possibility of a thought other than that which is always already structured and fabricated by, and within, the managerial logics of neoliberal market forces. Therefore, consumption and citizenship forge a specific relation of continuity between contemporary thought and the postdisciplinary structures of the society of control (even though they might do so in the name of emergent counterhegemonies and profoundly postnational commonalities). As such, the irony of García Canclini's thought —its quest for the fabrication of an ethical neoliberal market/state configuration—cannot be lost on us. After all, this quest for the rearticulation of national (or, at least, of interregional or translocal) equivalences—of a hegemonic state capable, once again, of universalizing particularities and of reintegrating social sectors into the construction of a civil society that is grounded in the positive articulation of equivalences—tends to elide all questions and experiences of hegemony's other side; that is, the exclusions that all hegemonic relations within capitalism presuppose and construct themselves upon.

In contrast, however, and as Lloyd and Thomas suggest in their examination of the notion of hegemony, the refashioning of intellectual practice engaged now in the analysis and "worlding" of the negative— in the formulation of subaltern genealogies, practices, representations, and social agencies, and therefore in a reimagining of intellectual practice construed around and through hegemony's finitude—might be able to uncover, or at least to give a name to, that which has not been articulated and controlled by the formulations, formalities, constructed truths, and desires of the contemporary order. Consider the words of Lloyd and Thomas in this regard:

> As intellectuals we do not stand before, as examples representing a fuller capacity or as epigones of progress. We come after. We come after a whole repertoire of possibilities, of counter-hegemonic strategies and alternative imaginations, that we cannot claim as our inheritance. In the debris of their passing we find nothing to develop and nothing to mourn as foregone. For in the present, in the gradual collapse of our own inherited spaces and practices, we find alongside the specter of a consolidating and homogenizing capitalism, alternative openings and fluidities that are in no way "exemplary", so specific are they to their given historical moment and to its indeterminacies. Precisely in that different relation to the "ends" of humanity, in the negation of universal claims by contemporary social movements, we discover an unexhausted repertoire of renewed possibilities. (30)

Within this formulation a fundamental distinction is made between two forms of knowledge production and two forms of placing thought in the service of hegemony and of hegemonic reproduction. In the first place there is the method of reflection that epitomizes the Latin American lettered tradition, which consists in "stand[ing] before, as examples *representing* a fuller capacity or as epigones of progress" (emphasis mine). This, we might say, is the intellectual position represented by the thought of hegemony and of counterhegemony in which both are the thought of (national) modernization and progress. The second position, however, consists in "coming after" or "following." The prior form or procedure remains invested inevitably in delineating paths toward the future, and therefore in the potential consolidation of a particular point of view or domain of reflection. In the latter procedure, however, it is evident that coming after or following "*is not at all the same thing as reproducing*," for "one never follows in order to reproduce" (Deleuze and Guattari, *Thousand* 372). After all, as Deleuze and Guattari observe:

> Following is something different from the idea of reproduction. Not better, just different. One is obliged to follow when one is in search of the "singularities" of a matter, or rather of a material, and not out to discover a form . . . with the legal model [representing and reproducing], one is constantly reterritorializing around a point of view, on a domain, according to a set of constant relations; but with the ambulant model [coming after or following], the process of deterritorialization constitutes and extends the territory [of thought, for example] itself. (372)

Perhaps we should take up Lloyd and Thomas's proposal for an alternative intellectual engagement and consider further the possibility of thinking about moments of leverage that permit us to glimpse hegemony in its negative shades and in its multiple sites of fatigue. Of course, as Lloyd and Thomas might suggest, such a project could only emerge from within the nonexemplary contingencies, dislocations, and constitutive outsides of contemporary cultural/capital formations in Latin America. As such, their formulations could offer no completion and certainly no resolution for disciplinary thought. Indeed, the inevitable incompletion, insufficiency, and open-endedness of such a reflection would be inherently dissatisfying for the discipline's traditional development-bound investments in Latin American (Creole) hegemony. Having said this, however, its very (indeed, its necessary) incompletion would certainly allow us to eschew the banality of consensus and to become possessed, once again, by the drive to question; to be overtaken, in other words, by the affective drive that returns us once again and without end to the theoretical question of futurity, and therefore to the necessary incompleteness of the political terrain.

Through the critical explorations included in the chapters following I will avoid the possibility of neohegemonizing claims and representations and, as Jean Franco puts it, will monitor "those places where hegemonic discourse ceases to make sense" ("Latin" 270). I will do this in order to uncover the promise of a repertoire of renewed critical, socioeconomic, and cultural engagements that are grounded no longer in the active constitution of Creole fictive ethnicity and its national hegemonies (as seen in chapter 1); nor in the logics of metropolitan intellectual populism (as examined in chapter 2); nor in the neohegemonic articulations of market-based consumption, citizenship, and hybridity (as seen in this chapter).

In contrast, the reflections contained in the chapters that follow are an attempt to shed light on the notion of subalternity as the effect of a process of becoming outside to hegemony and to hegemonic relations. This process uncovers the demand for a new telos from which to think: a telos grounded in hegemony's dislocation and finitude. As already suggested in the final sections of chapter 2, the relation between hegemony and its constitutive outsides renders subalternity thinkable. Yet within this thinkability the very same relation produces an aberrant disequilibrium and destabilization of cultural and political language. Subalternity thereby leans toward the degrounding promise of what remains beyond, stands up against, and suspends the suturing (and silencing) articulations of the hegemonic.[24]

Therefore, through the idea of the neoliberal order as a moment of uneven passage and of incomplete transition from the already partial order of national discipline to that equally incomplete order of trans- or postnational control; through the idea, therefore, of the present as a moment structured by the logics of radically differential intensities, by uneven networks of domination and subordination, by dispersal, redistribution, and dislocation (rather than by the place fixity of core areas or the constancy of centers and peripheries); through the idea that we can no longer uphold an intrinsic relation between the construction of hegemony—the fabrication and representation of subjectivity as agency and as a mediated institutional effect of the state or of statist social movements—and the notion of commonality, I will examine particular moments, social configurations, representations, and insurrectional practices that trace the intricate circuitries, displacements, and redistributions of contemporary processes of capitalization and subjectivization, while upholding at all times the need to "grasp the genealogy of social movements and emerging subjectivities not as reformist pressures on the existing order, but as elements of a new constituent power" (Hardt and Negri, 308).

Through these analyses I will challenge the value of neoliberal ideas and structures of domination in Latin America and strive to circumvent forms of cultural reflection that are directly invested in the thought and reproduction of hegemony/counterhegemony. I will embark, in other words, on an itinerant path that is designed to uphold the possibility of fracturing the institutionalized fabrication and social reproduction of capital's—that is to say, of neoliberalism's—desired truths and practices. Furthermore, in the following chapter I will turn to literature in order to set the scenes and the underlying grounds for such an itinerant critical possibility.

Intermezzo . . . Hear Say Yes

4

Hear Say Yes in Piglia
La ciudad ausente, Posthegemony, and
the "Fin-negans" of Historicity

> Politics has become a practice that decides what a society can *not*
> do. Politicians are the new philosophers: they decree what can be
> understood by the real, by the possible, and by the limits of the truth.
> The same goes for culture. Immediate politics defines the field of
> reflection. It seems that intellectuals can only think about the problems
> that politicians are interested in. . . . To think in the place of the
> politicians is the hegemonic tendency. Intellectuals speak as if they
> were ministers. They speak of reality with the care, calculation,
> commitment, and involuntarily parodic style used by those who
> directly exercise power. . . . Why should I have to think with the same
> categories as the minister of the interior?—Ricardo Piglia,
> *Crítica y ficción;* translation mine

Ernesto Laclau opens his *New Reflections on the Revolution of Our Time*
with the following observation:

> Every age adopts an image of itself—a certain horizon, however
> blurred and imprecise, which somehow unifies its whole experience.
> The recovery of a past which gave access to the natural order of the
> world for the Renaissance; the imminence of the advent of Reason for
> the Enlightenment; the inexorable advance of science for positivism:
> all were unifying images. In each case, the different stages of what has
> become known as "modernity" were conceived as moments of tran-
> sition towards higher forms of consciousness and social organization,
> holding the promise of a limitless future. (3)

In contrast, Laclau continues, the intellectual climate of recent decades
has been dominated by the growing and generalized awareness of limits.

This awareness challenges not only the notion and possibility of unifying images but also the sustainability of the idea of successive stages within a process of historical development:

> Firstly, limits of reason, as has been pointed out from very different intellectual quarters—from epistemology and the philosophy of science to post-analytical philosophy, pragmatism, phenomenology and post-structuralism. Secondly, limits, or rather slow erosion of the values and ideals of radical transformation, which had given meaning to the political experience of successive generations. And finally, limits arising from the crisis of the very notion of "cultural vanguard" which marked the different moments and stages of modernity. (3)

It is hardly surprising, then, that Laclau should conclude this opening section of *New Reflections* by affirming that after decades, or perhaps even centuries, of announcing the arrival of the new, it is as if we had reached a point of exhaustion and now mistrusted the outcome of all forms of experimentation (3).[1]

The unifying image of our time, in other words, is that of the exhaustion of unifying images. Thus, and as Laclau points out elsewhere in *New Reflections*, "the novelty of the present situation . . . lies in the fact that the nodal point around which the intelligibility of the social is articulated does not now tend to be displaced from one instance to another, but to dissolve. The plurality of dislocations generates a plurality of centres of relative power, and the expansion of all social logic thus takes on a terrain that is increasingly dominated by elements external to it" (59).[2]

Contemporary reflection is conditioned by a potentially productive circularity. Although it is always unsatisfactory to reflect on the present using exhausted notions of historical ground and becoming, our critical languages remain inevitably indebted to the history of exhaustion's coming into being. After all, "the *being* of what we are *is* first of all inheritance, whether we like it or know it or not. And . . . , as Hölderlin said so well, we can only *bear witness* to it. To bear witness would be to bear witness to what we *are* insofar as we *inherit*, and that—here is the circle, here is the chance, or the finitude—we inherit the very thing that allows us to bear witness to it" (Derrida, *Specters* 54). The current dilemma is that the intensification of globalism—in the case of Latin America, the exhaustion of the possibility of national fictive ethnicity brought about by the crisis of national capitalism's uneven and incomplete organizational structures and modes of representation—has exposed us, in extremely violent fashion, to the fact that while certain imperatives persist (freedom, justice, community, for example) the conceptual systems

The Other Side of the Popular

from which these imperatives have drawn their meaning in the past no longer appear to be viable (Fynsk viii).

As such, bearing witness to exhaustion is the condition of possibility for sustained reflection in the present and is therefore more necessary than ever. However, it is also an increasingly thorny venture. Bearing witness to history and to historical meaning in terms that remain (or that wish to remain) faithful to that modern inheritance merely reproduces the current postmodern dilemma by situating critical reason once again on the side of real or imminent exhaustion. As a result, the inheritance of exhaustion marks both the condition of possibility and the condition of impossibility of all contemporary reflection.

Exhaustion both traces and upholds, yet, curiously, it fails to inaugurate the ultimate demise of modernity's (predominantly national) histories. As Laclau puts it, it signals the end of a certain conceptualization of history, which can be understood as the historical unfolding of a permanent transition toward higher forms of consciousness and more advanced forms of collective political and social organization. But the end of that history of (predominantly) national modernization and progress is not the end of thought. Neither is it the demise of historicity. Postmodern exhaustion signals the end of a particular notion of history that sutured it (often implicitly and, of course, oversimplistically) to the promise of a limitless future. But the end of this conceptualization of history is neither cataclysmic nor apocalyptic. It is not revelatory either. Rather, postmodernity brings into view the subtraction of modernity's developmentalist sense of history from the regimes of signification that are available to us today. Subtraction, in other words, gives us the nihilistic gift of exhaustion, as the weakening of "a composed and complete order (from) within which to find a place, a dwelling, and the elements of an orientation" (Nancy, *Sense* 4). Thus, the postmodern order is the weakening, unworking, and redistribution of modern capitalist history's (that is, the nation-state's) modernizing ground. This is our inheritance and, according to Derrida, our chance ("here is the circle, here is the chance, or the finitude" [*Specters* 54]).[3]

Inheriting and supplementing Lyotard's formulation that the contemporary world signals the waning of modernity's metanarratives, Laclau's observations challenge and undermine the foundational premises of the Hegelian philosophical system (at least as they were translated into classical marxism). Indeed, Laclau both bears witness to, and displaces, Hegelian philosophy's underpinning of the notion of the universal in its relation to the geographic boundaries and interactions of the capitalist world economy and, in particular, in its relation to the nation-state form, which by the mid-1960s, of course, had become the hegemonic form of social organization almost throughout the globe.

In increasingly postnational times, however, the Hegelian conception of social objectivity and contradiction (in which the history of the nation is considered to be the history of the dialectical unfolding of higher and higher forms of social organization) have been quite literally opened up and dispersed—exposed to their finitude—by the radically contingent nature of global capital. In the words of Laclau:

> The Hegelian notion of negativity is that of a *necessary* negativity and as such was conceived as *determinate* negation. That is to say that the negative is a moment in the internal unfolding of the concept which is destined to be reabsorbed in the *Aufhebung*, or higher unity. It is not even necessary here, as has been occasionally claimed, for the final term of the dialectical movement to be positive; even if the system is conceived as a successive movement between positivity and negativity, the latter is always internal to it. Contingency itself is absorbed as a moment in the self-unfolding of the necessary. (*New* 26)[4]

As I have suggested in previous chapters, the self-unfolding of the Hegelian notion of negativity sheds light on the repeated and sustained outside-inside dialectic of recovery that characterizes, for example, institutionalized center-periphery positionalities, neo-orientalist intellectual maneuvers, and state-region relations during the populist phase of national development in Latin America. Indeed, it was from within this dialectic that the notion of totality—the concept of (and desire for) the nation, for example, as the privileged terrain for social organization and for cultural and political thought in modern Latin America—could be sustained and imposed by the Creole/mestizo bourgeoisie as a process unfolding itself almost as a natural law (and most certainly as a moral imperative both on the Left and Right) within the periphery's developmentalist transition toward higher forms of individual and collective consciousness and of national social organization.

Laclau, however, provides added nuance to the place of negativity within the contemporary constitution of the social, as well as within the distinction between this and the political. Laclau recognizes and thinks through his debt to the Hegelian dialectic, which fueled and sustained the notion of the nation-state and of national capitalism as fundamental nodal points around (and against) which postcolonial social meanings, positionalities, and representations could be organized and construed. However, he opens up that essentially national dialectic to the possibility of political articulations that are consonant with the weakening of the underlying ground of the nation and with the increasingly emergent contingencies of globalism. In other words, he attempts to think about the place of negativity from within the exhaustion of modernity's nodal points of intelligibility (the nation-state, national culture, national identity, etc.) as well as from within the apparent exhaustion of the Hegelian philosophical system itself.

The internal unfolding within the national terrain of, for example, people/power bloc antagonisms or periods of struggle over the means by which to stabilize particular social or cultural contents; the development of struggles over the means by which to fix meaning around particular discursive nodal points such as *mestizaje,* transculturation, *indigenismo,* Perón, Frente Sandinista de la Liberación Nacional (FSLN), FMLN, and so forth do not represent true outsides since they are mobilized in the first place in order to be recuperated by the contesting ideologies of nation formation. As such, they merely make themselves present in order to be recovered by the inside (the nation) under the banner of national hegemony. Social contents such as those emerging from a national people/power bloc antagonism allow for the social sphere to "be regarded as a trench war in which different political projects strive to articulate a greater number of social signifiers around themselves" (*New* 28). In other words, the national people/power bloc antagonism allows for the potentially universalizing articulation and representation of distinct outsides in the name of hegemony construction, nation-state formation, and national identity consolidation.

However, since hegemony is always constructed on the successful concealment of the exclusions on which it is grounded, the expanded articulation of social signifiers around the unifying image of, say, the nation-state or national identity also strives to exorcise society of its potential nonnormative identities and unacceptable practices. Processes of hegemonization operate on the historical and social terrains in such a way as to allow for, to extend, and to perpetuate social coherence as the necessary active forgetting of dislocation, potential antagonism, and difference. In this sense, these processes labor actively against the possibility of alternative (nonnormative) "worldings" that remain heterogeneous to those already represented within, and articulated by, hegemony's universalizing repertoires. As Laclau states:

> Insofar as an act of institution has been successful, a "forgetting of the origins" tends to occur; the system of possible alternatives tends to vanish and the traces of the original contingency to fade. In this way, the institution tends to assume the form of a mere objective presence.

> This is the moment of sedimentation. It is important to realize that this fading entails a concealment. If objectivity is based on exclusion, the traces of that exclusion will always somehow be present. What happens is that the sedimentation can be so complete, the influence of one of the dichotomous relationships' poles so strong, that the contingent nature of that influence, its *original* dimension of power, do not prove immediately visible. (*New* 34)

Hegemony is the expansion and deepening of social intelligibility, translatability, appropriation, and knowability (the fabrication of specific chains of representational equivalence, in other words) within the boundaries of any given field of force. As such, it is always carried out as both a potentializing force and as an active cover-up and silencing of those heterogeneous realms that expose (from within) the empirical impossibility or the violence of its language. As such, and as Derrida indicates, hegemony's active forgetting of its exclusions is never complete, for "hegemony . . . organizes the repression and thus the confirmation of a haunting. Haunting belongs to the structure of every hegemony" (*Specters* 37).[5]

Thus, it is actually the inherent incompletion of hegemony, rather than the full realization of its internal rationales, that brings Laclau back to the notions of negativity and contingency in *New Reflections on the Revolution of Our Time* as the possible bases for a renewed politics of radical democracy.

As has already been noted, in the Hegelian operation negativity is the contingent objectivity whose potential *recovery* is constitutive of an internal structure. Negativity is, then, a form of outsidedness whose recovery upholds hegemony's signifying processes, representations, and unifying images while remaining ultimately sedimented within, and constitutive of, the dialectical unfolding of the field of hegemonic social intelligibility itself. Dialectical negativity extends an outside to its own structure of signification that nevertheless allows the system from which it distinguishes itself to complete itself and, thereby, to achieve closure. In other words, it conjures up a limit as a necessary resistance to itself, recuperates that limit, and labors always against any possible death of signification that might arise from the limit that it conjures up. Dialectics therefore places itself on the side of the constitution and maintenance of production and knowability, as an incessant labor against the possibility of intelligibility's breakdown and collapse.[6]

Laclau, however, strives to assert a politics grounded in the constitutive impossibility of hegemonic representation and intelligibility. He strives to establish the contours of a negativity that is capable of not being

The Other Side of the Popular

recovered, of not being put to work in the name of hegemonic reproduction and, for that matter, of not being reabsorbed nor sublated in a community's utopic drive toward higher forms of self-consciousness and of social organization. Laclau asserts the possibility of a negativity that exposes the radically contingent nature of all social objectivity by interrupting or suspending hegemony's signifying processes and its necessary destitution of heterogeneity. This, then, is a dislocating negativity. It is a destituted and destituting negativity that labors on the side of impropriety and interruption rather than on the side of the passage toward higher forms of consciousness and social organization. As Laclau indicates: "If the negativity of which we are speaking reveals the contingent nature of all objectivity, if it is truly constitutive, then it cannot be recovered through any *Aufhebung*. It is something which simply shows the limits of the constitution of objectivity and cannot be dialecticized" (*New* 26).

How, then, could we characterize the negativity that Laclau seems to evoke as a space that is potentially constitutive of an alternative approach to politics? Perhaps we could say that it signals a posthegemonic site; a place within the social field in which hegemonic articulations and signifying processes no longer work, in which hegemonic discourses cease to make sense (Franco, "Latin" 270). Such a site would appear to ground itself not so much in the incorporation of subalternity as an inferior position within a hegemonic articulation but, rather, in the opening up of the political field to a certain form of unintelligibility that marks the "absolute limit of the place where history is narrativized into logic" (Spivak, "Subaltern" 16). It denotes an outsidedness that is so radically constitutive of hegemony and of hegemonic thought that it both suspends the completion of the social field (by signifying the impossible universalization of particularities) and, at the same time, opens up that field to the knowledge that in knowledge there is an *other* thought that is not thought by hegemony. This thought thinks and measures hegemony's force; it resists appropriation by interrupting hegemony's signifying processes; and it does not coincide with hegemony even when it converges with it. This is, in other words, the opening up of thought (and, in particular, of thought's institutional investments in the securing of hegemonic rationales) to the exposure of radical alterity, and therefore to the opening up of reflection to an outside that is capable of signaling the possibility of an entirely different telos from which to think.[7]

It is the affirmation of this *other* thought within thought—this disjunctive, interruptive, and heterogeneous remainder to, and within, hegemonic reflection—that brings forth the finitude of hegemony, that uncovers "the infamous death that is the beginning of the mind" (Blanchot, *Infinite* 35), and that extends what Derrida has called the formal structure of promise: the persistence of a spectral site of untranslatability within thought, and within the social field, that remains irreducible to any hegemonic recovery or deconstruction, and that therefore upholds the contours of both sustained reflection and of emancipatory promise. For Derrida such a site inscribes the Benjaminian notion of a "*weak* Messianic power" (Benjamin, "Theses" 254). As Derrida notes, it indicates "perhaps even the formality of a structural messianism, a messianism without religion, even a messianic without messianism, an idea of justice which we distinguish from law and even from human rights—and an idea of democracy—which we distinguish from its current concept and from its determined predicates today" (Derrida, *Specters* 59).

It is the site of a dislocation within the hegemonic socio-hermeneutic field that keeps the supply lines of reflection open to the notion of the Other—open to the promise of the Other (wo)man, open to (wo)man as other, and open to thought as a practice of difference. It is, then, the limit and finitude of hegemony at which all politics (and all political reflection) both stops and (potentially) begins.[8]

Although hegemony is the effect of a politics that labors on the side of intelligibility, guaranteed translatability, and systematic coherence (on the side of an intelligibility that is therefore ultimately directed against nonnormativity, divergence, and heterogeneity), Laclau's opening to a radically democratic politics grounded in the destituted (dislocated and ungrounded) objects of hegemony's exclusions preserves an opening to dislocation—to a certain unknowability haunting the social terrain—that is, at one and the same time, the sustained chance of "an affirmed or, rather, of a reaffirmed future" (Derrida, *Specters* 37).

As Derrida notes in his discussion of Marx's communist specter, this haunting site is "the future, it is always to come, it presents itself only as that which could come or come back; in the future, said the powers of old Europe in the last century, it must not incarnate itself, either publicly or in secret. In the future, we hear everywhere today, it must not re-incarnate itself; it must not be allowed to come back since it is past" (39). In order to maintain order's order (in order to preserve capitalist hegemony against its finitude) the specters of dislocation that haunt and inhabit the horizons of contemporary experience (the word "communism," for example) must be excluded without reserve, and therefore placed beyond the fabric of all possible meaning. This is, at least, what we are told by the mechanisms and calculations of the contemporary order. As such, history's disappeared specters must remain absolutely

The Other Side of the Popular

disappeared and therefore disappeared beyond all possible relation. But, of course (and here is the circle, here is the chance or the finitude), exclusions never stop signifying, and it is in their sustained yet often displaced and spectral signification—and in their potential reactivation—that hegemony continues to envision its point of exhaustion; the finitude of its signifying processes. The current regime of capitalist accumulation never ceases to give the disappearing logics of hegemony a positive force and value.[9] The task of *posthegemonic* thought, however, is to displace (to abandon, to unwork, to suspend) the positive grounds and signifying processes of that regime and its knowledge formations.

As Walter Benjamin reminds us in "Theses on the Philosophy of History," the past places a particular injunction on the present that obliges that critical reflection labor on the side of, and in the name of, mnemonic reactivation: "The past carries with it a temporal index by which it is referred to redemption. There is a secret agreement between past generations and the present one. Our coming was expected on earth. Like every generation that preceded us, we have been endowed with a *weak* Messianic power, a power to which the past has a claim" (254). No doubt we must act and think from within the ground of this Benjaminian injunction. The question, of course, is how?

If hegemonic articulations guarantee the repression of alternative worldings and of multiple options that were perhaps open in the past but were discarded or disappeared on the way (Laclau, *New* 34); and if the social field (the nation, for example) is considered not to be an organic topographic totality (a site of completion) but a historically heterogeneous and deeply fissured embodiment of multiple dislocations (a site of ongoing and sustained incompletion, in other words), then reflection is immediately opened up to possibilities of multiple and indeterminate rearticulations that might be capable of working in the service of those spaces that remain at least partially freed from the full presence of the hegemonic field's coercive force (42–43). Hence, the reactivation of thought on the side of subalternity—on the side of those limits at which hegemonic power and knowledge are exposed to their finitude and incompletion—presupposes the possibility of a politics that can announce the terms of another telos for historical reflection on the relation between culture and politics.

Posthegemonic reactivation cannot be a question of merely uncovering or of restituting the *original* meaning of acts. Nor can it be a question of recuperating, or of attempting to reproduce (in so-called faithful fashion), the terms of originary exclusions in order to uphold the undeniable truth of historical injury. Rather, posthegemony is a question of opening up the present to alternative possibilities and heterogeneous discourses and practices—to the fabrication of a certain sense of alternative histories—that haunt the inherent incompletion of hegemony's social articulations. Posthegemonic reactivation, then, calls attention to (and takes advantage of) the ways in which the social field has failed to constitute itself as a result of modernization's systematic exclusions and processes of subalternization. Within this process, and as Laclau upholds, "these three dimensions of the relationship of dislocation—temporality, possibility and freedom—are mutually involved" (44). Indeed, we might add, it is subalternity—the relational exposure of structural incompletion, of finitude, interruption, and of epistemological dislocation, limiting and unhinging the hegemonic field of power/knowledge relations—that affirms the possible spectral return of the Benjaminian injunctions of the past. However the question, once again, is how to envisage or imagine the terms of subaltern mnemonic reactivation—this future posthegemonic narrative—when, as Fredric Jameson notes in *The Seeds of Time*, "we do not have the terms and categories ready to describe what succeeds civil society as such, when the latter's collapse is not a regression, but rather the accompaniment of an even more advanced form of development" (155).

In *The Exhaustion of Difference* Alberto Moreiras takes on Ernesto Laclau's notion of exhaustion and equates it with the notion of denarrativization: "We have undergone a world-historical experience, which ended with the collapse of so-called 'actually existing socialism' and the ongoing destruction of the welfare state. . . . Actually existing socialism was no enemy of modernization and imperial reason. The conflict between the so-called First and Second Worlds was an internal episode in a dialectic of consciousness that has now come to reveal itself as the false dialectic of modernization. The rupture with such false dialectic is a historical moment of denarrativization" (50–51). The emergence of the current regime of global accumulation—which has brought about a moment of radical rupture with the false (First/Second World) dialectic of modernizing consciousness—is, Moreiras continues, "ultimately a rupture with all false dialectics, with all melodramas, with all narratives of identity, and with all narratives of difference" (51). Exhaustion, then, as the (dis)unifying image of our time, comes hand-in-hand with the disclosure of a historically grounded narrative fissure in contemporary consciousness, which can only be understood "objectively, in the sense of 'the fissure in narrative' (that is, not as 'the fissure of narrative'). It affects all narratives, and not selectively so, including all (post)modern

The Other Side of the Popular

narratives of difference and all (post)modern narratives of identity and including subaltern narratives wherever they exist" (51).

If, as Moreiras suggests, the telos of contemporary consciousness is the effect of a fissure in narrative itself, then surely the task of contemporary reflection is to be alert to the risk and potentiality of the instabilities that arise as a result of that fissure. Such a task would oblige us (perhaps) to desire no longer a thought of the system, and no longer the establishment of a unified theory, and not even the possibility of encompassing a particular body of knowledge in its totality (all of which would now be little more than reactive critical practices grounded in the false realization of preconceived theoretical programs, paths, theses, spaces, or destinies). Rather, perhaps the task of contemporary reflection is to think from within the finitude of such critical repertoires.[10] Such a strategy (which obviously challenges the efficacy of upholding now the value of, for example, national cultural traditions, objects, identities, and aesthetics in precisely the same way they have been construed throughout modernity) opens up reflection to the idea of what remains to be thought, to be done, and to be lived (Derrida, *Politics* 38).

Obviously, the notion of the present as the effect and reproduction of a historical fissure in narrative—as the opening up of a process of radical denarrativization that ungrounds the historical telos of modernization and its hegemonic projects—obliges that we explore the limits of a *new* kind of historical narrative; a narrative that is capable of exploring dislocation and of opening up its destructuring structures to future possibilities. But such a thought could only be effective if it evoked logics other than those dominated by the topographic stability of the national or the regional, or if it had the potential to interrupt the culture ideology of consumerism and the postmodern reduction of difference to manageable practical limits or to mere replicas of former models and ways of being.

This *other* narrative (a narrative constructed as a result of, and from within, the fissure in narrative itself) could strive to establish the parameters of a negative regional cultural logic, in which regional would be understood perhaps no longer as a "rural place that resists the nation and its power structures but rather [as] a whole culturally coherent zone (which may also correspond to political autonomy) in tension with the standardized world system as a whole" (Jameson, *Seeds* 191–92). Such a zone might be capable of upholding the possibility of singular worldings, of narrating a certain sense of historicity that belongs to alternative repertoires (of articulating "linguistic intersections, cultural knots in which the weight of certain histories, of certain ways and forms of narrating, can be found" [Piglia, *Diálogo* 28; translation mine]), while at the same time refusing to reproduce the standardized, rationalized, and homogenized narratives and topographies of (post)modern accumulation.[11]

In theory, this form of critical engagement might be able to construct a narrative that would be "opposed to modernism and postmodernism alike" (Jameson, *Seeds* 193). It might thereby uncover itself as a "name of the theoretical possibility of a residual outside to global consumerism, of an 'outsid-ing' trace" (Moreiras *Exhaustion* 53). In other words, it might be a practice that could strive to distinguish between culture as a globalizing commercial enterprise, and culture as that which allows for the inscription and rearticulation of disjunctive singularities and of singular (dis)encounters. The name of this new kind of historical narrative, as I understand it (a name originally coined by Kenneth Frampton) is "critical regionalism."[12]

Critical regionalism is an attempt to think beyond imposed and historically accepted rationales and hegemonic models in order to combat the standardization and naturalization of traditional power/knowledge configurations and in order to explore the limits of narratives not necessarily dominated by the false consciousness of metropolitan discourses of difference and identity. As an interrupted and interrupting narrative rendered possible because of denarrativization and exhaustion, it strives neither to lament nor reconstitute the contours of its lost objects (collective identities, identifications, cultural objects and practices, tools and forms of interpretation, etc.). Neither does it strive to overcompensate for their loss through the massive redistribution of their eclipsed categories (as can be seen, for example, in the almost manic proliferation of microsubjectivities and identitarian redemptions that have emerged in recent years as a result of, and in response to, the advent of the "death of the subject"). In contrast, critical regionalism strives to deconstruct previous and existing hegemonic logics and articulations in order to redirect them toward the realm of an *other* historicity (again, neither modern nor postmodern) as well as toward the possibility of coming, and as yet-unheard-of, commonalities.[13] In this sense the promise of critical regionalism lies in the fact that it is the product of denarrativization's ungrounding effects. However, it attempts to think and affirm the possibility of negativity from within that process of denarrativization.

But what are the narrative inscriptions, scenes, and stagings—the active distributions, in other words—through which critical regionalism might be glimpsed? Through what objects and articulations can something that resides outside of, and that remains unconstituted by and yet exists within, globalism's messianic celebration of a historical ending be affirmed? How can we be alert to the unstable and destabilizing possibility of a posthegemonic affirmation from within the homogenizing and dehistoricizing drives of globalized capital?

Perhaps the local, regional, and national literary traditions of Latin America are the placeholders of cryptic narrative cartographies that would allow us to "hear say yes," once again, in increasingly postnational times. The radically hybrid bearing of Latin American literary expression—a hybridity that emerges as a result of the historical realities of uneven and combined development; as a result of the disjunctive simultaneity of its subaltern/metropolitan articulations; and ultimately as a result of Latin America's profoundly nonunitary geopolitical location within world history—embodies and reproduces (perhaps) the discursive tensions (the encounters and disencounters) that are capable of opening up the supply lines of reflection to a certain sense of futurity.[14]

Ricardo Piglia's critical positioning of Macedonio Fernández in opposition to Domingo Faustino Sarmiento in Piglia's *Crítica y ficción* is, I think, an interesting point of departure in this regard:

> Sarmiento expresses better than anyone the idea of a *true* writing that ties fiction to the necessities of political practice. He writes from the position of the (future) state, and, in *Facundo,* uses fiction in all its artifice in order to define it as the enemy's basic way of writing history. For Sarmiento fiction condenses the (seductive) poetics of barbarism. Macedonio Fernández is the antithesis of Sarmiento. He inverts all of Sarmiento's presuppositions, and inverts the presuppositions that define Argentine narrative from its very origins. He unites politics and fiction rather than having them confront each other as if they were two irreducible practices. The novel maintains encrypted relations with the machinations of power. It reproduces them, uses them, and constructs their utopic counter-figure. It is for this reason that in *Museo de la Novela de la Eterna* there is a president at the center of the fiction. The president as novelist; once again, the narrator of tribal power. The utopia of the future state is now grounded in fiction rather than against it. Since there is a novel there is a state. That is what Macedonio says. Or, rather, since there is a novel (intrigue, belief, Bovarism) there can be a state. Are the novel and the state born together? In Macedonio the theory of the novel forms part of the theory of the state. They were elaborated simultaneously and are interchangeable. . . . In the unedited world of that secret museum the other history of Argentine fiction is constructed. That never-ending book announces the future novel, the fiction to come. Prologues proliferate in the *Museo* and Macedonio defines a new enunciation; the frame of the Argentine novel to come. . . .

Macedonio Fernández (not Manuel Gálvez) is the great social novelist. (204–6; translation mine)

Between *Facundo* and *Museo de la Novela de la Eterna,* observes Piglia,
we encounter a peculiar inheritance, a culturally coherent zone, or a kind
of discursive/literary niche in which the foundational relationship between mimesis and the state—between the intellectual and the production of political and cultural hegemonies in Argentina—can be uncovered and interrogated. As already noted in these pages, such hegemonies
have always been defined around the formation and expansion of the
nation-state and around the complicit proximity, or absolute distance, of
the intellectual to and from those processes. Piglia, however, appears to
be attempting to interrupt the foundational grounds of Argentine literary political culture—and the violent determinations that it has effected
and reproduced—by opening up reflection to another site of elaboration:
neither complicit proximity to, nor absolute distance from, stateliness,
but the forging of a radical shift in the way we can make political sense
of culture.

Piglia, it seems, is thinking (from within the postdictatorial neoliberal
order) of the ways of degrounding and therefore of unthinking the hegemonies that have underpinned culture's relation to the history of nation
formation and to the violent (often neocolonial) consolidation of (and
resistance to) the nation-state and national culture in Argentina. Indeed,
this interruptive labor of unthinking is designed to open up thought to residual relations and articulations between culture and politics that remain
to be constituted and that can only be carried out through an alternative
inscription of the cultural. Thus, Piglia points toward the possibility of
glimpsing, within certain literary moments and fleeting expressivities, an
other (unnamed and perhaps unnameable) space of elaboration that is
not defined by hegemonic and counterhegemonic modes of intellectual
engagement:

> If politics is the art of the possible, the art of the "full stop", then lit-
> erature is its antithesis. There are no pacts or transactions, and reality
> is not the only truth. Before the vigilant language of *realpolitik* we have
> the Argentine voice of Macedonio Fernández. . . . That *slight* voice an-
> nounces the antipolitics, the counter-reality, the feminine space, the
> stories of the Ranquel chieftain, Borges's *rhönir,* Marechal's *miry* phi-
> losophers, Roberto Arlt's copper rose. It announces what is to come.
> The tradition of that politics that demands the impossible is the only
> politics that can justify us. Beyond the barbarism and horror that we
> have lived, in a few pages of our literature I think that a memory per-

sists that allows us not to be ashamed of being Argentine. (206–7; translation mine)

It seems that this is a memory not of state-related injunctions allowing for the foundation of omniscient systems and totalizing orders of analysis. Nor does it appear to lend itself to consideration of the transparent realities and consensual demands of the social sphere. Rather, it is a memory of narrative residues and of leftover fragments within narrative that might be capable (within Piglia's formulation) of disrupting the suturing of history's traditional literature-politics/power-knowledge relations, be they hegemonic or counterhegemonic. This is, then, a search for an affirmation of alternative articulations of culture—"beyond the barbarism and horror we have lived"—from within the telos of contemporary cultural and social systems.

Such a politics of memory allows us (Piglia suggests) to trace the possibility of a residual outside to the shameful history of hegemony/counterhegemony in Argentina—to think beyond imposed and historically accepted rationales and dominant models of representation—in order to redirect reflection toward the realm of an *other* historicity, and toward a new scene from within which to articulate sense, the promise of culture, and the notion of futurity in neoliberal times. As we will see in our analysis of Piglia's *La ciudad ausente* (The absent city) this politics of memory searches for the possibility of a new scene of writing and reflection. Moreover, it does this from within the residual and fragmentary constellations of postdictatorship and its relation to globalism.

Ricardo Piglia's *La ciudad ausente* is a novel constructed for the sole purpose of representing, and of attempting to shed light on, the peculiarities of contemporary (postdictatorial) inheritances. As such, it is a reflection on the production of meaning and on the possibility of narrating a meaning at a time in which the signifying processes of Argentine modernity have brought about the exhaustion of the grounds and unity of meaning, and therefore also of knowing. In a manner reminiscent of *Finnegans Wake* (though always on a minor scale) the indeterminacies of *La ciudad ausente*'s speaking voices become so overwhelmingly complex (and yet often so understated) that the reader can only have a blurred impression that something is actually being told.[15] As such, Jean-Michel Rabaté's observations in relation to Joyce's text also hold true for *La ciudad ausente*: "As soon as we try to pinpoint the 'events' of a story, it trails off elsewhere, and we have to discover to our surprise that we are in the middle of another narrative. Nevertheless, we retain a constant and insistent feeling that some kind of storytelling is going on in a text which relies so much on speaking voices to tie up all the fragments" ("Narratology" 137). But as in *Finnegans Wake* the fragments of *La ciudad ausente* are never fully sutured to each other. Rather, each narrative is a residual storytelling that becomes the source for the possible yet fragmentary production of difference.

In *La ciudad ausente*, Junior—the novel's phantasmatic protagonist and named embodiment of inheritance—emerges into the nonspace of the object world as an eclipsed agent who is attempting to define the sense of a history made "under circumstances directly encountered, given and transmitted from the past" (Marx, *Eighteenth* 15). He is a journalist of English descent who finds himself, by chance, embarked upon an almost incomprehensible mythical journey/travel narrative/detective investigation into the threatened closure of Macedonio's machine, and, therefore, into the end of the production of social narratives that this seems to imply. The novel, then, takes on the form of a journey to the place (to the *museo* where the machine is located) from which all stories are said to generate. It therefore promises the form of an archival uncovering of origin and, hence, of meaning.

However, through Junior's journey toward the mnemonic machine—and through the narratives that it has generated—the journey itself becomes a machine containing matrixes of matrixes of stories that never provide insight into the revelation of the meaning of the original machine. The novel, in other words, refuses to answer any demand for a revelation of meaning as "dwelling, haven, habitation, safeguard, intimacy, community, subjectivity: as the signifier of a proper and present signified, the signifier of the proper and the present as such" (Nancy, *Sense* 3). It only allows us to perceive, through its constant logic of narrative assimilation, displacement, and deferral, a movement toward a certain sense of historicity in which narratives can only be made to make sense from within the very opening up of thought to the abandonment of sense itself.

The novel, then, presents itself as a hunt for the revelation of the machine's order and significance. But *La ciudad ausente* also participates in the machine's narratives; it stems from the machine itself and follows it as a ghostly double of itself. The reader can establish no distinction between the grounds of these projects—the search for the origin of Macedonio's magical invention and the coming into being of *La ciudad ausente* itself—for the novel produces itself as the constitution of a ghost effect that continually degrounds all notions of self and other.

The novel considers the notion of historical transmission to be an act of constant displacement and deferral rather than a given ground from which to think historically. In what appears to be an oblique evocation of the schemas of communication and code that characterize much of *Finnegans Wake*, as well as the foundational role of radio in the formation of popular culture and politics in Argentina, *La ciudad ausente* opens with an ear, and with a certain hearing, for the transmission of absent voices, for the spirits of the past, and for the Joycean "soundsense" of cultural and sociopolitical inheritances, repetitions, and differences in the present.

Thus Junior is the active re-presentation and farcical return, in the present, of Argentina's foundational narratives of nation formation and of national progress and development:

> Junior always said that he liked to live in hotels because his forefathers were English. When he said English he meant the English travelers of the nineteenth century. . . . Solitary and nearly invisible, they had invented modern journalism because they had left their personal histories behind. They lived in hotels and wrote their chronicles and maintained sarcastic relations with local governors. That is why when his wife left him and went with their daughter to live in Barcelona, Junior sold everything remaining in the house and dedicated himself to traveling. . . . He thought that his daughter was a version of himself. She was what he had been, but living like a woman. In order to escape this image he traveled twice around the republic by train, rental car, and provincial bus. (9–10)[16]

Alert to the phantom voices of absent storytellers and of history's narratives of dislocation, Junior lands a job at *El Mundo*, at which, it is said, "he alone controlled all the news before the events actually happened. All he had to do was pick up the telephone and he would get the stories with two hours advantage over everybody else" (10). But this uncanny ability not just to uncover the truth but, indeed, to predict it by keeping his ear to the ground, is nothing more than a historical return of the same in difference, for Junior is, within the narrative itself, the repetition and re-inscription of previous acts of hear-say: "Junior's father had been delirious and disturbed just like Junior. He would stay up all night in Patagonia listening to the BBC's shortwave transmissions from London. He wanted to erase all traces of his personal life and live like a lunatic in an unknown world, hooked to the voices that came to him from his country" (11). This act of re-call—which, along with the image of the English journalists of the nineteenth century, is the origin of Junior's magical ability to reveal/invent the truth in the present—quickly generates another site of re-call, another spectral site of narration and of hear-say in the history of Argentine national progress and development:

> According to Renzi that paternal passion explained the speed with which Junior had picked up on the first defective transmissions of Macedonio's machine. "A typically British reaction," said Renzi, "to train the son with the example of a father who spends his life with his ear stuck to a shortwave radio." "It reminds me," said Renzi, "of the years of the resistance, when my old man stayed up all night listening to Perón's recordings, which were brought to him clandestinely by one of the movement's envoys. They were the tapes from the first period that would fall out and unravel. They were brown and slippery and you'd have to put them on a head about so big, and then close the lid of the tape player. I remember the silence at the beginning and the buzz of the tapes before hearing Perón's exiled voice, which would always begin its messages with "Comrades," and then pause as if waiting for the applause. We would sit around the kitchen table at midnight absorbed just like Junior's father, but trusting in that voice that came out of nowhere and that always sounded just a little slow and distorted. (11–12)

The accumulation of peripheral hear-says with which *La ciudad ausente* opens — hear-says that all involve being alert to an affirmation and for the possibility of hearing say yes, of locating a soundsense in the other and in alterity — are all forms of addressing the possibility of affirming historical continuity and common ground. But, as Renzi seems to know, that affirmation of common ground is always a little out of place and a little untimely:

> "It should have occurred to Perón to speak through shortwave radio, don't you think?" said Renzi, and he smiled at Junior. "From Spain, in nighttime transmissions, along with all the electrical discharge and interference — because that way his words would have arrived at the very moment they were spoken. Don't you think? Because by the time we heard the tapes everything had already changed and it all seemed behind the times and out of place. I remember that," said Renzi, "every time I hear about the machine's recordings. It would be better if the story came straight out, the narrator should always be present. Of course I also like the idea of stories that seem to be beyond time, beginning whenever you want them to." (12)

It is at this point — with Renzi in a get-together telling the story of his father trying to hear an affirmation in the Peronist resistance; with Renzi telling this story in response to Junior's uncanny ability to address

The Other Side of the Popular

contemporary hearsay; with Junior as the re-presentation of his father's desire to re-call the developed world in Patagonia; and with Renzi presumably surrounded by a group of people hearing him give voice to his father's hear-say (and all this in the first five pages of the novel) — that *La ciudad ausente* begins to tell its own story: the story of the generation of stories from within the contemporary grounds of fragmentation, disconnectedness, and exhaustion.[17]

It is hardly surprising, then, that the narrative should begin with an interruption, a phone call, a phantom voice, and a hear-say grounded either in truth or in simulation:

> They had gone down to the bar to get a sandwich after work, and while Renzi talked about Perón's voice and the Peronist resistance and began to tell the story of a friend of his father, Monito showed up to tell Junior that he had a phone call. . . . Junior thought that it was that woman calling him again. "It's her," Junior thought, "for sure." An unknown woman would call and give him instructions as if they were lifelong friends. The woman must have been familiar with the articles he was publishing in the paper. Ever since the confirmation of certain imperfections in the machine a number of eccentrics had begun to forward him confidential information. "Listen," said the woman, "you have to go to the Hotel Majestic on Piedras and Avenida de Mayo. Got it? Fuyita, a Korean, lives there." . . . She spoke in code, with the allusive and slightly idiotic tone of those who believe in magic and predestination. Everything meant something else. . . . "There's a woman in a can who's Fat-Man Saurio's girlfriend. Are you getting this down?" she had said. "They're going to close the museum so hurry up. Fuyita is a gangster working as a security guard." . . . Junior hung up and went back to the bar. Renzi was already relaying another chapter from his life story. (13–15)

The novel begins, then, not just with an ear to the accumulation and transmission of disembodied voices, soundsenses, and self-projections, but with the active interruption of Renzi's Peronist/post-Perón story of hearing say yes in the relation between Peronist hegemony-lost and Peronist counterhegemony. Moreover, it is at this point — at this site of interruption — that a new circulation of stories begins (" 'Did I give you the recording?' said Renzi. 'Here,' he said, and handed over the cassette. 'Listen to it and fill me in later.' 'Perfect,' said Junior" [18]). It is at this point that the novel really begins: "Miguel Mac Kensey (Junior), an English traveler. The lighted subway train sped through the tunnel at eighty kilometers per hour" (19).

After an apparently senseless (dis)encounter with the mysterious woman of the Hotel Majestic, Junior takes a taxi to the *museo*. In transit to the place—the supposed origin—at which all stories are generated (including *La ciudad ausente*) Junior begins to listen to Renzi's tape and to the final story generated by the machine before its closure; that is, before the end of its history: "He put on the Walkman. He heard *Crime and the City Solution*. . . . He had the recording Renzi had given him. It was the last known story from the machine. A testimony, the voice of a witness telling what he had seen. It happened in the present, on the edge of the world, the signs of horror marked on the earth" (31). Junior's listening (and the reader's reading) of the tape signals the hear-say of a narrative about the unearthing of the gravesites of the *desaparecidos*. As such, it is also the hear-say of a narrative about the revelation of a language that hesitates, that appears on the point of collapsing, as it confronts the unspeakable horror of state-sponsored terror. This, the final known narrative of Macedonio's machine, bears witness to the exhaustion of language's ability to express. As such, it slowly stutters to a halt before the unmarked graves of the disappeared:

> "You know" he says to me, "this is the map of hell. On the ground, like a map, what I am telling you, I give you my word, was a map, I mean, of unmarked graves, with one section frosted like a tombstone and then earth or grass. You can't keep on covering it over because in the end the frost, the moved earth, can be seen, of course the harm was already done by then. . . . A map of tombs like we see here in these mosaics, like that, that was the map, it looked like a map, after the ground was frozen, black and white, immense, the map of hell." (39)

Junior (along with the reader) has begun to wander through the disparate micronarratives and cartographic coordinates of postdictatorship: an intellectual journey through underground networks of leftover storylines that emerge like the coordinates of a subway map, moving in multiple registers at any one time (91). Finally Junior encounters the haven of the *museo*, ironically "in a remote part of the city, near a park and behind the Congress" (43). The *museo*, of course, is home to all the narratives and logics of Macedonio's machine. But it also signifies what promises to be lost if the machine is forced to reach the definitive end of its history, its disseminations, and its potential readings.

Macedonio's machine—producer and reproducer of myths and of images creating and re-creating collective cultural memory—has been growing increasingly aware of its own machinations (and therefore of its own limits). It has begun to bear witness to the horrors of the cultural archive that it itself has helped to constitute and project from past to present. Indeed, the cultural memory computer's more self-reflexive stories of dislocation are now being copied clandestinely, and are being circulated throughout the city. Up until this moment of self-consciousness the archive-producing machine had always produced local narratives as if they were positive supplements of inherited models. As such, rather than translating those originals faithfully, the machine would transform them into an endless movement of cultural/narrative difference. Thus, when a metropolitan story such as Edgar Allan Poe's "William Wilson" was fed into the Argentine archive it was transformed into the supplementary and expanded narrative of "Stephen Stevensen." Macedonio explains this peripheral logic of cultural and epistemological translation in the following terms: "We wanted a translation machine and we have a machine that transforms stories. It took the theme of the double and translated it. It makes do with whatever it can. It uses whatever's available and what appears lost is brought back transformed into something else. That's life" (43–44). The question for Macedonio, however (indeed, as it was throughout the history of national capitalism in Argentina), is how to construct common narratives from within the periphery's dependency on metropolitan models, and from within the subsequent production of uneven cultural/mnemonic difference. The question, then, is how to constitute a shared peripheral cultural memory that is capable of preparing for its moment of nondependency: "The machine had grasped Poe's narrative form and had changed its storyline. Therefore it was a question of programming it with a variable set of narrative nuclei and of letting it get to work. The key, Macedonio said, is that it learns as it narrates. Learning means that it remembers what it has already done and that it gains more and more experience. It will not necessarily make better stories as it goes along, but it will know the stories that it has made and it might end up creating a common plot for them" (44).

The initial logic of Macedonio's culture machine is founded on error, yet the supplementary ground of the social memory that it can create promises both continuation with metropolis and the production of local originality. As such, its initial recycling of external forms and models promises to generate a form of homespun narrative development: the promise of a commonality in which the multiple generation of differences could finally inaugurate a unified and unifying storyline no longer grounded in dependency but in a local form of sovereignty. As such, the possibility of futurity is promised implicitly within the structure of dialectical unfolding that Macedonio's utopic mnemonic machine produces:

> Junior was beginning to understand. In the beginning the machine makes a mistake. Error is the first principle. The machine "spontaneously" breaks up the elements of Poe's story and transforms them into potential nuclei of fiction. That is how the initial plot had emerged. The myth of origin. All the stories came from there. The future meaning of what was happening depended upon that story about the other and what is to come. The real was defined by the possible (not by being). The true-false opposition had to be substituted by the possible-impossible opposition. (103)

The machine produces, from within the unfolding and expansion of its differential narratives, the promise of a common plot and, therefore, the grounds of a limitless future.

But Macedonio's utopic narrative machine, together with the *museo* that houses it, are threatened with closure and therefore with the beginning of the end of history's errant stories and commonalities. It seems to have passed beyond its productive narratives of identity/difference and appears to have confronted the question of what is left to narrate after the exhaustion of production. The machine, then, has achieved its own limit: "It has begun to talk about itself. That is why they want to stop it. It is no longer a machine, but a more complex organism. A system of pure energy. In one of its last stories there is an island, on the edge of the world, a kind of linguistic utopia about future life. A survivor constructs an artificial woman. . . . The castaway constructs a woman with the leftovers that the river brings him" (111).

Junior is sent one of the archive's last and most secret stories. It is a cybernarrative of antistate techno-resistance and lumpen misery entitled "Los nudos blancos" (The white knots), an encoded title referring to the unveiling of an experiential nodal point that is capable of providing meaning to social existence after the closure of Macedonio's machine, and after the eclipse of its programmed storylines.[18] For Junior this is "an explosive story, the paranoid ramifications of life in the city. That's why there's so much control, thought Junior. They're trying to erase everything recorded in the street. The flash that lights up the pallid faces of the innocents in police mugshot manuals" (68). It is in this deliriously futuristic (yet always uncomfortably contemporary) narrative of advanced technology and of underground struggle against a transnational culture—against a world that has become so global that whole populations are now obliged to live in the dark so that the news at eight can be seen everywhere at the same time (76)—that a resistance group attempts to open up experience to the "white knots." These are "zones of condensation" inscribed within memory that, "like myths . . . define the grammar of experience" (74). It is also in this final and clandestine narrative that Macedonio's machine makes mention for the first time of a linguistic configuration about the future—"La isla de Finnegans" (Finnegans Island)—located "way up the Paraná, on the other side of the River Liffey" (76).

In "Los nudos blancos" a woman, Elena (de Obieta? "la Eterna"?), emerges as either a drugged psychiatric patient or a torture victim, or both, under interrogation (it appears) regarding the whereabouts of a ghostly resistance leader named Mac (Macedonio? Junior?). In the end she gives up the name not of Mac but of Grete Müller, who, it seems, signals an oblique movement from individualized hear-say to the promise of a common grammar of experience in the future:

> In the market basement . . . Grete Müller was developing the photographs that she had taken that night in the aquarium. The signs of a lost language could be seen on the shells of the turtles. The white knots had originally been marks on the bones. The map of a blind language common to all living beings. The only trace of that original language were the patterns on the shells of sea turtles. . . . All the languages of the world had developed through the centuries from those primitive nuclei. Grete wanted to get to the island because with that map it would be possible to establish a common language. In the past we had all understood the meaning of every word, the white knots were engraved on the body like a collective memory . . . nobody conserves the memory of life anymore. We see the future as if it were the memory of a childhood home. She had to get to the island, discover the legend of the woman who was going to come and save them. Perhaps, thought Grete, she is motionless in the sand, lost, on the empty beach, like a rebellious replica of the future Eve. (84–85)

After an accumulation of fleeting narratives, Junior (and, of course, the reader) is exposed finally to the utopic linguistic world of Finnegans Island. But this exposure is once again contingent on hear-say, for it is the product not of direct experience but of the narrative of a former inhabitant of the island, Boas. Boas states that it is here, on the limit of the world, that a "white knot"—a collective grammar of experience—has been opened up. The island is a kind of utopia totality-enclave whose constructive principle lies in *Finnegans Wake*: that private grammar of experience beyond standardization and homogeneity whose transformational singularity, absolute indetermination, and total recall reproduces a totality of the world of radical hybridity and contingency in miniature: "It is an island, on the bend of a river, inhabited by English and Irish and Russians and people from all over, pursued by the authorities, threatened with death, political exiles. They have been hiding there for years and years; on the shores of the island they have built cities and roads and they have explored the land following the course of the river and now, in that region, all languages have become mixed together. Every voice can be heard. Nobody arrives or if they do they never want to leave. Because that is where the dead have found refuge" (123). On Finnegans Island all languages and marginalized voices have come together in the performative contingency of post-babelic babble. All currents in the island's *riverrun* of language are to be found there in their differential singularity, yet no one can inhabit the island—it cannot be the site of a "dwelling, haven, habitation, safeguard, intimacy, community, subjectivity" (Nancy *Sense* 3)—for there can be no notion of the nation to unify, standardize, nullify, or repress the eternal production of differences. The island then is a "river"—a *riverrun* of postnational language—"where all riverbeds are and where nobody can live because nobody has a homeland. Insomnia is the great disease of the nation. The rumor of voices is continuous and its changes can be heard night and day" (124).

Finnegans Island, then, has no single ground or telos. Rather, it is a point at which experience is opened up to the shifting tides that underlie the relation between language and the world. In this world all things are defined in terms of the practical and experiential mobilization of ungroundedness and finitude:

> The unstable character of language defines life on the island. One never knows with what words present states will be named in the future. Sometimes letters arrive written in signs that can no longer be understood. Sometimes a man and woman are passionate lovers in one language and hostile strangers in another. Great poets cease to be so and become nothing, witnessing the emergence of living classics (who are also forgotten). All masterpieces last only as long as the language in which they were written. Only silence persists as clear as water, and always exactly the same. (127–28)

Finnegans Island reflects an operation between language and history in which transparency and immediate intelligibility are degrounded by the impossibility of translating one language to another on the basis of common signifying structures. Language, in other words, opens up a common grammar of experience that unveils the world as the coming into itself of constant ungroundedness. Indeed, being-in-common is the experience of this ungroundedness, and the underground resistance of "Los nudos blancos" believes that this new telos is the nonfoundational foundation of a collective grammar of freedom. The Joycean *riverrrun* of language promises the possibility of interrupting the contemporary order's rationalistic telos of guaranteed translatability, given homogeneity, and systematic coherence. And this is done by suggesting the existence of an archive that is grounded in finitude; an archive that embodies the labor of historical incompletion, disjuncture, interruption, and heterogeneity.

Perhaps we could say that a narrative such as that of Finnegans Island traces the grounds of a communitarian space that is anchored in radical difference and in the collective experience of constitutive negativity. Indeed, perhaps one could even suggest that the absolute incompletion of the social sphere that the island seems to signify implies a nonunitary space in which radical historicity and political community come to each other as continual incompletion and absolute heterogeneity. After all, there appears to be no single conclusion to be reached in, and no end to, the languages that this totality enclave can articulate. As such, there is no hegemonic ground to be consolidated, no single sense to be made, and therefore no place from which to exorcise difference and negativity. In this sense, Finnegans Island promises the nonfoundational telos of a posthegemonic world.

Having said this, however, *La ciudad ausente* cannot appropriate and represent that world. It can merely present it as a hear-say and as an oblique affirmation in the words of a character/witness (Boas). The island itself, in other words, remains an absent space within the novel. It is the constitutive outside of the narration itself—an outside that cannot be dialecticized and recuperated for representation—for the machine that generates the story of Finnegans's totality enclave, and that plants the seed of a potential collective experience of posthegemonic ungroundedness, is closed down and the production of histories and futurities interrupted. All that remains after the closure of the cultural history machine—and after the end of a certain national history of narrative production—is the intermittent generation of a distant, untimely, yet ultimately affirmative female voice (or accumulation of female voices) from beyond the grave. The island allows for the final emergence within *La ciudad ausente* of funereal voices marked by finitude, negativity, and the intimations of an affirmation:

> I am the one who narrates. . . . I am anachronistic, so anachronistic that they have buried me in this white basement. That is why they want to isolate me, keep me under control, under the exclusive care of Fuyita the Korean, like an embalmed corpse. . . . Sometimes I get confused, I think I'm in the hospital. I think and think and see a cor-

ridor in my memory, and then another. . . . I am Amalia; if you hurry me I will say I am Molly, I am her, locked up in the mansion, desperate, the 'mazorca', I am Irish, . . . I am her and I am the others, I was the others, I am Hippolyte. . . . I remember, during the time of Richter, when Perón fell into the German trap . . . Evita used to slap the ministers around . . . she would slap them across the face, slap, slap. That was the beginning of the Peronist resistance. . . . Who knows what she was dreaming when she died. I remember the hospital room, the poor people who visited me, they would stand at the bottom of the bed with their cloth caps in hand, they are here to offer their condolences. . . . I am in a glass room on exhibition like a doll, I am the queen bee mounted on the velvet cushion, the tiepin has a pearl and pierces the butterfly's body. . . . I know they abandoned me here, deaf and blind and half immortal. If only I could die or see him again or really go crazy, sometimes I imagine that he is going to return and sometimes I imagine that I will be able to get him out of me, to stop being this interminable foreign memory, I construct memory but nothing else. I am full of stories, I can't stop . . . I am the singer, the one who sings, I am on the sand, near the bay, on the water's edge I can still remember the old lost voices, I am alone under the sun. Nobody comes near, nobody comes, but I will carry on, before me lies the desert, the sun burns the stones, sometimes I drag myself, but I will go on, to the water's edge, yes. (168–78)

Through this funereal voice of a female plurality—a plurality that seems to evoke the specters of Elena de Obieta ("la Eterna") in Macedonio's life and narrative world; the embalmed and disappeared corpse of Eva Perón in the years of Peronist resistance; and even the unearthing of Hullo Eve Cenograph in *Finnegans Wake* (a figure that embodies "a new form of writing [*kainos*], but also an empty writing [*kenos*] . . ." that, like Elena de Obieta and Eva Perón, re-calls "an entombed female subject commemorating a body buried elsewhere" [Moreiras, *Tercer* 104; translation mine])—indeed, through all of these possible connections, we hear say nothing more than the taking place of language as time. The novel, then, comes to a close through the enunciation of a machinic female orality (or accumulation of female oralities). Each possible voice branches into the next and into the next as consecutive nuclei of differentiation apparently embarked upon a movement of final becoming. The closing pages of the text, in other words, offer us the image of "an entity, an incorporeal ecosystem, whose being is not guaranteed from the outside. . . . It is not an object 'given' in extrinsic coordinates but an assemblage of subjectivation giving meaning and value to determinate existential Territories" (Guattari, *Chaosmosis* 94). It is the movement—

The Other Side of the Popular

the "machinic processuality" (90)—of a discursive labor for life born from within the finitude of literary history.

The closure of *La ciudad ausente*, then, bears witness to spectral female voices that are quite literally, at the end, a "have-been." But it is not simply the performance of pastness—of having been and of no longer being—that persists in this final passage. For the final affirmation, "yes," affirmed on the water's edge—at that limit of experience and of language that both joins and separates the funereal voice(s) to and from the utopic futurity of Finnegans Island—promises the re-call of a praxis that is capable of persisting into the future: "I can still remember the old lost voices. . . . I will carry on, before me lies the desert, the sun burns the stones, sometimes I drag myself, but I will go on, to the water's edge, yes" (178).

But this affirmation of collective re-call and of potential continuity—of a narrative machine populated explicitly by a multitude of women's voices reflecting from within, and through, the horrors of history—comes into being only by giving voice to the full knowledge and sharing of finitude and of fatality: to that which "remains there out of sound and out of sight, linked up in advance to some 'gramaphone in the grave'" (Derrida, "Ulysses" 596). The novel ends, then, with a sharing, but not with a constituted communion. On the contrary, what is shared by all is a limit that opens them (and the novel itself, and, therefore, literature itself) to being-in-common as being-for-other and through others. In the words of Jean-Luc Nancy:

> When the text recounts its own story, when it recounts it unfinished, and when it interrupts itself—and when it goes on to recount this interruption, but in the end interrupts itself again—it is because it has a stake, an end, and a principle beyond itself. In one sense, literature only ever comes from literature, and returns to it. But in another sense—which continually interferes with the first in such a way that, with each interference, it is myth that is interrupted—the text, or the writing, stems only from the singular relationship between singular beings. . . . The text stems from, or *is this relationship;* it renders its ontological vein: being as being *in* common is (the) being (of) literature. (*Inoperative* 66)

As such, *La ciudad ausente* inaugurates and performs a new knowledge and a new language grounded in finitude and in finitude's active perpetuation and redistribution; a posthegemonic thought handed over to the liminality of past and present agencies, in which the past is re-activated thanks to the almost hallucinatory quality of history's leftover traces and fragments. But as the final pages of the novel seem to suggest, hearing what these fragments have to say cannot serve to recuperate the notion of a particular ground—a new site for mastery, in other words—from which to grasp historical understanding. It cannot be a question of reestablishing the coordinates of an infrastructure or of a superstructure representative of ground and of history's immediate intelligibility.

On the contrary, *La ciudad ausente*, like *Finnegans Wake* before it, cannot describe the reactivation of history and of historical understanding in mimetic fashion. It is not about some specific thing, and is, therefore, not a question of mastery over an object-world or a language. Rather, it is about mastery's *lapsus* and about the spreading of the signifiers of that moment of denarrativization.

Hence, *La ciudad ausente* is the nonoriginary and degrounded thing that it writes. Like *Finnegans Wake* it is its own performative utopia of nonmastery (Rabaté, "Lapsus" 87); the being itself which produces and transfigures itself without reinscribing the false aura of preexisting cultural icons or future paths. In other words, it is its own posthegemonic affirmation: *yes*. And, indeed, like any *yes*, "it must entrust itself to memory" (Derrida, "Ulysses" 596).

In the end, *La ciudad ausente* opens up reflection to the demands of a thought of finitude. In *The Inoperative Community* Jean-Luc Nancy observes in passing that "when a voice, or music, is suddenly interrupted, one hears just at that instant something else, a mixture of various silences and noises that had been covered over by the sound, but in this something else one hears again the voice or the music that has become in a way the voice or the music of its own interruption: a kind of echo, but one that does not repeat that of which it is the reverberation" (62). *La ciudad ausente* is the communication of cultural history's (the machine's) suspension. It is the tenuous affirmation of the remaining distant sound-senses that resonate as echoes, as discontinuous alterities, and as haunting singularities from within the remains of interruption's enactment. In conclusion, it is a mnemonic narrative machine that allows us to hear say yes in that which remains, in curious and promising suspension, on the other side of (counter)hegemonic cultural, historical, and social configurations. As such, its posthegemonic language can only lead us forward toward further reflection.

Perhaps

5

*The Dispersal of the
Nation and the Neoliberal Habitus*
Tracing Insurrection from Central America
to South Central Los Angeles

> It is not enough to try to get back to the people in that past out of
> which they have already emerged; rather we must join them in that
> fluctuating movement which they are just giving shape to, and which,
> as soon as it has started, will be the signal for everything to be called
> in question. Let there be no mistake about it; it is to this zone of occult
> instability where the people dwell that we must come; and it is there
> that our souls are crystallised and that our perceptions and our lives
> are transfused with light. —Frantz Fanon, *The Wretched of the Earth*

> Trying to be South in the South, North in the North, South in the
> North and North in the South. —Rubén Martínez, *The Other Side*

The previous chapter opened up the terms of my discussion to the possibility of thinking beyond the historically accepted rationales and hegemonic circumscriptions of local/national cultural and political traditions.
My reading of Ricardo Piglia's *La ciudad ausente* (in conjunction with
Piglia's appropriation of Macedonio Fernández and James Joyce) extended the possibility of a posthegemonic critical practice designed to
guide reflection away from the standardized and homogenized narratives
and topographies of (post)modern accumulation. The purpose of the
previous chapter, then, is to redirect attention toward the possibility of
examining still-unheard-of transnational/transhistorical cultural articulations and potential political commonalities.

The purpose of this chapter is, quite simply, to continue this line
of inquiry—this potential praxis of difference in neoliberal times—in
order to suggest the possibility of a subaltern negativity located within

the contingent grounds of contemporary social experience. This, of course, is easier said than done. After all, any thought of subalternity supposes a critical practice that hesitates (perhaps necessarily) before its objects of analysis. This political, epistemological, and philosophical hesitation is the direct result of the unresolvable tension between the historical fabrication of modernity's dominant narratives and the position within such power/knowledge configurations of subaltern subject positions that unwork them (often by representing and reproducing themselves as "the absolute limit of the place where history is narrativized into logic" [Spivak, "Subaltern" 16]). This unresolvable tension between history's dominant logics (and representations) and the subaltern specters that haunt, challenge, and undermine them from within simultaneously upholds the possibility of subalternist reflection and undermines it as a productive site for conclusive argumentation and/or resolution.

Indeed, perhaps it could even be said that the notion of resolution within the thought of subalternity would merely transform the subaltern subject position into a nodal point of social intelligibility around which neohegemonic intellectual programs or populist political solutions could once again be affirmed. Such practices, however, would tend to reflect little more than a thought invested in the neohegemonic stabilization of the subaltern's destabilizing force. In this sense, it would be a thought grounded in the constitution and maintenance of social intelligibility and of immediate translatability, over and above the destabilizing promise of subaltern heterogeneity and difference. The question, of course, is how to think about subaltern heterogeneity and difference from within institutional thought.

In "In Defense of the Fragment" Gyanendra Pandey calls attention to the foundational tension within subaltern studies between subaltern knowledge and institutional knowledge. Pandey does this by pointing out that reflection on the history and representation of social violence in contemporary India is seriously hampered by one simple fact: it is almost impossible to establish anything like the facts, never mind the details, of the stories that bear witness to the subaltern experience of revolt and insurrection (9).[1] The truth of subaltern experience often remains hidden, in other words, even though spectral part-narratives do continue to circulate in an often unknowable fashion among more or less reticent subaltern populations (19).[2] As such, Pandey notes, official reflection on historical processes and, in particular, on the subaltern experience of those processes hesitates when confronted with the fragmentary and partial discourses that it encounters. In the face of subaltern fragments official historiography confronts the flimsiness of its own foundations;

the point at which the fabrication of a historiographical discourse based on the security of critical distance and/or omniscience flounders.

Pandey posits that subaltern histories can only be represented through what is available at the limits of hegemonic narratives. This means opening up historiographical discourse—and historical reflection—to an accumulation of partial, fragmented, and often fragmenting subaltern narratives that might be able to convey a certain sense of subaltern experience, and might be able to challenge dominant accounts of subaltern knowledge, representation, and experience:

> What the historians call a fragment—a weaver's diary, a collection of poems by an unknown poet (and to these we might add all those literatures of India that Macauley condemned, creation myths and women's songs, family genealogies, and local traditions of history)—is of central importance in challenging the state's construction of history, in thinking other histories and marking those contested spaces through which particular unities are sought to be constituted and others broken up. If the provisionality of our units of analysis needs stressing, so does the provisionality of our interpretations and of our theoretical conceits. The arrogation of "total" and "objective" knowledge is no longer anywhere near as common as it used to be in historical writing. Nevertheless the temptations of totalizing discourses are great. The yearning for the "complete" statement, which leaves out nothing of importance, is still with us. (28–29)

In Pandey's important formulation the innately unsatisfactory nature of subalternist reflection—in other words, its self-conscious engagement with the discursive fragments and residues that lie on the margins of hegemonic narratives—renders thought on subalternity, and on the social violence that often accompanies it, inherently unstable. As a result of this instability official historiography often merely posits subalternity as curiously supplementary to the intellectual enterprise itself. However, we could also posit that within the intellectual's drive to open up institutional reflection to what exceeds it, subaltern studies could unsettle, in creative and imaginative ways, the premises of knowledge production to which it belongs. If this were the case, subaltern studies could potentially promise a knowledge grounded in a foundational paradox: the better it is the worse (or at least the more unsatisfactory) it is for the hegemonic reproduction of institutional knowledge. The subaltern fragment, in other words, could limit the ability of the field of knowledge production to reproduce itself (thereby tracing a limit to the realm of disciplinary power) and simultaneously expose thought to a demand for richer evaluations of the relationship between the production of knowledge, the historical fabrication of reason on the capitalist peripheries, and the possibility of future political communities.

A "good enough" subaltern studies could not overcome, nor resolve, its foundational conditions of (im)possibility. Indeed, I would add that subaltern studies cannot even strive for the resolution of its conditions and representations. If it were to do so it would overstep immediately both the limits of its inheritance and the weight of its historical injunctions. And on doing this it would merely enter the essentialist and potentially authoritarian realm of absolute representation. On the other hand, by heeding the strength of Pandey's formulations we can suggest that subaltern studies is a critical affirmation that is alert to its own instabilities. And it does this in order no longer to think a thought of the system (be that colonial, national, imperial, global, neoliberal, etc.), no longer the establishment of a unified theory, and not even the possibility of encompassing a particular body of knowledge in its totality. Rather, subaltern studies strives to think something else and otherwise. It attempts to think from within the finitude of order's hegemonic repertoires—to think its fragmented leftovers and the fissures in our critical narratives that they presuppose—in order to open up reflection to the emergence and agency of momentary and partial glimpses into subaltern subject positions that arise from the experience (and understanding) of social conflicts, while also saying something about the parameters and limits of our own understandings as intellectuals and institutionalized thinkers.

The question, of course, is how to think subaltern fragments from within the fragmentary; that is, from within a critical site that does not merely reproduce within reflection an underlying desire for the authoritarian and homogenizing notion of a complete statement (which ultimately promises an order of knowability grounded in the always already hegemonic). Needless to say, the dilemma underlined in Pandey's work on the fragment in subaltern studies is by no means an example of South Asian exceptionality. I would even go so far as to say that the problematics underlined in "In Defense of the Fragment" hold true for the analysis of the postnational era in general.

For example, in the relation between the neoliberal restructuring of the state in Latin America, the messianic emergence of the marketplace in official discourse, and mass subaltern migration from Central America to the North, it appears that an analogous dilemma to that which Pandey signals for subalternist reflection in India emerges in relation to our ability to think through (rather than merely describe) the hybridity and violence that characterizes current North/South exchanges and inter-

actions. Given the current weakness of national paradigms and epistemologies, and given the destabilizing force of the subaltern fragment
within those paradigms, what are the grounds for a thought of, for example, subaltern migration in postnational times?

As a result of its accumulation of fragmentary and fissured realities,
architectures, experiences, and part-narratives, this chapter presents a
critical-regionalist reflection on the passage from civil war in El Salvador to the migratory lines of flight that characterize contemporary postwar articulations. Indeed, in this chapter I offer a practical evaluation for
subalternist critical practice of our (in)ability to grasp Salvadoran migration in conjunction with contemporary circuits of transnational social
violence. For reasons already outlined, the following discussion continually confronts and (to an extent) reproduces its own constantly shifting
foundation. In my own defense, however (and, once again, in defense of
the fragment as a privileged site for, and limit to, subalternist reflection),
to reproduce a sense of foundation—and therefore of order, continuity,
translatability, and completion—when trying to think through itinerant
subaltern realities produced by the Central American civil conflicts of
the 1980s would merely smack of placing thought once again on the side
of system, and therefore on the side of unitary paths toward a conclusion, toward a resolution of sorts, or toward a development. In contrast
to the shallow homogenizing drive of such epistemological formalities, in
this chapter I defend a Central American insurrectional and migratory
fragment, its potential thought, and that thought's limits when articulated from within the slippery ground of a Latino/a American subaltern
studies.[3]

The outlines traced in this chapter, then, cannot be evoked as parts of
a unified structure nor as assemblages within the formation of a singular
unit of argumentation. Rather, the unregimented constellation presented
here—its challenge to structural linearity in unhinged and dislocating
times such as those of the present—takes up what Gilles Deleuze and
Félix Guattari term a "line of flight," an accumulation of strides within
thought and within the relationality of things, bodies, societies, and geo-
economic configurations such as those that used to be called the Third
World and that are now euphemistically called emerging markets.

Needless to say, Latin America finds itself (along with most regions on
the planet) at a moment in the history of development to which it belongs
without belonging. It is an estranged partner in the aperture and redistribution of culture/state relations; a sidelined player in a historical moment
that inscribes development, once again, as an insurmountable aberra-
tion. Within this horizon the market is a necessary mutation given over to

The Dispersal of the Nation

transforming, once and for all, the organizing concepts of Latin American nation-state formation. Obviously, there is nothing new in the idea of historical mutation in Latin America given the effects of its peripheral position within the colonial and imperial orders. However, what is new is the intensity and astounding speed and depth of mutation that has taken over since the economic collapse of the 1980s, the fall of the Berlin Wall, and the end of the so-called revolutionary era. Without doubt, what we are witnessing is a transformation in the articulations between culture and organized power, a radical shift in collective and individual forms of belonging, and the systemic undermining of the ways contemporary experience can be grasped for thought.

Nietzsche, of course, stated that all affects are configurations of will to power (as described in Heidegger 45). If this is the case, then perhaps contemporary experience tells us that what we call the present is the effect of multiple and differential shifts in the accumulation of affects and of capital intensities that have swept over and seized us in sudden and turbulent fashion, transforming (probably forever) categories such as the state, the nation, the notion of commonality, and the idea of the people as social force or agent. Indeed, it is the never-ending turbulence of transnational capital's seizures that constantly undermines our ability to grasp singular objects of reflection, or to capture in conclusive terms the conditions of individual and collective belonging. Derrida's words in this regard appear to be particularly appropriate:

> We *belong* (this is what we take the risk of saying here) to the time of this mutation, which is precisely a harrowing tremor in the structure or the experience of *belonging*. Therefore of property. Of communal belonging and sharing: religion, family, ethnic groups, nations, homeland, country, state, even humanity, love and friendship, lovence, be they public or private. We belong to this tremor, if that is possible; we tremble within it. It runs through us, and stops us in its tracks. We belong to it without belonging to it. Within it we hear the resonant echo of all the great discourses (. . . Bataille, Blanchot and Nancy . . .) where they assume the risk and responsibility, but also where they give themselves over to the necessity of thinking and formalizing, so to speak, absolute dislocation, borderless disjoining. (*Politics* 80)

The systemic ungroundedness of market forces seems to impede us from upholding the revelation of particular truths, for it appears now that there is simply too much shifting in the post–cold war world for one to assume the burden of resolution, to take on the unilateral defense of a particular set of thoughts or strategies, or to propose conclusive horizons. As Richard Beardsworth notes in his critique of method in times of so-called globalization, "a thinker with a method has already decided *how* to proceed, is unable to give him or herself up to the matter of thought in hand, is a functionary of the criteria which structure his or her conceptual gestures . . . [and] this is irresponsibility itself" (4). Indeed, if we are talking about the neoliberal social order in Latin America—and therefore about collective displacements wrought by transnational economies of violence and by the projection into the future of truth regimes built on market forces—then we can only talk and think in the registers of circulation, exchange, and deterritorialization that remain to us after the weakening of previous modes of culture administration, political being, and reflection.

As Adorno put it in other times, "there has been an essential change in the relation between culture and organized power" ("Culture" 100). What, though, is the nature of this most recent "essential change"? Uncovering such a thing is no easy matter. It even appears that what we term "thought" is increasingly nothing more than another manifestation of commodity production generally, in which knowledge resonates institutionally only to the degree that it is able to insert itself into administrative circuits of academic market value in order to perpetuate the increasingly technocratic image of choice and difference, which remains so central to the reproduction of the marketplace's truths and modes of governmentality. Thus today's circuits of knowledge production increasingly inscribe thought as an appendage to the transnational market machinery, positioning us (that is, both northern and southern intellectuals) as potential performers within the real subsumption of society under capital.

The question at present, indeed the question *of* the present, is how to address what Adorno called the "nature of the essential change in the relation between culture and organized power." This, in turn, immediately produces the dilemma of how to think about the present negatively—that is, against it—when the agency of the outside is constantly privileged, and immediately eclipsed, from within the contemporary order itself. The so-called global system constantly produces its own outsides —countless differential voices, identities, and oppositional others—by promoting certain bodies of knowledge (identity politics, for example) as the ideal means of disseminating the value of difference. But such identitarian formalities merely mean that resistance and difference can be generated only after having already internalized and perpetuated the exhaustion of negativity per se. In the words of Wendy Brown, in late modernity "it is freedom's relationship to identity—its promise to address a social injury or marking that is itself constitutive of identity—that yields the paradox in which the first imaginings of freedom are always constrained by and potentially even require the very structure of oppression that freedom emerges to oppose" (7). And this phenomenon, she says, is directly linked to recent transformations in the dynamics of the state under capitalism. She argues further that critical theory "turned its gaze away from the state at the moment when a distinctly late modern form of state domination was being consolidated: when expansion and extension of state power transpired not through centralization but through deregulation and privatization, through localizing and 'contracting out' its activities—in short, through what some have identified as characteristically 'postmodern' techniques of power" (18). Thus, and as I argued in chapter 3 for example, the nature of the essential change in the relation between culture and organized power is located in the dispersal of state processes and in the domination of market forces—in the formulation of what Deleuze called the society of control—rather than in Foucault's formulation of disciplinary enclosure as formative of national state processes.

What appears to be at stake, then, is our ability to reflect on the effects of the transition to postmodern techniques of power and to trace the shifts in culture/state relations that emerge as a result of the passage away from the greatest state violence of military dictatorship and civil war (which, of course, characterized much of the 1970s and 1980s in the South) and toward the highest anxiety of peacetime market flows such as those of the new millennium. The challenge is to reflect on the intensification of forces—the differential economies of violence—that facilitated and guaranteed the traumatic and always incomplete passage from the national to the trans- or postnational, when the current order is not just a hegemonic response to crisis, but is itself a process through which historical knowledge of the world is opened up as a gaping hollow in the signifying projects of the formation of the nation-state, economic independence, and national cultural identity in Latin America. In this sense the challenge lies in our ability to think about the shifting terrain underlying the dissolution of centralizing master narratives such as the nation-state, the national, and the national-popular. It lies in our ability (or inability) to consider the present as a historical rift; as Derrida puts it, as a harrowing tremor in the structure and experience of collective being and belonging.

In the case of Central America (and, in this chapter, in the particular case of El Salvador), we would do well to reflect on the history that allowed for the insertion of democratic forms in order then to consider the extremely fickle hegemony of neoliberal governmentality. Thus we should examine the prehistory of neoliberalism's rationalities of control and, from within the historical framework of the state as the persistent site of confrontation and of increasing competition between subjectivities (Negri 11), we should consider the limits between global capitalization and contemporary processes of subject formation. But in order to do this we should also remain conscious that we are thinking at a time in the history of development in which the formalities of political subjectivity and of collective belonging are as sensitive to fluctuation and to external flows as the stock markets are to events on the other side of the planet.

For Walter Benjamin, of course, the critique of historical becoming and, in particular, the critique of its foundational violences demanded the philosophy of violence's history. As he states: "The 'philosophy' of this history because only the idea of its development makes possible a critical, discriminating, and decisive approach to its temporal data" ("Critique" 251). This is a very important formulation. What is at stake for Benjamin in such an assertion is the possibility of constructing a genealogical critique of violence's coming into being; a laying of grounds and structures that is capable of capturing and displacing the logics of violence's eruption. Thus Benjamin's philosophy of the history of violence is also the presentation of a negative or nihilistic schema that positions genealogy in the redemptive service of the present, as a means of preparing for another politics, for another law, and ultimately for what he later invokes as divine violence: revolution. In this sense, Benjamin's philosophy of the history of violence strives to uphold, in the Nietzschean sense, a nihilistic devaluation of the value and order of state violence as a precondition for a new order of value, a new order of thought, practice, and belonging; in his words, "a new historical epoch" (252).

Of course, Benjamin's notion of the inherited "weak Messianism" of all present generations ("Theses" 254), together with his conceptualization of thought given over to "the 'time of the now' . . . shot through with chips of Messianic time" (263), are a little disconcerting in a geo-economic system characterized by the systemic emptying out and redistribution of history's signifying processes. A transnational order constructed on the generation and intensification of "absolute dislocation, borderless disjoining" (Derrida, *Politics* 80) and grounded in continual mutations in the structure and experience of individual and collective belonging, scarcely lends itself to Benjamin's haunting image of "the strait gate through which the Messiah might enter" ("Theses" 264). At first glance, messianism in such circumstances (no matter how weak) must be disconcerting. Yet a critique of the harrowing tremor in the structure and experience of neoliberal belonging can hardly be posited without it.

In order to initiate such a reflection we should first (and always) "blast open" (Benjamin's phrase) those accounts of neoliberalism that place it at the redemptive service of the present. In other words, we should critique those evaluations of neoliberalism that reproduce, however unintentionally, its almost evangelical faith that emerging markets can overcome the time lapse of perpetual backwardness by breaking with the past, by embracing liberal democracy's electoral and market model, and by signing up for what the North represents as its intrinsic genesis toward the freedom of choice.

Surely if we think of the transition from brutal civil war to the democratic marketplace as a national journey from total war toward historical transcendence; from fratricide toward the potential resolution of historical antagonisms; and from collective slaughter toward the positive evocation of the present as completely different from the past, or as the potential return of institutional legitimacy, then we merely sustain the conceptual violence of development's masterful demands. By not reflecting on, for example, the complex and often violent nexus between neoliberal capitalization and historical processes of subjection we run the risk of overlooking, or of covering up, liberal democracy's originary violences and affects and of misrecognizing their traumatic redistribution throughout the contemporary social sphere.

Needless to say, an example of what could be called the neodevelopmentalist critique of development in Central America is in order. This critique will allow us to analyze the foundational affects of civil conflict in El Salvador during the decade of the 1980s and, from there, move into a thought of the contemporary that responds to, and challenges, the logics of contemporary neodevelopmentalism. Thus we will examine the complex and violent nexus between subject formation and capital that underlies and upholds contemporary cross-border flows. First, however, we need to consider the neodevelopmentalist critique of development.

In his 1997 book *Coffee and Power* Jeffrey Paige assures us, through his reading of Barrington Moore, that " 'a revolutionary break with the past' is necessary for the development of democracy" (335). "Of all the Latin American countries currently involved in transitions to democracy," Paige observes, "only Costa Rica, El Salvador, Nicaragua, and possibly Mexico have made such a revolutionary break with the past" (335). In Paige's formulation El Salvador's revolutionary break with the past—its move away from armed conflict and toward market-based liberal democracy—is the direct result of what he calls the agency of "socialist revolution from below" and of the nation's institutional transformations implemented as the result of the Chapultepec Peace Accords of 1992. Thus, he states, "in some respects, . . . the conditions for the consolidation of democratic rule . . . are actually better in Central America than they are in many democratic 'transitions from above,' in Latin America and elsewhere, where there was no revolutionary break with the past and the institutions of the old regime remain intact. . . . The road to democracy through socialist revolution from below has profoundly changed the political and economic institutions of Central America" (336–37).

This is a strikingly unnuanced evaluation of Salvadoran historical and institutional processes, and a strangely utopic vision of the Salvadoran state's willingness to redefine itself as a result of the revolutionary configuration of the 1980s. Indeed, this is particularly surprising since *Coffee and Power* provides an insightful examination of the development of the Salvadoran conflict and of the passage toward the electoral model. *Coffee and Power* examines the internal wranglings of institutional power and the revolutionary threat by reconstructing the author's interviews with numerous members of the Central American coffee-producing elites and, in the case of El Salvador, of the nation's so-called fourteen families. This analysis of the Salvadoran elite allows Paige to unmesh the intricate circuits of kinship relations within coffee-growing circles and organizations, to untangle their internal and external alliances and political power-mongering during the years of civil war, to analyze the ideological limits to their self-proclaimed legitimacy, and to paint a complex picture of agrarian versus agro-industrialist relations during the course of the nation's civil strife. In turn, this mode of analysis then allows Paige to conclude, in convincing fashion, that the civil war resulted from a crisis in the oligarchic state brought about by increasing leftist activism in the 1970s, the realignment against the oligarchy of certain forces within the post-1968 Salvadoran church, the persistent power and autonomy of the military, the victory of the Sandinista revolution of 1979 in neighboring Nicaragua, and the land reforms of 1979 that promised to disrupt traditional relations of production in the Salvadoran countryside. The war only came to a peaceful close, continues Paige, when certain factions within the coffee elites (the Cristiani dynasty, for example) successfully took over Roberto d'Aubuisson's right-wing nationalist ARENA (Alianza Republicana Nacionalista) party, allied themselves to transnational capital other than that of U.S. military aid, and, in conjunction with the fall of the Berlin Wall and the FMLN's second "general offensive," had the foresight to distance themselves periodically from the increasingly murderous military.

For this faction of the oligarchy, then, prolonged civil strife was, put simply, not good for business. Although the military and some factions within the state elites had been convinced for quite some time that internal social antagonisms required a total war—not just a war of annihilation against an opposing army but a war centered once and for all on the entire population (low-intensity conflict doctrine)—in the end (Paige informs us) business-minded members of the coffee elites were able to forge a tense yet peaceful settlement with the FMLN and to dilute the crippling effects of civil war by incorporating the guerrilla into an electoral configuration. These events both form the backbone of what Paige calls El Salvador's "revolutionary break with the past," and the basic ground for his evaluation of the present as a moment of historical transcendence.

Paige's narrative is praiseworthy as a critical anthropology of the coffee elites in Central America, and it is particularly interesting due to its compositional form. The book's portrayal of the coffee elites' ability to reposition themselves and to reemerge as a hegemonic force at the end of the 1980s remains at all times fixed firmly on center stage. This obviously allows us to penetrate the inner workings of the oligarchy's multiple and very often contradictory articulations. However, both the FMLN and the military in this account remain conspicuously absent as state and anti-state forces, even though the Salvadoran armed forces had retained direct control of the state (with the exception of a few very brief attempts at civil government) since the military coup of 1931, and even though the conflict of the 1980s had been (at least in part) a conflict about the means of transferring power to civilian institutions (or of not doing so). The importance of this is that in spite of Paige's critical anthropology of coffee elites, El Salvador's history and collective experience of violence remains, for all intents and purposes, absent. In this sense *Coffee and Power* is testimony to the fact that "the history of violence is . . . almost always about context—about everything that happens around violence. The violence itself is taken as 'known'. Its contours and character are simply assumed: its forms need no investigation" (Pandey 1).

Indeed the book cannot conceptualize, nor call attention to, the astounding intensities and economies of violence that have perpetuated Salvadoran social relations since the years of the Great Depression. At no point, for example, does *Coffee and Power* provide the means by which to think through the almost unimaginable tension, the equilibrium of forces and of collective affects, by which oppositional camps could render violence so durable, so lasting and intense and so unbearable, while at the same time keep it away from total annihilation.

There is, in this sense, a point at which Paige's valuable reconstruction of the transition to democracy and to market-based capitalism in El Salvador shies away from considering the economy of violence that gave birth to the political realities and epistemological limits that it aspires to uncover. Indeed, *Coffee and Power* leaves us with a series of formulations about democracy's "revolutionary break with the past" that remain enormously problematic, if not profoundly flawed, for our understanding of the contemporary order. If El Salvador's passage from total war to peace and democratization bespeaks the emergence of "socialist revolution from below," working in tense conjunction with the oligarchy's willingness to "break with the past," as Paige suggests, then we face recent history as an almost seamless passage toward what Francis Fukuyama called the "good news" of the last quarter century: that liberal democracy, preceded or followed by a liberal revolution in economic thought, "remains the only coherent political aspiration that spans different regions and cultures around the world" (quoted in Derrida, *Specters* 57). True, the FMLN's ability to sustain the equilibrium of antagonistic forces during the general offensive of 1989 allowed it not just to survive but to force certain sectors of the oligarchy to the negotiating table. But, in hindsight, we have to recognize that this has by no means brought about a revolutionary break with the past. Indeed, it is only by overlooking the agency of the military, the peasantry, and the FMLN, together with the affects that drive the perpetuation and redistribution of social violence in the transition to market-based democracy, that one can claim historical transcendence for El Salvador's democratic present. With this in mind, one can only conjecture as to how Paige's reading of El Salvador's recent history could account for some of the most striking characteristics of contemporary social reality: namely, the astounding persistence and systemic dissemination of fear and loathing throughout El Salvador's national and postnational social configurations (which now include, of course, Los Angeles and Washington, D.C.).

As Philip Williams and Knut Walter demonstrate in their analysis of militarization and demilitarization in El Salvador, the 1992 Peace Accords ultimately failed to address the military's position within the state because the negotiated peace settlement fell seriously short of dismantling the army's network of social control in rural areas and failed to attend to the persistence of its institutional and political autonomy (163). In this sense, the accords did not establish the armed forces' subordination to civilian authorities (169). If this is the case, of course, then

the transition to democracy can hardly be considered to be a revolutionary break with the past instigated by "socialist revolution from below,"
as Paige suggests. Consider the following details: while the civil defense
patrols and the *servicio territorial* were dismantled, after the Peace Accords members of units continued to serve in the military forces' paramilitary network of control in the countryside, gathering intelligence and
intimidating the civilian population (160–61). Meanwhile, Cristiani's
democratic ARENA government continued to appoint military officers
to key positions within the administration as had been the tradition for
decades (164), and the military "continued to be the only state institution not held accountable for its expenditures" (168). In fact, to this day
democratic legislators still do not have access to the details of military
budgets (168). Moreover, the editorial of the July 1993 edition of the *Revista militar* (Military review) demonstrates just how little military atti-
tudes toward the FMLN and its supporters changed during the forging
of negotiated peace, as the editors accuse the Left of actively fomenting
criminal activity, stating that through the accords the FMLN was bringing the military to " 'a new form of war and a new battlefield,' " a new
level of antagonism that raised the question for the armed forces: " 'What
should be the armed forces' battle plan in this new class of war?' " (173).
In July 1993 the Party of National Conciliation nominated General Juan
Rafael Bustillo as its presidential candidate for the 1994 elections, in spite
of the fact that Bustillo had been singled out in a report by the Truth
Commission for his involvement in planning the murder of six Jesuits
and their two aides during the FMLN general offensive of 1989 (173). In
the same month President Cristiani called the army out to patrol national
highways in order to "protect the coffee harvest" (173). During June
through September 1993 the United Nations Observer Mission in El Salvador documented an increase in human rights abuses and other illegal acts, including torture, arbitrary detentions, and executions by the
national police, as well as the assassination and attempted assassination
of several FMLN leaders (175). In 1994 the Joint Group for the Investigation of Politically Motivated Illegal Armed Groups announced that
death squads had branched out into organized crime, while active duty
officers and members of the national police were becoming increasingly
implicated in politically motivated violence and even banditry (180–81).
Finally, and topping what appears to be the perpetual ungovernability
of peace in El Salvador, in 1995 a new death squad, Sombra Negra
(black shadow), began targeting suspected members of L.A. street gangs
who had been deported back to El Salvador after the Los Angeles riots

sparked by the police beating of Rodney King in 1992 (DeCesare, "Children").

All of this leads to the most astounding of national statistics. As Donna DeCesare has noted, according to the Pan-American Health Organization "El Salvador's per capita homicide rate of 150 per 100,000 is the highest in the hemisphere, surpassing even Colombia. This means that violence—if defined by the annual homicide rate, the most commonly cited measure of crime and violence in general—is greater in El Salvador now than during the 1980s, when civil war grabbed international headlines and hundreds of thousands of peasant refugees escaping mayhem and economic collapse sought sanctuary in the crowded slums of Los Angeles" (DeCesare, "Children" 23).[4] The total war of the revolutionary era may have been surpassed, then, but the transition to peace and the collective experience of the liberal democratic order is (potentially) just as terrifying. After all, negotiated peace and democracy seem to reveal themselves as an opening experienced as the peace of impending terror, in which the social sphere that plays host to such a system apparently re-articulates, redistributes, and perpetuates civil war's affects, albeit now by other institutional and structural means.

The question, then, is not how to think of the present as the inscription of development's promise, as the waning of war's affects, or as the historical transcendence of past conflicts (in other words, as Jeffrey Paige presents it, as an institutional break with the past that opens up the way for the reinsertion of El Salvador into the league of emerging markets). The question, rather, is how to construct meaning around the lines of force that still seize, stir up, and govern the formation of national and transnational subjects and of their harrowing being-in-common; how to read the contours of market-based democracy when that order has been constructed on the aftermath of civil war's exterminatory logics.

It appears that we are dealing with a social order that is still governed by an overwhelming surplus of danger and fear, as well as by state practices that now contract out, for private and for democratic gain, what used to be called the state's monopoly of legitimate physical force. In the transition from national antagonism to globalism and liberal democracy we witness the emergence of what goes by the name of social cleansing in other parts of the world. As such, in the privatization of the state's death work, and in the accumulation of the democratic order's new cadavers—the bodies of postideological undesirables such as gays, street kids, beggars, petty thiefs, gang members, garbage dwellers, transvestites, prostitutes, drug addicts, or maquiladora workers suspected by management of talking about organizing—we witness a social order that seems to be anchored in the sustained production and accumulation of the dead, almost as an unpopular "magical harnessing of the dead for stately purpose" (Taussig, "Magic" 3).[5]

There is, of course, nothing new in the harnessing of the dead for the purposes of the state. After all, in the history of modern El Salvador from the 1930s through to the 1980s the state always constructed itself on such a war machine. What *is* new, perhaps, is the way in which the contemporary order has brought about a new war that appears to have emerged as a result of the harrowing tremor in the historical telos of national collective identifications. Needless to say, before thinking through the terms of that harrowing tremor we should examine in further detail the originary violences of neoliberalism's predecessor: that is, the war *for* the nation-state in El Salvador before the fall of the Berlin Wall and before the establishment of neoliberalism's openly violent peacetime.

"Thinking," affirms Benjamin, "involves not only the flow of thoughts, but their arrest as well. Where thinking suddenly stops in a configuration pregnant with tensions, it gives that configuration a shock, by which it crystallizes into a monad. A historical materialist approaches a historical subject only where he encounters it as a monad. In this structure he recognizes the sign of a Messianic cessation of happening, or, put differently, a revolutionary chance in the fight for the oppressed past" ("Theses" 262–63). In the networks of exchange between a novel's publication, the launching of a guerrilla offensive, and a military massacre—between the publication in 1980 of Manlio Argueta's *Un día de vida* (translated in 1991 as *One Day of Life*), its wink from within literary culture to the FMLN's first general offensive, which was about to occur while the novel was being written, and the military massacre of hundreds of peasants in the hamlet of El Mozote in December 1981—we behold the monadic figurations (both literary and real) of a vast horde of dead pressing through Salvadoran history, from the originary violence of the 1932 massacres through to the civil war of the 1980s.

This vast horde of the dead, we might suggest, holds the key to the redistribution of being-in-common in neoliberal El Salvador. For it is in their historical articulation on one another that we witness the contours of a particular historical monad; a singular image of competing subjectivities that testifies both to the incomplete formation of the nation and of the nation-state, as well as to the violent opposition between the statist and antistatist authority and value of the dead for the present. "We were all born half dead in 1932," wrote the Salvadoran poet Roque Dalton in reference to the collective inheritance of the peasant massacres of that year in El Salvador (42). As we will see, the violence of the civil war and its redistribution in the neoliberal order was, and still is, a collective struggle over the terms of that inheritance: a struggle over the atonement or damnation of history's living dead. But in order to understand this verse and the continued collective spectrality of being-in-common in neoliberal El Salvador, we need to examine two cold war parables in further detail: namely, Manlio Argueta's evocation in *One Day of Life* of national popular history and of the potential for social transformation in the days leading up to the emergence of the FMLN between 1979 and 1980; and Mark Danner's *The Massacre at El Mozote,* an outstanding piece of journalistic investigation unearthing the gory details of a military massacre in the Red Zone of Morazán on December 10, 1981, and of Washington's ill-fated cover-up of those events. Examining the conflictive circuits of affect that these two texts embody will then allow us to move into the thought of liberal democracy as civil war by other means.

Argueta's *One Day of Life* is a narrative grounded in the formulation of subaltern affect and in the enhancement of popular power and plenitude through the embodiment—the possible coming into being, the revenant—of the specters of history's living dead. In this sense the novel is about the potential coming into being of collective rapture and about national salvation as the result of the resurrection of the dead body of the politicized peasant as Christ the Savior, "El Salvador." Body of Christ, body of the peasant, and body of the nation; a textual holy trinity of redemption and origin of the essence of revolutionary creation posited as the form-engendering force of the national popular.

The novel itself is based on a divine plan of personal and collective salvation, and it could not be more simple. Taking place during Holy Week and, therefore, firmly grounded in the death and resurrection of "El Salvador," it is a personal account of a day in the life of Lupe, a peasant woman from Chalatenango whose husband, Chepe, toils on the local coffee plantation and avoids sleeping at home because of his political activism and the potential dangers that could befall him. In this sense, the novel is immediately about displacement. However, intertwined with Lupe's apparently simplistic autobiographical narrative—her almost childlike tale recounting everyday experience and the insignificant details of her daily grind, her position within the domestic sphere, her thoughts on her kids, her loving identification with the family puppy, and even her identification with the birds that accompany her in her mundane chores—we enter a complex web of individual and collective relations that slowly begins to reveal the accumulation of dead and mutilated bodies underlying, upholding, and structuring the narrative of this single day.

Lupe's chronological account of twelve hours of daily life in Chalate is introjected with the testimonies of other women. The first of these is by Lupe's daughter, María Pía, who lives in the provincial capital and who is incapable of doing anything about the National Guard's abduction, torture, and murder of her husband, Helio Hernández, whom she has to deny knowing in order to survive. The second testimony is that of fifteen-year-old María Romelia, Lupe's neighbor in Chalate, who witnessed Lupe closing her eyes and walking away from the body of her son, Justino, who was decapitated by the single stroke of a machete and shot seven times in the back by the authorities some three weeks before the opening of Lupe's account. The final testimony is by Adolfina, Lupe's teenage granddaughter (and daughter of María Pía and Helio Hernández), whose political activism takes her from village to provincial capital to national capital and, ultimately, to the military siege of Archbishop Romero's cathedral in a perpetual political nomadism of resistance and clandestine organization. In this work, three generations of female subject formation and agency are thus presented, as well as three distinct forms of positioning oneself within the Salvadoran social sphere, ranging from the grandmother's and the daughter's local denials of kinship to the granddaughter's active mediation between the distinct geographical, generational, and political spaces of the nation.[6]

There appears to be, then, a considerable distance between the way the three generations of women position themselves, and are positioned, within the social. But the apparent distinction and perhaps even contradiction between these forms of belonging within the local/national slowly begin to unravel as, toward the end of the novel, the third and final Christlike denial of *One Day of Life* slowly takes form. At midday members of the military come to Lupe's home looking for Adolfina, who is traveling from Ilobasco to visit her grandmother in Chalate. When Adolfina arrives we witness the final scene of collective recognition and denial around which the whole narrative revolves. A group of soldiers appear with the battered and mutilated remains of a man whom they present to Lupe and Adolfina for identification. Knowing that the sacrificed figure they have before them is Lupe's husband, Chepe, both women, arm in arm and in direct defiance of the guardsmen they have before them, deny knowing him (192–93). And it is only at this point—after the women are obliged for the third time to deny knowing their loved ones—that we see how Chepe's political knowledge "assumes transmissable form at the moment of his death" (Benjamin, "Storyteller" 94), for Lupe begins to draw discursive authority from death, summoning the dead man's language and ideology to the arena of the living in the interests of resurrecting his specter for the redemptive service of the present.[7]

In what amounts to an uncharacteristic critique of the gendered division of labor, the aging peasant grandmother, Lupe, assumes the discursive authority of the husband she had to deny knowing and initiates her own process of self-embodiment, her own entrance into revolutionary consciousness: "You can't expect more from the men. From that point of view we peasant women are slaves, but it is not their fault. At bottom we help produce the wealth of the landowners when we take care of the children by ourselves, because we are also giving men the time to work in peace from sunup to sundown. That is to say, we are giving our time to the landowners so that our husbands can produce more, can be better exploited" (204). This simply does not sound like Lupe. For a moment she appears to be lifted up beyond herself in an almost rapturous evocation of a social bond that seems to suggest a "bodily takeover by the dead" (Taussig, *Magic* 187), a takeover that, through the incorporation of the authority of the dead, allows her to appropriate the discursive and ideological spaces previously reserved exclusively for Chepe and Adolfina. In other words, through Lupe's unexpected critique of the gendered division of labor we see what amounts to a harnessing of the dead for popular purposes in which liberation theology—the resurrection of Christ in the body of the peasant, El Salvador—achieves plenitude.

Indeed, it is only after Lupe's active harnessing of the dead for the redemptive service of the present that the novel's nod toward impending insurrection, toward the embodiment of the peasant as a coming community—and as national redemptive promise—is revealed to us. At 5 P.M., and just three hours after the novel's central recognition scene and denial, Adolfina has a vision of violent atonement:

> You know something, Grandma: all of a sudden I saw the corpse of Private Martínez. I say: "Where child?"
> She tells me: "In my imagination, it came upon me like a revelation. His eyes and his mouth were open, and no matter how much they tried to shut his eyelids, they would open again, and no matter how much they pulled on his big toes, his mouth would not close. Standing around his body, his mother and his sisters were crying. And as they could not close his mouth, they put a lemon in it, so flies would not be able to get in, and so he wouldn't get wormy inside."
> And I tell her: "Oh, child, that's a nightmare!" She tells me: "No, I think it's true, it has to be true."

I tell her: "But that's not possible, how could that be?"
She tells me: "My heart told me, and up to now my heart has never lied to me."
A shiver runs through my body as I light the candles. (214-15)

Adolfina denies that this is a nightmare (and therefore a dreamlike state) and insists that it is the truth of impending insurrection, communicated as an enhancement of force and plenitude and anchored in the intertwining of the peasant body politic—Chepe's mangled corpse—with the image of the suffering body of Christ the Savior/El Salvador. Peasant retribution and redemption intermingle in the collective experience of Christian rapture, and Christian rapture becomes the form-engendering force of insurrection's content. Lupe, meanwhile, lights candles and remains physically and secretly stirred, herself quietly transported and possessed by Adolfina's revelation of a redemptive future. Such is the sacred authority of Chepe's corpse, and such are the magical circuits of affect that inscribe the images of peasant salvation—of the national-popular—in *One Day of Life*. In the end, then, we are faced with the narrativization of an impending insurrection whose violence is arranged around collective martyrdom, sacrifice, and rapture as will-to-power.[8]

The state, on the other hand, had its own death work; its own magical ways of seizing, moving, and of lifting erect bodies beyond themselves and into the performative evocation of stateliness. It had its own violent sacrificial dance that was also anchored in the harnessing of the dead. However, in this case it was no longer a harnessing of the dead carried out for insurrectional purposes but rather for insurrection's violent dismemberment.

Mark Danner's investigation in *The Massacre at El Mozote* exhumes the brutality of cold war logics in El Salvador. In a particular section of the book he speaks of a peculiar rite of passage, a bizarre symbolization of anticommunist manliness that allows us to capture the foundational death work of state-generated affect in the Red Zone of Morazán. Speaking of the elite U.S.-trained Atlacatl Battalion, one of the army's Immediate Response forces (the BIRIs), Danner comments that from the Atlacatl's inception it was revered and feared by both civilians and military alike, because the soldiers of the Atlacatl had what Danner calls a "*mística*—a mystique" (50), a series of rumored animalistic practices that set them apart from the rest:

"They shot animals and smeared the blood all over their faces, they slit open the animal's bellies and drank the blood", a lieutenant in another unit told me. "They were a hell of a raunchy lot. They had no discipline of fire, none at all. I mean, they saw something moving out there, they shot it—deer, pigs, whatever. You'd be out there in the field trying to sleep, and all night those assholes would keep shooting at things". According to one reporter, the men of the Atlacatl celebrated their graduation by collecting all the dead animals they could find off the roads—dogs, vultures, anything—boiling them together into a bloody soup, and chugging it down. Then they stood at rigid attention and sang, full-throated, the unit's theme song, "*Somos guerreros*":

> We are warriors!
> Warriors all!
> We are going forth to kill
> A mountain of terrorists! (50)

"By the fall of 1981," Danner continues, "the Atlacatl was well on the way to building that mountain" (50). Indeed, in the series of operations that came to be called the massacre at El Mozote, the Atlacatl harnessed some 767 deaths for nation-state consumption and continuity (280–304).[9]

So what of this rite of bloody consumption and of the death work of the state; this disseminated rumor of monstrosity that surely attests to subaltern cognition of the position and protagonism of the state in their daily lives? Needless to say, we have before us the performance of the state's internalization and neutralization of the inherently unproductive objects of the Salvadoran countryside: dead dogs, vultures, etc. Moreover, this incorporation of the countryside's unproductive forces into the phallic body of the militarized state is the precondition for a peculiar brand of state-related anthropophagy, in which the persistent presence of the oligarchic state within rural Morazán depended on the continuous passing away of the body of the people. It is in this passing away of the people—in the abject slaughter that inevitably accompanies this rumored ritual—that the blood of the unproductive spews out once again for its definitive consumption by the land. Thus it would appear that through the production of the Atlacatl affect one enters Bataille's evaluation of the ritualistic enchantment of consumption and war as foundational to the workings of the modern state. Through the state's performative ritualism and its direct relation to massacre, the Morazán peasant is interpellated by the state as profoundly unproductive, entirely severed from the circuitry of profitable activity. Indeed, as Bataille puts it, "this separation has the sense of a definitive consumption," for "the victim is a surplus taken from the mass of *useful* wealth. And he can only be withdrawn from it in order to be consumed profitlessly, and therefore utterly destroyed. Once chosen, he is the *accursed share*, destined for violent consumption" (58–59). Quite literally, in the staging of the Atlacatl affect the only good Morazán peasant is a dead one, for this is what saves the state, its dissolute order, and its privileged subjects from absolute ruin.[10]

Of course, neither should we overlook the fact that the Atlacatl affect is an exercise in representational syncretism. Its violent consumption of the bodies of the unproductive uncovers a parody of precolonial indigenous rites of sacrifice, as well as a parody of colonial and national Catholic communion. Indeed, it is probably not by chance that this violent representation of symbolic *mestizaje* should emerge at this particular historical juncture. For this performance of symbolic sacrifice and unholy sacrament is without doubt choreographed (in one way or another) as a response to the state's definition of the cold war as a crusade against the post-1968 communism of Salvadoran Catholicism. In this light we should also note that this ceremonial bloodletting coincides with the emergence of the Pentecostal evangelical churches, which were beginning to challenge the increasing politicization of Catholic liberationist Christianity throughout rural Central America.

If all of the above can be read into the Atlacatl affect, and I would hazard to say that this is the case, then nothing, it seems, escapes the state in the performance of death's harnessing and redistribution. There appears to be no surplus and nothing left out, for the Atlacatl affect's symbolic value is all-encompassing and all-consuming. It is, quite literally, the performance of a "world of bodies gobbling other bodies, swelling with power" (Taussig, *Magic* 72) and finally announcing the ever-threatening body of the subaltern as handed over to the state in a rationale of extermination performed as mystical sacrifice. It is a statist performance, in other words, by which the production and reproduction of the conditions of exploitation are there for all to see, to imagine, or to know as rumor, hearsay, and impending fear.

Through the performances of the Atlacatl affect and of Manlio Argueta's popular Catholic counterpart—narratives that, when placed side by side, attest to the intensity of a war of collective fantasies and, indeed, to the astounding symmetry of affective divisions in the people/power bloc antagonism of the 1980s—we can see how "revolutionary and counter-revolutionary crises condense into a single dramatic sequence of various phenomena that display both the break-up of class representation and the polarization of society into antagonistic camps" (Balibar, "Class" 160). Between rapture and consumption at all costs, and with both orders linked inextricably to the relation between the Catholic embodiment of the revolutionary class struggle and its abject dismemberment, we witness the equilibrium of intensities that maintained itself during the years of civil war in El Salvador. In other words, we see the imagistic foundation of the people/power bloc antagonism's overarching articulation: the magical harnessing of the dead for redemptive Christian/subaltern purpose versus the state's harnessing of the dead for the neutralization of any potentially transformational use of human capital within the national space.

What is to be said, however, of the present? What is to be said of the economies of violence that shed light on the passage from the struggle for state hegemony to the nation's increasing insertion into postnational cultural, economic, and political configurations?

I would suggest that what we witness at present is transnational capital's powerful redistribution of the peoples and places of national space, national patrimony, and of the national-popular. It appears that foundational categories such as national fictive ethnicity and the national-popular have been diluted, at least in part, by thousands of bodies moving northward, en masse, like cross-border floating organs propelled toward new forms of daily experience; toward new circuits and new relays of personal and collective memory, as well as to as-yet unnameable and perhaps-unheard-of forms of cultural and historical embeddedness. Within the recent scenario of massive and generally impoverished migration, the uprooting and displacement of peoples, classes, genders, and ethnicities becomes the essential terrain from which to evaluate the exhaustion of the nation (as the exclusive threshold for collective cultural identifications) and of the nation-state (as the sole horizon for political organization in the present).

As I suggested at the outset of this chapter, the national telos, and its relation to the evaluation of post–civil war and post–cold war El Salvador, is in a state of radical redistribution. The Salvadoran nation-state was never very good at representing itself as an active site of mediation between the interests of the nation/people and the interests of the elites and their relation to outside forces. With transnationalism, this lack of representation is more obvious than ever. The reason for this is that with the post–cold war insertion of peripheral nations (emerging markets) into global chains of production (as well as into the transnationalization of the war on drugs and the control of international terrorism), power is becoming increasingly structured through expansion and extension; that is, through the flattening out of distinct social, cultural, and governmental topographies. While we cannot go so far as to say that we are experiencing the demise of the nation, neither can we ignore the fact that in the new world order the "urban becomes the social in general, and both of them constitute and lose themselves in a global that is not really their opposite either . . . but something like their outer reach, their prolongation into a new kind of infinity" (Jameson, *Seeds* 29).[11]

With such expansive circuits already in motion, any critical insistence on the permanence of national culture as a singular, discrete, and exclusive locus of experience and meaning production tends to resonate now as little more than "sentimental localism" (Jameson, *Seeds* 191); a neoregionalist compensatory desire for cultural identity, difference, and ground, governed ultimately by reactive investments in the visible and tangible policing of national (cultural) frontiers. Having said this, however, transnational circuitries (which we are calling the postnational, for want of a better word) do not signify the end of the history, nor of the actuality, of the nation. Salvadoran mass migration during and after the civil war, for example, might indicate a certain incalculable exhaustion within the idea of the nation, but it does not denote the end of the signifier *El Salvador* nor its definitive demise as a locus of, and target for, popular affects and collective identifications. Indeed, as we will see in the remainder of this chapter and through what is perhaps *the* paradigmatic experience of the contemporary (that is, postnational subaltern migration), the national and even the notion of the national-popular do circulate in spectral fashion as haunting sites of collective experience and as vehicles for sustained affects and identifications. The national and the national-popular, in other words, become ghostly revenants within certain Salvadoran migrant realities.

As such, Salvadoran subaltern migration to the United States since the 1980s reveals the ways in which national culture can now be engaged as much from a location beyond the dividing lines and given borders of the nation as they can from within them. The forced displacement of thousands of rural and urban Salvadoran bodies into less conflictive departments, into refugee camps on the other side of the Honduran border, or, more significantly, into other neighboring countries to the north (including, of course, the ghettos of Washington, D.C., and the spatial grid of MacArthur Park/South Central Los Angeles) redistributed the terrain and topography of Salvadoran experience, commonality, and collective affect forever. As Mario Lungo Uclés states:

> Quite possibly, the 1980s marked the greatest transformation of El
> Salvador's demographic structure in the country's history. The main
> cause of these changes was the war and its attendant consequences
> (many of them not yet documented). The Salvadoran transformation
> is something new. It is not a function of the well-known pattern of migration from the countryside to the city stemming from the penetra-

tion of capitalist production into rural areas and the exhaustion of the agricultural frontier. Nor is it the result of alterations in the age makeup of the population due to changes in health conditions. It involves, instead, a new context—one in which the greatest share of the migrants leave the country. In the meantime, within El Salvador itself, the conditions of war have assured that young people make up most of the seventy thousand killed since 1980. . . . Despite the resettlement programs, the number of internally displaced approached 750,000 by the end of the decade. The Fundación Salvadoreña de Vivienda Mínima (Salvadoran Foundation for Low-Cost Housing) showed that 40 per cent of the urban population was living in San Salvador metropolitan area, where 700,000 people lived in 170 shantytowns, 364 illegal colonies, and 55 camps. Exact data on Salvadoran citizens living in the United States is harder to obtain, since there are no reliable registries. Nevertheless, . . . Segundo Montes states that "despite the suppositions and the limitations of the calculations we have made, it can be sustained that the number of Salvadorans living in the United States is approximately 1,000,000." (102–105)[12]

Within this process of demographic (as well as cultural and political) redistribution, we witness the corporeal and affective movements that, in a bizarre twist of transnational logic, permitted the Salvadoran oligarchic state to ride out the economic ravages of civil conflict in the 1980s, as well as those of its so-called transition to democracy during the 1990s. According to Lungo Uclés, monetary remittances sent by Salvadoran migrants living abroad during the 1980s totaled about \$1.4 billion per year, a capital flow "equal to U.S. aid and the country's total export income combined. The remittances are more than double the latter and almost double the annual national budget. Nothing in Salvadoran history can match this stream of money" (105). "One cannot ignore," he continues, "the levels of distortion, dependency, and vulnerability that this flow brings to the existing structural problems of the national economy" (105). According to Segundo Montes, these monetary remittances made up 47 percent of the total income of the families who received them, thereby creating the paradoxical situation in which the Salvadoran elites were able to maintain an export economy thanks in part to the affective capital remittances of displaced Salvadorans who sustained the economy by providing it with a considerable portion of its foreign currency (cited in Lungo Uclés 106).[13]

In El Salvador, as in so many places, it was the corporeal and capital redistribution of national frontiers—migration's massive extension of bodies and of historically constituted forces and affects—that preceded the emergence of what could be called low-intensity democracy; that is, the new ideological and structural ground for the insertion of El Salvador into a transnational order grounded in the flows of the global marketplace.[14] Obviously, market-based contingency—Derrida's notion of the contemporary structure of social order as the dissemination and intensification of absolute dislocation, of borderless disjoining (*Politics*) —redirects and redistributes collective experiences of impotence and of powerlessness toward the "culture-ideology of consumerism" (Sklair). Furthermore, it does this in order to leave previous collective identities, organizations, and ideologically grounded social positions "nakedly individuated" (Brown 69) by deterritorialization, by contemporary bodily and capital flights, and by the deregulated demands of the informal economy and the maquiladora networks.

Indeed, this has enormous consequences for the post–civil war critique of violence. In the case of El Salvador, perhaps it would not be erroneous to suggest that the conjuring up of liberal democracy after the signing of the Chapultepec Peace Accords has allowed for the redistribution, extension, and expansion of deregulated and privatized social violence as a peculiarly powerful method of holding in check, controlling, or of simply exterminating the phantom subjectivities of the contemporary order. After all, and as I noted in the opening pages of this chapter, violence in recent years is now directed in increasing intensity toward peripheral group subjectivities that are no longer identified exclusively with a particular ideology or with a transformational or potentially threatening vision of the future. Rather, violence is directed increasingly toward those subjectivities identified by the market (and by its privatized and deregulated representatives, such as countless collectives of small business owners who band together to carry out the market's death work for it) as unproductive groups of bodies whose mere visibility in the streets attests to the ungovernability of the social sphere. Society's death work, in other words, is no longer channeled and directed exclusively toward ideology and the counterhegemonic threat of social transformation (which is not to say, of course, that such a death work is not in itself ideological). It is now displaced toward, and circulated among, those subjects who are most ostensibly dominated not only by global configurations of political and economic powers but by the problematic of post–cold war history itself; in other words, by "the late modern rupture of history as a narrative, history as ended because it has lost its end" (Brown 71).

As such, the contemporary appears to reveal the experience of subalternity as continual exposure to a war without ends or end. As Wendy

Brown puts it, in this experience "the extent to which 'the tradition of all the dead generations weighs like a nightmare on the brain of the living' is today unparalleled, even as history disintegrates as a coherent category or practice" (71). "We know ourselves to be saturated with history," she continues, "we feel the extraordinary force of its determinations; we are also steeped in a discourse of its insignificance, and, above all, we know that history will no longer (always already did not) act as our redeemer" (71). With this in mind, what does war without ends or end actually look like? What is its contemporary transnational design?

I would suggest that the visible architecture of the present as war without ends or end can best be seen through the migratory lines of flight that animate the new transnational El Salvador and its hitherto unmapped topographies. But we cannot reflect on such a cartography, nor on the present as a harrowing tremor in the structure and experience of belonging, nor on the transition from national civil war to liberal democracy and globalism, without taking into consideration the astounding militarization of life in recent years, and without considering the U.S.-Mexico border as paradigmatic of the proliferation (in the years leading up to and following the fall of the Berlin Wall) of low-intensity policies that have been designed in order to effect social control over targeted populations and their movements. My discussion of the architecture of the present as war without ends or end will lead toward further reflection on subaltern agency—on the subaltern knowledge of insurgency—and on the particular nexus between capitalization and the forms of subject formation that structure North/South articulations between El Salvador and South Central Los Angeles.

In *The Militarization of the U.S.-Mexico Border, 1978–1992* Timothy Dunn traces the process by which the Pentagon's cold war policy of low-intensity conflict affected the border adjoining the United States and the Third World. As Dunn notes in his analysis:

> Counterinsurgency doctrine was originally formulated in the early 1960s by the Kennedy administration as a rather panicked response to the growth and success of revolutionary guerrilla insurgencies around the world—especially the Cuban Revolution of 1959. The principal threat of these movements, as perceived by U.S. policymakers through their Cold War interpretive framework—was their role in the world-wide spread of communism. Counterinsurgency doctrine was constructed to have a distinctly internal focus—meaning that military and security forces came to view the *enemy within* the nation (e.g., internal subversives) as a grave threat to "national security" (broadly defined)—rather than the more traditional military focus on defense

against external threats (e.g., foreign armies). As a result, domestic civilian populations rather than geographic territory became the contested ground, as it were. This approach entailed the development of elaborate internal-security infrastructures to conduct surveillance and coercive strike operations. While theoretically designed to be used selectively, these measures often led to widespread repression and human rights abuses, including, in a disturbing number of cases, "death squads"—the ultimate means of securing social control. (22–23)

Dunn's account is a detailed examination of escalating low-intensity policies—what U.S. Army Colonel John D. Waghelstein, a commander of the U.S. military mission in El Salvador during the 1980s, called "total war at the grass-roots level" (quoted in Dunn 24)—throughout the Carter, Reagan, Bush, and Clinton administrations. But, more important, it is the account of low-intensity conflict's domestication and increasing extension and expansion into the everyday realities of contemporary migratory flows and state (re)formation in the United States (and, of course, beyond). For example, the insertion of counterinsurgency logics into U.S. domestic politics can account for the fact that in 1984 (the height of the Central American conflicts, of course) Ronald Reagan signed a National Security Decision Directive that in 1987 resulted in a U.S. cabinet-level task force on terrorism devising the following profile of, and blueprint for, the U.S. state's identification of potential foreign terrorists: "Fully 60 percent of the Third World's population is under 20 years of age; half are 15 or less. These population pressures create a volatile mixture of youthful aspirations that when coupled with economic and political frustrations help form a large pool of potential terrorists" (26). But this oversimplified globalization of youthful aspirations and terrorism is by no means a phenomenon exclusive to Reaganism and to the years of the Central American civil conflicts. Neither is it a phenomenon exclusive to the state's control of the U.S.-Mexico border. After all, according to California Legislature and State Penal Code no. 186.22—itself a response to the advent of the profoundly ethnicized transnational war on drugs—membership in a street gang in California now falls under the auspices of the "California *Street Terrorism* Enforcement and Prevention Act" (emphasis mine). In this legislation a gang is loosely defined as "any ongoing organization, association, or group of 3 or more persons, whether formal or informal . . . which has a common name or common identifying sign or symbol, whose members individually or collectively engage in or have engaged in a pattern of criminal gang activity" (Statutory Framework, Penal Code 186.22 [1]).[15] Thus the low-

The Other Side of the Popular

intensity militarization of the border over the last twenty years—which is now accompanied by border patrol strongarm performances such as San Diego's Operation Gatekeeper in 1994, the construction of new border walls, further plans for triple-layer fence barriers (Dunn 174), and a dramatic increase in human rights abuses—has far wider social ramifications. Obviously, examples of these ramifications include the landslide passage of Proposition 187 in California (which tried to enlist health care workers, teachers, and social service agencies in reporting the presence of undocumented workers [Nagengast 40]), the 1995 repeal of affirmative action in the University of California system (rescinded in 2001), the continuing erosion of the boundary between architecture and law enforcement in downtown Los Angeles (Davis, *Ecology* 366), and the simple fact that during the early 1990s, "while California's colleges and universities were shedding 8,000 jobs, the Department of Corrections hired 26,000 new employees to guard 112,000 new inmates. As a result California is now the proud owner of the third largest penal system in the world (after China and the United States as a whole)" (416).

California's intensifying siege mentality—the state's increasingly "reckless gulagism" (416), which is ultimately designed to keep out that 60 percent of the Third World's population under twenty years of age, or, if not out, at least under bodily control—has given rise to what José David Saldívar has called "our home-grown *intifada*" (129); a war without ends or end in Los Angeles in which law enforcement becomes increasingly "retrenched behind the supervision of security macro-systems (maintenance of major crime data bases, aerial surveillance, jail systems, paramilitary responses to terrorism and street insurgency)" (Davis, *City* 251), while the redistribution of downtown space after the Watts riots of 1965 becomes increasingly "programmed to ensure a seamless continuum of middle-class work, consumption and recreation, without unwonted exposure to Downtown's working-class street environments" (231).[16]

As part of the state's multifrontal (almost metastasizing) counterinsurgency against ethnic poverty and the poor in Los Angeles, in the late 1980s the Los Angeles police department's CRASH (Community Resources Against Street Hoodlums) program launched an offensive in the MacArthur Park district to destroy the Salvadoran Mara Salvatrucha street gang. "As the leader of the INS agents explained," states Davis, "gang *membership*, not necessarily criminal activity, was the qualification for deportation. 'If a gang member is out on the street and the police can't make a charge, we will go out and deport them for being here illegally if they fit that criterion.' Fifty-six of the 175 youth deported were returned to El Salvador, to uncertain fates at the hands of the military and death squads" (Davis, *City* 287). Indeed, as Timothy Dunn informs us, during the Los Angeles riots in 1992 some four hundred border patrol agents, part of a contingent of one thousand federal law enforcement agents sent to Los Angeles to help the military and police to restore order, were deployed alongside local police in Latino immigrant barrios located in or near the riot zone, arresting some one thousand undocumented immigrants who were then turned over to the INS for deportation, even though most were never formally charged with riot-related criminal activities (168).[17] Meanwhile, however, the privatization and increasing militarization of public space provided a different experience of the riots in Bunker Hill, for the physical boundaries and architectural partitions that guarantee the continued separation of corporate capital from the ethnic neighborhoods—the insulation and segregation of white-collar workers from the old downtown—only proved to expand future business opportunities:

> The 1992 riots vindicated the foresight of Fortress Downtown's designers. While windows were being smashed throughout the old business district, Bunker Hill lived up to its name. By flicking a few switches on their command consoles, the security staffs of the great bank towers were able to cut off all access to their expensive real estate. Bullet-proof steel doors rolled down over street-level entrances, escalators instantly froze, and electronic locks sealed off pedestrian passageways. As the *Los Angeles Business Journal* pointed out, the riot-tested success of corporate Downtown's defenses has only stimulated demand for new and higher levels of physical security. (Davis, *Ecology* 366)[18]

At this point the question is how can we evaluate what "can no longer be exclusively located within the border-patrolled boundaries of the nation-state" (Saldívar 128)? In other words, how can we conceptualize the new symbolic mediations and experiential flows that ground the contemporary order and the border-crossing stories that it tells itself about itself? Indeed, what can we do with the question of the subaltern cognition of the contemporary when thought—subaltern and nonsubaltern—is increasingly determined by the displacement of the nation-state's foundational and predominantly developmentalist myths, and confronted by transnational forms of control that range from migration and social cleansing to the architectural *intifadas* of contemporary post-urban experience? In other words, how can we keep the notion of commonality alive from within the expansive logics of the society of low-intensity democracy and control?

Perhaps nobody has expressed more succinctly, and more symptomatically, what it means to experience Salvadoran postnational history—this harrowing tremor in the structure and experience of historical belonging—than Mirna Solórzano. She is "a 22-year old single mother of three" (DeCesare, "Children" 27) living in South Central Los Angeles, as well as an active member of the notorious Eighteenth Street gang that, thanks to the gulagism of contemporary transnational circuits and deportation flows, is now organized not just in South Central but throughout El Salvador (and Mexico D.F.) as well. Reflecting on her traumatic inheritance as the daughter of deterritorialized Salvadoran exrevolutionaries, Solórzano evokes the historical (dis)continuity of postnational subaltern agency in the following disturbing, yet thought-provoking, part-narrative: "The way I see it, it's all the same thing. If you're from the FMLN you're hard core. You fight for your country, program, whatever. That's how gangstas are. If somebody disrespects our neighborhood we throw down, we fight" (27).[19]

Such a statement upholds, yet challenges, the notion of historical continuity. It also seems to suggest a traumatic shift in the orders of collective identification and affect wrought by transnational capital and its cross-border flows. As such, this fragment-*testimonio* can only be the grounds for further reflection. However, it probably will not be the grounds for answers, conclusions, and resolutions, for it merely exposes analysis to what appears to be the provisionality of any possible interpretation.[20]

Los Angeles's Salvadoran gangstas as the FMLN of the postnational and postideological present! Surely one is left wondering how such a border-crossing conviction—such transnational subaltern common sense—can be processed and articulated for meaningful reflection rather than suppressed and silenced once again in orderly fashion. Perhaps we would do well to take into consideration Pierre Bourdieu's notion of habitus as a means of continuing reflection on this radical subaltern *frontera* experience (the subaltern experiential architecture, let's say) of contemporary liberal democracy.

In *The Logic of Practice* Bourdieu presents the notion of habitus in the following terms:

> The conditionings associated with a particular class of conditions of existence produce *habitus,* systems of durable, transposable dispositions, structured structures predisposed to function as structur-

ing structures. . . . The *habitus,* a product of history, produces individual and collective practices—more history—in accordance with the
schemes generated by history. It ensures the active presence of past experiences, which, deposited in each organism in the form of schemes
of perception, thought and action, tend to guarantee the "correct-
ness" of practices and their constancy over time, more reliably than
all formal rules and explicit norms. . . . The *habitus,* embodied history, internalized as a second nature and so forgotten as history—is
the active presence of the whole past of which it is the product . . . and
so ensures the permanence in change that makes the individual agent
a world within the world. (53–56)[21]

Through the notion of habitus, then, we can insert an economy of
production—and of life—into what neoliberal logics would surely call
a profoundly useless and nonproductive part-narrative. If Mirna Solórzano's arc of memory (or at least her representation of an arc of memory,
South Central/El Salvador) provides us with an example of what it means
to think from within the seismic event that Derrida has called the time
of mutation—the present as a harrowing tremor in the structure and experience of belonging—then this particular subaltern experience comes
to us structured by a tremor in previous forms of cultural embedded-
ness and of historical sedimentation. The end of a history begins (the
exhaustion of the FMLN in its relation to the construction of a revolutionary Salvadoran national popular), yet remains alive in intermittent
and ghostly fashion (through the spectral revenant of the FMLN in Los
Angeles's Eighteenth Street). As such, the contemporary experience of
location as dislocation appears to reveal the haunting experience of belonging as spectral otherness.[22] If this is the case, then the ritual repetition
of gang violence—its "rigid, stereotypic, conventional, conservative, in-
variant, uniform, redundant, predictable, and structurally static" character (Margaret Thompson Drewal, quoted in Roach 29)—can be understood as a form of mnemonic reserve; as a displaced transmission and
adaptation of historic practices to changing conditions in which "popular behaviors are resituated in new locales" (28).

Needless to say, the gang member's conscious displacement of historical social agency—the perhaps spectral presence of the FMLN in
Solórzano's South Central formulation—demands that we consider the
continuity of thought and of subject position to be both necessary and
yet, perhaps, impossible. For while it might be tempting, and probably very easy, to draw a clear line of demarcation between the popular
struggles in El Salvador of the last fifty years and the often ritualistic or
merely self-serving violence of South Central Los Angeles, we cannot

The Other Side of the Popular

deny that through a ruse of life and of reason the FMLN has stayed alive (whether it wants to or not), firmly welded into the experience of Mirna Solórzano as an economy of life that conserves, circulates, produces, and reproduces meaning both locally and (now that the Eighteenth Street is in El Salvador and Mexico D.F.) perhaps transnationally.

With this economy of life in mind, it scarcely befits us to uphold the realm of the nonproductive or to content ourselves with the subject position of the subaltern as one of a negativity without reserve (as an abjection beyond all relationality and knowability). For to do this is merely to uphold the Salvadoran poor in Los Angeles as the absolute renunciation of social and/or historical meaning, and therefore to position them within thought as a negativity that could never take place.

In contrast, by refusing to draw a clear line of demarcation between so-called productive and nonproductive agencies—between, for example, Solórzano and the ways in which some of El Salvador's repopulated communities have succeeded in challenging traditional economic assumptions and structures through popular democratization, local control of scarce resources, and collective efforts to build social and physical infrastructure alongside forms of community governance—perhaps we can begin to gain a far more complex insight into the experiential grids of patterned representation that inscribe and reproduce Salvadoran subalternity in the first place.[23] After all, in Solórzano's fleeting formulation the L.A. gang member—perhaps *the* ethnicized U.S. criminal par excellence—appears as none other than the repopulated Morazán-FMLN community in a different modality, in its otherness.

Obviously a part-narrative such as this—which, at first sight, appears to be little more than a performative contradiction stating something like "we're the FMLN because we're not the FMLN"—denotes a paradoxical, aporetic, impossible manner of reflecting on transformational agency, communal belonging, historical continuity, and individual and collective location. After all, it merely appears to testify to the presence of misguided or misplaced fantasies acted out as a result of migration and the shifts in collective identification and affect that accompany this phenomenon. Perhaps.

In one way or another we are reading the fragmented leftovers of the prolonged effects of civil war, of the end of the cold war, and perhaps even the effects of a transnational order of democracy defined in exclusively institutional terms as the selection of leaders through competitive elections (Samuel Huntington, quoted in Robinson 50). If this is the case, then Solórzano and her fellow gang members are, at least in part, the cultural effect of "political power deposited in a democratic state through which classes and groups may withdraw or utilize their share of power in accordance with their resources and their organizational capacity," but in which "the distribution of material resources is determined [purely] in the socio-economic sphere, and the particular distribution [determines] the relative strength of groups and group access to political power" (Robinson 53). This, of course, might be the case, but can subaltern fragments be taken so far? Have I taken this one far enough?

Low-intensity democracy affords us a certain insight into the domains of organized power that haunt Solórzano's dislocated account of historical continuity. Her location—her position as a Salvadoran gang member in South Central Los Angeles—challenges the notion that low-intensity forms of governmentality still process and dilute social antagonisms in order to anchor and guarantee the fabrication of hegemony. Indeed, perhaps her border-straddling subject position could be taken to be the embodiment of the postnational order's inability (or lack of desire) to universalize particularities and to uphold the notion of consensus. For this is a discourse that must be read as emerging from within the breakdown of institutional administration, organized power, neoliberal governmentality, and hegemony. Having said this, however, neither does Solórzano's discourse fall resoundingly on the side of the notion of popular will, of counterhegemony, or of transformational negativity. She merely marks, experiences, and constantly re-presents the limit of both hegemony and of counterhegemony—the limit to the idea of an intensifying antagonism between symmetric forces—for her cross-border identification appears to indicate the outer limit to hegemonic rationales and signifying processes.

On the one hand, then, Solórzano's migratory discourse appears to indicate the absolute disorientation and discontinuity of the national-popular hegemonic articulation that made its mark during the revolutionary configuration of the 1980s in El Salvador. As such, it signifies the eclipse of the revolutionary subject and, therefore, represents a part-genealogy of what appears to be no more. Yet, on the other hand, and as Allen Feldman informs us in his treatment of political violence and its redistribution throughout the social sphere in Northern Ireland, in oral accounts that organize themselves around allegories of real or symbolic genocide—and Solórzano's account is surely the symbolic effect of such violence—the dead always come back to haunt the living (and the ways they live) as uncanny mirror images of each other. And they do this almost in an attempt to reverse, or at least to control, the grounds of social upheaval:

The Other Side of the Popular

The genealogy of the dead is a direct inversion of the positivities of kinship and residence. . . . The production of ethnicity is partially grounded in the mnemonic recitation. Social reproduction becomes organized around an absence: one's own dead and the dead of the other side. This doubled chain of corpses forms temporal and spatial magnets that sublate and redirect the social relations of the living. The lineage of the dead and the sociation of the living—exist side by side as mirror images of each other. The synchrony of the two social orders is a tensioned trope of the immanent inversion of the living by violence, past and present. (66)

Indeed, in Solórzano's part-narrative perhaps we can imagine precisely this: that the lineage of the absent (the FMLN) and the subjectivation of the living (the Eighteenth Street gang) exist side by side as mirror images of each other. If this is the case then her account inscribes the folding back onto itself of the dead (the FMLN's and the gang's) in the form of the promise of continuity between past counterhegemonic articulations and the present. At any point, and at any moment, the dead of the gang could add themselves to, and become equal to, the dead of the FMLN, through an immanent inversion of the living by violence. In this sense, it could be said that Solórzano presents us with a part-narrative— a fragment perhaps of a wider but silent genealogy of the dead—that organizes the individual and collective historical experience of political violence, and the historical rift of deterritorialization, into a localized narrative capable of underscoring and upholding the overarching possibility of insurrectional continuity, and perhaps even of transformation. But, once again, can reflection and the fragments it strives to think about be carried this far? Are the terms of the discussion excessive? Insufficient?

Of course, when confronted by this gang member discourse on Salvadoran inheritance—this collective genealogy of post–civil war disorientation and discontinuity but also of the paradoxical unfolding of discontinuity's spectral otherness—we cannot position ourselves on either one side of the *frontera* between the cognitive instability of Solórzano's formulation and the promise of the future that it implicitly upholds. To do so would be to overlook the way in which subaltern location—this postnational habitus located in dislocation—disjoints the idea and experience of social and historical order by interrupting order's structures of signification. Thus, to fall on the side of resolution—and state here and now that what she says and how she positions herself makes perfect sense or that it signifies nothing more than an absolute loss of meaning, abstract negativity—to come down on either one side of this interface is to refuse to confront the risk of instability in one's own thought. It would be to fall immediately into programmatic thought, into causality, and, ultimately, into just another discourse upholding the history of development, of ethnicized and gendered underdevelopment, and of identitarian essentialism.

In other words, if we are going to think of Solórzano's account as symptomatic of a postnational subaltern habitus—or, for that matter, if we are going to think through any fragmentary account of subaltern migratory experience in neoliberal times—we cannot do so by sidestepping the tension between the simultaneous inconsistency and the spectral promise that orients her analysis of history. Perhaps it is not by chance that she represents what some might consider to be the radical disjuncture between past and present experiences and subject positions by actively folding them into each other: "The way I see it, it's all the same thing," she says, "if you're from the FMLN you're hardcore . . . that's how gangsta's are." Is this not a sublimation of Salvadoran popular agency— of the promise of the national-popular as revolutionary force—that preserves and maintains what is sublated, allows its agency to survive in spectral form, and maintains its promise no matter how paradoxical it may appear? Perhaps.[24]

The problem, of course, is that there is apparently no resolution for, or from, Solórzano's words, because they are profoundly unstable and unreliable in their evocation of agency, location, and continuity. Having said this, however, we have to wonder whether the lack of resolution—the apparent inconsistency of her border-straddling formulation—is perhaps something more than the reproduction of mere indetermination or of an underlying subaltern nonknowledge (what the state or disciplinary authority might call ignorance). For it is very possible that her apparent refusal of resolution itself "supposes a certain type of resolution and a singular exposition at the crossroads of chance and necessity" (Derrida, *Politics* 29–30). It might be a *frontera*-straddling maneuver designed to consist in not consisting, to consist in eluding consistency and constancy and therefore to consist in destabilizing any concept of truth that might be associated with, or imposed on, her and her *vato* (homie) commonality. On the limit between the ideological and the postideological, between El Salvador and Los Angeles, between civil war and liberal democracy, between the struggle for hegemony and hard-core negativity (but without pertaining anymore to a history of counterhegemony), her posthegemonic part-narrative remains, as Derrida would put it, "as undecidable—and therefore as decisive—as the future itself" (29).

If this is the case then Solórzano's dislocated and perhaps paradoxical manner of representing agency, memory, belonging, place, and con-

The Other Side of the Popular

tinuity opens us up necessarily to the risk of instability in the production of knowledge itself. But it also opens us up to the question and to the threshold of the possible, because it is only by maintaining the notion of possibility—and, ultimately, of the Benjaminian notion of the messianic—within her apparently impossible formulation that we can begin to imagine the distant, and as yet unnameable, stirrings of possibilization. Meanwhile, however, it is only by calling attention to, demanding, and disseminating subaltern instability into the production and institutional reproduction of knowledge (thereby destabilizing the border-patrolled boundaries and epistemological *fronteras* of late capitalism's liberal democratic truths and so-called consistencies) that we can consider the possibility of upholding and of advancing the domains of intellectual necessity and responsibility. Perhaps.

But, in the end, what do our violent lines of exchange—the multiple conceptual border circuits and fragments that form the disembodied corpus of this chapter—actually leave us with? Needless to say, the question of what remains to us demands a final reflection on the experience of postnational belonging and on the political thought that might be glimpsed through its spatial organization. It remains to be seen, however, whether subaltern studies (or any other form of critical engagement at this time) has the language to answer in satisfactory fashion the question of what remains to us, and embedded for us, within the topographic-ideological boundaries of postnational subaltern deterritorialization. After all, if political culture is engendered and represented through prescribed forms and "available and recombinant grids of depiction" (Feldman 36), then it appears that the violent post–civil war contours of the El Salvador/South Central interface hardly suggest the emergence of a specific political culture.

Rather, the interface appears to uphold the ghostly myths and agencies of nationhood and of the nation-state while simultaneously interrupting, redistributing, and recirculating what it upholds. In other words, the interface kills original practices and agencies, yet, through displaced transmission, intermittent signals, transpositions, and electrified affective shocks of borderland experience, manages to keep the dead body of collective agencies alive. Having said this, however, it is also the shifting terrain of transnationalism that upholds contemporary experience and thought as the fragmented effect of war without ends or end; as the result of an accumulation of differential intensities and "homegrown *intifadas*" that follow "much more a pattern *à la* Hobbes, in which there is a 'war' of each against each, than a Marxian-Hegelian pattern of growing antagonism between symmetric forces" (Balibar, "Ambiguous" 51).

Within such political, social, and cultural horizons, then, subaltern studies hesitates before its injunction to grapple with the meaning and intelligibility of, say, commonality when the world is no longer structured by rival powers—by competing universalizing drives—struggling to incorporate external national arenas into the limits and inner workings of their core domination. Rather, the world is now structured around "the scattered meaning of the universal" (49), around global capital's ability to penetrate peripheral states through diverse direct and indirect means, to incorporate multiple modalities, to multiply centers, to transform peripheries constantly, and to form transnational networks (NAFTA, Mercosur, EEC, etc.) that are designed to transcend, displace, and redistribute the logics underlining the previously fixed topographies of peripheral national/local experience. Thought hesitates before the counterinsurgency logics of a social organization in which the undeclared enemies are those members of an emergent but scattered universal: the migratory and informal sectors, political and economic refugees, nonnormative deviants, and ethnicized criminals.

With this in mind, what do the border-straddling circuits of the present do to the notion of commonality after the eclipse of the national-popular and the demise of national fictive ethnicity? The response to this question is both very simple and enormously problematic: in postnational times there is no single ground from which to contemplate, or even to imagine, an original or origin of commonality. And since there is no single ground or unique telos from which to contemplate commonality, there is no single horizon from and toward which to think of identity and difference. In other words, there is no definitive revelation or relation of immanence to be found in postnational commonality.

Mirna Solórzano's South Central knowledge attests, perhaps, to the notion that the days of a Salvadoran national unity construed around the sacred closure and hypostasis of the Catholic national-popular are over as such. But, of course, this does not signify the demise of being-in-common. For even though transnationalization eclipses the potentially absolutist character of categories such as identity and difference, it also appears to set in their place the somewhat shadier notion of like-being. Indeed, it appears to be like-being (rather than identity or difference) that structures and upholds Mirna Solórzano's reading of historical transnational violence and everyday life in the Latino barrios of the North: "If you're from the FMLN you're hard core. You fight for your country, program, whatever. That's how gangstas are."

It is neither identity nor difference, then, but the very breakdown of such formulas in the face of this hybrid grid of border-crossing ex-

The Other Side of the Popular

change. The El Salvador/South Central interface circulates subjectivity and innumerable othernesses with such rapidity and force that identity and difference falter inevitably before the radical undecidability of hybrid like-being. Moreover, through like-being we stumble upon the affective, corporeal, and post-ontological borderlands of collective identity/difference's other side: namely, opaque resemblance, open exposure, and actively unprogrammatic contagion. It seems, then, that along the interfaces of the postnational there can be no original nor origin of political identity and no common place for difference. As such, the origin of being-in-common in the transnational order is nothing more than the death work of immanence and communion; the constant finitude and contagion that occurs along the endless circuits of individual and collective *frontera* experience. It is in this sense that in like-being "we are alike because each one is exposed to the outside that *we* are *for ourselves.* The like is not the same. I do not rediscover *myself,* nor do I recognize *myself* in the other: I experience the other's alterity, or I experience alterity in the other together with the alteration that 'in me' sets my singularity outside me and infinitely delimits it" (Nancy, *Inoperative* 33–34).

It is through the like-being that emerges from collective exposure to the outside that we glimpse the intimations of a scattered (and therefore fragmented and fragmentary) universal being-in-common, which is nevertheless "always already beyond any simple or absolute unity," and "therefore a source of conflicts forever" (Balibar, "Ambiguous" 72). Like-being signals the postnational as the revelation of a contingency at which reflection on politics both stops and begins; an aporetic and abyssal ground, in other words, that opens up politics simultaneously to undecidability and (perhaps) to savage possibility.[25]

Postnational being-in-common—neoliberalism understood as the harrowing tremor in the structure and experience of belonging—is the active unworking of the notion of commonality and of common place as sanctuaries of individual and collective identitarian affirmation. Mirna Solórzano's subject position and part-narrative of life on the El Salvador/South Central interface signals (indeed, *is*) an active labor of interruption in the orders of fusion and communion that have grounded the mirages of national-populist hegemony, thought, identity, and critical practice for decades. It is the effect of a historical process of becoming outside to hegemony. Indeed, it is this very process that destabilizes the signifying processes of hegemonic thought, politics, and culture (my own, of course, included).

Having said this, however, the cognitive instability of Solórzano's part-narrative does not denote the closure, nor the suspension, of commonality's history. Rather, it denotes a subject position and a fragment of subaltern knowledge that attests to "an absolute solitude, . . . an extremely populous solitude, like the desert itself, a solitude already intertwined with a people to come, one that invokes and awaits that people, existing only through it, though it is not yet here" (Deleuze and Guattari, *Thousand* 377).[26] From within South Central, Solórzano turns commonality toward a ghostly outside—toward a spectral FMLN—rather than directing commonality toward an internal gathering of forces around the hegemonic configurations of a transcendent and abstract community or nation-state, even though she herself is simultaneously part of the history of such processes and configurations. Is she alone in this maneuver?

Solórzano does not provide us with an answer, nor with a methodological formulation for challenging the hegemonic articulations of capital. She places South Central thought in a relation of immediacy with the outside (El Salvador) and provides us with a vision of contemporary postnational experience that succumbs to no method and to no conceivable reproduction, only to "relays, intermezzos, resurgences" (Deleuze and Guattari, *Thousand* 377). Indeed, it is precisely because Solórzano remains unrecuperable in her state of exposure that she has to be taken seriously as an affirmation, rather than discarded or denounced in the name of a more intelligible, realist, material, or even aesthetic program of reflection or of social change. For what she exposes is the fact that in her part-testimony there is no room for statist common sense, and perhaps therefore no register from which to construct consensus. After all, she posits a form of worlding and a realm of reflection that remains on the outskirts of such formalities as identity and difference or of hegemony and counterhegemony thinking. Her language, in other words, is itself the embodiment of the *frontera:* a spectral and violent world replete with the promise of a savage and postpopulist vox populi.

In the final analysis (and, of course, there is no such thing) the fragment knowledge of Mirna Solórzano reveals and embodies the performative violence of commonality as it emerges along the interface between hegemony and counterhegemony's other side. She signals a contact, a contagion, "a touching, the transmission of a trembling at the edge of being, the communication of a passion that makes us fellows, or the communication of the passion to be fellows, to be *in* common" (Nancy, *Inoperative* 1991, 61). And surely her linguistic transmission of cognitive trembling—her active self-insertion into, and communication of, the harrowing tremor in the structure, experience, and language of postnational belonging—promises, embodies, and disseminates the

The Other Side of the Popular

eclipse of both the grounds of popular incorporation and the desires of disciplined institutional reflection.

In short, it is the intensified dispersal of this ground that makes sub-alternist thought hesitate (necessarily) before the transurban interfaces of market-based control. However, it is also this very same realm of ex-tension, control, and hybrid transmission—this "zone of occult insta-bility where the people dwell" (Fanon 182)—that brings us to a thresh-old of promise, to a nonpopulist fragment from which to reflect on, and perhaps from which to affirm, the nomadic savagery of subaltern insur-rectional commonality . . . perhaps. . . .

6

Of Pishtacos *and Eye-Snatchers*

Neoliberalism and Neoindigenism

in Contemporary Peru

> The bourgeoisie, by the rapid improvement of all instruments of
> production, by the immensely facilitated means of communication,
> draws all, even the most barbarian, nations into civilization. . . . It
> compels all nations, on pain of extinction, to adopt the bourgeois
> mode of production; it compels them to introduce what it calls
> civilization into their midst, i.e., to become bourgeois themselves. In
> a word, it creates a world after its own image. — Karl Marx and
> Friedrich Engels, *The Manifesto of the Communist Party*

> There are no doubt many bad things about our era, but there is one
> very good one, without precedent in history. Countries today can
> *choose* to be prosperous. . . . The internationalization of modern life —
> of markets, of technology, of capital — permits any country, even the
> smallest one with the fewest resources, if it opens out to the world and
> organizes its economy on a competitive basis, to achieve rapid growth.
> — Mario Vargas Llosa, *A Fish in the Water*

> Every white man is, more or less, a Pizarro, a Valverde, or an Areche.
> — Manuel González Prada, "Nuestros indios"; translation mine

By examining the underlying dynamics of the Salvadoran people/power
bloc antagonism of the 1980s, the expansion of the North's security and
economic agendas, and the nomadic cultural identifications that result
from migrant displacement, the previous chapter analyzed the logics of
a transnational "war without ends or end" that appears to be extend-
ing itself in increasing intensity from North to South and back again. In
the current restructuring of the nation and of its national frontiers we

seem to be able to glimpse the mechanisms and calculations of a war machine that appears to anchor itself in the sustained peace of violence and deterrence. In this regard Gilles Deleuze and Félix Guattari note the following:

> This war machine is terrifying not as a function of a possible war that it promises us, as by blackmail, but, on the contrary, as a function of the real, very special kind of peace it promotes and has already installed; . . . this war machine no longer needs a qualified enemy but, in conformity with the requirements of the axiomatic, operates against the "unspecified enemy", domestic or foreign (an individual, group, class, people, event, world); . . . there arose from this a new conception of security as materialized war, as organized insecurity or molecularized, distributed, programmed catastrophe. (*Thousand* 467)

With my examination of the dispersal and redistribution of national antagonisms, in the previous chapter I turned toward the subaltern limit of this dispersal; toward the potential disruption (in the form of a radical heterogeneity) of that regime's structures and calculations. In order to accomplish this I called attention to the role of savage nomadic hybridity in contemporary political, cultural, and epistemological configurations. In contrast to the ways in which hybridity has been construed in mainstream cultural analysis in recent years—that is, in contrast to the notion of cultural or ethnic hybridity as a flexible dialogue between individual and collective identity and difference—savage hybridity appears to undermine all forms of positive identitarian production. As noted in my analysis of Mirna Solórzano's *fronterizo* part-*testimonio*, what Bhabha (158) and Moreiras (*Exhaustion* 289–297) call savage hybridity promises to make the boundaries of neoliberal hegemony unpoliceable because it destabilizes the grounds and limits of hegemony's processes of signification. In this sense, the abyssal foundation that savage hybridity exposes in its relation to hegemony holds out the possibility of taking "history to its limits" (Chakrabarty, "Marx" 16) and, ultimately, of uncovering the gaps and fissures that uphold the history of contemporary liberal democracy in Latino/a America. Hence the nexus between deterritorialization, low-intensity democracy, and savage hybridity uncovers the possibility of inscribing horizons of radical heterogeneity into (and of unworking) what Dipesh Chakrabarty has referred to as the contemporary "time horizon of capital" (14–15).

The relation between low-intensity democracy and savage hybridity is, of course, proper to the current time of capital and to the structural specificities of the regimes of accumulation that crisscross contemporary

Latino/a America. How, though, can we think about savage hybridity in light of those specificities? In other words, what are the shifts that structure and condition its existence, its potential emergence, and its possible conceptualization?

Savage hybridity, like all current forms of hybridity, is a disjointing site and an internally fissured effect of the overlapping yet distinctive co-existence of (at least) two historical movements. At present, one movement is descending (the Keynesian/Fordist era of the national-popular and of national development), while another (the postindustrial era of finance capital, of market domination, and of informal labor processes) is ascending. As I noted in my analysis of the emergence of the Latin American *testimonio* in chapter 2, the cold war signal crisis of the dominant U.S. regime of accumulation, a crisis that inaugurated the shift toward neoliberal economic and social policy in the metropolitan industrial centers as well as the initiation of the debt crisis in Latin America and elsewhere, has its origins in the decade that preceded the emergence of the Reagan/Thatcher/"Chicago-boy" network of influence. As Giovanni Arrighi discusses in *The Long Twentieth Century*, it was in the early 1970s that the world system began to switch its capital in increasing quantities from trade and production to financial intermediation and speculation (215). This switch, Arrighi notes, holds the key to the origins of contemporary globalization and to the neoliberal social orders that guaranteed its extension. He states:

> The switch is the expression of a "crisis" in the sense that it marks a "turning point", a "crucial time of decision", when the leading agency of systemic processes of accumulation reveals, through the switch, a negative judgement on the possibility of continuing to profit from the reinvestment of surplus capital in the material expansion of the world-economy, as well as a positive judgement on the possibility of prolonging in time and space its leadership/dominance through a greater specialization in high finance. This crisis is the "signal" of a deeper underlying systemic crisis, which the switch to high finance none the less forestalls for the time being. (215)

Indeed, as Arrighi continues, it was generally thought that the switch could do more than just forestall an imminent crisis. It was thought that it could effectively restructure the world economy and "transform the end of material expansion into a 'wonderful moment' of renewed wealth and power for its promoters and organizers, as to different extents and in different ways it has done in all four systemic cycles of accumulation" (215).[1]

The switch in the metropolitan countries toward high finance and technoscientific forms of capitalization has produced an intensified drive to liberate capitalism from the grounds and limits of abstract labor and production, as well as from the geographical specificity, place fixity, and people of the nation and of national forms of institutionality. It thereby strives to initiate a new era of accumulation grounded in a free-floating state of money market speculation and media information, in which, as Fredric Jameson indicates, "content . . . has definitively been suppressed in favour of the form, in which the inherent nature of the product becomes insignificant, a mere marketing pretext, while the goal of production no longer lies in any specific market, any specific set of consumers or social and individual needs, but rather in its transformation into that element which by definition has no content or territory and indeed no use-value as such, namely money" ("Culture" 153). As Jameson observes, finance capital's meteoric expansion in recent years is a dematerializing and deterritorializing process in which capital itself becomes its own object of desire. Dematerialization is guaranteed through a system of speculative/monetary accumulation that feeds off its very own processes, nourishing itself on its own abstract metabolism in order to establish a system of circulation that exists without apparent reference to a former content, ground, or mode of production.[2] Speculative globalization, in this sense, is "a kind of cyberspace in which money capital has reached its ultimate dematerialization, as messages which pass instantaneously from one nodal point to another point across the former globe, the former material world" (154).

But this is only a partial consideration of the logics and realities of the current regimes of accumulation. After all, as Arrighi notes, the material limit to finance capital's increasing dematerialization, and the limit within the real world to globalization's wonderful moment of free-floating expansion, resides, at least in part, in the fact that entire communities, regions, countries, and even continents (from, for example, the inner cities of the United States to the shantytowns of Latin America; from Chiapas to sub-Saharan Africa) have been declared redundant or wholly superfluous to this increasingly abstract economy of accumulation on a world scale (330). Indeed, finance capital's generalized declaration of actual or potential redundancy on a global scale now uncovers the imprints of a limiting human world; a potentially negative universality that is composed of a multiplicity of imminently residual, redundant, or superfluous peoples, places, cultural practices, and histories.[3]

As described in the previous chapter, the extension of postnational architectures and cultural configurations continually raises the question of the relation between security, population, and government—or, to put it in different but related terms, between hegemony, conduct, and force—as paramount to our understanding of the contemporary order and its forms of representation in Latin America. Judging by the human and spatial architecture of the El Salvador/South Central interface, low-intensity democracy strives actively to *police* the remaining sediments of so-called archaic utopias. It no longer strives to incorporate them into the state's disciplinary/pedagogical processes in order to produce new forms of citizenship. New forms of citizenship are now the purview of the Nongovernmental Organizations or of market forces. The state, rather, strives to control cultures, histories, and collective practices that now find themselves fully integrated into the logics of the marketplace and yet simultaneously on the verge of becoming part of an increasingly un-represented and unrepresentable multitude.[4]

Contemporary structures of violence and hybridity formation bring us inevitably to the notion of neoliberalism as an art and artifice of government and of governmentality; as a specific political rationality or police (a particular governmental disposition) that is governed in-creasingly through market forces. As we will see, questions of neoliberal police, and, therefore, questions pertaining to the relation between the market and the people, are intimately related to a foundational shift in the notion of temporality that has been effected in recent years as a result of the switch to speculative finance capitalism.

As a consequence of finance capital's recent overall pattern of as-cendency, it now appears that the era of national development and of national production (an order that often upheld and extended feudal re-lations of production, of course) is descending. Having said this, how-ever, it has not been, and cannot be, fully laid to rest. This can be seen in the fact that production processes have merely been displaced and dis-persed thanks to the proliferation of the transnational maquiladora net-work, and to the floating flexibility of the informal economy throughout the South. Furthermore, and in a similar though inverted process, while the postindustrial era of finance capital is ascending, and often advertises itself as effectively liberated from the trivial archaisms of local history and from the troublesome provincialisms of national or regional culture, it never comes fully into its own. It does not liberate itself absolutely from attachments to real bodies and places, nor to abstract labor's new-found flexibility. Rather, it simply exists as a relation of distinction from (and to the extent that it can feed off) all notions of ground, place fixity, historical continuity, or demographic constancy. Indeed, in Latin America the dis-persal and superimposition of differential temporal layers (which can be

The Other Side of the Popular

seen, for example, in the recent emergence and increasing extension of highly organized premodern barter economies organized, nevertheless, on the Internet) both potentialize and limit the absolute ascendency of technoscientific capitalization. These layers produce cultural forms and processes of social organization that signal the human limit to finance capital's ability to actually come into its own. As such, a completely new stage in the time horizon of peripheral capitalism cannot be announced by the cybersystems of the new world order.

The current regime of speculative accumulation cannot, and does not even really desire to, fully surpass the limits of its previous modes of capitalist and precapitalist production per se. Nor does it strive to fully abandon old-order strategies such as the violent coercions that were reminiscent of the liberal and populist phases of national development in Latin America. It merely strives to place such premodern or pre-postmodern forms alongside, and in distinction to, the naturalized and supposedly consensual realities of transnational market forces and capital flows.

Needless to say, this layered, disjunctive, and internally fissured structure and experience of the current pattern of accumulation and of social organization—this vision of the present as the effect of a multiplicity of coexistent, overlapping, often antagonistic, and cannibalistic ascending/descending movements—is not unproblematic. The fact that an absolute other side of the national-popular and of national development never fully comes into its own, and therefore never fully distinguishes itself from any previous order as a new stage of development or as a distinctive mode of production within the history of Latin American capital, suggests that the neoliberal social order does not move toward any horizon in particular. It does not move toward a projected and potentially utopic reality or historical stage grounded in difference from the present or from the past. Rather, it fuels its processes by feeding parasitically in the present off the organs, mechanisms, and forms of the past.

Thus, from within the current configuration, history in Latin America is no longer a linear narrative of postcolonial backwardness from which underdeveloped collectives and nation-states are trying to awake. Underdevelopment, in other words, is no longer the negated ground on which future development and difference (both capitalist and national-popular/socialist) can be forged. Rather, the time horizon of national development and of national production is no longer projected toward the future. It is projected toward a state of things passed, to which the new order can now return at will and cannibalize or "spin" for its own perpetual consumption and redistribution in the present. In this sense, the new world order in Latin America really is described in most convincing terms by the discursive shift that has been effected recently in official public-policy circles, in which discourses of Third World underdevelopment have given way to discourses dealing with what are now called the emerging markets of the South. The new regime of accumulation in Latin America really has taken on the guise of a *machina ex machina* grounded in the continual emergence of emergence, and nothing else.

Latin American capitalist modernities strived to organize themselves within the borders of the nation, and by means of the universalization of the nation-state and of national culture as complementary sites for the resolution of the long-standing question of national sovereignty. Within this process the notion of development was tied intimately to the utopic figure of death. It was tied to the point of finitude in the future at which the painful process of nation-state formation would reveal itself in its achieved completion (in other words, the point at which the postcolonial liberal or populist order would become the post-postcolonial order, and would therefore acquire the name and visage of a truly sovereign state). In this sense the development that would come with sovereignty, it was thought, resided on the other side of underdevelopment's finitude. The historical and structural persistence of underdevelopment continually displaced the utopic figure of death. It also maintained the promise of futurity that grounded the national-popular stage of development in Latin America. In this sense, the utopic figure of death fueled both the revolutionary era and its violent oligarchic and military responses in the 1970s and 1980s. As mentioned in chapter 1, this developmental process spanned the years preceding the Great Depression through to the defeat of Unidad Popular and, in some cases, even carried through to the fall of the Berlin Wall.

Now, however, that strong (idealistic) notion of futurity—the utopic figure of death announcing the possibility of national development's definitive completion—has been diluted and displaced as the future ground of the sovereign nation. The advent of global capital flows has finished off the ideal finitude that, for decades, upheld the promise of development and of the sovereign national future. But this, of course, does not denote the absolute demise of the nation. Nor does it signify the complete demise of the future or of its relation to underdevelopment's utopic figure of death. Now, however, the term "underdevelopment" is displaced by the weaker signifier "emerging." This maintains the notion of underdevelopment's finitude, but keeps it explicitly and permanently unfinished (a question of perpetual emergence rather than the effect of a definitive event). Ultimately, emergence empties the utopic figure of death of all depth, transcendence, and signification other than that pro-

The Other Side of the Popular

vided by the emergence of emergence itself. As such, the new order is a perpetual nonfinishing of the past and, simultaneously, the dilution and unfinishing of the figure of death that structured national capitalism's promise of a sovereign future. Of course, it is the marketplace that takes charge of this permanent labor of past/future unfinishing. Meanwhile, the present feeds off the images and realities of the past in order to establish the parasitic autopoeisis of a new order that does not, and cannot, finish doing away with that past. Such maneuvers leave both the past and the promise of emergence unfinished and intentionally unachievable.

Thus while underdevelopment was always a function of a movement toward futurity, and therefore a function of the possibility of a utopic unveiling of distinctive sovereignty, the current time horizon of capital (that is, the continual promise of emerging markets in the South) is never more than a function of the past/present. The present continually displaces the possibility of a utopian figure of death—it displaces the point of finitude in the future at which the current order would reveal itself in its achieved completion, and therefore in its difference—and it does so by never finishing finishing in the present. This means that the new order takes it on itself, persistently and repeatedly, to transform in the present all images of the past and to systematically exhaust all previous promises of future sovereignty (revolution, national liberation, socialism, communism, etc.). As such, the new order returns to the past constantly in order to empty it of signification and to devoid it of potential exemplarity. It thereby exposes it continually as little more than a spectral trace or marketable image that is capable of signifying little more than the perpetual incompletion of the past in the present. However, and more important, in this very unfinishing of the past in the present the new order values only the past's ability to transform its contours in order to enter the consumption-dominated present. It is in this sense, of course, that the specter of Che Guevara can now exist as the diminutive figure of a chihuahua dog in commercials for Taco Bell's "revolutionary taco." The past exists to the extent that it can uphold market "spins"; and if, by some quirk of embedded culture or some form of irreducible belief system, language, or mode of production something cannot be captured immediately by the market's mobile centers of appropriation, it too is brought into the structures and circuits of the system by merely being represented as always already residual, redundant, or superfluous. Thus, as Jean-Luc Nancy puts it, under such circumstances "worldly man— man according to humanism—is man exposed to a limit or an abyss of grounding, end, and exemplarity," because, he continues, this world of perpetually unfinished finishing, the world of, and as, the marketplace "is the world of spacing out, not of finishing; because it is the world of the intersection of singularities, not of the identification of figures (of individuals and masses); because it is the world in which, in short, sovereignty is exhausting itself (and at the same time resisting with gestures at once terrifying and derisory)—for all these reasons, and from the very heart of the appropriative power of capital . . . sovereignty is *nothing*" (*Sense* 50–56).

But it is more than this, for in order to be *nothing* it must exhaust itself continually, and must therefore be *everything* in order to then reveal itself persistently as *nothing*. Indeed, it is for this very reason that neoliberal globalization is nothing more than market autopoeisis: the new order's machinic production and reproduction of itself exclusively as the result of "the consummation . . . of the old one," in which "the presumed epic battle between neoliberal globalization and collective identities is really not a battle for the future but is rather the very face of the past as it evolves into the present" (Moreiras, *Exhaustion* 274). This is a very important formulation (indeed, it is worth restating: the present of neoliberal globalization is not a battle for the future but, rather, a battle for the visage of the past as it evolves into the present), because it uncovers the temporal machinery that anchors the unfinishing labor of the "neo" in neoliberalism.

Neoliberalism cannot be considered merely a singular (one-time) return to, and reworking of, previous economic, social, and cultural doctrines and practices of government (conjured up, once again, by the powers that be for the benefit of future development and for the current regime of accumulation). Rather, through the spectral temporalization of the neoliberal we can see that its formulas of rule are grounded in the permanent unfinishing and perpetual emptying out—converted into social and cultural ideology, policy, and into societal and institutional reorganization—of all potential returns to the exemplarity of histories, ideas, practices, and languages other than those that are always already constitutive of the dominant order itself. In this sense, laws designed to dictate the movement of collective historical knowledge—such as Punto Final (Full stop) (imposed after the military dictatorships in Argentina) or Alberto Fujimori's full amnesty of military officers directly responsible for the human rights abuses during the 1980s in Peru—are profoundly positive techniques of government. They are absolute institutional and societal necessities and preconditions for the establishment, regulation, and perpetuation of neoliberal governability and freedom, for they expose liberal democracy and the opening up to the transnational marketplace as global capital's ability to openly and actively forget differential and potentially destabilizing mnemonic reserves and histories.[5] Thus they are an act of absolute institutional transparency because they explicitly disclose the truth of the present for what it is: the repeated and perpetual erasure of the face of the potentially transformational past as it evolves into the postsovereign present and the hypostasis of the global marketplace. These laws, in other words, are a permanent reminder of the need to forget. They are the very foundation of a political rationality that is constructed on the demand not to forget the past, but to remember to forget the past. Therefore they guarantee the perpetuation of the end of the past, together with the reconversion and refunctionalization of individual and collective freedom as a technical condition of consumption and of entrepreneurial and competitive conduct, rather than as the condition and effect of collective utopian drives and potentially antagonistic affects and insurrections.

As such, the notion of temporality must remain paramount to our ability to think about, challenge, and potentially disrupt the power structures and relations of force that uphold the current regime of accumulation and contemporary governmentality (understood in Foucault's sense of the term) in Latin America. After all, in order to claim the continuous successes of finance capital's "wonderful moment" of renewed wealth and power, the neoliberal practice of police—the practice of contemporary population control as well as of the management (and representation) of happiness and prosperity—must persistently open up and redistribute potential radical heterogeneity by diluting and displacing previously incommensurable languages, codes, practices, temporalities, or modes of production. Indeed, this perpetual labor of aperture, exposure, and circulation uncovers the ways in which market forces predicate themselves on the continual production of cultural/ethnic hybridity as an emptied-out and internally (re)functional fabrication of heterogeneous universes.

However, as Dipesh Chakrabarty suggests in "Marx after Marxism," there are differences and then there are differences. Moreover, and in the terms of our present discussion, there are hybridities (flexible identitarian formalities) that pertain to the neoliberal political rationality of the present and then there are savage hybridities or radical incommensurabilities that disrupt the current order's ability to reproduce itself either in real or epistemological terms. The presence of the first upholds the anthropological mechanisms of the everyday. The presence of the second, on the other hand, opens up and produces the radical ungrounding of the first, and perhaps also that of the order to which it belongs. The question, of course, as Chakrabarty indicates, is how to uncover, represent, and think about disruptive incommensurabilities from within the contemporary order. How to engage in a "worlding of the world" that does not commit thought to "a bloodless liberal pluralism that only subsumes all difference(s) within the Same" ("Marx" 13) (which is, of course, what mainstream discourses of cultural hybridity and of public policy ultimately tend to do).

In "Marx after Marxism" Chakrabarty traces relations between con‐ temporary governmentality, history and the practice of representation, and the haunting figure of incommensurable difference in light of the re‐ lation between notions of real and abstract labor.[6] For the Chakrabarty of *Rethinking Working Class History,*

> "real labour" refers to the labor power of the actual individual, labor power "as it exists in the personality of the labourer"—that is, as it exists in the "immediate exclusive individuality" of the individual. Just as personalities differ, similarly the labour power of one individual is different from that of another. "Real labour" refers to the essential heterogeneity of individual capacities. "Abstract" or general labor, on the other hand, refers to the idea of uniform, homogeneous labor that capitalism imposes on this heterogeneity, the notion of a general labor that underlies "exchange value". It is what makes labor measurable and makes possible the generalized exchange of commodities. (*Re‐ thinking* 225–26)

For the Chakrabarty of "Marx after Marxism," this difference be‐ tween real and abstract labor takes on added significance because, as he claims, it holds the key to our ability to think about the possibility of radi‐ cal heterogeneity within the contemporary horizon of capital. Real labor, he argues, should be read as socially/culturally produced and therefore capable of referring to "different kinds of 'social' and hence to differ‐ ent orders of temporality" (14). "It should in principle even allow," he continues, "for the possibility of these temporal horizons being mutually incommensurable. The transition from 'real' to 'abstract' is thus also a question of transition from many and possibly incommensurable tempo‐ ralities to the homogeneous time of abstract labour, the transition from 'non-history' to 'history'. 'Real' labour, therefore, is precisely that which cannot be enclosed by the sign 'commodity' while it constantly inheres in the latter" (14).[7] As such, continues Chakrabarty, the tension between real and abstract labor invites us to reflect further on forms of tempo‐ rality that challenge the apparent seamlessness of social organization, for "if 'real labour' . . . belongs to a world of heterogeneity whose various temporalities . . . cannot be enclosed in the sign History, then it can find

The Other Side of the Popular

a place in a historical narrative of capitalist transition (or commodity production) only as a Derridean trace of something that cannot be enclosed, an element that constantly challenges from within capital's and commodity's—and by implication History's—claims to unity and universality" (14).

As a result, continues Chakrabarty, the notion of precapital becomes particularly important for a sustained reflection on radical heterogeneity, for precapital "speaks of a particular relationship to capital marked by the tension of difference in horizons of time. The 'pre-capitalist' can only exist within the temporal horizon of capital, and is yet something that disrupts the continuity of this time precisely by suggesting another time that is not on the same, secular, homogeneous calendar (which is why what is pre-capital is not chronologically prior to capital). This is another time which, theoretically, could be entirely incommensurable with the godless, spiritless time of what we call 'history' " (14–15).[8] In this sense, and as already noted in these pages, subalternity for Chakrabarty "is not the empirical peasant or tribal in any straightforward sense that a populist programme of history-writing may want to imagine" (15). It is not, in other words, a given subaltern cultural identity, but a disruptive site that "fractures from within" the unitary signs underlying national and global narratives of capitalist development and/or emergence. The subaltern, in other words, is the heterogeneity effect that marks the limit between different coexistent thresholds of consistency, temporality, and meaning production within the time horizon of capital itself.

Within this configuration, then, precapital attests in the present (though always retroactively) to the violence of the transition from real to abstract labor. It is the momentary site within abstract labor—within the time horizon of capital per se—of a specter of irreducible heterogeneity that conjures itself up (again, in the present) as the ghost of another order or as an alternative process of worlding, that remains at all times incommensurable to capital's dominant modes of governmentality. As such precapital is, as John Kraniauskas observes, "the site for possible re-memoration rather than reification" ("Hybridity" 112). It is the suggestion of an erased otherness or alternative worlding to capital that emerges from within capital, disrupting it in such a way "that governmentality—in Foucault's sense of the term—all over the world has to subjugate and civilise [it]" (Chakrabarty, "Marx" 15).

Thus, it is precisely in governmentality's uneven and incomplete subjugation of heterogeneity that the new order emerges as an ongoing battle, not over the terms of the future but, on the contrary, over "the very face of the past as it evolves into the present" (Moreiras, *Exhaus-*

tion 274). Contemporary governmentality, in other words, remains at all times haunted by spectral objects, languages, and practices that bear witness to thresholds of alternative openings, worldings, indeterminacies, and possibilities. It is haunted by phantasms that uphold the potential to shake the edifice of hegemonic thought when they are unleashed from within the differential thresholds of consistency that pertain to capital itself. As such, any effective reemergence of incommensurable alterity—of the specter of real labor or of precapital as a site of subaltern difference or perhaps even of insurrection—would be accompanied invariably by the return of a nondevelopmentalist utopic figure of death: namely, by the promise of the breakdown in the structural, political, and epistemological limits of capitalist governmentality itself.

As noted in chapter 3, Marx and Engels evoked the disruptive potential of capitalist order—the exposure of a trace of something that cannot be enclosed—in the following terms: "Modern bourgeois society with its relations of production, of exchange and property, a society that has conjured up such gigantic means of production and of exchange, is like the sorcerer who is no longer able to control the powers of the nether world whom he has called up by his spells" (*Manifesto* 11). If this is the case then perhaps we could suggest that the disclosure of the marxian netherworld is the site of subalternity: the site of the spectral reemergence of precapitalist difference, of real labor's evocation of different orders of temporality and of alternative worldings that fracture (from within) the seamlessness of capital's contemporary narratives. It is a site that stands within/without and alongside/against—always connecting and standing between radically different entities, consistencies, and intensities—and that persistently challenges governmentality's (the "sorcerer's") ability to account fully for the definitive meaning of the face of the past as it evolves into the present.[9]

In the previous chapter, of course, the unsettling labor of radical heterogeneity was uncovered through the historical knowledge, the violent transnational interface experience, and the *frontera* language of a Salvadoran/L.A. gang member. In the pages that follow I will examine the logics and limits of neoliberal governmentality's subjugating and civilizing mission—the "way in which the elites take charge of the interaction of different historical temporalities" in order to elaborate a global project within them (García Canclini, quoted in Kraniauskas, "Hybridity" 126)—in order to trace the eruption of governmentality's other side; that is, radical heterogeneity's netherworld promise. I will do this, however, not from within the circuits and affective flows of the order of postnational

The Other Side of the Popular

deterritorialization and migration (as I did in chapter 5) but, rather, I will concentrate on the situated practices and narrative strategies that still persist within the borders of intranational migration and redistribution.

Thus I examine the practices of the body and of violence (both real and epistemic) that direct, orient, and extend the interactions, agencies, affects, and circuitous demographic flows that uphold the "borderland temporalities" (Chakrabarty, Kraniauskas) of the Andes/coast interface in contemporary Peru. As I show later in this chapter, ultimately what is at stake in this analysis is the site to be assigned in contemporary reflection to the notion and thought of savage (nomadic) hybridity in postmodern Peru.

IMPALING JOSÉ MARÍA ARGUEDAS

In *The Illusion of the End* Jean Baudrillard provides us with a formulation that sheds light on the relation between history and the emergent orders of the South: "There are those who let the dead bury their dead, and there are those who are forever digging up to finish them off. Having failed both in their symbolic murder and their work of mourning, it is not enough for them that others should be dead; they have to disinter them once again to impale them—this is the Carpentras complex . . . the desecration complex" (24). It is only in light of this desecration complex that we can begin to understand postmodernity's sojourns into the realm of cultural history. Furthermore, it is only in light of this drive to perpetuate the perpetuation of death infliction that we can approach, and think through, the essays contained in Mario Vargas Llosa's *La utopía arcaica* (The archaic utopia).

In this collection Vargas Llosa resurrects the figure of the indigenist novelist, anthropologist, and ethnographer José María Arguedas (almost thirty years after his suicide), only to reinter him finally as no longer of this world, as no longer of the now. Thus, in the book's final paragraphs Vargas Llosa declares the effects of Peru's economic structural adjustments and subsequent cultural transformations—the emergence in the 1980s and 1990s of Lima's burgeoning migrant informal sector and the insertion of the nation-state and of national culture into global capitalist networks—as the final proof of the demise, already postmortem, of José María Arguedas and of his so-called archaic utopia: literary indigenism. It is worth citing here Vargas Llosa's burial of the dead body of Arguedas and of indigenism in its entirety:

It is obvious that recent events in Peru have inflicted a mortal wound on the archaic utopia. No matter if we view the informalization of Peruvian society in positive or negative terms, it is undeniable that that traditional, communitarian, magical-religious, and quechua-speaking society that strived to uphold the collectivist values and the atavistic customs that nourished the ideological and literary fiction of "indigenismo" no longer exists. Furthermore, and regardless of the political changes that might occur in the coming years, it will not reconstitute itself. Future utopias, if they emerge, will be of another kind. Regardless of whether democracy or authoritarianism take hold, and regardless of whether we sustain current economic policy or allow it to follow more social-democratic or socialist paths, everything indicates that Peru is now a society that definitively rejects archaism, and perhaps even utopia. . . . Although opinions vary on many issues—perhaps on *all* issues—Peruvians of all races, languages, economic conditions, and political persuasions agree that the Peru of the future will not, and should not, be a revival of Tahuantinsuyo. It should not be an ethnically defined collectivist society, a country at odds with the "bourgeois" values of commerce and wealth. It should not be closed off to the world in defense of its immutable identity. Neither Indian nor White, "indigenist" nor "hispanist", the Peru that is emerging and that is here to stay is still an unknown quantity. However, we can assure with utmost certainty that it will not correspond in the slightest to the images with which it was described—through which it was invented—in the work of José María Arguedas. (335; translation mine)

Basically, it seems, Arguedas and people like him were misguided. He and the social, religio-anthropological, linguistic, economic, and political authority of the world he represented (in both the literary and the experiential senses of the word) have been displaced by the forceful drive of national and transnational history itself. In this sense, contemporary Peru emerges in Vargas Llosa's formulation as a privileged protagonist on the center stage of Francis Fukuyama's "good news" of the neoliberal "end of History."[10]

Arguedas's indigenist worlding, according to Vargas Llosa, can no longer be evoked in terms of historical exemplarity, imitation, or identification. Rather, it can be decoded exclusively in the name of an archaic utopian fiction that, in a fashion similar to the demise of the Buendía lineage at the end of *One Hundred Years of Solitude,* will never have a second opportunity on earth. But such a comparison between collective literary deaths, both past and present, is an oversimplification, for there is a fundamental distinction between the apocalyptic demise of the Buendía lineage in 1967 and the end of Arguedas/indigenism in 1996. In contrast to García Márquez, Vargas Llosa does not condemn Arguedas and his literature absolutely—for time immemorial and forever more—to the dustbin of history. On the contrary, Vargas Llosa represents himself as still very much invested in redeeming his objects of analysis from the absolute oblivion that comes with being the embodiment of the "end of History." As we will see, however, it is precisely his redemptive promise that guarantees their death over and over again, because, he says, it is only by reading them as fiction, and nothing else, that their repeatability as the end of History can be guaranteed and recycled ad infinitum. Thus, as he continues (and as he ends his book), "needless to say, this discrepancy does not impoverish these works. On the contrary, it allows for their literary nature. It highlights their inventiveness and consecrates them as fictions that, thanks to the skill of a creator who intertwined personal experience, the avatars of the society in which he lived, together with the generous and violent desires that inspired him, appeared to portray real Peru when they really constructed a dream" (335–36; translation mine). On the one hand, Vargas Llosa disinters Arguedas and literary indigenism in order to impale them. Yet, on the other hand, by impaling them he perpetuates their (literary) life by, of all things, emptying them and the collective cultural and political tradition to which they belonged (and for which Arguedas stood and perhaps died) of all significance or value other than that of the purely aesthetic. Thus, according to Vargas Llosa, the value of reading Arguedas as a profoundly decontextualized and depoliticized literary literature, written by the individual dreamer and auteur (Arguedas), is that it allows us a greater understanding of the present as a distinction from the past, even though it does not teach us how to think about the present per se at all.

Ironically, then, by condemning Arguedas to the dustbins of history Vargas Llosa declares the end of the history of Arguedas (and of indigenism) as simultaneously the end of the dustbins of history. While Arguedas/indigenism are actively condemned, Vargas Llosa's insistence on literary value for the sake of literary value allows us to save them perpetually from their own condemnation (precisely, however, by condemning them perpetually to the dustbins of history). The past, in other words, can only be reincarnated for the present to the extent that it can transform its contours in order to signify the present as distinct from the past. This, of course, reproduces the temporal movement of the "neo" in neoliberalism, in which insistence on the value of literary value, for example, and nothing more, allows us to value the recycling of history as the necessary precondition for us to ground ourselves firmly within a present that is nothing more than an order that sustains itself by feeding off the perpetual ending of previous multiple collective histories.

In Vargas Llosa's formulation Peru's social restructuring in recent years has carried the nation beyond national antagonisms of identity and difference. It has opened up the nation to the flexible hybridities of the global cultural economy. In this process the present is the perpetuation of a distinction from the past: "Neither Indian nor White, 'indigenist' nor 'hispanist', the Peru that is emerging and that is here to stay is still an unknown quantity. However, we can assure with utmost certainty that it will not correspond in the slightest to the images with which it was described—through which it was invented—in the work of José María Arguedas" (335; translation mine). The present, then, is present—is contemporary, is "the end of History"—only because it produces and feeds off a distinction with the past that it manufactures continually for itself in the present. Thus Arguedas's dis-/re/dis/reinterment allows Vargas Llosa to fabricate and maintain the presentness of the present—the contemporaneity of the contemporary—as nothing more than a distinction in which the present is the present—and Arguedas/indigenism's collectivist history has come to a close—because the past was . . . well, not like this. Thus Arguedas/indigenism are the site of the most banal distinction possible between past and present, in which they are continually exposed as archaic because . . . they belong to history and all history is always already archaic.

Furthermore, as Vargas Llosa himself seems to suggest, this necessarily vacuous distinction can even be the ground for a contemporary Peruvian cultural politics of consensus, in which national cohesion can be achieved through the collective recognition that both Arguedas and indigenism are no more: "Peruvians of all races, languages, economic conditions and political persuasions agree that the Peru of the future will not, and should not, be a revival of Tahuantinsuyo. It should not be an ethnically defined collectivist society, a country at odds with the 'bourgeois' values of commerce and wealth. It should not be closed off to the world in defense of its immutable identity" (335; translation mine). National consensus, in other words, can be achieved by all Peruvians who can agree on what they are not, or can no longer be. This, indeed, is the great innovation of the new order: to ground the conditions of success (prosperity, democracy, order, governmentality, civilization, etc.) not as a function of the possible future—and therefore not as a positive function of desire—but as a function of the perpetual and positive negation of the past and therefore as a function of what one does not desire.

And how, we might ask, is this intentionally banal yet apparently foun-

dational distinction in the order of desire to be maintained ad infinitum; that is, beyond the current moment and therefore into the future?
How, in other words, does this profoundly uninsightful foundation forge
culture? Quite simply, by making contemporary and future readings of
Peruvian cultural history the perpetuation of a Peruvian "aesthetic of absence" (Jameson, "Transformations" 130), in which the subject to be
rendered absent repeatedly in the present is the limiting Andean object
world. In this sense, what Vargas Llosa proposes as a contemporary reading of past forms, discourses, and desires is nothing more than the maintenance of a repetitive and reactive ideological maneuver that is achieved
most effectively through the sustained performance of the loss of Andean
meaningfulness; in other words, through the sustainable and repeatable
extinction of Andean culture.

Furthermore, within Vargas Llosa's formulation such a necessary
loss of meaningfulness is upheld and structured by the evocation of the
present as little more than a mystery—as a non-sense—that remains
somehow beyond questions of identity and difference but also beyond
the domain of contemporary reflection: "Neither Indian nor White, 'indigenist' nor 'hispanist', the Peru that is emerging and that is here to stay
is still an unknown quantity" (335; translation mine). The cultural authority of the present, then, is to be located in the fact that it resides in
a relation of hybrid distinction from the monumental opposites of the
past, such as Indian/White and indigenist/hispanist. But within this process the present defines itself, in positive terms, as a relation to that which
is no longer: no longer Indian, no longer White; no longer indigenist,
no longer hispanist. The present, in other words, is a "something else"
that cannot be named in and of itself, and therefore cannot be negated.
It remains, in this sense, absent from the grounds of reflection and of
negative practice, other than in its capacity to fuel the emptying out of
the signifiers of the past and, from within that emptying out, its ability
to construct consensus on what "we" are not.

CHOLAJE

The most curious thing about Vargas Llosa's evocation of the present
as a necessarily positive-negative relation—"We can agree that we're
not Indian, not White, not indigenist, and not hispanist and that's what
makes us contemporary Peruvians"—is that the present in Peru *does*
contain a name that remains curiously silenced in Vargas Llosa's neoindigenist formulation. It is, however, a name "that sows confusion be-

tween opposites and stands between the oppositions at once" (Bhabha 128). It is "an act of ambivalent signification, literally splitting the difference between the binary oppositions or polarities through which we think cultural difference" (128). Indeed, it is in the enunciatory performances of its sustained splitting that it "creates its strategies of differentiation that produce an undecidability between contraries or oppositions" (128). This signifier, which in Vargas Llosa's formulation must remain unnamed, silenced, and actively displaced as a potentially aporetic signifier of a postindigenist present, is *cholo*.[11]

Cholo—the urban Indian laboring for the most part in the informal economy—is the limit between different coexistent thresholds of consistency, temporality, and meaning production within contemporary Peru. As such, it is the ambivalent and disruptive border between the Andes and the coast at which everything—modernity, progress, development, civilization, barbarism, indigenism, hispanism, national identity, nation, hegemony, counterhegemony—can be brought into question, reterritorialized, or deterritorialized forever. As such, it is the name for the site at which contemporary history—the time horizon of peripheral capital—can envision its own threshold of precapital non-sense: a potential disruption of historical meaning brought about by "inscriptions of an uncertain colonial silence that . . . display the alienation between the transformational myth of culture as a language of universality and social generalization, and its tropic function as a repeated 'translation' of incommensurable levels of living and meaning" (Bhabha 124–25).

In spite of Vargas Llosa's apparent labor of active forgetting, *cholaje* raises the question of neoliberal wisdom and of its ability to know (that is, to know how to control) its new populations.[12] It marks the end of the territorial and cultural binarisms that founded both Creole and indigenist notions of modernity in Peru. Hence it brings to the traditional urban spaces of Creole authority customs, habits, ways of acting and thinking—forms of self-government in other words—that undermine the historical foundations of Creole sovereignty. It calls attention therefore to the historical limits of the modern state's attempts to represent the communal interest of all (as Marx and Engels state in *The German Ideology*) through seamless projections of national progress and development.

It is therefore hardly by chance that in recent years the powerfully ambivalent site of the *cholo* should have produced critical discourses in which hybridity and flexible informality have been evoked as both the names for impending popular insurrection and the site for the sustainability of capitalist development in globalizing times.

As José Matos Mar observed in *Desborde popular y crisis del Estado*—

The Other Side of the Popular

an essay written as a response to the Shining Path's declaration of war on the Peruvian state in 1980 and to the mass subaltern migration from the countryside to Lima that resulted — the foundational presuppositions of modern thought in Peru have become increasingly undermined by the emergence of new social actors and new political identities; by alternative popular practices and epistemologically undefinable cultural configurations that can no longer be conceptualized through the rubric of a strict White/Indian, colonizer/colonized, costeño/andino, city/country, modern/traditional, or civilization/barbarism duality. Matos Mar notes that in recent decades mass indigenous and peasant migrations from the Andes have flooded the streets of Lima, thereby producing a popular overflow whose unpredictability is, the author suggests, an increasing force to be reckoned with. As Matos Mar viewed the situation at the height of Peru's *manchay tiempo* (time of fear), recently urbanized and predominantly informal actors unravel the epistemological and political limits of national cultural politics and state practices and challenge the elite's dualistic conceptualizations of Peruvian national identity. Hybridization is, in other words, the site for the promise of a popular hegemonic articulation uncovering the agency of an ungovernable and unintelligible collective Other existing within the very borders of the oligarchy's urban center itself. Matos Mar states:

> The incapacity of the governmental apparatus to assure and guarantee the universal legitimacy of its legal processes can be seen in the phenomenon of Peruvian "informalization". With its authority weakened and its power undermined, the State apparatus begins to spin out of control. . . . The process under way corrodes and dissolves the old Creole illusion of national identity and challenges the Nation-State's institutional structures. For the first time, these two problems (which have been buried in the recesses of national consciousness since the Conquest) can no longer be ignored. The spectacle of a State whose already questionable authority is now weakened, and the legitimacy of whose institutions is no longer recognized by the masses, together with an official culture that remains unaware of the language and traditions of the majority while still expressing itself in foreign languages and forms, opens up new questions regarding the legitimacy of the State and the definition of nationality. . . . Official Peru will no longer be able to impose its conditions. It should enter into dialogue with the overflowing masses in order to foment the true integration of emergent Peru's emergent institutions. (103–4; translation mine)

However, at the other end of the political spectrum the migrant informal sector and the uneven processes of *cholaje* that emerge with it have also been construed as a new source of human capital for the current regime of accumulation. Thus, in Hernando de Soto's *The Other Path* (for which, incidentally, Mario Vargas Llosa wrote the foreword), informals represent a potential entrepreneur culture that is thought to be capable of consolidating and expanding the grounds for future national development (to the extent that they can be integrated into judicial structures and kept away from the idea of owning the means of production). Thus, as de Soto outlines in his response to the crisis of the 1980s, to the intensification of mass migration from rural to urban centers, and to the concentration of mass urban poverty:

> Competitive business people, whether formal or informal, are in fact a new breed. . . . They may be neither likable nor polite—remember what many people say about minibus drivers and street vendors—but they provide a sounder basis for development than skeptical bureaucracies and traffickers in privileges. They have demonstrated their initiative by migrating, breaking with the past without any prospect of a secure future, they have learned how to identify and satisfy others' needs, and their confidence in their abilities is greater than their fear of competition. . . . Every day they face dilemmas: what and how are they going to produce? What are they going to make it with? At what prices will they buy and sell? . . . This ability to take risks and calculate is important because it means that a broad entrepreneurial base is already being created. In Peru, informality has turned a large number of people into entrepreneurs, into people who know how to seize opportunities by managing available resources, including their own labor, relatively efficiently. . . . Wealth is achieved essentially by one's own efforts. It is earned, little by little, in an active market where goods, services, and ideas are exchanged and people are constantly learning and adjusting to other's needs. Wealth comes from knowing how to use resources, not from owning them. (243)[13]

Obviously, in the distinction between Matos Mar's "revolutionary" articulation (his interpretation of informal *cholaje* as an emergent people/power bloc antagonism in the 1980s) and de Soto's entrepreneurial reading of informality for contemporary Peru, we come face to face with the emergent figure of the *cholo* as the screen or interface that simultaneously separates and unites potential insurrection—ungovernability— from, and to, the formalities of contemporary police. The migrant *cholo* is the uncanny embodiment of the relation between Andean precapital transferred to the coast and the homogeneous order of abstract labor. It is potentially a singular embodiment of, and site for, enmeshed yet different and coexistent thresholds of consistency, temporality, and meaning production within the time horizon of contemporary capital in Peru. It can be a fully acculturated or subsumed subject or it can be a spectral site within the contemporary social axiomatic that haunts its order with alternative worldings and indeterminacies.

For neoliberal governmentality, then, the urban *cholo* is desirable as an acculturated, integrated, and thoroughly de-Andeanized economic subject exposed to, and fully incorporated into, the flexible urban circuitry of transnational market forces. The problem is that the *cholo*'s Andean identifications can be inherently disruptive to that order because (paraphrasing Chakrabarty) it can mark a site within the current regime of accumulation that unconceals the tension between real and abstract labor. It thereby has the potential to make capital reveal the heterogeneities and incommensurabilities that are inscribed at all times within its own core. The mere presence of the *cholo*, in other words, has the potential to take the history of capitalist development, order, and progress to its limit, thereby (potentially) rendering "its unworking visible" (Chakrabarty, "Marx" 16) or, at least, imaginable.[14]

It is as a result of this potentiality that, for neoliberal governmentality, the *cholo* interface should always be subject to a form of control in which the thing to be controlled is the visage of the Indian/peasant/Andean past as it evolves into the informal processes of the increasingly urbanized, and transnationalized, coastal public sphere. The success of neoliberal governmentality, in other words, resides in its ability to articulate the Andean past as archaic and, in this unfinishing labor of representation, to empty it continually of signification in order to transform it, in the present, into a tamed realm that is capable of negotiating the realities of the transnational cultural economy. It is for this reason that Alejandro ("Choledo") Toledo's recent rise to presidential power in Peru is so important for the sustained symbolism of the neoliberal order. Thanks to his years at Stanford University and the World Trade Organization, Toledo has become a poster boy for the benefits of tamed *cholaje*. His is an emblematic story of the local *cholo* who "did good"; the archetypal story of the successfully globalized former Indian who, in his political campaigns, now relies on his Belgian wife in order to communicate in Quechua with the impoverished Andean highlanders.

Needless to say, the struggle for the terms of neoliberal police and governmentality is ongoing in Peru. As we will see in our discussion of Mario Vargas Llosa's *Death in the Andes* (*Lituma en los Andes*), as well as in Francisco Lombardi's award-winning film *Bajo la piel* (Beneath the skin), the labor of active forgetting, the active enunciation, articulation, and disavowal of the archaic (the Andes, the Indian, the colonial, precapital) takes center stage and replays itself continually in the new order's armory of cultural representation.

DEATH IN THE ANDES

It is as a result of the question of potential *cholo* incommensurability that Mario Vargas Llosa returns to our field of reflection; on the one hand as a critic of contemporary Peruvian social and cultural configurations (as already witnessed in his examination of Arguedas and of literary indigenism), but, on the other, as a critic intimately linked to the upholding of the thought and logics of the neoliberal state. Before engaging Vargas Llosa and the scope of his portrayal of the Andes and of *manchay tiempo* in *Death in the Andes* (his first novel published after failing in his bid for the presidency in 1990) I will lay the interpretive groundwork by reflecting briefly on the relations that the Peruvian novelist establishes with Nietzsche's *The Birth of Tragedy*, as well as with the figure of José Carlos Mariátegui, founder of Latin American marxian thought, modern revolutionary *indigenismo*, and Peruvian socialism.

As shown in the examination of national fictive ethnicity in chapter 1, Mariátegui strived to establish the contours of an indigenous national-cultural identity for Peru. By doing this he attempted to lay the epistemological and political foundations for Peru's insertion into the major ideological currents of industrial modernity. As such, Mariátegui tried to give shape to a compensatory regeneration of the figure of the Indian as *the* modernizing revolutionary force. As Ofelia Schutte reveals, one of the most remarkable and perhaps dumbfounding characteristics of Mariátegui's work, and of his *Seven Interpretations of Peruvian Reality* in particular, is the relation of debt that he immediately establishes with the writings of Friedrich Nietzsche. As Schutte notes, apart from heading the *Seven Interpretations* with a Nietzschean aphorism from the period of *The Wanderer and His Shadow* (27), in his preface Mariátegui refers to Nietzsche as a thinker whose spirit is intimately linked to Mariátegui's own: "I bring together in this book, organized and annotated in seven essays, the articles that I published in *Mundial* and *Amauta* concerning some essential aspects of Peruvian reality. Like *Escena contemporánea*, therefore, this was not conceived of as a book. Better this way. My work has developed as Nietzsche would have wished. . . . And if I hope to have some merit recognized, it is that—following another of Nietzsche's precepts—I have written with my blood" (xxxv).

Indeed, in "El hombre y el mito" Mariátegui's debt to Nietzsche is repeated, as he identifies the underlying spirit of the Peruvian social classes in terms that echo the German philosopher's treatment of Wagner (as well as Sorel's notion of class as mythical unity):

> What most clearly and obviously differentiates the bourgeoisie and the proletariat in this era is myth. The bourgeoisie finally has no myth. It has become incredulous, skeptical, nihilist. The reborn liberal myth has already aged. The proletariat has a myth: the social revolution. It moves toward this myth with a vehement and active faith. The bourgeoisie denies; the proletariat affirms. The bourgeois mind amuses itself with a rationalist critique of the methods, the theories, the technique of the revolutionaries. What incomprehension! The revolutionaries' power is not their science; it is in their faith, their passion, their will. It is a religious, mystical, spiritual power. It is the power of myth. (*Heroic* 144–45)

Mariátegui's life-affirming social myth of proletarian passion, transgression, and unconstrained revolution in Peru appears to construct itself, at least partially, on the appropriation of Sorel, on the reworking of Nietzsche's *Birth of Tragedy,* and, in this regard, on the distinction that the latter establishes between the Apollonian and the Dionysian spirits. As Steven Cresap informs us, this fundamental distinction in the history of thought refers to the conflict of two classical world structures representing two opposing formulations of communal life (107). Apollo is the founder of states, etymologically the "shining one," the deity of light, *principium individuationis,* the limits of a single image of the world, a restraining boundary, freedom from wilder impulses, the order of civilization. Dionysus is the destruction of individuality, a mystical sense of commonality, transgression, the orgiastic spirit, the netherworld, the ecstasy of ceremonial bloodletting, the experience of "the supreme gratification of the primal Oneness amidst the paroxysms of intoxication" (Nietzsche *Birth,* 18). As Nietzsche puts it, in the transgressive rites of Dionysus "the slave is a free man [and] now all the rigid and hostile boundaries that distress, despotism or 'impudent fashion' have erected between man and man break down" (*Birth* 17).

Mariátegui's definition of the Indian proletariat as a life-affirming revolutionary spirit redirects and retranslates the interactions of the Apollonian and the Dionysian orders in *The Birth of Tragedy* and locates the birth of Peruvian modernity in the struggle between the forces of social production that originated in, and that imposed, the constraints and restraining boundaries of colonialism and those ungovernable collective and liberational impulses that emerge as the affirmation of primordial sundering from within the hostile boundaries of that order. Thus, as Mariátegui affirmed in his prologue to Luis Valcárcel's *Tempestad en los Andes:* "It is not civilization nor the White's alphabet that raises the soul of the Indian. It is myth, the idea of socialist revolution. Indigenous hope is absolutely revolutionary" (10; translation mine).

Moreover, these are precisely the forces that inhabit Mario Vargas Llosa's reading of *manchay tiempo* in Peru. As we will see, however, like Mariátegui before him Vargas Llosa recuperates the specter of Nietzsche's distinction between the Apollonian and the Dionysian spirits as foundational to the birth of the modern Peruvian tragedy. But he does so by effectively sidestepping Mariátegui's revolutionary appropriation of the mythical indigenous/indigenist "labor of Dionysus" (Hardt and Negri). Rather, Vargas Llosa wipes the founding father of Latin American marxism off the political and cultural map and returns to Nietzsche in order to filter the Apollonian and the Dionysian through a *hispanista* reappropriation of Sarmiento's civilization versus barbarism paradigm, obviously as a means of laying the body and history of *indigenismo*—and of Peruvian marxism in particular—to rest.[15]

Death in the Andes is a border text that traces "the topographic-ideological boundary sector that physically and symbolically demarcates" (Feldman 28) the traditional dualism of ethnic communities as construed through colonial and postcolonial configurations. If, as Mark Thurner has pointed out, the struggle for the coming into being of the Peruvian nation-state and of national culture in the nineteenth century underlined the historical passage from two republics (the more or less assymetrical complementarity of Indian/Creole worlds in the colonial order) to one divided (the internally fissured unified state of national culture), then it could be said that *Death in the Andes* locates itself on the internal cultural division that has grounded national state and culture formations throughout the postcolonial history of Peru. In this sense, it reproduces the foundational geographic, economic, linguistic, and cultural binarisms that have fueled both oligarchic power in the nineteenth and twentieth centuries as well as its protohegemonic counterparts: populism and literary indigenism.

Death in the Andes, then, is the narrativization of "a spatial construct preeminently linked to the performance of violence" (Feldman 28) in which the frontiers between conflictive temporalities, modes of production, and the accumulation of antagonistic cultural interactions allow for the examination of the "significatory boundaries of cultures, where meanings and values are (mis)read or signs are misappropriated" (Bhabha 34). The novel, therefore, presents itself as an enunciative site that is based on the critique and reproduction of boundaries; of readings and misreadings, of the presentation and critique of the state's command of space, and of the relationship between community, boundary, boundary transgression, and power. Thus it strives to constitute, and to think through, cultural difference and the ways in which difference animates the boundaries between potentially antagonistic notions of knowledge, power, and agency.

For Homi Bhabha, cultural difference's meanings are played out along the epistemological, political, and aesthetic borders between the representation of cultural supremacy and the enunciation of significatory or representational undecidability. As he notes in the following passage from "Commitment to Theory," the notion of enunciation holds the key to the disclosure and praxis of the radical heterogeneity of difference:

> The concept of cultural difference focuses on the problem of the ambivalence of cultural authority: the attempt to dominate in the *name* of a cultural supremacy which is itself produced only in the moment of differentiation. And it is the very authority of culture as a knowledge of referential truth which is at issue in the concept and moment of *enunciation.* The enunciative process introduces a split in the performative present of cultural identification; a split between the traditional culturalist demand for a model, a tradition, a community, a stable system of reference, and the necessary negation of the certitude in the articulation of new cultural demands, meanings, strategies in the political present, as a practice of domination, or resistance. . . . The enunciation of cultural difference problematizes the binary division of past and present, tradition and modernity, at the level of cultural representation and its authoritative address. It is the problem of how, in signifying the present, something comes to be repeated, relocated and translated in the name of tradition, in the guise of pastness that is not necessarily a faithful sign of historical memory but a strategy of representing authority in terms of the artifice of the archaic. (35)[16]

As I will show in my reading of *Death in the Andes,* Vargas Llosa installs the notion of cultural supremacy yet continually calls attention to the limits of the cultural authority of supremacy's authoritative address in the Andean highlands. In this sense it is, on the surface, a complex engagement with the "limit-text of culture" (Bhabha 34), with culture's relation to development and to precapitalist underdevelopment, and, ultimately, with the latter's articulation across the Andes/coast interface.[17]

As I have already established, the novel presents itself as an active engagement with the notion of cultural difference in contemporary Peru. Yet it is precisely in the novel's presentation of itself as an engagement with cultural difference that the limits of the text themselves are uncovered. After all, in spite of its active engagement with difference the novel shies away from thinking of the border that inaugurates it in the first place. In other words, *Death in the Andes* is a novel that presents itself as a representation and reproduction of the problematics underlying the Andes/coast interface. It therefore presents itself as an evocation of the epistemological, political, and cultural limits and violence of contemporary transcultural interactions. Yet it systematically steps back from considering the hybrid/transcultural interface as a specific space of reflection and representation. Quite literally, the novel signals the problematic of cultural ambivalence yet quickly displaces it (actively strives to forget it) in favor of the maintenance and order of identity/difference investments.

As Homi Bhabha has noted, although the dissemination of radical ambivalence deterritorializes binary divisions between past and present, tradition and modernity, or the contemporary and the archaic, and although the neoliberal social order (and Vargas Llosa with it) declares that the present is the unnameable and profoundly hybrid other side of the archaic, when faced with the realities and lived experience of that other side—with the zone of occult ambivalence where the savagely hybrid people dwell—neoliberalism's conceptual tables are quickly turned. As we will see, in *Death in the Andes* hybridity (what the new order calls for, let us not forget) is rapidly resignified as the perpetuation of a backward and primordially archaic tradition. And neoliberal thought does this—declares the postmodern archaic, in other words—by returning to, and reinstalling, the reactive epistemological and political models (Sarmiento's civilization versus barbarism, for example) that it purports to have condemned to the dustbins of history.

In other words, when neoliberalism is confronted by the realities that it itself creates (*cholaje*, for example) it declares them to be archaic, even when they are often more contemporary than the thought that calls them archaic in the first place. From within the order of such a limited, and limiting, philosophical and political structure, there can be no room for hybridity-thinking other than that which defines hybridity as what it no longer is (no longer Indian, no longer traditional, no longer Andean, etc.). Ambivalence, for example, cannot be thought through and affirmed as such because it preconditions the choice between civilization and chaos. It can only be disavowed in the name of order and signification, while cultural authority or supremacy remains authoritative because . . . well, just because. In other words, hybridity's potentially radical ambivalence can only be overcome either by active disavowal (by emptying out the face of the past as it emerges into the present) or by naked force: that is, by the return of the law as law.

As we will see in the discussion that follows, the active disavowal of ambivalence in *Death in the Andes* — its inability to inscribe the *cholo* interface as anything more than a potential loss of meaning that has to be forgotten and lost in order to maintain the logic of logic and the order of order — becomes an unstable haunting of the body of neoliberal thought and representation. This dynamic is by no means limited to this novel. Rather, I would hazard to say that it underlies generally the temporal borderlands of the Andes/coast interface in contemporary Peru.

Death in the Andes is a murder mystery without a crime, a body, or a weapon, and therefore with nothing to investigate. In other words, it is detective fiction without the power of reason. In the novel the representative of Creole state law, Corporal Lituma, has been posted to Naccos, a frontier encampment uncomfortably close to one of the Shining Path's so-called liberated zones in the Andean highlands. There Lituma finds himself enmeshed in a series of inexplicable disappearances for which no one has the answers, particularly not Naccos's Indian laborers who are constructing a road to no one knows where.[18]

The object of Lituma's investigation is ultimately the interface between the Creole rationality of cause and effect and the Andean netherworld and the indigenous system of belief, which is represented in the novel as perhaps the prime structuring force of the cultural landscape. Through the corporal's repeated contact with the mysterious shamanistic figures of Dionisio (the bisexual tavern owner and suspected instigator of nocturnal high jinks) and Adriana (Dionisio's wife, a renowned witch and slayer of evil spirits, who, Lituma suspects, hands herself over to the orgiastic spirit with men other than Dionisio), Lituma becomes increasingly convinced that the Naccos disappearances belong not to the realm of the modern world's material interests of production and exchange, nor to the resistance to those interests as represented in the novel by the brutality of the Shining Path, but, rather, to the mysterious experience of the ritualistic and the sacred in what is portrayed as everyday Andean life. As it turns out, the disappearances belong somewhere on the border between the material and the sacred. As a means of placating the evil spirits of the Andes, who have been offended by the construction of the road through the sierra, Dionisio and Adriana incite and orchestrate a series of human sacrifices aimed at avoiding a potentially impending apocalypse, thereby keeping the Indian laborers in a job while also keeping intact the community that keeps their carnavalesque tavern open for business.[19]

The victims, it is suggested, are outsiders or social marginals who are hurled down a mine shaft in a state of total intoxication (the same state, it is later revealed, in which the anonymous executioners perform their transgressive functions). *Death in the Andes* is, then, an investigation into the logics of the outsides to Creole state reason, law, and morality (the powerful spirits—*apus, huancas, chancas, pishtacos,* and *ñacaqs*—of the Andean cultural landscape), whose sustained outsidedness remains at all times constitutive of Creole order and hegemony. The novel is, in other words, an examination of the outside-inside borders to Creole/coastal hegemony in the Andes, and it confronts the unsettling ambivalence that surfaces when that constitutive outside (so-called Andean worlding) comes a little too close for comfort (or, for that matter, for sustained order and governability).

The narrative of Lituma's somewhat pathetic attempts to unlock both the mystery of the disappearances and the secrets of the Andean people, language, and culture are interspersed with narrative sequences depicting the barbarism of terrorist violence and persecution against the civilizing forces of white educated innocents, state representatives, a merchant, and foreign capital. Thus we are presented with two French students bludgeoned to death by the Shining Path as they travel by bus to Cuzco; a Belgian ecologist captured in a liberated zone while carrying out research who then is interrogated and stoned to death at dawn; a herd of vicuñas belonging to a foreign enterprise that is mercilessly destroyed by the Shining Path in the highest reaches of the Andes; the respected governor of Andamarca who escapes a Shining Path attack by the skin of his teeth and, from a grave in the cemetery in which he is hiding, witnesses the violence of Maoist popular justice only to "be disappeared" later in Naccos under a pseudonym; and, finally, an albino merchant who takes advantage of a young indigenous girl on his travels and is later confronted by a Shining Path death squad, which is led by the adolescent victim who is now hell-bent on seeking revenge. The albino merchant escapes miraculously but then disappears in Naccos under suspicion of being a *pishtaco,* an Andean fat-extracting evil spirit.

Throughout the novel the Andean cultural terrain is portrayed as a place of apocalyptically perverse enjoyment. The civilizing boundaries and foundational restraints of the state-forming, homeland-producing Apollo—the idealistic dream-state of the "shining one," in other words—have become displaced, inverted, and retranslated into the perverse nightmare of the Shining Path's dogmatic war machine against the state and its ties to international capital. On the other hand, those Indians not directly linked to the Sendero ("innocent" Indians, in other words) are suspected of congregating in Dionisio's tavern late at night and of engaging in drunken reveling, shadowy orgiastics, homosexuality, spirit worship, sacrifice, and ultimately even cannibalism. The logics of the Shining Path, the novel suggests, can only be understood within the broader context of unenlightened transgressive Indian practices. What is at stake in the reappearance of the Apollonian and the Dionysian in *Death in the Andes,* then, is no longer the transformative or modernizing potentiality of the Indian, as in Mariátegui's portrayal of the underlying spirit of the Peruvian social classes, but, rather, the Indian's apparently barbaric relationship to enjoyment; to an enjoyment that is viewed by Lituma (the uniformed embodiment of Creole state reason) to be a lack of enjoyment, a deprivation, an enjoyment in what is profoundly displeasurable or perverse to decent coastal culture. Indeed, this Indian pleasure in the profoundly displeasurable is played out through both guerrilla and nonguerrilla practices. It is all-pervasive, omnipresent, natural to the barbaric forces of Andean life, it would seem: "This fucking life was a bitch. Weren't the terrucos killing people left and right and saying it was for the revolution? They got a kick out of blood too" (18); " 'After you and I leave, I'm sure all kinds of faggot shit goes on in the cantina,' said Lituma. 'What do you think?' . . . 'Sure, disgusting stuff goes on. Dionisio makes them all drunk and then he gives it to them up the ass. You want to know something, Corporal? I don't feel sorry when Sendero executes a faggot' " (59).

The Andes, in this sense, is always a space located beyond the limits of state law and intelligibility, a frontier landscape in which language, morality, reason, justice, sexuality, and nation transgress their boundaries and disintegrate into an undefinable, ambivalent, and unthinkable Indian commonality. Thus the Andes in the novel stands for the apocalyptic horizon of epistemological breakdown that undermines, it would seem, modernity, the nation, the state, and civilization.

Quechua is little more than "savage music" (3), while the apparent inevitability of abject violence only serves to stereotype indigenous ties of kinship and community as they actively exclude the gregarious Corporal Lituma from their logics: " 'All those deaths just slide right off the mountain people,' Lituma thought. The night before, in Dionisio's cantina, he had heard the news of the attack on the Andahuaylas bus, and not one of the laborers who were eating and drinking there had a single thing to say. 'I'll never figure out what the fuck's going on around here,' he thought" (25). Potentially wild, brutish, devoid of selfhood and ultimately unrepresentable in their threatening commonality, the serrano becomes the coast's (and therefore the nation's) heart of darkness, to be constituted exclusively through effacement: " 'Do you believe in pishtacos?' Lituma asked the men at the next table. Four faces, half hidden by shawls, turned toward him. They all seemed made from the same mold—skin burned by hot sun and cutting cold, evasive, inexpressive eyes, noses and lips livid with harsh weather, unruly hair—and it was difficult for him to tell them apart. 'Who knows?' one of them answered at last. 'Maybe'. 'I do', one of the men in a hard hat said after a moment. 'They must exist if so many people talk about them' " (53).[20]

Throughout this Creole/coastal condemnation of all things transgressive/Andean the only redemptive space is to be found in the sections of the narrative that recount Lituma's contact with the outside (non-Andean) world. Lituma's assistant, Tomasito, is a serrano who nevertheless looks like a mestizo and speaks both Spanish and Quechua (5). Tomasito lies in bed at nights and recounts his one-sided love affair with a young prostitute from Lituma's home town of Piura, situated on the northern coast of Peru. After a series of picaresque adventures that carry the couple to the point of criminal excess, the coastal prostitute finally abandons Tomasito and takes his savings with her. However, at the end of the novel she reappears in Naccos, deus ex machina, searching for the Spanish-speaking, that is, acculturated/transculturated serrano who had been almost a slave to her well-being. The final heterosexual union of an acculturated (tamed) serrano and a now redeemed (i.e., an inherently good) coastal woman comes to represent the only space in the novel somehow beyond the logics of impending Andean apocalypse. But, of course, this beyond-space is nothing less than a re-presentation of nineteenth-century *hispanista*-styled romanticism: serrano redemption through hispanization and the love of a good (non-Indian) woman.

Ultimately the novel presents itself as the repeated revelation of the unintelligibility of Andean cultural practices and belief systems, which are invariably portrayed as naturally violent, ancestrally antidevelopmental, inherently transgressive, and profoundly illogical. This is only part of the picture, however, for of particular importance in the novel is the panic with which the coastal state representative—this embodiment of contemporary police and governmentality—portrays the threatening specters of increased urban Andeanization (*cholaje*) in recent years.

At one point the unintelligible events of Naccos are portrayed almost as a microcosm of the state of the nation as a whole, as Lituma reflects on the potentially cataclysmic consequences of mass Andean migration to the capital, and therefore on the possibly sustained translation to the coast (a space historically equated with Creole civilizing forces, of course) of collective practices and beliefs considered to belong exclusively to the Andean spiritual netherworld:

> "I'm sorry, Tomasito", Lituma interrupted in the darkness. "That article in the Lima newspaper about people stealing children's eyes really got to me. I'm not up to hearing about your love life tonight. Let's talk about the eye-thieves instead. Or about Dionisio and the witch." . . . "The paper didn't talk about pishtacos but eye-cutters, or eye-robbers," Lituma said. "But you're right, Tomasito, they're like the serrucho pishtacos. What I can't get through my head is that even in Lima people are beginning to believe this stuff. How can that be? It's the capital of Peru!" . . . "Something serious is happening in this country, Tomasito," Lituma interrupted again. "How can a whole district in Lima get so crazy they believe a story like that? Gringos putting five-year-old kids in luxury cars and cutting out their eyes with ultrasonic scalpels. Sure, maybe a few crazy women say those things. Lima has its Doña Adrianas, too. But a whole district believing it and people keeping their children home from school and looking for foreigners to lynch: it's incredible isn't it?" . . . "The paper said that last month people went crazy like this in Chiclayo, and in Ferrañafe, too", Lituma continued. "They said a woman saw four gringos in white robes taking a boy away; they found the body of another boy in a ditch, and his eyes were missing and the eye-robbers had left fifty dollars in his pocket. They formed patrols, just like in Ayacucho when there were rumors about the pishtaco invasion. Lima, Chiclayo, Ferrañafe, they're all catching the serrucho superstition. No different from Naccos. It's like an epidemic, isn't it?" . . . "I can't help seeing Dionisio and the witch in all this" said Lituma. "It's like those two savages were turning out to be right, not civilized people. Knowing how to read and write, wearing a tie and jacket, finishing school, living in the city—it's not enough anymore. Only witches can understand what's going on. . . . Peru is being overrun by devils and lunatics, and all you can do is go on about that woman." (159–63)

What is in danger of extinction in contemporary Peru, it seems, is the postcolonial Creole notion of the city as progress, of the nation as universal singularity, and of self-government as the foundation of a morally grounded national culture. Eminently ecstatic, orgiastic, barbaric, the Andes is a threatening cultural space whose potential expansion through migration promises the end of the history of Creole-led modernity and modernization in Peru; a space beyond thought, not even a limit-experience of Creole historical knowledge, but, rather, that knowledge overrun by chaotic bodies, rumors, and superstitions creeping into the very moral fabric of the nation-state and undermining the civilized polis from within.

But this invective against the effects of urban *cholaje* does not lead to further reflection within the novel. Apparently it cannot be thought through. It can merely be displaced once again and silenced within the text as just one more symptom of the hybrid present's mysterious loss of meaning in Peru. Needless to say, later in this chapter I will return to this outstanding and active labor of silencing.

"So what is to be done with the Andes?" seems to be the underlying question of the whole novel. In the end Lituma reveals what could either be an implicit solution to the question or the recognition of the impossibility of the art of coastal government in contemporary Andean Peru. Both possibilities are equally problematic. After discovering the truth he has been looking for—the truth of collective sacrifice and cannibalism, of a differential Andean relation to labor and consumption, or a barbaric ungovernability signifying little more than the exhaustion of the state— he simply walks away dumbfounded, incapable of further reflection and further interaction:

> "I'm sorry I tried so hard to find out what happened to them. I'd be better off just suspecting. I'll go now and let you sleep. Even if I have to spend the night outside so I won't bother Tomasito. I don't want to sleep next to you or near those guys snoring back there. I don't want to wake up tomorrow and see your face and have a normal conversation with you. Son of a bitch, I'm going to breathe a little air".
>
> He stumbled to the door of the barracks and walked out. He felt a blast of icy air, and despite his confusion, he could see the splendid half-moon and the stars shining in a cloudless sky, still shedding their clear light on the craggy peaks of the Andes. (275–76)

The Andes is worse when you know the details of its secrets, it seems, for the Creole state's final unraveling of the mystery cults of the highlands only leads to "confusion," and hence to the state abandoning (or so it is suggested) the sierra to its own devices. Naccos is a (pre)capital threshold space that upholds the specters of alternative worldings and of cultural indeterminacies that fracture (from within) the coast's (Lituma's) seamless narratives of order, progress, and civilization. Naccos shakes the edifice of hegemonic thought by exposing the limits between different and coexistent thresholds of cultural consistency, temporality, and meaning production within the time horizon of Peruvian capital itself. Naccos, then, is the site of an irreducible heterogeneity. It remains at all times incommensurable to the successful and orderly subsumption of difference under hegemonic forms of governmentality and of social reproduction.

This said, however, *Death in the Andes* cannot think such realities within the edifice and artifice of its own processes of signification. It can merely rally against them. It can lament the loss of meaning that they induce and expose them as the continual revelation of an archaic and barbaric world that makes a non-sense of coastal hegemony and of traditional notions of progress, development, and civilization. Quite literally, in the final pages of the novel the state's recognition and enunciation of cultural difference—Lituma's experience of "confusion" (276) (the anxiety that is produced by the exhaustion of all possible recognition and mutual understanding)—merely produces the disavowal of cultural difference and the initiation of abandonment ("I don't want to sleep next to you or near those guys snoring back there. I don't want to wake up tomorrow and see your face and have a normal conversation with you. Son of a bitch, I'm going to breathe a little air" [276]). Moreover, it is upon this act of disavowal—this final suggestion within the novel of an unfinished labor of active forgetting—that coastal cultural superiority, and, therefore, the perpetuation of the inferiority of the Andes, can be fabricated. *Death in the Andes* is, in this sense, a neoindigenist novel that strives to establish a hermeneutic process that naturalizes the necessary loss of Andean meaningfulness for the present.

Within Vargas Llosa's formulation the need for disavowal is upheld and structured by the evocation of the present as little more than a mystery—as a non-sense—that remains somehow beyond the domain of critical reason. Within this loss of meaningfulness the cultural authority of the nation-state (as represented in the figure of Lituma, the uniformed Piuran), can only lament and define itself, and renegotiate the terms of its authority, in relation to what it thinks it is not: not Indian, not Andean, not archaic, not transgressive, not Quechua-speaking, not gay or bisexual, and so forth. The nation-state in the novel, then, is nothing more than the embodiment of a suspect nostalgia for an order lost as a result of the confusion or undecidability that characterizes intense exposure to precapital difference and to unorthodox relations to the notion of production.

Before the state's exhausted political, epistemological, and aesthetic edifice the novel can only police its boundaries and, therefore, struggle for the face of the past as it emerges into the present by negating the cognitive instability of the transcultural contact zone. Moreover, it can only do this by presenting itself as an aesthetic resuscitation of the specter of Domingo Faustino Sarmiento. In other words, it is only through the resuscitation of the historical "clash of civilizations" (Huntington) in Peru that Vargas Llosa's neoindigenism—his developmentalist critique of indigenous/indigenist archaism in Peru—can uphold the promise of order or of contemporaneity. Equally, it is only through Sarmiento's spectral revenant that Vargas Llosa can disinter, and simultaneously fetishize, both Mariátegui and Arguedas as cultural relics lost to the inevitability of Peru's "end of History."

Meanwhile, however, the radical ambivalence of *cholaje*—the increasingly intensified urbanization, internalization, and proliferation of the coast-Andes/civilization-barbarism interface—remains conspicuously absent within such reflections. As we will see later in this chapter, however, *cholaje* remains at all times the constitutive outside—the traumatic outside-inside; the cultural/political unconscious—of the new order's archaic representations of postindigenist order and police.

As seen in this discussion of *Death in the Andes,* Corporal Lituma is deeply disturbed by news in Lima of widespread popular mobilizations against an outbreak of gringo eye-snatchers. Lituma reads such reports as little more than the enunciation of the end of civilization and of state hegemony in the metropolitan centers of Peru. In spite of the silence with which the novel itself very quickly disposes of such reports, however, it is in Lituma's (and therefore the state's) inability to grasp the complex insurrectional language of the Dionysian that we can begin to open up reflection to the dissemination of subaltern knowledge and *cholo* ambivalence in neoliberal Peru.

At the height of *manchay tiempo* (that is, of Lima's time of fear during the 1980s) a series of remarkable events swept across the shantytowns—the *pueblos jóvenes*—of Lima. Indeed, we would do well to examine these events in greater detail than Vargas Llosa does (or can) in *Death in the Andes,* because they represent not something as simplistic or as superficial as Lituma's reading of indigenous superstition and rumor translated into the city but, rather, they portray subaltern rumor as "a sign of a Messianic cessation of happening, or, put differently, a revolutionary chance in the fight for the oppressed past" (Benjamin, "Theses" 264–65).[21]

Indeed, it is through these events that we can begin to examine the ongoing struggle over the signifying processes of the past and present, of subaltern knowledge, and of the complexity of hybrid forms of social agency in Peru. In other words, it is through *cholo* sites of intervention that we can begin to bring the sedimented specter of Mariátegui back to the question of the Dionysian—and, of course, back to the spectral and radically heterogeneous emergence of real labor—in order to challenge the suspect nostalgia of Vargas Llosa's "end of civilized History" paradigm.

As Gonzalo Portocarrero Maisch, Isidro Valentín, and Soraya Irigoyen inform us in their volume *Sacaojos,* between the end of November and mid-December 1988 a popular uprising occurred in the poorest sectors of Lima. At a time of enormous economic and social hardship, with the Shining Path already active in the city and the government incapable of doing anything to counter their penetration, and on the eve of a suspected package of austerity-based reforms that promised to cut in half the buying power of the urban poor almost overnight, an incredible rumor circulated among Lima's popular (predominantly *cholo*) sectors: gringo doctors carrying machine guns, and with black aids or bodyguards, were entering the shantytowns, kidnapping children, and extracting their eyes with ultradynamic scalpels in order to sell the eyes abroad. Some rumors had the gringo doctor and his aides driving around the streets in an ambulance or a yellow Volkswagen, others stated that the doctors left the children blindfolded on a particular street corner with a princely sum of money left in dollars in an envelope. Other rumors even described the machine that the doctors used for the macabre extraction, and some stated that they also extracted the child's kidneys or their body fat. All agreed that the doctors existed, that they were gringos, white, armed, diabolical, and that they exported the children's body parts.[22]

Between 29 and 30 November hundreds of mothers—all of them first- or second-generation *cholas,* daughters or granddaughters of migrant Indians and, as Kraniauskas indicates, "new political subjects" ("*Cronos*" 15) in the capital's increasingly informal economy—took to the streets of Lima and congregated vociferously around local schools in order to get their children out and home as quickly as possible, for their lives were endangered by the white gringo doctors, their black assistants, and by their powerful connection to accumulation and machines of extraction. Populations organized nightly patrols—*rondas nocturnas*—through neighborhood streets. People throughout the shantytowns remained on a state of alert while the authorities could do nothing to quell the tension of the situation. Indeed, as Nathan Wachtel notes, far from appeasing the population the incredulous, dismissive, or ironic articles that appeared in the Lima press, together with the solemn televised denial by the Peruvian minister of health, only aggravated the problem (85).[23] On December 9 three young French tourists in José Carlos Mariátegui shantytown were detained by the local population and almost lynched for the kidnapping of twenty local children. The three French tourists were rescued by the police and taken to the Canto Grande police station where hundreds of mothers soon congregated shouting, "Poke their eyes out, burn them, child-killers" (Portocarrero Maisch et al. 48–49; translation mine). On December 10, local neighborhood leaders in Atusparia met with the people to discuss means of protecting themselves from the *sacaojos* outbreak. On the evening of December 12, a medical team from the Nutrition Research Institute was attacked by a raging multitude, most of whom were, once again, *chola* women. The medical team was saved from a lynching only by the arrival of three police tanks and one hundred fully armed civil guards (49–53). This was, however, the climax of the crisis, and from this point on the rumors of gringo eye-snatchers began to dissipate. But they did not by any means disappear, for many believed that although the *sacaojos* had gone into hiding because they had received too much publicity, they would return when the time was right.

According to Portocarrero Maisch et al. the *sacaojos* is a modernized, urbanized, *cholo* transfiguration or stylization of the Andean figure of the *ñacaq* or *pishtaco,* an evil spirit of the Andean netherworld who attacks lone figures on mountainous roadsides, throws magic powder in their face, and then proceeds to extract their body fat through the anus or simply rip them apart. The victim either dies immediately or suffers a few days before he or she disappears or wastes away as the result of a lack of body fat. As Michael Taussig (*Shamanism*) informs us, in the early 1950s the Peruvian ethnographer Efraín Morote Best discovered that the *ñacaq* almost invariably extracts fat from bodies in order to sell it to pharmacies where it is used in medicines, or to people who use it to grease machines, to cast church bells, or to shine the faces of the statues of the saints (238). The *ñacaq,* or *pishtaco,* is nearly always said to be white or mestizo.[24]

Events similar to those in Lima had been reported a year earlier in Huamanga in the Andean province of Ayacucho, this time in the center of Peru's civil conflict between the Shining Path and the Peruvian army. In Huamanga a number of mutilated bodies had been found, and rumors of *pishtacos* and *ñacaqs* immediately began to circulate. The perpetrators were believed to be *ñacaqs* who had been released on the populace by the government and had even been seen carrying "an ID card signed by 'presidente Alán' [García]" (Portocarrero Maisch, et al. 54; translation mine). According to local newspaper reports it was believed that the *ñacaqs* were extracting fat from their victims for export in order to create a medicine that could only be made with human fat. The money from this export was then believed to be used to pay off the nation's astronomical foreign debt. In other versions, the victim's meat was to be sent to restaurants particularly frequented by high-ranking members of the armed forces (Portocarrero Maisch, et al. 54). In Huamanga, one young merchant was stoned and hacked to death with machetes because, when confronted by a large crowd of people, he could not prove that he could speak Quechua and was immediately identified as an outsider, a *ñacaq* (54).

The question, of course, is what does all of this mean? Obviously we cannot resort to models of Andean savagery or wildness, since they merely re-present the developmentalist logics of neoliberalism and of *Death in the Andes:* the unintelligibility and absolute unrepresentability of an indigenous/*cholo* urban cultural landscape dominated by ancestral backwardness and archaism. Like Vargas Llosa's novel before it, this interpretation would simply fail to account for the extent to which such occurrences articulate differential or subversive relationships to, and challenge (no matter how momentarily), the seamlessness of historically constituted hierarchies and narratives of progress.

These astounding events have their roots in the colonial relations of the present and in the enunciation of a subaltern knowledge that articulates anticolonial protest at a historical moment in which the subaltern sectors of Lima were becoming increasingly cornered by the transition to free-market policies and economic liberalism. Indeed, the astounding affective circuitry of this insurgent performance allows us to glimpse the ways in which the transition to a new axiomatic of national and local social organization—the violent intensification of state intervention, of transnational market forces, and of outside gringo influence in everyday life—produces this *chola* reenactment of a haunting history of dismemberment, corporeal expropriation, deterritorialization, and exploitation. Within this political fantasy *pishtacos* and eye-snatchers "are clearly postcolonial and transcultural signs of contemporary social processes, evoking as they do the cultural memory of changes in the social experience of the body and its perceived invasion and colonisation by new institutions (medical) and regimes (technologies): modern doctors having taken the place of colonial priests in an ongoing history of dispossession" (Kraniauskas, "*Cronos*" 152).[25]

The emergence of the eye-snatcher rumor signals a ground-level response to, and subaltern knowledge of, a shift in the balance of local and world forces dominated by superhuman and supernatural powers outside and independent of the subaltern collective. Viewed as a surface on which power relations are inscribed, the body is construed as a central and active site for the historical appropriation and expansion of white/gringo neocolonial power. The extraction of fat, or of other body parts through technologically advanced means, comes to be viewed as a form of obtaining power or of wielding it over others and inevitably attests to the shantytown knowledge that the subaltern body is colonialism's and late capitalism's fetishized commodity par excellence, painfully joining and separating colonizer and colonized, white and Indian, gringo and *cholo* on the multifarious battlegrounds of colonial, national, and postnational history. The *sacaojos* episode conjures up an interface of complex and ambivalent contamination between past and present colonizations, knowledge and superstition, body and spirit, materiality (shantytown poverty) and immateriality (finance capitalism, the national debt, the IMF, market forces), the machinic and the magical, precapital and abstract labor, family and state, coast and sierra, male and female, affect and reason, and the penetrating force of the secular (medicine) and the sacred (the priest). It presents all of these contaminations (and no doubt more) in its spectral apparition, but displaces them right away *in* the apparition, in the very coming of the revenant that is the return of the specter of colonial relations.

Subaltern knowledge of the eye-snatcher, then, belongs to a realm of experience that one does not and cannot know precisely; in the words of Derrida, "one does not know if precisely it *is,* if it exists, if it responds to a name and corresponds to an essence. One does not know: not out of ignorance, but because this non-object, this non-present present, this being-there of an absent or departed one no longer belongs to knowledge. At least no longer to that which one thinks one knows by the name of knowledge. One does not know whether it is living or if it is dead" (*Specters* 6). It is, quite simply, the unleashing onto the field of signification of a radical interruption in the link between critical reason and power.

A question remains for us: how has the hybridity of the *sacaojos* episode been represented and thought through by those directly involved in its analysis?

For Juan Ansión, for example, the chaotic, vociferous, and disordered eruption of hybridity is a direct challenge to the sustainability of hegemony, ordered governmentality, and modernity in Peru. In his introduction to the collection of essays included in *Pishtacos de verdugos a sacaojos* Ansión characterizes the eye-snatcher rumor as sustained proof of a failed project of national transculturation. He thus positions the dissemination of subaltern knowledge as emblematic of the nation-state's crisis of hegemony, which, he says, has fueled the reemergence onto the terrain of national culture, politics, and state formation of ethnic irrationality, sectarianism, and ancestral backwardness. In this sense the eye-snatcher episode fractures the seamlessness of peripheral modernity and undermines its proposed passage from backwardness to development.

Having said this, however, he views this episode not just as an impediment to the consolidation of order and progress—not just as the eruption of *cholo* babelic babble onto civilization's processes of signification—but also as the limit from which a new process of hegemonization, now under the rubric of a politics of multicultural recognition, must be articulated and negotiated. As can be seen in the extensive passage below, in which multiple references to the specter of José María Arguedas suggest the author's sustained investment in an integration-oriented transcultural national fictive ethnicity, the eruption of the *sacaojos* is a double-edged sword exposing both hegemony's conditions of possibility and its conditions of impossibility in the struggle for the face of the past as it emerges into the present:

> Rumor is dangerous because it feeds hopelessness and undermines the possibility of forging a future with the support of a new knowledge. It indicates a moment of disconcertedness before the advance of the great social and cultural admixtures that are currently being produced in the capital city. This turn back into the self [*este repliegue hacia lo propio*] can perhaps be useful in times of great tension and confusion in which signs of order are desired. But it impedes one's ability to confront the real problems. It conspires against the unity of all popular forces. It generates radical, regressive, and exclusivist responses in moments in which great audacity is required in order to invent new social relations with the non-sectarian contributions of all the bloods. As a symptom, belief in the eye-snatcher allows us to bear witness to the urgent need to resolve the ancient problem of the cultural schism between diverse ethnic groups; and particularly between the Andean-Amazonic axis and the culture of Hispanic origin. It shows that it is more necessary than ever to work toward a fruitful encounter between the fox from up above and the fox from down below, as José María Arguedas put it, in order to consolidate multiple forms of alliance and mediation that would be capable of fomenting an authentic cultural mestizaje from below, which, rather than suturing opposites, could construct a new culture grounded in admixtures that are no longer fearful of multiple "contaminations." This would allow for a fearless unity in which it would no longer be necessary to turn back into the self, because the basis of unity would be grounded in the respect for difference. (14–15; translation mine)

A number of misconceptions are at play in what is, for the most part, a sympathetic reading of *chola* hybridity's affective emergence onto the Andes/coast interface. Ansión, like Lituma, reads the *sacaojos* as a cultural return to a primordial and profoundly antidevelopmental Andean origin (a "turn back into the self," as he puts it) that is capable of undermining the order and progress of the nation and of the nation's traditional modernizing projects and transcultural social alliances. By doing this, Ansión, like Lituma, reinstalls the foundational binarisms of national fictive ethnicity construction: identity and difference. He thereby overlooks the fact that this moment of radical incommensurability emerged from within, and as the effect of, the transcultural habitus—the ambivalence of an "authentic cultural mestizaje" negotiated "from below," that is capable of denoting "a new culture grounded in admixtures that are no longer fearful of multiple 'contaminations' "—that he apparently supports and calls for as a means of once again putting Peruvian modernity back onto the path toward progress. If this is the case then what, in Ansión's opinion, is the problem of the eye-snatcher and its effects? What is the threatening limit that is represented by this *chola* reading and performance of the colonial present? The answer is quite simple: the Andean past that emerges through this hybrid, urbanized, and informal performance remains untamed and untameable ("an unknown quantity" as Vargas Llosa might put it). It is unrecuperable and unproductive when viewed from within the historical, political, and epistemological paradigms of modern Peruvian nation-state formation.

Although modernity's processes of state-led transculturation (of national fictive ethnicity) were designed to fabricate hegemony by producing and incorporating the people as the subordinate position within the postcolonial universalization of particularities, the emergence of the eye-snatchers testifies to the failed incorporation and production of the people, who now actively desuture the representational processes of the universalization of particularities, and therefore also of hegemony, from within. The eye-snatcher rumor thereby wreaks havoc on the possibility of constructing a hegemonic articulation between distinct agents and differential social and ethnic positionalities. Perhaps it even fractures the possibility of thinking hegemony as a sustainable category in contemporary Peru. It unglues the dialectic of identity and difference that has for years grounded and preconditioned the promise of the nation-state and of a modern national culture. As such, it undermines the figure of death that upholds the promise of national sovereignty and of economic and cultural development in the future. The *sacaojos* is overburdened (and indeed overburdens the social) with semantic excess because it is

The Other Side of the Popular

both self-evident in its emergence and yet profoundly impenetrable. It is simply too subaltern, too hybrid, and too unrecuperable an enactment for the good of sustained hegemony, order, and progress. From within the boundaries of hegemony thinking, it provides no ordered resolution for "the ancient problem" of so-called archaism, cultural difference, and backwardness. It can only offer epistemological chaos—the affirmation of a Dionysian netherworld of savage hybridity—that is incapable of covering up the gaps and limits in the edifice of hegemonic thought that it itself fractures. It is therefore unable to provide resolution for its own eruption. In this sense, the emergence of its conditions of possibility (transculturation, hybridity, *cholaje*, informalization, the demise of populism/socialism and the transition to economic liberalism) are precisely the conditions of impossibility of a sustained hegemonic thought, for it denotes (just once, just this time) the emergence of the subaltern as the effect and performer of an irreducible violence that momentarily fractures the signifying processes of neoliberal capital and governmentality.

Thus the implicit question that remains unanswered at the end of Ansión's introduction is how to tame such an enactment of savage hybridity in order to keep the promise of national hegemony and national police alive. For Ansión, of course, the answer lies in the reformulation of national fictive ethnicity; in the hegemonic reuniversalization of particularities and in the politics of recognition between "the fox from up above" and "the fox from down below." As we will see in our continuing discussion of the representations of Peruvian neoliberalism, Francisco Lombardi's film *Bajo la piel* (Beneath the skin) provides Ansión's neo-hegemonic desire with a powerful model of figuration.

BENEATH THE SKIN

Francisco Lombardi's 1996 film *Bajo la piel* intervenes, it seems, at precisely the point at which Lituma's Andean investigation ends (in the disavowal of cultural difference) and at which Ansión's call for a return of authentic (and, presumably, state-led) national fictive ethnicity is unseated by *cholaje*'s radical subaltern hybridity.

The film is set in the small town of Palle on the northern coast of Peru, on the eve of the town's anniversary. In this desert topography renowned for the violent human sacrifices and sacred decapitations of the pre-Incan Moche warrior-priests (a cultural terrain that was later assimilated by the Incan empire of Tahuantinsuyo), Captain Percy Corso

investigates a string of mysterious murders in which the heads of adolescent males between the ages of sixteen and twenty are found carefully
decapitated, with their eyes perfectly extracted, in what appears to be
almost a restitution of Moche sacred tradition to the present.

As in *Death in the Andes*, in *Bajo la piel* archaic social violence erupts as
a surface expression of deeper ethnic, socioeconomic, and/or ideological contexts that are located within, and on the margins of, the nation-
state, national identity (Peruvianness), national culture, and, therefore,
the time horizon of contemporary development itself. In other words, as
in *Death in the Andes* and the *sacaojos* episode of 1988 before it, the reemergence of dismembered bodies in *Bajo la piel* upholds the violence
of a topographic-temporal ethnic boundary that both distinguishes and
unites the heterogeneous faces of the past as they emerge into the Peruvian present.

The questions underlying the development of the film are as follows:
Do these bizarre decapitations belong to the order of the immediate, to
transparency and the world of evidence? Do they pertain to the contemporary world? Or do they disclose history as the perpetual gravedigger
of the present, thereby suggesting that the motives underlying the eruption of social violence in Palle remain beneath the skin, as an affirmation
of an unthinkable netherworld of transcultural ties that bind that promise little more than the sustained impossibility of national development
and progress?[26]

Curiously enough, though, and in contrast to our previous readings of Indian/*cholo* corporeal dismemberment, this is a film explicitly
grounded in the pursuit and successful achievement of happiness. Indeed, it presents itself as the active remembrance and restructuration of
the road from indigenist chaos and dismemberment (from an apparently
Moche crime wave in which, the film suggests, the cyclical return of precolonial passions and antidevelopmental indigenous affects still hold the
key to understanding the eruption of social violence up to and including
the Shining Path) to individual hispanized contentment, order, and fulfillment. As such, the film can be read as an extension and sustained interrogation, in the present, of the place of the foundational *hispanista/in-
digenista* debates of early Peruvian modernity. It is hardly surprising,
then, that the film returns us not just to the ancient Indian past, but also to
Nietzsche and to Hellenic conceptions of history and culture, as a means
of thinking about the services that transcultural Euro/Indian "history is
capable of performing for life" (Nietzsche, *Untimely* 77).

Indeed, in *Bajo la piel* Percy Corso's Palle is almost a reproduction of the Hellenic struggle against heterogeneity and its threat to the boundaries of the ordered polis. In this sense, Nietzsche's comments in *Untimely Meditations* ring almost uncannily true for Lombardi's examination of both the everyday and the underlying forces that produce the violence of postcolonial cultural history in Peru:

> There were centuries during which the Greeks found themselves faced by a danger similar to that which faces us: the danger of being overwhelmed by what was past and foreign, of perishing through "history". They never lived in proud inviolability: their "culture" was, rather, for a long time a chaos of foreign, Semitic, Babylonian, Lydian, Egyptian forms and ideas, and their religion truly a battle of all the gods of the East. . . . And yet, thanks to that Apollonian oracle ["the god of Delphi cries to you his oracle: 'Know thyself'"], Hellenic culture was no mere aggregate. The Greeks gradually learned *to organize the chaos* by following the Delphic teaching and thinking back to themselves, that is, to their real needs, and letting their pseudo-needs die out . . . after hard struggle with themselves and through protracted application of that oracle, they even became the happiest enrichers and augmenters of the treasure they had inherited and the first-born and models of all future cultured nations. This is a parable for each one of us: he must organize the chaos within him by thinking back to his real needs. (122–23)

As we will see in the discussion that follows, *Bajo la piel* simulates the precolonial order of sacred warfare and sacrifice, as well as the Hellenic quest for, and revelation of, self-knowledge as the precondition for the organization of chaos. In the end, however, the needs of the present in the film are formulated and controlled through the active disavowal of archaic Indianness, while hispanization is placed once again at the service of the present, of life, and of happiness. In this sense, the film is about Peruvian modernity's competing knowledges and about the usefulness of those knowledges for the present and the future. But it also provides these knowledges and discourses with a language that is capable of placing the nation's foundational intellectual discourses firmly within the present.

The film opens with a modern-day tropical *locus amoenus* and with the figure of a mestizo man (Captain Percy Corso) rocking gently in a hammock and reflecting silently to himself about the road to personal well-being: "They say happiness doesn't exist, that it's just an idea, just an illusion. Until a few months ago I thought the same."[27] This tranquil scene then cuts to the beginning of his history; that is, to the origin of his quest for happiness now fulfilled and known, and, therefore, to the revelation of what it is exactly that makes happiness happiness in the Peruvian present.[28]

But the film's mnemonic process does not begin with the origin of the ritualistic crime wave. Rather, Corso's road to happiness begins *en media res* with the uncovering of a fourth eyeless and decapitated head, which is discovered in the garbage by a young soccer player. The film willfully disavows three prior moments of violence. It actively condemns them to the dustbin of history and therefore banishes them to representational insignificance for once and forever more. In this sense, the film openly gives itself, *a posteriori* as it were, a past in which it would like to originate (the origin of the process toward happiness) in opposition to that in which it did originate (the three prior decapitations). Thus the order of representation in *Bajo la piel* embodies the selective forgetting of certain zones of experience within its own process of coming into being. Quite literally, the film allows its pseudo-needs to die out.

Furthermore, what constitutes the foundation of life and happiness for the present is the silent weaving of a second crime into the logics of the first; the surreptitious choreographing of a crime of individual passion that is firmly rooted in and responds to the state's (Captain Corso's) perceived needs of the immediate present, rather than to those imposed by the spectral return of collective precolonial and colonial subaltern histories or cultural practices. Happiness, then, is the effect of an active cover-up imposed by an individualized crime of passion that successfully subsumes, diverts, and resignifies the ritualistic fourfold eruption of Indian/indigenist worlding. The success of the second crime, which is itself the mimetic reenactment and commemoration of the four previous murders, simulates and displaces the sacred ritualism of violence's potentially precolonial eruptions. It also allows for the opening up of the social realm to the experience of individual peace, order, and tranquility with which the film is framed.[29] The film reenacts forgetting as a precondition to the forging of individual and collective contentment. And the force behind this creative construction of collective peace and tranquility is the man of police himself, Captain Percy Corso, the mestizo embodiment of law and order in Palle.[30]

In his investigation of the pre-Columbian/colonial/contemporary decapitations and eye extractions, Percy Corso finds himself drawing on, and passing between, two competing visions of what is potentially *bajo la piel* (beneath the skin; on the underside of the everyday) and presumably at the innermost core of human nature (Peruvianness, for example). In the state's quest to uncover Palle's most intimate drives and

The Other Side of the Popular

historically grounded secrets we encounter two distinct yet intimately intertwined bodies of knowledge; two forms of epistemological intervention into the individual and social body; two modes of reconstructing life postmortem. Between forensic pathology and archaeology Percy uncovers two knowledge markets and two mnemonic models engaged in the revelation of historical truth. And it is through the law—through Percy Corso himself—that these two bodies of knowledge begin to interact within the film in such a way as to create the conditions by which individual mestizo police and happiness can be enjoyed in the end. In other words, it is through the suicide and disposal of the body of the representative of one form of knowledge (archaeology) and Corso's sustained desire for the female representative of the other (forensic science), that the film reconstructs itself as the Peruvian road to order and individual well-being.

Percy becomes convinced very early on in the film that Professor Pinto, the director of the Museum of Anthropology at the University of Palle—who, it is later revealed, also worked at the University of Cajamarca between 1979 and 1982—holds the key to this macabre re-enactment of pre-Columbian sorcery. Indeed, from the very moment of Percy's first suspicion the remainder of the film is dedicated to proving him to be right.[31] However, it is only with the combined articulation of modern western science (as seen in the town's beautiful Spanish-educated pathologist) and of northern high culture (as revealed in reference to Edgar Allan Poe's "The Pit and the Pendulum"), rather than through archaeology's unearthing of indigenous pasts and of heterogeneous subaltern knowledges, that instrumental reason can be put to work and the case pieced together.

The female Spanish-Peruvian pathologist suggests that the sacrificial knife used by the murderer must have been shaped like a pendulum similar to that in Poe's macabre tale. This find immediately sends Percy back to the Museum of Anthropology in order to recuperate a Moche dagger that he suddenly suspects to have been the murder weapon. The pathologist finds traces of blood on the sacred weapon and Pinto is duly arrested for a series of murders designed, it seems, to conjure up the gods of the past, to evoke the historical continuity of the Indian collective subject, or to restitute indigenous worldings to contemporary Palle.[32] The archaeologist, however, refuses to confess and thereby refuses to hand over his knowledge. Finally he commits suicide in his cell (a private act of resistance imitating Indian mass suicides in the face of Spanish colonization) at the height of Palle's anniversary celebrations. The day after his suicide a jar of eyeballs is found in his home by the police, obviously suggesting that the decapitator/eye-snatcher has finally been exposed, and the case closed.

But it is at this point that *Bajo la piel*'s second narrative begins to take form, and, indeed, to take over (to become hegemonic) within the film. It is at this point that Percy begins to emerge as the Peruvian incarnation of the Eighteenth Brumaire of Louis Bonaparte; the protagonist, in other words, in a reenactment of previous history that is designed to empty out that past of its previous contents, and of its former transformational potentials.[33]

Percy and the Spanish-Peruvian pathologist, Marina, have become lovers, consummating their relationship first on the Moche sacrificial stone at the local pre-Incan ruins and later in her laboratory, shortly after discovering the traces of blood on the Moche dagger while Percy gazes out (in horror?) at the specimen bottles lining the walls (an obvious foreshadowing of the archaeologist's carefully guarded jar of eyeballs). But their relationship is an accumulation of explicitly noncoincidental desires, investments, and affects. Marina finally rejects Percy in favor of Gino—the mayor's son and a renowned philanderer. After spying on the couple making love, and in a moment of drunken self-pity, Percy accidentally runs over and kills his dog, Napoleon, and buries him in the garden of his home. This chance event, together with the archaeologist's unexpected suicide, allows Percy to uncover his entrepreneurial (specifically strategical) side, and to forge a new symbolic order by constructing the fifth decapitation and eye extraction—the film's second murder mystery that simulates the details of the first. By doing this Percy choreographs a masquerade that is designed to lure the representative of European science and knowledge (the pathologist) back into the private world of the lawman and, in the process, lay the foundations for the revelation of a Peruvian road to contentment and order.

At the height of Palle's anniversary festivities, and with the police guards either absent or sleeping, Percy discovers the archeologist hanging in his cell. He "disappears" the body and fakes Pinto's escape while hiding the cadaver in his home. He then lures the mayor's son to his home, shoots him in a fit of envy, and proceeds to decapitate him and extract his eyes in the bathroom, using the Moche knife previously confiscated from the Museum of Anthropology. Under the protection of darkness he drives the two corpses—one the simulation of a precolonial decapitator (Pinto) and the other the simulation of his victim (Gino)—into the desert sands, and buries them one on top of the other. However, as he is digging he is spied by a lone horseman passing in the darkness. As such, his perfect crime—a crime made possible by its explicit accumulation of corporeal simulacra—is perhaps not quite so perfect.

As in the previous killings, the head of the mayor's son turns up in the town garbage, while news of the decapitator/eye-snatcher's escape and apparent reemergence exposes the local authorities' inability to control and apprehend the now quite farcical return of history's tragic order of cyclical decapitation and eye extraction. With the arrival of a state investigator, however, together with the emergence of forensic results that indicate methodological inconsistencies with the previous four decapitations, Percy's account of events begins to raise suspicions. The Spanish-Peruvian pathologist, meanwhile, returns to Percy without explanation and, when asked if she was sleeping with the mayor's son, assures him that she was not. Percy actively condemns what he witnessed to the dustbin of history, apparently deciding that the end of discourse and truth preconditions the establishment of the emergent social order: "That's fine. I won't bother you again with this," he says. Finally, when the anonymous horseman informs a local newspaper reporter that he witnessed Corso digging in the desert in the middle of the night, the imperfection of his simulation appears to have been exposed and Percy's fate is sealed. He is driven into the desert and forced to dig at precisely the spot where he buried the archaeologist and the decapitated body of the pathologist's lover.

However, under the watchful eyes of the state investigator, the mayor, the reporter, the witness and, at a distance, the pathologist, Percy (looked at from all sides) dupes the collective seekers and representatives of truth and of scientific and popular knowledge by exposing, on the smooth lines of the desert, the cadaver of Napoleon (his dog) who, it is now revealed, had been previously exhumed from his garden, reburied in the desert topography on top of the other two cadavers, and now, once again, disinterred as a screen designed to reestablish the contours of collective knowledge. With the exposure of the dog's second death on the flat surface of the desert sand, Percy substitutes the layered depths of collective history with the smooth surfaces of a new ground of objective signification.

A new order of signification emerges, capable of installing and of upholding objective truth by displacing the weight of the violent past and by emptying it of its exemplarity or value for the present. With the exposure of Napoleon, truth is uncovered, collectively recognized as credible, and instituted—Napoleon is dead; he is a mere ghost of his former self. But this offering up of credibility for all to see (its obvious transparency, in other words) disappears truth (Pinto and Gino are disappeared and dead thanks to the police) and withdraws it from the realm of know-ability. Thus, the exposure and reenactment of the death of Napoleon is both the only thing to see (the revelation of credibility as absolute truth) and the proof that there is absolutely nothing to see (no truth) other than that of a decomposing signifier inhabiting and giving life to the present and to its sustained social relations. The ghostly presence of Napoleon is a sign that fabricates the present by making collective history, embedded-ness, sedimentation, and knowledge disappear (and appear otherwise, at exactly the same time). It is, in this sense, an act of institution.[34] Thus the indigenist restitution of the precolonial past to the present is quite liter-ally subsumed by the repeated exposure and recycling of the ghosts and names of the bourgeois past (Napoleon). This opens up a movement of exposure that allows, on the one hand, that meaning still be produced, but, on the other, that that meaning will mean little more than its own immediate credibility.

Through the revelation of Napoleon we are presented with the simu-lation of historical significance. But the meaning of Napoleon's cadaver is to be found only in the fact that it allows Percy to lift the veil on the fact that an event has *not* taken place. Local cultural history, in other words, has been sequestered. In the meantime, the meaning of history—of his-tory understood as depth and embeddedness, and as the potential emer-gence from below of alternative worldings—collapses, or at least enters the first stages of collective fossilization.

Percy's crime of passion and envy (of *invidia, videre,* to see) is covered up in such a way as to arrest the eye of the law, of justice, and of his-tory because the rehabilitation of Napoleon as dead provides Percy with a mask, a double, that he can give to be seen to those around him in order to uncover himself as the nonperpetrator of the perfect crime (the theft of collective history itself). It is with the rebirth of Napoleon as dead again that a foundational disjuncture in the order of seeing and knowing opens itself up to *Bajo la piel*'s gaze. The viewer, who now has to recog-nize that she did not know that the "real" bodies had been covered over by Napoleon, is for the first time confronted by a nonknowledge that can only be recognized anamorphically; after the fact, so to speak. As such, she is now exposed as always already caught and tamed in both Percy's, and in the film's, representational trap.

The exhumation of Napoleon forces us to lay down our gaze before the effect of seductive imagery and superior representation. Thus the film effects a temporary coup on reflection. It is a coup that constructs itself surreptitiously in the space opened up between the two deaths of Napoleon: that is, between the tragedy of his "real" death (in which he is hit by Percy's truck and buried), and its farcical resymbolization (in which he is publicly exhumed before the eyes of the state and exposed as dead, thereby taming the state judicial system and declaring its symbolic order ineffective). The film's between-space, the place between the two deaths (and symbolic lives) of Napoleon (a space that also accounts for the death of the representative of indigenist knowledge as well as for Percy's rival in love) exposes Napoleon's body as the nonhistorical kernel around which the symbolic network of Percy's brave new individual world can be articulated.

Like the precolonial Moche, Napoleon is caught within the web of death and put to the service of the present. The difference, though, is that the dis/re/disinterment of Napoleon's dead body empties out the history of Moche archaism and of indigenist restitution. It produces consensus around the signs and meanings of the present, resutures the imaginary and symbolic order of the world, and ultimately produces an order of tranquility grounded in the renegotiation of silence as sustained happiness, consensus, and objective truth. Thus, at the end of the film Marina confronts Percy for the last time:

> PERCY: You are accusing me too?
> MARINA: The only thing I want is for you to be sincere with me. I need to know the truth, whatever it is. I'd never tell anyone. Did you have anything to do with Gino's death?
> PERCY: This is the last time I'm going to talk about this either to you or to anybody else.
> MARINA: Did you do it?
> PERCY: . . . No.

It is at this point that the *locus amoenus* reappears, that Percy's silent monologue of peace and contentment reestablishes the new order of the present, and that a pregnant Marina glances over and smiles (presumably carrying the heir to this individualized story of hispanic consensus production). Thus *Bajo la piel* draws to a close with the promise of *real* de-Indianization. Meanwhile, indigenism and indigenist knowledge have been subsumed and silenced forever. As Percy Corso narrates at the film's close: "It was a bad dream. A nightmare from which I've already awoke. Now I have everything, or almost everything. With Marina you can never know, but I accept her as she is and that is enough. Sometimes I think I don't have the right to be so happy and that everything I did could turn against me some day. But then I think of Pinto, of Pinto and what he used to say about the Moches. They did atrocious things too. But who cares about that now?"

The order of peace, tranquility, and material well-being—and therefore the reinscription of the European Enlightenment notion of police—
is achieved through the entrepreneurial construction of a radical illusion
that is made possible by adapting to chance circumstance and by laboring at all cost to place individual and collective history exclusively at the
service of the immediate present. It is Percy's construction of simulation—of a simulation guaranteed by conjuring up the spirits of the bourgeois conservative past (Napoleon), by putting them to the service of the
present and borrowing from them names, battle cries, and costumes in
order to present the new scene of local history in this time-honored disguise and this borrowed language (Marx, *Eighteenth* 15)—that re-sutures
truth to the real, that voids the past by mimicking it, and that fabricates
the silence of consensus as the foundational vehicle for the dissemination
of truth and happiness. Thus, happiness is negotiated by enlisting the
services of the signifiers of the past and by then running them through
the performative mill of the death drive, in order to transform collective
historical tradition into the continual erasure of the past in the present.

Percy opened the film by stating "they say happiness doesn't exist,
that it's just an idea, just an illusion. Until a few months ago I thought
the same." By the film's end we see that the term illusion is no longer in
opposition, nor counter, to the real or the possible. In the end it is only
by making the unreal real, through the fabrication of collective consensus around the meaning of the present, that happiness can be sustained
and the present rendered distinct from the past. Thus, in the end, illusion does not undermine the real. Neither does it stand against it as its
outer limit. Rather, it is the name to describe the order of simulation that
subsumes and supplants colonial histories in the present, thereby fabricating the collective reality of a new (harmonious) social order. And it
does this by placing the new order's temporal index firmly on the side of
the unfinished, and of the unfinishing, death drive.

Indeed, so successful is Percy in his simulation that by the film's end
the question of happiness (happiness as a desire or as a utopic drive)
can no longer be posed as a historically valid question because it is revealed as always already achieved and silently agreed on by all. Alongside
Mario Vargas Llosa in *La utopía arcaica*, Percy Corso reveals himself as
having succeeded in actively forgetting indigenism ("Who cares about
that now?"). He has successfully negotiated the eclipse of collective indigenist history precisely by simulating it and exposing it for the world
to see as no more.

As such, within this new social configuration there really is no longer
any need for language or for discussion on the signifiers of the past, for

The Other Side of the Popular

Percy has always already revealed and put into practice the image of his entrepreneurial plastic power. In this sense, *Bajo la piel* ends with the active subsumption of indigenist history, and silences the heterogeneous faces of the colonial past as they emerge into the Peruvian present. *Bajo la piel* is, then, an homage to the individual's ability to bypass the reemergence of history's collective and transformational colonial ghosts.

The film continues to manufacture history, but it does so in order to fuel the end of Peru's utopian notions of indigenist restitution and of collective indigenous social formations. Thus in *Bajo la piel* indigenism in the present is deterritorialized by the Benjaminian "storm from paradise." That storm, of course, is the signifier of progress, or, rather, of potential emergence, and it "constantly calls for new victims, for new events, so as to be done with them a little more" (Baudrillard, *Illusion* 22). As such, in *Bajo la piel*, as in Vargas Llosa's work on José María Arguedas, it is finally to indigenism that it will have fallen to fuel the end of collectivist formulations of the Peruvian past and present. Moreover, it is also to indigenism that it will have fallen to nourish the massive revisionism of the new world order that, to this day, defines the unstable contours of the Andes/coastal interface in Peru.

The model of structuration in *Bajo la piel* uncovers the passage of history as a low-key yet "triumphal procession in which the present rulers step over those who are lying prostrate" (Benjamin, "Theses" 256). Within this process the spoils are carried along in the procession as indigenous cultural treasures and sacred practices that are successfully silenced, tamed, and reconverted into the archaeological fossils of the future. *Bajo la piel*, then, is a model of figuration that represents itself as having effectively deterritorialized the specters of cultural difference, while having kept alive the notions of hegemony and of police.

Thus *Bajo la piel* stands almost as a methodological response to Juan Ansión's anxious call for a project of rehegemonization after the *chola* eruption of the final days of 1988. But hegemonization in the film is little more than a statist process of neohispanic de-Indianization designed to subsume the violent eruption of Peru's colonial specters under a self-satisfied simulation of stately police.

As such, the film turns us once again toward Mario Vargas Llosa's final evaluation of José María Arguedas and of literary indigenism in *La utopía arcaica*. It turns us toward the dynamics of the neoliberal clash of civilizations, in which the loss of indigenist meaningfulness is guaranteed by a reactive ideological maneuver that is designed to uphold the conditions of hegemony production as a function not of the present or of the future, but as the positive negation of the past. Let us recuperate momentarily Mario Vargas Llosa's reading of José María Arguedas:

> Everything indicates that Peru is now a society that definitively rejects archaism, and perhaps even utopia. . . . Although opinions vary on many issues—perhaps on *all* issues—Peruvians of all races, languages, economic conditions and political persuasions agree that the Peru of the future will not, and should not, be a revival of Tahuantinsuyo. It should not be an ethnically defined collectivist society, a country at odds with the "bourgeois" values of commerce and wealth. It should not be closed off to the world in defense of its immutable identity. Neither Indian nor White, "indigenist" or "hispanist", the Peru that is emerging and that is here to stay is still an unknown quantity. However, we can assure with utmost certainty that it will not correspond in the slightest to the images with which it was described—through which it was invented—in the work of José María Arguedas. (335; translation mine)

But *Bajo la piel* appears to do more than simply call for the need to fuel the end of indigenism's history, for the film actually gives body to what Vargas Llosa fails to elaborate in *Death in the Andes*. While in *Death in the Andes* we are left with little more than cultural disavowal and with a nostalgic lament for coastal/Creole hegemony lost, in *Bajo la piel* we face hegemony's refabrication through an emptying of history that is carried out in the service of coastal police.

But this is far from being the end of our story, because hegemony's final revelation in *Bajo la piel* recognizes its potential and perhaps imminent dismemberment. The hegemonic articulation embodied by Percy's *locus amoenus,* the moment of resolution with which the film both begins and ends, recognizes within its boundaries the threatening specters of hegemony's potential finitude. Thus in the film's final scene Percy slips in the apparently insignificant comment: "With Marina you can never know, but I accept her as she is and that is enough. Sometimes I think I don't have the right to be so happy and that everything I did could turn against me some day." This is obviously more important than it appears at first glance because it indicates Corso's knowledge of the limits of his fabrication of police, order, progress, and happiness. Corso's knowledge of the present is the knowledge of a potential future event that is capable of inaugurating "an interruption in the normal course of things, a radical dislocation" (Laclau, "Universalism" 73). Like Vargas Llosa before him, Corso reinscribes the notion of the present as inherently unknowable and unstable (as an unknown quantity) when viewed from within the epistemological edifice of hegemony's processes of signification. It is for this reason that the present must be continually emptied of historical significations other than those pertaining to the history of the new order's coming into being.

In this sense, the Peruvian road to happiness in *Bajo la piel* is profoundly anti-Benjaminian. Although the film is structured around Percy's ability to seize hold of a memory as it flashes up at a moment of danger (that is, around his ability to seize the revenants of indigenous coastal history), he quickly guides the specters of history away from the possibility of dislocation and directs them once again toward the notion of order. Thus hegemony in *Bajo la piel* emerges as a positive response to a moment of danger. It is hardly surprising, then, that the film should end before dislocation can reemerge and direct itself against the order, police, and simulated transparency of Percy's replete present. The film's final act, then, is that of silencing any possibility of difference as a result of Percy's regime of hegemonic reproduction. As such, *Bajo la piel* labors explicitly on the side of guaranteed and fully constituted intelligibility, given homogeneity, and systematic coherence in their absolute forms.

In contrast, however, *Bajo la piel*'s fleeting suggestion of future dislocation (represented in the film as little more than the possibility of a minor hiccup in the new individualized order of utopia) is the desuturing terrain toward which reflection on subaltern cultural politics should be directed. Having said this, however, the contours of such a reflection cannot be forged from within the film's production of hegemony itself. The film merely silences us, renders us speechless, "subalternizes" us. In order to trace the possibility of an alternative pathway we have to leave *Bajo la piel* behind and return to the site of the *cholo* as a telos that safeguards the possibility of an *other* history.

Cholaje challenges neocolonial modernity's monumental ideals of order, rationality, and progress. Its ambivalent hybridity exhausts the notion of identity and simultaneously provides no ground from which to think about difference. Thus it remains firmly rooted in the histories of modern and (post)modern development in Peru yet always sustains the possibility of a semiotic break with development's signifiers and dominant discourses. It is partial hispanization and partial de-Indianization simultaneously. However, its ungrounding ambivalence scarcely stabilizes the grounds of modern culture formation and its forms of contemporary political organization. In this sense, *cholo* is potentially the embodiment "of a shifting boundary that alienates the frontiers of the modern nation" (Bhabha 164).

The question, however, is how can we direct the notion of *cholaje* toward the possibility of new cultural perspectives and new readings of cultural history that do not merely subsume it under the homogeneous narratives of capitalist development, order, and police in Peru? What, in other words, can be presented for reflection within *cholaje* that is other than just another mainstream postmodern discourse on cultural hybridity's ability to guarantee the notion of transnational capitalist development and integration? How can we somehow uphold a promise that remains beyond *Death in the Andes*'s suspicious lament for hegemonic loss; beyond *Bajo la piel*'s silencing production and naturalization of consensus; beyond Matos Mar's already eclipsed faith in the national-popular revolutionary configuration; beyond de Soto's evaluation of informalization as the ground for national development's consolidation; beyond Ansión's nostalgic reenactment of the transcultural national-popular; beyond mainstream cultural hybridity, and beyond the idea of the collective as a Dionysian/Sorelian mythical unity? Within the context of the current discussion, how can we uphold a *cholo*—that is, a savagely hybrid—promise that is capable of affirming a critical perspective that lies beyond the limits of national hegemony and on the outer limits of our current forms of knowledge production?

In order to suggest this possibility—in order to advance reflection on subalternity and to do so by "establishing a conception of the present as the 'time of the now' which is shot through with chips of Messianic time" (Benjamin, "Theses" 263)—we must return to, and end with, the *sacaojos* outbreak that erupted in the shantytowns of Lima on the eve of the IMF's austerity measures in November and December 1988.

As already noted in my discussion of this spatio-temporal borderland insurrection, much has been made of the ancestral identitarian question and of the notion of sustained ethnic archaism as the placeholder and guarantor of perpetual national backwardness. Within this line of thought the specters of Sarmiento reinscribe *chola* insurrection as the symptomatic point of breakdown of a nation-state that is in urgent need of hispanic/coastal remodernization and rehegemonization.

Nothing, however, has been made of the real question of alterity in this insurrection: namely, the singularly antagonistic relation between the collective *chola* body (in relation to its offspring and, therefore, to future generations) and the gringo machine's perverse quest for corporeal penetration, dismemberment, and accumulation. Nothing, in other words, has been said of the place of the interface relation between the female body and the machinic that seems to uncover itself here as a result of the imminent dominance of global finance capital (the imposition of IMF austerity measures). As such, nothing has been said of the relationship that this insurrection establishes with the penetration of invisible global forces into the everyday life of Lima's informal *pueblos jóvenes*. This insurrection enacts a form of being that could be called "being for a chain of others." Within the insurrection, being for a chain of others is being opened up to being for the IMF, being for the World Bank, being for finance capital, and being for unimaginable quantities of foreign debt. Nevertheless, nothing has been said of the opaque "relations of syntagmatic linkage" (Guattari, *Chaosmosis* 35) that uphold this profoundly gendered "zone of occult instability where the people dwell" (Fanon 182).

Obviously, this insurrection is a response to cultural deterritorialization. But it is not just thinkable in terms of migration from the Andes to the coast. Nor is it imaginable merely in terms of identity-based underdevelopment. Rather, it is imaginable in terms of a gendered and ethnicized transition to a new order of finance capital that constantly deterritorializes with one hand and reterritorializes with the other; that imposes de/reterritorialization as the order of both global speculation and of the intensified wanderings of the informal sector in contemporary Lima. Within this context it appears that these *cholas* conjured up neither a space of deterritoriality nor a zone of reterritoriality—neither absolute displacement nor complete subsumption, in other words—but, rather, what Deleuze and Guattari have called a neoterritoriality; the eruption within the time horizon of capital of an unstable site that sows confusion between opposites and that promises to unwork the regulatory and controlling effects of modernity's binary oppositions and polarities. The following is Deleuze and Guattari's definition of neoterritoriality:

> Neoterritorialities are often artificial, residual, archaic; but they are archaisms having a perfectly current function, our modern way of "imbricating", of sectioning off, of reintroducing code fragments, resuscitating old codes, inventing pseudo codes or jargons. Neoarchaisms, as Edgar Morin puts it. These modern archaisms are extremely complex and varied. Some are mainly folkloric, but they nonetheless represent social and potentially political forces (from domino players to home brewers via the Veterans of Foreign Wars). Others are enclaves whose archaism is just as capable of nourishing a modern fascism as of freeing a revolutionary charge (the ethnic minorities, the Basque problem, the Irish Catholics, the Indian reservation). Some of these archaisms take form as if spontaneously, in the very current of the movement of deterritorialization (neighborhood territorialities, territorialities of

the large aggregates, "gangs"). Others are organized or promoted by the State, even though they might turn against the State and cause it serious problems (regionalism, nationalism). (*Anti-Oedipus* 257)

Neoterritorialities are, then, volatile zones of alterity or sites of emergence that are capable of splitting "the discourse of cultural governmentality at the moment of its enunciation of authority" (Bhabha 131).[35] They are interface zones of occult instability that belong to, stand alongside, and uphold the potential to erupt against "the abstract universality of wealth-creating activity" (Marx, *Grundrisse* 104). They thereby promise to fracture, from within, the naturalized edifice of hegemony and of abstract labor's history of development and expansion. In this sense, neoterritorialities suspend the abstract mechanisms of the capitalist social axiomatic in order to, perhaps, take on the posthegemonic functions and promises of real labor in globalized times.

In the case of Lima in November and December 1988, *chola* neoterritoriality exposed an underlying movement of history in which both gender and ethnicity became momentarily transferred onto the workings of disembodied, and disembodying, transnational machinic apparatuses and networks. This transferential movement unveils the *chola* as the potential site of still-unheard-of identifications, for in this insurrection she enacted herself as a body explicitly "singularized at the crossroads of heterogeneous machinic universes, of differing dimension, of foreign ontological texture, with radical innovations, with benchmarks of ancestral machinisms previously forgotten and then reactivated" (Guattari, "Machinic" 17). Lima's 1988 *chola* insurrection did not perform subalternity as a meaning that one can assign exclusively to questions of national or regional cultural identity, or to a lack thereof. Moreover, it certainly did not perform subalternity as a meaning assignable exclusively to the national elite's history of nation-state and hegemony formation. And therefore, it did not play itself out purely as the revelation of an originary or derivative ethnic identity. Rather, it played itself out as the unworking of originary and derivative identities.

Furthermore, I would suggest that the insurrectional quality of this insurrection lies in the relation that it establishes between gender, precapital, neoterritoriality, and the pressures of global finance capitalism that are experienced on a daily basis throughout the shantytowns of the South. If we take into consideration the fundamental fact that this insurrection was performed on the eve of Lima's insertion into the violent austerity measures of the IMF, perhaps it could be said that these groups

The Other Side of the Popular

of *cholas* enacted themselves as beings increasingly exposed to a new configuration that is grounded in "being toward becoming worldwide."

Needless to say, current institutional thought cannot accede to, nor arrive at, the constitution of this being's possible signification, for it would require a thought that is capable of withdrawing completely from the fulfillment of hegemonic (national) knowledge as we know it. However, this is not to say that such a form of being is not already underway. Being toward becoming worldwide presents us with the challenge of grappling with the notion of universality. It uncovers the traces of an unconstituted subaltern mass—a negative universality—that haunts the current social axiomatic with all its multiplicity and heterogeneity. It is a multi-faceted human limit within the current regime of accumulation that upholds the promise of a call to thought: to hear say yes in, and to begin to think through, the intensifying relation between migration, cultural hybridity, global subalternity, gender, and the neoliberal extension of finance capital.

In the relation between migration, gendered *cholaje*, and being toward becoming worldwide—in which both gender and cultural hybridity are fully exposed to the relation between shantytown life, the IMF, and, therefore, the World Trade Organization—we encounter a major stumbling block for hegemony thinkers who are seeking to reuniversalize the signifiers of specifically national cultural forms and traditions. This relation is, perhaps, "a place for the destabilization of all ontopologies, for a critique of totality—*and* a place for the possibility of an *other* history" (Moreiras, *Exhaustion* 294). If this is the case, then within the context of increasingly heterogeneous and highly coordinated mass protests against the current terms of capitalist expansionism (as seen, for example, in Seattle in 2000 or in Genoa in 2001), we might be able to suggest that the relation between migration, gendered *cholaje*, and being toward becoming worldwide announces just one of the potential heterogeneses of real labor. Perhaps it announces radical heterogeneities that cannot be fully subsumed by current metropolitan/masculinist discourses of national knowledge production or by contemporary forms of cultural commodification. We might be able to conjecture that such a relation announces the aporetic spot within the contemporary social axiomatic at which hegemonic (national) thought confronts (and attempts but fails to disavow) the "conception of the present as the 'time of the now' . . . shot through with chips of Messianic time" (Benjamin, "Theses" 263).

We might be able to affirm that it upholds the different coexistent thresholds of historical and cultural consistency, expressivity, temporality, and meaning production that fracture contemporary Peru from within. Finally, we might propose that it marks (potentially) the promise of savagely hybrid neoterritorialities; posthegemonic configurations that turn the notion of community outward—toward a scattered negative universality—rather than gathering them inward toward the false cohesiveness and factitious intelligibility of a stable hegemonic ground. With all of the above in mind, perhaps we could suggest that the relation between subaltern migration, gendered *cholaje*, and being toward becoming worldwide signals from a distance the Benjaminian portal "through which the Messiah might enter" (264). Needless to say, we can only speculate. One thing appears to be sure, however: being toward becoming worldwide leaves us with the affirmation of *perhaps* ringing in our ears and suspended on the tips of our tongues . . . perhaps. . . .

7

Operational Whitewash and the Negative Community

> How not to search that space where, for a time span lasting from dusk
> to dawn, two beings have no other reason to exist than to expose
> themselves totally to each other—totally, integrally, absolutely—so that
> their common solitude may appear not in front of their own eyes but
> in front of ours, yes, how not to look there and how not to rediscover
> "the negative community, the community of those who have no
> community"?—Maurice Blanchot, *The Unavowable Community*

> The visage . . . is that experience I have when, facing the face that
> offers itself to me without resistance, I see arise "out of the depths of
> these defenseless eyes", out of this weakness, this powerlessness, what
> puts itself radically in my power and at the same time refuses it
> absolutely, turning my highest power into im-possibility.
> —Maurice Blanchot, *The Infinite Conversation*

The opening section of this book, "Closure," traced some of the practical and theoretical limits pertaining to three of the most important Latin Americanist critical discourses of recent years. In chapter 1 I reviewed certain intellectual investments in the thought of transculturation, and through the examination of a number of specific cultural and political settings I analyzed their critical and historical relation to the wider field of modern populist nation-state formation in the South. In chapter 2 I traced the emergence of the notion of the subaltern in northern Latin Americanism as a cultural, political, and epistemological response to the overall crisis of the nation, the nation-state, national developmentalism,

All photos in this chapter are from the book *El infarto del alma* by Diamela Eltit and Paz Errázuriz. Reprinted with the permission of Paz Errázuriz.

the rise of Reaganism in the North, and the debt crisis of the 1980s. In that chapter I called attention to the relation between the crisis of the integration-oriented national-popular model in Latin America, and the emergence of an identity-based politics of microdifference, as a political and cultural alternative to the monumental cultural politics of nation formation. The purpose of this analysis was to shed light on the epistemological, ideological, and geopolitical constraints of northern intellectual interventions (including those included in these pages) that are grounded in the recuperation and representation of the notion of peoplehood and of common subaltern identities and agencies. Needless to say, the limits in question emerge in particular when those identities and agencies are negotiated from within the dominant structures and hegemonic paradigms of the postmodern U.S. academy. Then, in chapter 3, and in specific reference to the important critical contributions made by Néstor García Canclini in recent years, I traced the somewhat problematic relation that he establishes between the notion of cultural hybridity and categories such as consumption, citizenship, civil society, and cultural democratization. As I indicated in chapter 3, the positive relations of equivalence that García Canclini establishes between these notions tend to uphold transnational market forces as the essential ground for an ethical postnational state apparatus that is capable of representing the interests of social groups who are now living in the (ongoing) aftermath of the nation. However, these same relations fail to conceive of the possibility of a thought other than that which is always already structured and fabricated by, and from within, the managerial logics of neoliberal market forces themselves. As such, these formulations tend to give to global capital what global capital needs in order to expand its frontiers and to extend its horizons.

The second section of the book, "Intermezzo . . . Hear Say Yes," turned to literature and to the relation between language and the affirmation, in Ricardo Piglia's *La ciudad ausente,* of a common grammar of experience grounded in what Derrida has referred to as the contemporary world's extension of "absolute dislocation, borderless disjoining" (*Politics* 80). Piglia's novel suggests the possibility of a future narrative of collective experience—the promise of a coming polis—that remains at all times unconstituted within the narrative itself, yet always imaginable from within the deconstructive and constitutive force and circulation of storytelling and memory. In this chapter, *La ciudad ausente* is read as an opening up of language to the demands (the intimations, the posthegemonic "hear-says") of a future political topos—a future relation to the production of language and to the relation between language and world—that remains on the other side of, and that interrupts or suspends, national history's constituted cultural and social hegemonies.

By now the reader will have noticed that in the final section of this book I have worked toward the relation between posthegemony—the theoretical and practical site at which both hegemonic and counterhegemonic discourses cease to make sense—and the notion of "perhaps." I have chosen this relation, together with a number of the critical paths that it uncovers, because perhaps is the greatest gift that posthegemony has to offer. In the same way the greatest gift of deconstruction is "to question the authority of the investigating subject without paralysing him, persistently transforming conditions of impossibility into possibility" (Spivak, "Subaltern" 9), the greatest gift of perhaps is the chance to link "an *affirmation* (in particular a political one), *if there is any*, to the experience of the impossible" (Derrida, *Specters* 35). This act of linking, observes Derrida, underlines and preconditions the "radical experience of the *perhaps*" (35). As such, the thought of the perhaps "engages the only possible thought of the event—of friendship to come and friendship for the future. . . . And there is no more just category for the future than that of the 'perhaps'. Such a thought conjoins friendship, the future, and the *perhaps* to open on to the coming of what comes—that is to say, necessarily in the regime of a possible whose possibilization must prevail over the impossible" (Derrida, *Politics* 29).

In this final section I have strived to trace a pathway toward the perhaps. I have done this in order to outline the possibility of a critical perspective that is no longer grounded in the active reproduction of historically constituted hegemonies and counterhegemonies. Because the underlying ground of any theory of change is anchored in the displacement of function between sign systems, the pathway traced out in "Perhaps" has displaced the function of hegemonic thought in "the name of reading as active transaction between past and future" (Spivak, "Subaltern" 5). This is not to say that the discursive displacements included in this section are successful accounts that uncover, in definitive form, the contours of an alternative critical perspective. The narratives included in these pages are to a considerable degree accounts of epistemological and political failure: that is, accounts of the limits that circumscribe and challenge my own attempts to displace the function of hegemonic sign systems.

Having said that, however, it is also evident that perhaps and its posthegemonic thought tends to both challenge and undermine traditional constituted powers and critical paradigms. They point toward their finitude and to the possibility of a theoretical (and potentially constitutive) other side. The relation between posthegemony and perhaps therefore exceeds hegemony, denaturalizes its relation to the reproduction of intellectual mastery, and unbalances mastery's authority. However, it does not replace it with another master discourse. Rather, the relation between posthegemony and perhaps uncovers languages, worldings, narratives, and relations that point us toward those realms of experience, knowledge, and commonality that promise meanings other than those that are immediately handed over to the history and reproduction of instrumental reason's relation to cultural and social hegemonies. It promises areas of experience and forms of reflection that remain extraneous, or foreign, to the interests and orders of hegemony and of hegemonic thought. As such, it does not tend toward unity. On the contrary, it tends to challenge critical perspectives that are invested in the forging of unification or in the fabrication of hegemonic relations of equivalence between different subject positions such as those of the intellectual/subaltern relation. As such, it leans toward those sites of dislocation that demand *other* relations and *other* forms of measurement between subjects, and, for that matter, between (subaltern and elite) epistemologies and knowledge formations.

The thought of the perhaps takes epistemological, cultural, and political dislocation as the very form and foundation of possibility and freedom. As Ernesto Laclau observes in *New Reflections on the Revolution of Our Time:*

> With dislocation there is no *telos* which governs change; possibility therefore becomes an authentic possibility, a possibility in the radical sense of the term. This means that there must be *other* possibilities, since the idea of a single possibility denies what is involved in the very concept of possibility. . . . Because structural dislocation is constitutive, the dislocated structure cannot provide the principle of its transformations. The dislocated structure thus opens possibilities of multiple and indeterminate rearticulations for those freed from its coercive force and who are consequently outside it. And the very possibility of this dislocation reveals the character of *mere possibility* of the articulatory ensemble forming the structure before dislocation. (42–43)

Dislocation, together with the radical experience of the perhaps that it inaugurates, desutures the relation between critical reason and those practices, narratives, genealogies, and institutional configurations that have been fabricated and hegemonized historically. In my analysis of Francisco Lombardi's *Bajo la piel* in chapter 6, I traced the ways in which constituted power (in this case, the coastal notion of police in contemporary Peru) attempts to defend itself against possible (in this case, indigenous/indigenist) dislocations by obscuring histories marked by distinctive worldings or potential ideological antagonism. It does this by forging official discourses, cultural practices, and critical languages that are capable of withdrawing presence from the open violences and antagonisms of the past (of withdrawing presence from history's wars of position, in other words). The purpose of this is then to replace those potential antagonisms with a seamless veneer of collective consensus, apparent transparency, and the immediate intelligibility of common sense. As I suggested in my analysis of *Bajo la piel*, through the incomplete and often imperfect whitewash of the past the current order of accumulation in Peru attempts to suture the excessively open dislocations, antagonisms, and wounds of the latter half of the twentieth century. Needless to say, daily reality shows us that such attempts are profoundly flawed. However, it is imperfection itself that produces the grounds of iteration.

Indeed, as Michael Hardt and Antonio Negri indicate in *Labor of Dionysus*, globalization in general never stops attempting to suture the world to the notion of consensus and to the apparently seamless logics of the transnational marketplace:

> Through the mediatic manipulation of society, conducted through enhanced polling techniques, social mechanisms of surveillance and control, and so forth, power tries to prefigure its social base. Society is made aseptic through mediatic and communicative operations designed to dominate the dynamics of transformation and simplify the complexity of reality. The crisis of collective identities is in this way pushed to the extreme; individualism is maintained as the supreme value and the antagonisms are manipulated by the mechanisms of compensation that participate in the repression or eclipsing of the historical and social events. Society has to dance according to the rhythm of power and every dissonance, every instance of cacophony must be reduced to the heart of the harmony in which power invents the rules in every case. The passivity of consensus becomes the fundamental rule; the reduction of social space is the norm of political space; political space produces the social event, which produces the social dynamics and creates consensus; and finally the social is annulled through communicative overdetermination and substitution. The concepts of legitimation and administrative and political responsibility are ground up in the same mill. (272)

In this passage Negri and Hardt seem to be referring to what Jean Baudrillard has called the global market's ideal "dissolution of negativity in a perfused euphoria" (*Transparency* 44). By this Baudrillard means late capitalism's profoundly flawed yet unceasing "operational whitewash" of all negative histories and undesirable socioeconomic and cultural traits through the communicative manipulation of both language and image (44). Operational whitewash, explains Baudrillard, is the aseptic effect of a contemporary "surgical compulsion that seeks to excise negative characteristics and remodel things synthetically into ideal forms. Cosmetic surgery: a face's chance configuration, its beauty or ugliness, its distinctive traits, its negative traits—all these have to be corrected, so as to produce something more beautiful: an ideal face, a *surgical* face. . . . To this end," Baudrillard continues, "a gigantic campaign of plastic surgery has been undertaken" from within the current global order (45). Furthermore, Baudrillard notes in his customarily apocalyptic tone, through the mechanisms and calculations of contemporary power "we are doomed . . . to a whitewashing of all activity—whitewashed social relations, whitewashed bodies, whitewashed memory—in short, to a complete aseptic whiteness" (45).

As I outlined in the previous chapter, neoliberal discourse in Latin America is deeply invested in the casting off, and in the consequent disappearance, of negative or so-called archaic histories, cultural identifications, or belief systems. As such, in a film such as *Bajo la piel* the sign (as seen, for example, in the exposure of the dead dog, Napoleon) functions in order to make the sordid realities of collective indigenous history disappear, while at the same time it masks that disappearance with the appearance of a consensus-producing (nonindigenous) transparency. The sign, in other words, is made to function in the name of individual happiness—perhaps in the name of a particularly neoliberal *jouissance*—as a means of guaranteeing the obfuscation of neocolonial histories through the simulation of consensus and hegemony in the present.

It must be noted, however, that this is not something that is exclusive to Lombardi's award-winning film or, for that matter, to Mario Vargas Llosa's reading of literary indigenism. Indeed, thanks to the astounding penetration of transnational market forces in recent years, previously marginalized subaltern lives are now being increasingly assimilated into the consensus-producing mechanisms and calculations of postmodern cultural performance, simulation, and power. As such, Andean populations that just a few years ago were caught up (either directly or indirectly) in the open violence of Peru's "time of fear" are now actors who are increasingly (yet by no means uniformly) integrated into the performative whitewash of previous forms of social antagonism and dislocation. "Heritage tourism" in Peru has become a privileged site from which to witness recent transformations in the nature and extension of exploitation in Latin America, as well as from which to view the (ongoing, incomplete, and uneven) transition from open violence, fear, and antagonism to the powerful and aseptic mastery of market-driven consensus.

Consider George Yúdice's observations regarding the new expediency of culture and of cultural identity among growing sectors of the subaltern classes in neoliberal Peru:

> On a visit to Puno, on Lake Titicaca, nestled in the Andes . . . tourists are taken to see a Quechua farmer perform who he is. The tour bus stops by his ranch on the way to the patrimonial site of Silluistani, where Incan rulers officiated in the 14th century. We see this descendant of the Incas pound the earth with a hoe to soften it and then poke it with a pick in order to sow kernels of corn. Then he takes us to his outdoor kitchen, where he makes a fire of llama excrement briquettes as his wife prepares one of the 200 varieties of potatoes and grinds quinoa grain for soup. After treating us to food, he takes us into his cottage and shows us how he weaves his alpaca rug and how he sleeps with his entire family, including some animals. ("Expediency" 17)

Andean populations increasingly act out their indigenous cultural identities for organized groups of northern tourists, in neoethnographic performances that no longer strive to obscure the effects of cultural expansionism and economic superiority/inferiority. In this enactment of subaltern cultural identity the notion of Andean cultural difference becomes marketable. It is a performative rite that upholds archaic images of historical cultural resilience and of premodern economic sustainability. Such archaic images are nevertheless tamed by their full integration into postmodern marketing networks. However, this enactment also performs the idea that the current regime of accumulation is no longer one of open domination. Rather, in this rite of North/South communication the current regime is an order of benevolence, mutual cooperation, and charity (he shows us his house and gives us food; "we," presumably, give him money in exchange for his hospitality).

Indeed, through heritage tourism it appears that it is no longer necessary for superiority to hold up a screen behind which to conceal its hierarchies, for the expansion of the neoethnographic encounter in the Andes now uncovers and empties out previously fixed images and hierarchical representations of cultural superiority and inferiority. It does this by making superiority and inferiority explicitly interactive: in other words, by making them performative operations anchored in the simulation of a charitable "horizontalization" of social relations. Heritage tourism obscures the old notion of exploitation by subsuming it under the relation between northern enjoyment and Andean necessity (perhaps it is difficult to know who enjoys, or reaps the benefits of, these encounters more). By doing this, heritage tourism gives exploitation a new name: the expediency of culture. As a result, exploitation and the vertical relations of power that produce it are designed to disappear from view, thanks to a cultural reconversion in which "the subject who is principally exploited . . . is recognized in its creative subjectivity but controlled in the management of the power that it expresses" (Hardt and Negri 281). In this northern recognition of Andean peasant culture and identity, the presence of subalternity and of historical processes of subalternization are subsumed by a veneer of mutual cooperation and benevolence. Furthermore, if the performance and consumption of subaltern cultural identity brings subalternity per se as close to insignificance as possible, then it must also weaken the notion, impact, and image of domination's historical relationship to vertical power structures. Thus, the operational performance of subalternity renders domination virtually untouched and untouchable in its absolute exposure, its immediate transparency, and its willed and fully organized ritualism. In this sense, the cultural reenactments of Andean heritage tourism promote the performance of subaltern culture and history as the operative and almost ceremonial whitewash of past heterogeneities and dislocations.

I do not mean to suggest that there was at some time an original identitarian negativity or subaltern subject position that is now (for the first time) under liquidation. What I do see as qualitatively distinct from the past, however, is that there is an intensified drive within globalization to have subalternity be subaltern and to have it perform and speak its subalternity—and to do so apparently free of all open violence—in a regulated, market-driven, and whitewashed environment. Subaltern culture in global times is increasingly operational and increasingly located "in the thrall of the performance principle" (Baudrillard, *Transparency* 47); or it is, quite literally, nothing at all (that is, dead or on the verge of extinction). For millions, the secret violence of this choice—"perform your position in the global cultural economy or starve"—is the underlying reality of globalization's increasingly horizontalized social relations.

In other words, heritage tourism grafts itself onto a history of recalcitrant subaltern worldings in order to incorporate the archaic (the supposedly premodern) past into the market forces of the present. Moreover, it does this in order to have subalternity perform itself as opened up and exposed to the outside world, as a tamed (that is, knowable, predictable, manageable, and governable) form of cultural difference that is capable of reproducing its own long-standing position within the global cultural economy. As such it is a performance that is choreographed by market forces for the specific purpose of withdrawing presence from any historical relation between subalternity and sustained heterogeneity, radical difference, or violent insurrection.

Thus, heritage-based cultural performance is fundamental to the sustainability and reproduction of neoliberal order in the Andes, for it obscures the open violences of historical domination with the consensual affirmations of market-driven subaltern assimilation (code word: cultural hybridity). In this sense, it uncovers the new management techniques of a social violence that no longer affirms itself as such—as open violence. Now, the underlying adage "perform your position in the global cultural economy or starve" uncovers the secret violence that grounds an increasing number of social interactions in the neoliberal worlds of the South (and, for that matter, the North).

At this point it must be noted that the operational whitewash of potential negativity—the attempt to suture both subalternity and its fields of social articulation to the interactions and seamless images of the marketplace—is by no means confined to heritage tourism's Andean performances. Rather, I would hazard to say that the suturing logics of operational whitewash lie increasingly at the heart of neoliberal institutionality as a whole (which is not to say, of course, that it is successful or even in its applications). The recent history of Chile is perhaps paradigmatic in this regard.

In *Chile actual* (*Present-day Chile*) Tomás Moulian examines the performative role of operational whitewash in the years of transition from dictatorship to postauthoritarian democracy in Chile. For Moulian the elite's successful negotiation of the transition to democracy after 1988 was the result of two simultaneous maneuvers: first, its campaign to manage and control the historical image of the dictatorship (transfiguring Pinochet the dictator and, therefore, assassin, into Pinochet the national republican figurehead and patriarch); and, second, its insistence on representing the military regime as an oppressive machinery that was capable of reemerging, quite literally, at any moment and with a vengeance in order to put an end to the process of transition itself.

In other words, the successful transition into the postauthoritarian era was the result of the political elite's ability (through the complex manipulation of media images and political language) to make people recognize that it was in their best interests to (actively) forget the dictatorial history and the institutional processes to which they had been subjected under military rule, even though they were still living in the shadow of that rule. Thus, like all masters of violence, by claiming sole propriety over the universal interests of the nation they set to "make the public see reason," and accept the terms of democratic transition as offered to them by dictatorship. The politics of democratic consensus, then, was designed to withdraw presence from Chile's history of open violence. Moulian formulates this phenomenon as follows:

> The strategic negation of "state reason." That is the field of planned and of pacted silences offered up as sacrifices in order to contain the supposed rage of the patriarch. The so-called transition worked like the barter system: stability, it was said, has to be bought by silence. This was the transition's cunning trick. Negotiations (in particular those carried out during Aylwin's government) appeared to be carried out in fear, as if inspired by a policy of appeasement. I think that the feeling of fear really did exist in the population. But the decision-taking elites were inspired by another strategy: the "whitewash" of Chile. They were moved by a cold, arrogant, and remorseless realism that allowed them to interpret the "common good": Chile's needs. That strategy was grounded not in fear but in complicity with the project of transition itself. They took fear—latent phantasm or avatism of the common man—as their justification. What they were really seeking, however, was the reconstruction of Chile as a valid and trustworthy country; the model, the perfect transition. In order to achieve this, plastic surgery, the transsexual operation that transformed the dictator into the patriarch, was necessary. (32–33)[1]

Quite simply, in the Chilean transition to democracy, democracy's surpassing of the dictatorial culture of fear was promoted by sustaining the dictatorial culture of fear as the necessary precondition for the possibility of a peaceful transition to democracy. Within this operational whitewash—in which democratization is guaranteed by suppressing democratization and by allowing for the positive extension of dictatorial social and institutional processes—sustaining Pinochet (and, of course, the dictatorship's 1980 constitution) as the guardian of, and as the ground from which to articulate, national democratic forms would prove to be less traumatic than the violence that would be exacted on the country and its population if it considered questioning the institutional processes of the military regime that had put democracy on the table in the first place.

Liberal democracy, in this sense, exposed its advent (and performed this advent) as little more than a gigantic dictatorial campaign of plastic surgery:

The Other Side of the Popular

The whitewash of Chile was necessary in order for the country to represent itself as the model of a mature neocapitalism that was capable of producing democracy as its natural environment, and, from there, of growing in economic leaps and bounds. This meant that Pinochet, the supreme symbol and conductor of the military regime, could not be viewed as exclusively responsible for the dirt and the blood. It also required that people recognize the need for a sustained role for Pinochet in the years following dictatorship. The despot had to become a man of providence. As such, he would unify all possible contradictions: he would keep the military from dishonor and thereby make the transition a peaceful one. He alone could impede his own repetition: the reemergence of Pinochet-the-new. (34)

As Moulian observes, and as has been widely commented in Chile, the democratizing whitewash of history reached its iconic apogee in 1992, when the newly democratic state decided to transport an iceberg to the Seville World Fair (Expo '92) as a symbol of what the New Chile could now offer to the global cultural economy. As Moulian notes:

> For a long time we thought that the iceberg was an ingenious device designed to compare us to northern modernity. . . . But the meaning of the iceberg exceeded such mercantile gestures. It was not merely a strategy by which the seller could show off his trinkets, nor was it a performance of Chile's distancing of itself from Latin America. The signifier did allow for these signifieds. But the least obvious signified was actually the main one. The iceberg represented New Chile's debut into society, now cleaned up, sanitized, and purified by its long ocean crossing. In the iceberg there were no traces of blood and no *desaparecidos*. Not even the shadow of Pinochet could be glimpsed. It was as if Chile had just been born. Neither the trained eyes of a geologist, not to mention those of an archeologist, could have glimpsed the uneraseable traces of accumulated suffering in the luminous beauty of the iceberg's petrified ice. (34–35)[2]

The iceberg is an antimnemonic operation that is designed to make the memories, signs, and sordid realities of dictatorial history disappear, while at the same time masking that disappearance with the image of an absolutely seamless luminescence through which the New Chile — the Chile of democratic consensus — projects itself. The iceberg, in other words, was the mythical icon of a new order that was brought into being by successfully whitewashing recent history's bloody violence, torture, exile, and economic restructuring. It was an incantation — the fetishistic effect of a peculiar communicative rite or socioeconomic cult — that was designed to produce a staged and choreographed horizon of transnational relations purportedly dominated by the common (globalized) language of democracy and lucidity. The iceberg embodied, in this sense, the foundational speech of neoliberalism's myth of market-based communitarianism, in which the social field reproduces itself through unambiguous icons that are designed to fabricate images of common immanence between the global marketplace and all individuals, collectives, traditions, nations, pasts, presents, and futures.

However, the iceberg was a mythical icon with a difference, because it was an icon that, while at some point presumably part of nature, had been separated and then refabricated by market forces for the strict purpose of becoming mythical. It was made to be (naturally) mythical and was, therefore, made to act as if it had arisen naturally from a community, as if it actually channeled collective (national) identifications.[3] In a single gesture—its transatlantic crossing—it announced what the New Chile was: naturally and unambiguously crystalline. Furthermore, it announced that the New Chile (and, for that matter, the world) could only agree to say that this was now the case. As such, it also said what saying means for the New Chile: namely, that it does not communicate any knowledge to itself or to the world other than that of its whitewashed luminescence; indeed, that it only communicates the communication of this knowledge. The New Chile is therefore so painstakingly transparent in its communications that it is, as Jean-Luc Nancy would put it, *tautegorical* (*Inoperative* 51). The iceberg, then, was the great icon of Chile's foundational democratic myth: that, thanks to its smooth sailing into the global cultural economy and to its postauthoritarian guarantee of democratic transparency, Chile and its history are now absolutely and naturally sutured to each other as well as to the rest of the capitalist world order. Dislocation, in this sense, is a thing that only existed prior to 1973.

Needless to say, through the iceberg the New Chile withdraws presence from the open institutional violence of the past. However, we must also recognize that the withdrawn element—open violence—lays the foundation for the existence of the democratic New Chile. Moreover, since the iceberg affirms the new democratic order as the end result of a peaceful and institutional transition from military to civil rule, then the open violence of the dictatorship is ultimately, and inevitably, the origin of the iceberg's silent affirmation. This is obvious. Dictatorship is, in this sense, the withdrawn presence that fabricates the silent violence of both the iceberg per se and democratic operational whitewash as a whole.

Having said this, however, the iceberg is designed to make this interpretation of a direct link between dictatorship and present-day Chile little more than a fanciful vision. After all, through the iceberg we can only imagine dictatorship as a presence or as a reality. The complete seamlessness of the iceberg and the inevitable consensus that it generates vis-à-vis its shimmering cleanliness disallows any notion of anything existing beneath the surface of operational whitewash's greatest icon. The iceberg/New Chile is, in other words, what it is: unambiguous and cleansed of sordidness, and there is nothing more to be said on the matter of its historical coming into being.[4]

Moulian, however, strives to give us something that stands in stark contrast to this icon; something that is designed to unsuture the iceberg and, most definitely, to exceed the terms of my discussion as it stands thus far. Moulian calls attention to the spectral presence and systematic silencing of potential dislocation:

> The iceberg was a successful sign—the architecture of transparency and cleanliness—in which all damage had become transfigured. The dry blood, the endless grief of those awaiting the return of the disappeared, the groans of the tortured, the remorse of those forced to betray, the nostalgia of the exiled, the dull pain of the thousands of people left unemployed and unable to work for years, had all been transformed into the purity of ice. In order to uncover the traces and confirm the sounds of suffering the geologist would have had to destroy the iceberg. But he would not have found anything inside it for it was a simulacrum, rather than a shell holding Pinochet at its core. (35–36)

Moulian brings us momentarily before the dictatorship's true story: spectral residues of incessant suffering, fear, and muted speech ("the dry blood, the endless grief of those awaiting the return of the disappeared, the groans of the tortured, the remorse of those forced to betray, the nostalgia of the exiled, the dull pain of the thousands of people left unemployed and unable to work for years" [35–36]). He momentarily opens up his critical discourse to the mention of phantom part-narratives and collective experiences that appear to have no real measure in their relation to the seamless positivity and factitiousness of the iceberg's (and the current order's) historical revisionism. And this raises the question that even if collective suffering indicates the true story of the dictatorship (in direct opposition, of course, to democracy's seamless iconography), what are we supposed to do with this true story?

Within *Chile actual* the residues of past suffering emerge as little more than anxious and, perhaps, frustrated signifiers of negative languages, part-narratives, fragmentary responses, affective residues, and fissured experiences that exceed, and that remain extraneous to, not just the managed transparency and consensual positivity of the current order but also the historical and epistemological limits of critical reason itself. Their presence in Moulian's critique of neoliberal transparency calls attention to a world of experience that is being silenced by the transition to democracy and the operational whitewash of Chile's violent recent history.

While the iceberg imposes a seamless relation between the past and the present that is grounded in the relation of the same with the same—in the unitary production of whitewashed commonalities and in a past that is (according to *Chile actual*) now as cleansed and emptied out as the present—Moulian introduces the Other: that is, a community of mute sufferers of no one knows how many ("the thousands of people," he says, but how to count them and when to stop counting them? What is the limit of their being-in-common?), who simply cannot fit comfortably into the dominant rationales, narratives, and symbolic structures of the official democratic order.

There is no ground from which to think about such a commonality, for this is a multitudinous Other that communicates, in muted fashion, the affective limits of a collective that one can scarcely call a constituted community. Moulian seems to evoke a spectral commonality that projects itself through, and as the result of, a foundational relation of dissymmetry between the hegemonic logics, representations, and iconography of liberal democracy (the iceberg, for example) and the violent truth of dictatorial history. Moulian, as such, seems to want to expose the myth of the New Chile, just for a moment, to the mumbled interruption of its claims to democratic transparency, commonality, and universality. He underlines the spectral and residual dissension of a potentially negative community (perhaps even the quiet yet powerful murmurings of a "community of those who have no community," as Georges Bataille put it) in an attempt to expose the logics of the iceberg to an unmeasurable relation to the unrecuperable, to the unconstituted, to the unworkable, and to the spectral speech of the defeated. Moulian, in other words, seems to suggest an affective world of signification that remains senseless (for democratic hegemony), and ungraspable for the order of disciplinary reason and for institutional knowledge as a whole.

As such, *Chile actual* cannot appropriate that affective realm of signification. It cannot constitute it and have it speak its negativity. Therefore, it signals it as truth but relinquishes its injunction immediately. It indicates the existence of a community of sufferers—the community of those for whom community and the communication of commonality would surely unwork the traditional notion of community—yet it can only articulate them as a spectral presence lying within "the lines of the syntax of reason" (Derrida, "Cogito" 37). It is not by chance, then, that Moulian should withdraw from the images of residual suffering and of tortured affect in order to revert, once again, both to reason's powerful syntax and to his (on the other hand, most convincing) examination of the institutional maneuvers that conditioned Chile's peaceful transition to democracy. By doing this, however, Moulian implicitly upholds the logics of his object of critique. He fails to displace operational whitewash—the dominant institutional sign system of the New Chile—and disavows the possibility of a reading that could be characterized as an active transaction between past and future (Spivak, "Subaltern" 5). The result, of course, is that in *Chile actual* operational whitewash is implicitly hegemonized from within the very critique of hegemony formation itself.

In contrast I would like to remain not so much within the main corpus of Moulian's impressive analysis as in the wake of his fleeting gesture toward an apparently unrecuperable world of spectral and affective ruin. After all, this gesture toward the world of historical affects reveals, momentarily, a space within *Chile actual* that indicates an apparent withdrawal from the text itself. It signals, in other words, an opening up within the text to that which remains residual to it, to that which remains extraneous to the hegemonic workings of operational whitewash and perhaps to the exercise of critical reason itself. As such, Moulian's glance toward the affects that exceed, and that perhaps suspend, the factitiousness of governmental transparency obliges that we reflect on whether or not there are common relations that challenge, interrupt, or suspend the rational transparency-producing machinery that grounded the transition to democracy in Chile. Is there an affective form of commonality that interrupts common measures for being-in-common? Is there a thought that is proportionate to such an interruption?

By obliging, just for a second, that we take into consideration those experiences that cannot fit into the transparent narratives of democratic neoliberalism, by obliging that we take into consideration that realm of affective commonality, Moulian uncovers a relation of extreme remoteness and of profound incommunication between critical/institutional reason, the contrived transparencies of operational whitewash, and history's pained and sometimes not-so-silenced residues. Just for a second it is as if we have been asked to establish a relation with an accumulation of spectral presences and affective part-narratives that are located both within, and simultaneously outside of, recent institutional history.

With this in mind, perhaps there is a secret interpellation in this gesture: namely, to envision (or, rather, to hear say) the possibility of an impossible critical intimacy with a world of residual affects that has been ·

included into democracy as democracy's zone of (necessary) exclusion. If this is the case, then perhaps such an interpellation is asking us to consider holding onto (and, perhaps, of establishing a hold over) that which disallows the possibility of any definitive hold (once again, history's dried blood, its endless grief, its moans, remorse, nostalgia, and dull pain). In other words, perhaps we are being asked to constitute a critical relation with the past, and with the devastated affective residues of that past in the present, that would require a completely new relation between reflection and the historical formation of the social order; that would require, in other words, a new theoretical telos from which to think of the political histories of subaltern affect.

Such a thing would require opening up Moulian's hegemonizing evaluation of the Chilean transition to democracy to thought's relation not just *to* the Other (to the grief, groans, remorse, nostalgia, pain, etc. of the past) but to a relation *with* the Other and with otherness that is, itself, Other. As such, *perhaps* we would have to take into consideration the singular relation between thought and its objects (between intellectual engagement and subaltern affect) that is, as Maurice Blanchot puts it, entirely Other (*autrui*):

> *Autrui* is entirely Other; the other is what exceeds me absolutely. The relation with the other that is *autrui* is a transcendent relation, which means that there is an infinite, and, in a sense, an impassable distance between myself and the other, who belongs to the other shore, who has no country in common with me, and who cannot in any way assume equal rank in a same concept or a same whole, cannot be counted together with the individual that I am. . . . I am definitely separated from *autrui,* if *autrui* is to be considered as what is essentially other than myself; but it is also through this separation that the relation with the other imposes itself upon me as exceeding me infinitely: a relation that relates me to what goes beyond me and escapes me to the very degree that, in this relation, I am and remain separated. (*Infinite* 52)

Within this formulation the relation established between, for example, intellectual practice and subaltern affect could not be measured in terms of immediate unitary (coalitional, solidarity-based, or representational) gestures between distinct identitarian or geopolitical subject positions. After all, such gestures invariably serve to bolster the intellectual's recuperation of the subaltern position; and, through that recuperation, the return of critical reason to the fabrication and reconsolidation of already-existing social, cultural, and institutional hegemonies.

Rather, in Blanchot's formulation the intellectual is obliged to establish a relation between the fabrication of knowledge and that which

The Other Side of the Popular

passes beyond it, draws it out of itself, and places it before its own point of breakdown. It signals the end of a certain kind of redemptive or developmentalist intellectual engagement, in which redemption and development have been sutured historically to the expansion and extension of western/northern reason. As such, it is a relation that opens up institutional reflection to a "desire for that with which one has never been united, the desire of a self not only separated but happy with the separation that makes it a self, and yet still in relation with that from which it

remains separated and of which it has no need: the unknown, the foreign, the *autrui*" (53). This is, in other words, a relation of intimacy between reason and history's affective residues, negative languages, fragmentary responses, leftovers, and fissured experiences, in which the latter remain on the outer limits of intellectual recuperation, on the outer limits of epistemological reproduction, and, therefore, on the outer margins of what thought (and its institutions) can make of them (or can produce through them). Perhaps.

Such a limit embodies an interruption in relations of unity, equivalence, or common measure between critical reason and its objects of analysis (all relations, of course, that ground the consolidation of western history's preexisting intellectual and institutional hegemonies). Such a relation, then, is the nonredemptive manifestation of reason's moments of powerlessness. As Blanchot observes:

> *Autrui* risks being as far from me as the sky from the earth, as uncertain and as empty. But this extreme remoteness is not only able to manifest itself, it presents itself to us face to face. In the visage whereby it offers itself to me openly, in the frankness of a gaze, in the nakedness of an approach that nothing prevents, it is presence itself; and Levinas gives precisely the name *visage* to this "epiphany" of *autrui*. When *autrui* reveals himself to me as what is absolutely outside and above me — not because he would be the most powerful, but because there my power ceases — there is the visage. (54)

The Other Side of the Popular

Thought's *Other* relation to history and to the politics of culture marks subalternity, for example, as a presence within institutional thought that that thought cannot hold. It is "a presence that I cannot dominate by my gaze, that always exceeds both the representation I make of it and any form, any image, any view, any idea by which I might affirm it, arrest it, or simply let it be present" (54). As such the visage—the epiphany of the *other* relation between, for example, intellectual and subaltern affect—exposes a form of commonality that promises to unwork productive relations of absolute immanence between beings.

Thus it opens up reflection to the contours of community's finitude. Indeed, negative commonality discloses a site at which the notion of being-in-common—or of solidarity, for example—becomes not the articulation of active relations of equivalence (not the articulation of common measures and transparency, in other words), but the constitution of an inoperative relation that uncovers "the ecstatic consciousness of the night of immanence" (Nancy, *Inoperative* 19). Through the exposure of the visage, community becomes not a project (and therefore not the epiphany of a historically constituted program, integration, progress, development, or institutional hegemony). Rather, it becomes the exposure of a taking-place of commonality's scattered or extended singularities and common finitudes. Thus, through the relation of thought to the visage, community exposes itself "not in a work that would bring it to completion, even less in itself as work (family, people, church, nation,

party, literature, philosophy) but in the unworking and as the unworking of all its works" (72).

Through the explicitly dissymmetrical relation between institutional reflection and hegemony's historical residues, being-in-common un-covers itself at, and as, the exposure and taking-place of community's finitude. It is the radical site of negativity (of a being-in-common exposed to its finitude) at which historically constituted conceptualizations of commonality confront their unworkability, both in the present and for the future. As Blanchot observes in *The Unavowable Community*:

> If the relation of man with man ceases to be that of the Same with the Same, but rather introduces the Other as irreducible and—given the equality between them—always in a situation of dissymmetry in relation to the one looking at the Other, then a completely different relationship imposes itself and imposes another form of society which one could hardly call a "community". Or else one accepts the idea of naming it thus, while asking oneself what is at stake in the concept of a community and whether the community, no matter if it has existed or not, does not in the end always posit the *absence* of community. (3)[5]

Indeed, how else but through the uncovering of this negative form of affective community—how else but through the exposure of the community of those who have no community, and through the relation of absolute dissymmetry that it imposes on its distanced witnesses (myself, you, others)—can we even begin to approach the community of insane

The Other Side of the Popular

and glassy-eyed lovers who give themselves to us, and to us alone (and we are how many?), in Diamela Eltit and Paz Errázuriz's *El infarto del alma* (The heart attack of the soul). Moreover, how else but through the immediacy of their unoperative affective commonalities can we think about the possibility of forms of being-in-common that are grounded in a telos other than that of the hegemonic will to realize transparent communitarian essences, systematically whitewashed positivities, and constituted communal powers?

El infarto del alma is the textual and photographic taking-place of a common communication (Eltit and Errázuriz's) that takes place at the site of community's finitude (in the Putaendo insane asylum outside Santiago de Chile) and that constitutes commonality—its community of those who have no community (its mad lovers)—as the limit of commonality's communicability. The question, then, is how do we think about these forms of commonality and what do we do with them? In order to do this we need to situate them in relation to intellectual history and to a certain genealogy of intellectual engagement with the notion of community.

There is an obvious relation of intimacy between Diamela Eltit and Paz Errázuriz's depiction of Putaendo's communities of mad lovers and André Breton's *L'amour fou* (Mad love). Delirium and the unconscious lie at the heart of both projects. Indeed, at one point Eltit even notes that, in the Putaendo asylum, "Breton inundates my memory and I for-

get my own thoughts" (n.p.).[6] *El infarto del alma*, however, is not interested in announcing surrealism as its direct genealogical antecedent. But
neither does it present itself as surrealism's open antagonist. Rather, it
is the negative exposure (the inversion, the photographic other side) of
French surrealism's liberational quest for the positive love of the irrational and for the pure creations of the mind. In this sense, *El infarto del
alma* is the point at which a certain intellectual history breaks with itself
from within its own genealogy.

In Breton the eruption of unreason—the materialization of reason's
negativity—is ultimately the result of an aesthetic-philosophical quest
for a relation between beings that is grounded in the redemptive revelation, in the common and irreducible experience, of the unconscious: the
Other. Breton's work is therefore anchored in the potentially radical reorganization of the ways in which collective perception, reality, the social
bond, or community can be apprehended and put to use in the future. In
Putaendo, however, the immediate presence of the Other—a presence
that is exposed to us repeatedly through the empty faces, glassy eyes, and
almost parodically ceremonial gestures of the asylum's mad lovers—uncovers the nonredemptive other side of Breton's messianic investments
in the disclosure of the Other. In other words, the Other in Putaendo
can no longer be an object of intellectual desire to be recuperated and
put to work in the name of new cultural or political programs, visions,
or hegemonies. It is no longer the epiphany of a process of intellectual

labor to be revealed and communicated in all its messianic glory. Rather, it is the exposure of abject, impoverished, speechless, yet dignified commonalities grounded in subaltern affect that challenge and undermine the notion of intellectual work and, indeed, make such a notion withdraw before its uncomfortable relation to abject love against all odds and without apparent reason.

There can be little doubt, then, that *El infarto del alma* positions itself in direct relation to the intellectual history of the international avant-garde. But in this very act of recognition it denarrativizes that tradition's investments in the promise of messianic revelations. Putaendo merely opens up such investments to their negative site of im-possibility. As such, *El infarto del alma* conceives of itself not as the communication of a liberational evocation of reason's finitude and not as the site for that finitude's aesthetic unleashing. Rather, it conceives of itself as a work that is carried out from within the very impossibility (from within the very finitude) of intellectual redemption. As Eltit writes:

> The alienated inhabitants of Putaendo already carry the signs of a fatality. Thus the hospital in the town of Putaendo rises up like a wall containing a fatality, as a means of controlling the impulses of those who opened themselves up entirely to an unintelligible universe. For they are intertwined, like a malignant plant, in a desire for the Other whose ultimate goal is strangulation. The patients are a material other exposed to the possibility of camouflaging themselves (of sheltering

themselves) within any other body; of penetrating any other mind; of inhabiting the Other at all cost. Perhaps they came so close to the sun—to the Other's deadly brightness—that their minds caught fire. They burned up following the same ritual of aesthetic suicide with which a moth seals its fate. They approached the incendiary gaze of God in such a way that they were blinded. As such, they ended up like the militant rebels of passion's anarchist movement, and were confined (forever?) to their own disorganized organicity. They rejected all forms of social negotiation other than that of illegal viscidity or the tragic upheaval of defeat. (n.p.)

At first glance *El infarto del alma* appears to be what surrealism would have wanted: the disclosure of a site at which the Other offers itself up for the expression and, perhaps, for the constitution of radical intellectual prophesies. On another level, however, it is the site of the disaster—of the disjointedness—of that intellectual history, because the abject reality of Putaendo merely wrecks masterful expressions and intellectual prophesies. As such, it marks almost an essential and perhaps necessary depoliticization of that intellectual project. *El infarto del alma* performs the exhaustion—the genealogical deconstruction—of its own genealogical schema, for, from within its obvious gestures toward genealogical continuity, it both upholds and unworks Breton's desire for the Other. As a result, in the images of mad lovers that we have before us we encounter portraits that attest to the creative relation between subaltern affect, sub-

The Other Side of the Popular

altern commonality, and the unraveling of the avant-garde's constructivist revolutionary projects and aesthetics.[7]

It is for this reason that Eltit finds herself asking: "What is the language of this love? For they do not even possess words, only the devia-
tions of a terribly fractured syllable. So what agreement, what instance,
what amorous aesthetic, mobilizes them?" (n.p.). Of course, these questions remain unanswered—or, rather, they are always already exposed
to their fundamental intellectual im-possibility—for Putaendo's community of mad lovers can only promise the radical unworking of all re-
demptive/constructivist intellectual languages, aesthetics, and consen-
sual/hegemonic projects.

El infarto del alma, then, inscribes itself within a particular genealogical schema. However, it simultaneously deconstructs the field of articulations that it presents as being its own. As such, it is a genealogical deconstruction of its own genealogy. Not an avant-garde prophesy
or intellectual directive, but a rearguard "a-genealogy" (Derrida, *Politics* 105) that inscribes and unworks the history of its own coming into
being. It is by no means a declaration of war against the surrealist intellectual tradition, but the search for the possibility of a cultural politics that is capable of beginning by breaking (and by calling attention
to the necessary break) with genealogy's apparent naturalness; with its
historically constituted acceptedness or transparency, and its inevitable
homogeneity.

In this sense, *El infarto del alma* strives to present itself as the site of an originary heterogeneity within an intellectual history that is grounded in and fully dedicated to the radical realignment of thought's relation to the world and to the promise of an Other politics of culture. As Nelly Richard puts it: "[*El infarto del alma*] moves the critical imagination toward the risk of a wager that appears to suggest that not all times or forms of subjective experience can be anticipated by, or converted into, the workings of the marketplace" (268; translation mine). With this in mind, we can only read *El infarto del alma* as preparatory for an intellectual engagement that is firmly grounded within those posthegemonic places at which hegemony (translatability, transparency, intelligibility) ceases to make sense (Franco, "Latin" 270). It is not preparatory for another masterful intellectual discourse designed to forge the contours of new paths and new developments into the future. Rather, it is preparatory for a peculiar friendship that is grounded in the possibility of "linking an *affirmation* (in particular a political one), *if there is any,* to the experience of the impossible" (Derrida, *Specters* 35). Perhaps.

In the radical disjuncture that lends structure to *El infarto del alma*—in the fissure between the almost incarcery centeredness of Errázuriz's camera (its thirty-eight black-and-white exposures with their intentionally authoritative immediacy and almost stifling objectivity) and Eltit's wandering narrative fragments that accompany them—we confront a work that is not invested in revealing the pure or liberational speech of

The Other Side of the Popular

unreason per se. On the contrary, we face a collective intellectual venture that is most definitely invested in exposing the fissured and fragmented expressivities of inoperative commonalities that exist other than toward instrumental reason's constituted history and social order in Chile.[8]

Within this process, Paz Errázuriz's portraits expose themselves as anything other than interpretations of postauthoritarian Chilean reality. As representations of the immediacy of subaltern affect, the book's portraits are little more than centered sites of capture in which the corporeal disclosure of being-in-common—the disclosure of dissymmetrical singularities touching each other and exposing themselves as near-twin images of each other, posing, perhaps, in the name of extinction's other side while remaining always incapable of sexual reproduction—emerges in dark contrast to (and as almost raised up out of and against) the emptiness of the page's oversized and whitewashed frame.

Each portrait is an exercise in negative spacing. Indeed, their spacing throughout the book's pages (as well as through these pages) also guarantees the separation of any one portrait from any other. In this sense, there is no such thing as unity within the unified visual field that they produce and belong to, for each exposure is a site of immediate singularity and negativity that is quite literally pulled away from (or perhaps carefully cut out of) any possible relation of equivalence that one might like to establish between portraits, between communities of lovers, and between their relationship to any external and all-encompassing herme-

neutic field. Quite literally, within the book the physical and measured separation of each portrait from its others, and the relation of radical separation and dissymmetry that each image imposes on its powerless beholder (myself/you), indicates the disclosure of an inessential commonality that is grounded both in the finitude of each community as well as in the scattered commonality of those finitudes.

As such, *El infarto del alma* is the taking-place of a peculiar form of thinking, of sharing, of participating in commonality, and of resembling that actively renders fraternity, proximity, equivalence, sameness, identity, and difference inoperative. In order to reflect on the arrest of absolute immanence between subjects—in order to think about the experience of finitude, the exhaustion of a substantive ground for reflection, and the demise of common measures—we are obliged to think from within a foundational double bind that lies at the heart of *El infarto del alma*. Errázuriz's portraits reveal the freedom of irreducibly Other commonalities that we cannot dominate with our gaze, that exceed any representation that we might make of them, and that might even transcend any idea that we might affirm in their regard. Having said this, however, her portraits expose this freedom, and the unmeasurable relation that they establish with us, by constituting a unified visual field that captures and holds that Other prisoner, in the same way the walls of the Putaendo asylum guarantee that such negative commonalities are never unleashed onto the outside world.

The Other Side of the Popular

In this sense Errázuriz's portraits seem to suggest that in order to think we should recognize that we are being asked—silently—not to even try to reproduce the logic of capture that has brought these defenseless eyes to us in the first place. After all, to attempt such a thing would merely turn our highest power—reason—into im-possibility (Blanchot, *Infinite* 54). As such, Errázuriz's work opens us up as witnesses, and as desiring witnesses, to the necessary devastation and annihilation of our own thought and of its potential relation to any critical desire to cross and to recuperate that which is uncrossable and unrecuperable.

Thus we are exposed to the demand to establish critical relations with subaltern affect that do not ground themselves in nor reproduce historically constituted (colonial, national, imperial, or neoliberal) notions of a subsistent ground or of a common measure for being-in-common. We are located before a world of commonalities that can no longer be thought of in terms of history's substantive grounds, common measures, or hegemonic forms of thinking about the relation between culture and politics. We are facing, in other words, such hegemonic notions of community exposed to their negative (other) side. And this demands a notion of the social that is grounded no longer in constituted intimacy, in closure, in communion, or in the promise of a completed collective identity of all in one. Rather, it demands a notion of commonality that is grounded in intimacy's and communion's dispersed and scattered interruptions, fissures, fragments, and residues. As Blanchot states it in his

reflections on the unavowable community: "The community of lovers—
no matter if the lovers want it or not, enjoy it or not, be they linked by
chance, by '*l'amour fou*', by the passion of death (Kleist)—has as its ultimate goal the destruction of society. There where an episodic community takes shape between two beings who are made or who are not made
for each other, a war machine is set up or, to say it more clearly, the possibility of a disaster carrying within itself, be it in infinitesimal doses, the
menace of universal annihilation" (*Unavowable* 48).

Errázuriz's portraits uncover the contours of a subaltern visage that
forces us to think from within, and to uphold the immediate presence
of, thought's relation to dislocation and to the im-possibility of a common telos for the relation between intellectual and subaltern. However,
they also strive to conjoin that im-possibility to a "regime of a possible
whose possibilization must prevail over the impossible" (Derrida, *Politics* 29). For this reason there is no site within these portraits that can lead
us toward a singular interpretation and nothing in them that is capable
of uncovering a particular revelation of signification.

We cannot think about the portraits in and of themselves, in other
words. Rather, we can think about them only in their relation to the aseptic whiteness that frames and incarcerates them and that they interrupt.
Indeed, if we turn these portraits toward, and against, their own outside
(rather than toward a potentially meaningful interiority) then we can invert the dominant order of the page—as well as the natural order of our
interpretation—in order to suggest that rather than offering or promising
the possibility of a hermeneutic paradigm the portraits are themselves
the internal point of breakdown of all hermeneutic paradigms. They
are the silent fissure at which the hermeneutic field becomes opened up
to the nontelos of structural and epistemological dislocation.

The portraits of mad lovers are, in this sense, the exposure of a negative site at which the page's aseptic whiteness—that symbolic space that
both joins and separates the community of lovers to and from the world
and that represents the limit of a seamless world that lies beyond the confines of Putaendo—is forced to give way to an internal negative point of
breakdown at which seamlessness ceases to function and to operate as
a structure or an order. The portraits are, in this sense, structural dislocations that are constitutive of an interruption in the aseptic whiteness
of the page. Furthermore, these constitutive dislocations are designed to
expose us to a relation with an Other that imposes itself on us and yet
exceeds us infinitely.

Love, in other words, is exposed in exemplary fashion—as posthegemonic subaltern affect; as the grounds of a politics of friendship—not

302   *The Other Side of the Popular*

through the establishment of subsistent grounds, nor through the forging of common measures for being-in-common, but through the finitude of ideals such as common measures and subsistent grounds for being-in-common. Love emerges, therefore, where reason lends itself to the exploration of subaltern sites of commonality that exist other than toward the social history of instrumental reason and its constituted powers. Love exposes itself in the radical deconstruction of reason's constituted histories, genealogies, institutional paradigms, and epistemological configurations.

Errázuriz's portraits, then, promise nothing other than the exposure of the negative community—the subaltern community of those who have no community—as a scattered and potentially multitudinous site of loving promise, at which institutional/administrative configurations (asylums, universities) cease to reproduce their mastery. Therefore, through *El infarto del alma* we are forced to confront, and to think from within, the im-possibility and finitude that the visage of subalternity offers and imposes on us and our signifying processes. This finitude is subalternity's affective affirmation of life and friendship. It is also the intimation, the hear-say, of an other side—of another (posthegemonic) telos—from which to think. Perhaps.

What, though, can be made of finitude's intimations and hear-says? What affirmation can be made on their behalf? In the final paragraph of *Labor of Dionysus* Michael Hardt and Antonio Negri observe that today "communism is revived . . . in the *ritorno ai principî* of a radical constructivity, stripped of the illusion that socialism or mature capitalism can interpret the path to freedom" (313). Within this theoretical return, they continue, "the only power that can be transcendent is that of human finitude, rich with all its powers. There, in finitude, the form of the constituent process and the subject of constituent power coincide" (313). If this is the case, then perhaps we can suggest that it is in the relation between hegemony's scattered other sides and the experience of the perhaps that they inaugurate that we can begin to elaborate the grounds of a possible radical constructivity. Furthermore, within this overall horizon of theoretical practice perhaps we can also suggest that it is only deconstruction—"a deconstruction, at once genealogical and a-genealogical, *of the genealogical*" (Derrida, *Politics* 105)—that can keep thought open to the potentially constitutive force of finitude; open, that is, to finitude's endless repertoire of possibilities and alternative imaginations that we have not been able to claim as our philosophical and political inheritances . . . perhaps. . . .

1 The State of Things Passed: Transculturation as
National-Popular Master Language

1 As Laclau indicates, the essential features of populism are (1) an elite imbued
   with an anti–status quo ideology, (2) a mobilized mass generated by a "revolution of rising expectations," and (3) an ideology with a widespread emotional
   appeal ("Towards" 152). A populist hegemonic articulation depends on the
   ability of the dominant class to "articulate different 'conceptions of the world'
   in such a way as to neutralise their potential antagonism" (177). Within populism the category of "the people" promotes widespread emotional appeal and
   neutralizes class conflict. For Laclau, "*the people* is a concept without a defined theoretical status; despite the frequency with which it is used in political
   discourse, its conceptual precision goes no further than the purely allusive or
   metaphorical level. . . . Populism is both an elusive and a recurrent concept.
   Now we understand why it is elusive: all the uses of the term refer to an ana-
   logical basis which, in turn, lacks conceptual precision" (165).
2 Cardoso and Faletto trace the history of popular incorporation in the following terms: "The distinctive feature of the transition period in Latin America
   in the relations among social groups and classes was the growing participation
   of the urban middle classes and of the industrial and commercial bourgeoisie
   in the system of domination. The social situation was expressed on an economic level by policies to consolidate the domestic market and to industrial-
   ize. . . . Countries that began to grow in these ways underwent a demographic-
   ecological transformation as a proletariat emerged and as a non-wage-earning
   popular sector developed in the cities. The growth rate of the latter sector usually was higher than the rate at which new jobs were generated by industrialization. This brought about the formation in Latin America of what came
   to be called 'mass urban societies' in insufficiently industrialized economies.
   The presence of masses, together with the beginnings of industry that produced more than just nondurable consumer goods, characterized the initial
   period of inward development. This period intensified during World War II
   and reached its peak in the 1950s. During this period, industrialization was
   'substitutive': it was made possible mainly by difficulties of importation and
   subsequently by lack of foreign exchange. It used and expanded the production base of the preceding period to meet domestic demand for consumer and
   intermediate goods. In the process, the role of the state increased and changed
   in character. The state had fundamentally expressed the interests of export-

ers and landholders and had acted as agent for foreign investment. Now it intervened to set up protective tariffs, to transfer income from the export to the domestic sector, and to create the infrastructure needed to support the import-substitution industry. . . . The masses were generally oriented toward participation and social and economic distributivism. The new dominant sectors generally favored continued national economic expansion, now directed to the domestic market. Their trend to nationalism made possible incorporation of the masses into the production system and, to varying degrees, into the political systems. The connection thus established gave meaning to 'developmentalist populism' " (128–30).

3   For a chronology of elite reform, mass incorporation, and immediate and long-term socioeconomic and political dynamics in Brazil, Chile, Mexico, Venezuela, Uruguay, Colombia, Peru, and Argentina, see Collier and Collier (22, figure 0.1).

4   Indeed, this search for a harmonizing totalization of the social sphere—always under the dominant rubric of the nation and of national identity—was precisely what Perón would later underline as the dominant goal of Peronist ideology in Argentina: "The dominant principle of our ideological system is the harmony of opposites, the equilibrium between extremes, the 'Third Position' " (*Filosofía* 121; translation mine).

5   As Bourdieu puts it, "The state concentrates, treats, and redistributes information and, most of all, effects a *theoretical unification*. Taking the vantage point of the Whole, of society in its totality, the state claims responsibility for all operations of *totalization* (especially thanks to census taking and statistics or national accounting) and of *objectivation*, through cartography (the unitary representation of space from above) or more simply through writing as an instrument of accumulation of knowledge (e.g., archives), as well as for all operations of *codification* as cognitive unification implying centralization and monopolization in the hands of clerks and men of letters" ("Rethinking" 7).

6   See Cornejo Polar's notion in *Escribir en el aire* of cultural heterogeneity as an important critical response to this dilemma.

7   In particular, see González Prada's "Discurso en el Politeama."

8   As Arguedas put it: "The *Amauta* movement coincides with the opening of the first roads" (quoted in Rama, *La novela* 222; translation mine).

9   Obviously, my argument in these pages relies heavily on the invaluable contributions made by Cornejo Polar in *La formación de la tradición literaria en el Perú*.

10 See Riva Agüero's *El Perú, histórico y artístico* and his celebration of Inca Garcilaso de la Vega's aristocratic *mestizaje* in *Los comentarios reales de los incas*. See also Belaúnde's *Peruanidad, elementos esenciales* and Raúl Porras Barrenechea's evaluation of the failure of harmonic *mestizaje* in *El cronista, Felipe Huamán Poma de Ayala*.

11 For a persistently harsh reading of Arguedas, however, see Mario Vargas Llosa, *La utopía arcaica*.

12 See José de la Cuadra and Adalberto Ortiz; see also Demetrio Aguilera Malta, Enrique Gil Gilbert, and Joaquín Gallegos Lara.

13 See Poppe; Barrios de Chungara; Encinas, Mayorga, and Birhuet; and Catoira. For further critique of the revolutionary state, see the multifaceted work of Jesús Lara (in particular *Repete* and *Yawarninchij = nuestra sangre*), as well as the remarkable work of the Bolivian filmmaker Jorge Sanjinés (particularly *Yawarmallcu*).

14 As Cornejo Polar (*La formación*) notes, one only has to think of the uncanny parallels in the representation of educational processes in novels such as Rómulo Gallegos's *Doña Bárbara* in Venezuela and the Colombian Clorinda Matto de Turner's *Aves sin nido* (from some fifty years before), to trace the problematic line between populist ideologies of mass education and incorporation and the civilizing Creole projects of the nineteenth-century liberal order. In Peru, Haya de la Torre (affectionately known by workers as "el maestro") was an outspoken admirer and follower of José Vasconcelos's Spengler-inspired notions of education, hispanization, and national peoplehood fabrication. Spengler's *The Decline of the West* also exercised considerable influence on Mariátegui (affectionately known by workers as "Amauta"), whose articles in *Variedades* (in particular those published between May and December 1927: "The Decline of England," "The Destiny of North America," and "Yankeeland and Socialism") address Spengler and his possible articulation with the writings of Lenin (see Mariátegui, *Heroic*).

15 It must be noted, however, that on the margins of Peronist culture Ezequiel Martínez Estrada's *Muerte y transfiguración de Martín Fierro* stands out as a forceful analysis and critique of national processes; Leopoldo Marechal's *Adán Buenosayres*, which was severely critiqued by González Lanuza in *Sur* yet later identified by Julio Cortázar as a precursor to *Rayuela*, is of interest due to its constant alternations between high and low linguistic and cultural modes, its parodic form, and its insolent anti-*Sur* heterodoxy (Viñas, *Literatura* 214). Meanwhile, according to David Viñas the contributors to *Sur*—beginning with Victoria Ocampo but also including Borges, Mallea, and Sábato—"lived the enclosure of their publications and their episodic conflicts with Peronism like 'a dramatic exile in their own country'" (207; translation mine). Finally, for a ferocious response to Peronism after Perón's departure from Argentina, see Martínez Estrada's *Qué es esto?*

16 See, to name just a few, Manuel Puig (*El beso de la mujer araña*), Ricardo Piglia (*Respiración artificial*), Osvaldo Soriano (*No habrá más penas ni olvido; Cuarteles de invierno*), Juan José Saer (*Nadie nada nunca; El entenado*), Luisa Valenzuela (*Cambio de armas*), Carlos Dámaso Martínez (*Hay cenizas en el viento*), Juan Carlos Martini (*La vida entera*), David Viñas (*Cuerpo a cuerpo*), and Miguel Bonasso (*Recuerdo de la muerte*).

17 Cuba's model of a revolutionary national identity (a New Man), which was construed as a relation of absolute immanence between the intellectual, the people (peasants and workers), the revolutionary vanguard party, and the anti-

imperialist sovereignty and economic independence of the nation-state, very quickly became the model for anti-imperialist mobilizations throughout the South. As Tomás Borge indicates, this immanentist form of fictive ethnicity also came to form an essential part of Nicaraguan Sandinismo after 1979: "The Sandinista Front is the vanguard of all Nicaraguan patriots. The Sandinista Front is the vanguard of national reconstruction. The Sandinista Front is the vanguard of the workers and the peasants, and is the vanguard of these social sectors; the Sandinista Front is the living instrument of the revolutionary classes, the guide toward a new society" (quoted in Marcus 28). Of course, the development of a so-called new society would require the fabrication of a new citizenry and of a new national peoplehood from which imperialism could be combated and cultural difference affirmed. For Borge, Sandinismo entailed the vertical (pedagogic) fabrication of a new national character designed to bind the heterogeneity of race, gender, and cultural difference not only to each other but also to the idea of national space and identity. As Borge puts it in a speech given to teachers' groups after the revolution: "Economic development will not alone be enough. . . . You teachers are the main workers in the ideological construction of our people. You ideological workers are directly responsible for the creative capacity, the critical spirit, the banishment of selfishness, the political strength, and the audacity of our new generations. . . . You have to confront the ideas of the past that contaminate our beautiful present. You have to confront the negative habits, the totality of soiled ideological remnants that imperialism and the exploiting classes imposed on us and whose presence still has not been entirely eliminated in the realm of ideas" (quoted in Marcus 79). Needless to say, the Miskito Indians were to Sandinismo what Canudos and Antonio de Conselheiro were to Euclides da Cunha in *Rebellion in the Backlands:* a hard-core kernel of subaltern difference, an interruption in the progress of tamed/orderly transculturation, and a resistance to the integration-oriented paradigms of the nation-state.

18 For further critique of Latin American literary modernism, see Larsen.

19 I take the term "hyperbolic doubt" from Pierre Bourdieu, who asserts that a rupture with the thought of the state should "subject the state and the thought of the state to a sort of *hyperbolic doubt*. For, when it comes to the state, one never doubts enough" ("Rethinking" 1).

2 Intellectual Populism and the Geopolitical Structure of Knowledge

1 The Catholic Church also played an important role in this ideological shift in global power relations. The election of Pope John Paul II in 1978 put the Catholic Church in a theologically conservative and politically antisocialist direction. The Vatican quickly set about countering prevalent leftist sympathies by appointing conservative bishops, putting an end to Jesuit influences both within the Vatican and beyond, and replacing those influences with Opus Dei mem-

bers who offered close ties to business and social elites. As Francisco Durand notes: "In 1979, the Latin American Bishop's Conference (CELAM) met in Puebla, Mexico, under the initiative of conservative clerics. The conference signaled the end of Liberation Theology as the most influential doctrine within the Latin American church, and its replacement by a more conservative, less critical vision of capitalism known as the Theology of Culture. While Theology of Liberation had centered its analysis on oppressive socioeconomic and political structures that needed to be changed, Theology of Culture emphasized the contribution of Catholicism to Latin America's culture, ideas, and values, while emphasizing reconciliation. The conservative trends in CELAM were consolidated in the Santo Domingo conference of 1992" (162). Such has been the success of Opus Dei under Pope John Paul II that the organization has constructed a seventeen-story U.S. national headquarters and conference center, to the tune of $47 million, on the northeast corner of Lexington Avenue and 34th Street in downtown Manhattan, just blocks away from the most powerful financial and political institutions in the world (*New York Times*, September 21, 1999, sec. 11, p. 1). Furthermore, in February 1999 Vatican-based members of Opus Dei interceded on behalf of General Augusto Pinochet in the Chilean ex-dictator's brush with Spain's judicial system and Britain's Foreign Office (*El Pais*, February 21, 1999, p. 1).

2   As Giovanni Arrighi indicates, the early 1970s marked the signal crisis of the U.S. regime of accumulation. The switch from the gold standard to flexible exchange rates in the early 1970s, the fourfold increase in the price of crude oil (producing an $80 billion surplus of petrodollars for the banks to recycle), and the elimination in January 1974 of all controls on foreign capital movements immediately created an overabundant supply of dollars that was released by the U.S. monetary institutions. This provided U.S. capital with the means for self-expansion not just at home but also abroad. However, it simultaneously undermined the state's ability to control the production and regulation of world money and threatened to destroy the U.S. credit structure and worldwide networks of capital accumulation on which U.S. hegemony depended (310–17). For Third World countries, who had constituted a latent and growing challenge to U.S. world power for a number of decades (321), the changes in the exchange rates guaranteed their inferior position in the capitalist world system by imposing on them a cycle of debt that was propelled by the fact that "they simply did not command the financial resources needed to hedge against fluctuations. Hence their main contribution to the growth of the 'financial casino' of Euro-currency markets has been on the demand side rather than on the supply side of the equation; that is, through their demand for funds to offset the devastating effects of financial crises rather than through deposits aimed at forestalling or taking advantage of these same crises" (311). The signal crisis of the early 1970s closed one cycle in the U.S. regime of accumulation, created the means for bringing the Third World nations to their knees, and opened

a new regime and cycle of accumulation grounded in the extension and control of finance capital. As Arrighi puts it, "the result was the *belle epoque* of the Reagan era" (314).

3 The conservative backlash against the national-popular period in Latin America (the repressive military regimes of the Southern Cone in the 1970s and early 1980s, initiated in September 1973 by Augusto Pinochet) established social reorganization programs designed to integrate Latin American economies into rapid projects of export-oriented modernization, to facilitate the downsizing of all state welfare programs, to weaken popular influence over economic processes, and to create the systematic privatization of state-run industries (together, of course, with the attempted extermination or exile of political opposition). In Central America, of course, antipopular backlashes bolstered local military regimes that maintained intimate links to the landed oligarchies and to U.S. views on hemispheric security. It also produced the "scorched earth" policies of "low-intensity warfare."

4 Responses from people such as Dinesh D'Souza, William Bennett (in Beverley, *Against Literature* 13) and, more recently, David Stoll are testimony to the success of *testimonio* as a form of political intervention both locally and internationally.

5 The International Solidarity Movement, under the rubric of organizations within the United States such as the Committee in Solidarity with the People of El Salvador, the National Network in Solidarity with the Nicaraguan People, Neighbor to Neighbor, and the lesser-known Network in Solidarity with the People of Guatemala, remained throughout the 1980s fundamental protagonists in lobbying Congress and protesting U.S. foreign policy in Central America.

6 Indeed, we could even broaden the scope of this statement to include the international culture industries as a whole. As a result of the editorial success of Rigoberta Menchú's *testimonio*, together with its award of the Nobel Prize in 1992, the canonization of *testimonio* no longer traverses just the university. Rather, this canonization suggests far wider ramifications for reflection on the production of contemporary culture. On April 14, 1996, the Spanish newspaper *El Mundo* included in its weekly supplement an article by Elizabeth Burgos Debray on Rigoberta Menchú ("Rigoberta Menchú: La india rebelde"). This was part of a series that the newspaper was running on "Mujeres de fin de siglo." The article itself basically reproduces the portrayal of Menchú already provided by Elizabeth Burgos Debray in her introduction to the original *testimonio* in 1983. What is remarkable about the piece, however, is that Menchú is presented as one within a series of exemplary women. In particular, she is afforded membership in an exclusive club of end-of-the-century female icons such as Sharon Stone, Martina Navratilova, Hillary Clinton, and Sophia Loren (65). Obviously, the critical possibilities are endless. On the less-popular (and less-glamorous) side of the culture industries—yet, nevertheless, for the

most significant contributions to debate on Latin American *testimonio*—see the essays collected in Vidal and Jara; Gugelberger and Kerney; Beverley and Achúgar; and Gugelberger. Also see Beverley and Zimmerman; Sklodowska; Beverley (*Against*); Larsen; and Zimmerman.

7 Indeed, Jon Beasley-Murray takes this observation one step further and notes, in his examination of *testimonio*'s critical foundations, that the genre was always as much about forging solidarity in the United States as it was about the local realities of Latin America: "*Testimonio* was a bit player less in a set of struggles over Central America . . . but rather, as its right-wing critics such as D'Souza were quick to notice and as [Mary-Louise] Pratt underlines, in a set of efforts to transform the (reading) public in places such as the United States. This was its more or less surreptitious, more or less innocent function, in which raising consciousness of US policy in Latin America became a lever to encourage a movement against US policy in the US. Through *testimonio* Latinamericanist intellectuals in the US were offered—and to a greater extent than before or since took—a chance to be critical intellectuals within the US" ("Thinking" 126–27).

8 Thus, political reason and the terms of its critique have shifted in recent years. As Barry, Osborne, and Rose indicate: "It has proved difficult and painful for much political theory and political sociology to abandon the oppositions that have sufficed for so long: State and civil society, economy and family, public and private, coercion and freedom. Yet contemporary movements in politics show just how clumsy and inept such oppositions are: each, in different ways, demands a form of government that combines action by political and non-political authorities, communities, and individuals. And the relations of force, of power, of subordination, of liberation and 'responsibilization', of collective allegiance and individual choice that are brought into being in these new configurations are difficult to visualize, let alone to evaluate, in the language of orthodoxy" (2).

9 For the genealogy of the group until 1993 and an evaluation of the emergence of the subaltern as a concept within the field of Latin American Studies, see the section of the founding statement titled "The Subaltern in Latin American Studies" (112–16). Also see Beverley (*Subalternity* 1–24). The discussion that follows appeared originally, in somewhat different form, as "The Fantasies of Cultural Exchange in Latin American Subaltern Studies," published in *The Real Thing*, edited by Georg Gugelberger. I would like to thank the former members of the group for their generous and critical reading of the original essay.

10 In *Against Literature* John Beverley expresses similar concerns regarding the presence of *testimonio* in the U.S. academic marketplace: "How much of a favor do we do testimonio by positing, as I do here, that it is a new form of literary narrative or by making it an alternative reading to the canon, as in [the] case of the Stanford general education requirement?" (85–86); and "Is testi-

monio . . . simply a new chapter in an old history of the literary 'relations' between dominant and exploited classes and groups, metropolis and colony, center and periphery, First and Third Worlds. Is it yet another version of a subaltern subject who gives us now—in addition to the surplus value her exploitation in the new circuits of global capital produces—something we desire perhaps even more in these times of the political economy of the sign: her 'truth', a truth that is, as stated at the start of *I, Rigoberta Menchú*, 'the reality of a whole people'?" (89).

11 Center-periphery positionalities are the product of what Alberto Moreiras terms "the auratic practice of the postauratic" ("Aura" 201). This refers to a self-legitimating form of critical practice that results from the "positing of two radically heterogeneous fields of experience . . . my or our experience and theirs" (201). This initial engagement becomes postauratic "because the relational mediation between the heterogeneous realms is no longer based on mimesis, but it is based precisely upon the impossibility of mimesis: a simulation, then, a repetition, whose moment of truth is the loss of truth itself" (201). This auratic practice of the postauratic, this foundational practice of self-legitimation enacted between a center that posits a periphery as the absolute auratic Other of the center, is also the object of Neil Larsen's excellent critique of the ways in which the North posits the South as the silent, and silenced, pole that enables the North to think and reauthorize itself.

12 Latin American Latin Americanists working in Latin America, or those working in the United States who presume to represent the position of Latin America within global cultural politics, are not immune to such essentializing logics. They merely implement them from what they perceive as being the other side of the geopolitical configuration. But this does not immediately signify a higher truth than that elaborated from within metropolitan critique. Recent interventions have criticized the internationalization of U.S. Latin American cultural and/or subaltern studies as just another neoimperial imposition onto the Latin American tradition (see Achúgar; Moraña ["El boom"]). In other words, they once again affirm Latin America as the periphery to the center's centrism. But the irony of the center-periphery binarisms that uphold such models of thought are that in order to arrive at the conclusion that cultural/subaltern studies is mere centrist neoimperialism or cultural colonization, they have to reaffirm the imperial structures—the center-periphery model— that they critique. In other words, because of their implicit center-periphery binary thinking they offer no outside to the strategies they contest. They merely reproduce neocolonial relations of power without thinking about the possibility of the deconstruction (or transculturation) of those relations and modes of production within knowledge production itself. For further critique of these internally antagonistic logics, see Moreiras (*Exhaustion* 239–63).

13 In "Can the Subaltern Speak?" Spivak critiques Foucault and Deleuze in terms strikingly similar to the self-positional transparency—or antipositionality— of the founding statement: "In the Foucault-Deleuze conversation, the issue

seems to be that there is no representation, no signifier (Is it to be presumed that the signifier has already been dispatched? There is, then, no sign-structure operating experience, and thus might one lay semiotics to rest?); theory is a relay of practice (thus laying problems of theoretical practice to rest) and the oppressed can know and speak for themselves.... Further, the intellectuals ... become transparent in the relay race, for they merely report on the nonrepresented subject and analyze . . . the workings of (the unnamed Subject irreducibly presupposed by) power and desire. The produced 'transparency' marks the place of 'interest'; it is maintained by vehement denegation: 'Now this role of referee, judge, and universal witness is one which I absolutely refuse to adopt' " (279–80). For Spivak there is no doubt that "this S/subject, curiously sewn together into a transparency by denegations, belongs to the exploiters' side of the international division of labor" (280).

14 "Spectacular redemption" "is only the shamefaced, embarrassed other side of disciplinary power/knowledge, working in spite of itself to give the discipline further legitimacy, providing it with an alibi, blind to the fact that the discipline speaks through us, always and everywhere, no matter what we say and what we do not say" (Moreiras, "Aura" 209–15). For the notion of disciplinary fantasy, see Williams.

15 This same logic is prevalent in the boom in Hollywood ethno-products that emerged in the early 1990s. Movies such as *Dances with Wolves, The Last of the Mohicans,* and *Geronimo: An American Legend,* and so forth all seem to share the same underlying fantasy scenario: they invariably express respect for the indigenous way of life (again, for subaltern "strong family relationships, community solidarity, an intimate relationship with nature," etc.) yet they simultaneously naturalize Euro/North American expansionism, indigenous subjugation to processes of modernity, cultural appropriation, displacement, and demise. Paraphrasing Žižek, these appropriations of the subaltern into U.S. cultural networks uncover an underlying fantasy scenario that, on the one hand, provides the hegemonic with a myth of the origins of a national heritage, yet, on the other, posits the subaltern as an ideological fossil that is created retroactively by ruling ideologies in order to divert attention away from contemporary antagonisms (232).

16 For outstanding discussions of the notion of de-orientalism, see Levinson ("Death" and "Latin Americanist").

17 For Scheper-Hughes, "anthropology exists both as a field of knowledge (a *disciplinary* field) and as a field of action (a *force* field). Anthropological writing can be a site of resistance. This approach bears resemblances to what Michael Taussig . . . and others called 'writing against terror,' what Franco Basaglia . . . referred to as becoming a 'negative worker,' and what Michel de Certeau meant by 'making a *perruque*' of scientific research. The latter tactic refers to diverting the time owed to the factory or, in this case, to the academic institution into more human activities. We can, offered de Certeau, make 'textual objects' (i.e., books) that 'write against the grain' and that signify solidarity" (24–25).

3 Formalities of Consumption and Citizenship in the Age of Cultural Hybridity

1 As noted in chapter 1, in the relatively marginal field of Latin American literary studies the boom/postboom model emerged within cold war conditions as a peripheral cultural and technical innovation of the metropolitan modernist canon. However, as Arif Dirlik notes, cold war conditions can no longer help us reflect on global relations that have emerged as a result of recent upheavals in the capitalist world economy. The emergence of what has been termed global capitalism, flexible production, and late capitalism has transformed relations that had previously been protected by such universalistic rubrics as colonizer/colonized, First World/Third World, or "the West and the Rest" (330). As noted in the previous two chapters, in Latin America new capitalist configurations are eclipsing national development (the cultural politics that nurtured the boom/postboom paradigm, for example) and have fabricated postnational neoliberalism as the dominant ideology and restructuring force of the present. This has resulted in a generalized crisis in the role of the intellectual because it is no longer clear what his or her relationship to the state or to popular culture is or could be. The dissolution of modernity's totalizing ideas of social change and collective transformation; the erosion of the ideology of progress, growth, utopianism, and instrumental rationality; the eclipsing of the avant-garde and of the aesthetic values of modernity; and, finally, the crisis of humanism and of the place of its traditional objects (in particular, of high literature and the very idea of the literary as a privileged space for cultural definition in an increasingly technological age) provide us now with the challenge of rethinking state/culture relations, community, civil society, the place of the lettered intellectual in the face of transnational flows, and the permanence of the political within postnational or nonnational cultural and social formations.

2 The new relation of the intellectual to neoliberal forms of social reproduction can be seen in the shift from state education to the decentralization and privatization of schooling at all levels. In Chile, for example, this has made education a profit-oriented business strictly linked to the logics of the transnational marketplace rather than being a right or a service to the nation's populace. Thus the radical restructuring of the education system in Chile from the early 1980s to the present, a restructuration that is now being reproduced to a greater or lesser degree throughout Latin America (in Mexico D.F., for example), has subsumed pedagogy under the logics of disciplinary consumption and institutional marketability. This has produced a new class of "taxi teachers" who, in order to make ends meet, teach up to fifteen classes per day in a myriad of institutions, with ever-fewer forms of collective organization or means of negotiation, and within a market logic that pays them not per pedagogical hour but per chronological hour (in such a way that in order to be paid for three classes they have to teach four [see Collins and Lear 132]). As Collins and Lear put it in their analysis of Chile's "free-market miracle", "the claim that thanks to

314   *Notes to Chapter Three*

free-market privatization young Chileans and their families now enjoy an array of higher educational choices proves to be a mirage visible only from certain neighborhoods. . . . From the viewpoint of the champions of the free-market model, the previous long-standing 'socialistic' model of a society striving to enable all who desire more than a minimal education to obtain it is to put fancy notions into the heads of the poor. In the words of the Chilean government's Social Report 1984–1985: 'Values that correspond to models of unattainable lives should not be fomented among the poorer sectors of society' " (148).

3 The following comments by John Beverley should be noted in our dealings with the term "civil society" under current conditions: "The current privileging of the concept of civil society—understood as free associations or relations among autonomous individuals governed by civil law but not under the direct tutelage of the state—is connected to a 'postmodernist' disillusion with the capacity of the state to organise society. Agency is transferred from the state to the forces that are said to be operating autonomously in civil society: to 'culture' and/or to the market" ("Theses" 312). As we will see throughout the course of this chapter, the postmodern privileging of the category of civil society is anchored in the establishment of an implicit positive relation of equivalence between consumption, the popular, politics, and freedom, which is particularly prevalent in cultural studies. Once again, as John Beverley indicates, "the equation cultural studies arrived at was something like the following. To the extent that mass culture is popular in the consumer sense—that is, 'pop'—it is also 'popular' in the political sense: that is, representative of the people, embodying the social will of the people, national-popular, progressive. The premium placed in cultural studies on analysing the activity of the consumer often led to the claim that consumption itself constituted a particular realm of freedom and low-level popular resistance to the ideological forms or 'reality principle' of capitalism" (307). As we will see in the course of my argument, this cultural studies premium has now also passed into social sciences discourse in Latin America. The purpose of this chapter, of course, is to shed light on the limits of this form of analysis under current conditions.

4 This is by no means to suggest that Foucault was mistaken in his analyses of the society of discipline. Indeed, as Michael Hardt notes, in 1978 Foucault himself suggested that the notion of discipline was becoming increasingly problematic: "In the last few years society has changed and individuals have changed too; they are more and more diverse, different, and independent. There are ever more categories of people who are not compelled by discipline, so that we are obliged to imagine the development of society without discipline. The ruling class is still impregnated with the old technique. But it is still clear that in the future we must separate ourselves from the society of discipline of today" (quoted in Hardt 41).

5 In Norbert Lechner's formulations, neoliberalism is a reform of the state on the grounds of reducing public spending, redirecting social policies, decentralizing and debureaucratizing state apparatuses, and increasing the economic

efficiency of state practices. All of this leads to the redistribution of the limits of the state and, in particular, to the construction of public policies that no longer confront the question of social integration. Rather, the state maintains the marketplace as the principle form of social control and mediation, while upholding at all times the so-called systemic competitivity of the nation in world markets. In this sense, every political decision in neoliberalism is always already overdetermined by its eventual impact on the economy ("Por qué" 65). Thus President George Bush's launching of the Enterprise for the Americas Initiative after the fall of the Berlin Wall has become the powerful backdrop for one of the most remarkable features of official hemispheric neoliberalism: the pan-American dream (officially excluding Cuba for now) structured through the ideal of a single marketplace that is governed by what has been called the "Washington consensus." As John Williamson puts it, the latter is the result of an assemblage of agreements forged in recent years between the political Washington of Congress and senior members of the administration, and the technocratic Washington of the international financial institutions, the economic agencies of the U.S. government, the Federal Reserve Board, and the think tanks (see Castañeda 315). Ultimately, it is as a result of the Washington consensus that Latin American state formations have been legitimately downsized, streamlined, denationalized and, when necessary, bailed out by the IMF when finance capitalism loses control of its own dynamics. It would appear, then, that what is really at stake in transnational neoliberalism is the renegotiation of the state's necessarily illusory "thereness." Berger's critique of Latin Americanism in *Under Northern Eyes* testifies to the increasingly overpowering thereness of the modern imperial state during the cold war; its mass, its homogeneous coherence and excessive visibility as an organ of domination superimposed on economically subjugated or dependent societies and economies whose elites, in turn, needed to assuage their increasing illegitimacy in the war against communism by transforming their historical antidemocratic practices. The neoliberal downsizing of the metropolitan and peripheral state apparatuses, and their more or less uniform acceptance of the so-called democratizing forces of the global marketplace, indicate the hemispheric attempt to conceal the state. The state is now more given to controlling through capital flows than it is to disciplining its populations and market territories through state unionization, national education, or the dissemination of a good *criollista* or *indigenista* bildungsroman.

6   This is not, however, the end of Gramsci. Indeed Gramsci's discussion of laissez-faire liberalism is almost prophetic: "It is asserted that economic activity belongs to civil society, and that the State must not intervene to regulate it. But since in actual reality civil society and State are one and the same, it must be made clear that *laissez-faire* too is a form of State regulation, introduced and maintained by coercive means. It is a deliberate policy, conscious of its own ends, and not the spontaneous, automatic expression of economic facts. Consequently, *laissez-faire* liberalism is a political programme, designed

to change—in so far as it is victorious—a State's leading personnel, and to change the economic programme of the State itself—in other words the distribution of the national income" (160). Since the economic crises of the 1980s the reabsorption of political society into civil society has been carried out by the transnational marketplace. After the final erosion of the national-popular state, the market (embodied in the emergence of NAFTA, Mercosur, the GATT agreements, etc.) stepped in to put things in their rightful place for global accumulation, guaranteeing the state as the sole negotiator of its own disappearing act by allowing it to be absorbed into and redistributed by market forces. This means that both culture and political representation are increasingly absorbed into each other and reconverted through the naturalizing processes of the culture ideology of consumerism. Within the long history of the liberal tradition neoliberalism has officially rediscovered the economy as constitutive of what is now not merely the national but the *international* division of labor and institutionality. And this very division has become constitutive of capital's new global civilizing process. Thus civil society, understood as an institutionalized democratizing force capable of challenging or even of subsuming the rule of the state, has been displaced by a civil society that produces new consensual/controlling practices structured and manipulated by the market/state and its images. For Marx, of course, "the sale of commodities, the realization of commodity capital, and thus of surplus-value as well, is restricted not by the consumer needs of society in general, but by the consumer needs of a society in which the great majority are always poor and must remain always poor" (*Capital* v. 2, 391). With this in mind, the advent of transnational finance capital, the real subsumption of labor under capital, and the demands of the international division of labor seem to suggest that Marx's comment on the consumer needs of society is still a fundamental challenge to contemporary considerations of civil society.

7 As Roger Bartra tells us, Latin American modernizing processes (populist national capitalism in particular) constantly conjured up and mobilized, from within their own dynamics, those very social identities that remained most threatening to the success of modernization. In what is without doubt a rearticulation and subtle inversion of Marx and Engels's famous celebration of proletarian revolutionary potential ("Modern bourgeois society with its relations of production, of exchange and of property, a society that has conjured up such gigantic means of production and of exchange, is like the sorcerer who is no longer able to control the powers of the nether world whom he has called up by his spells" [*Manifesto* 11]), Bartra describes peripheral capitalism as a war machine of containment, identification, and subjectivation: "Modern developed capitalist societies continuously nurture a series of symptomatic contradictions that determine what could be called the 'Jezebel syndrome', characterized by a constant creation, provocation, stimulation and repression of society's marginal areas. These areas contain aggravated, dominated and exploited classes in addition to certain ruling class segments. In brief, it is a

manipulation, refunctionalization and recreation of certain aspects of the class conflicts. These manipulative processes become the powerful ideological apparatus exerting control over the deepest (and potentially revolutionary) forms of social conflict. This apparatus bears a similarity to Jezebel who, pregnant with terror, gave birth to a vast horde of strange beings, including criminals, revolutionaries and madmen" (17).

8   Needless to say, this is a profoundly Rousseau-like formulation of social organization: the rational civil order is diametrically opposed to the irrational disorder of nature and of natural society, while the passage from the latter to the former is deemed to guarantee the inevitable movement of universal civilization. Sarmiento, for example, has to be read in light of such formulations.

9   Once again, as we saw in chapter 1, such valorizations (present of course throughout the postindependence period from Bello and Sarmiento through to Fernando Ortiz and beyond) have been synonymous historically with both the construction of the nation-state and also with the perpetuation, ultimately, of populism and its monolithic and often authoritarian conceptualizations of pluralism, community, development, and identity.

10 It is at this point, of course, that we trace the passage from Rousseau to the Hegelian notion of the pedagogic state, in which civil (bourgeois) society is structured through "a process of formal subsumption, a process whereby particular differences, foreign to the universal, are negated and preserved in unity" (Hardt 29). In other words, we witness the emergence of an attempt by the state to organize capitalist civil society through the fabrication and incorporation of a subjugated and tamed (effectively subsumed) labor force.

11 We should not underestimate the historical successes of such movements and encounters by the state. As Carlos Vilas informs us (with a noticeable charge of nostalgia and idealization): "In the Keynesian-Fordist model, the state regulated economic activity and intervened in specific sectors, including the establishment of state-owned enterprises. Increases in economic productivity led to salary increases and expanded employment, which benefited the population as a whole. Social policy in this model reinforced the process of capital accumulation to the degree that it created externalities for private enterprises. For example, public investment in education, health care, worker training, and low-income housing represented a savings for the private sector, which would otherwise have had to invest in these areas. Meanwhile, employment, wage and pricing policies improved the purchasing power of individual workers and the domestic market as a whole. Social policy was seen as an element of investment, not an expense. Both economic and social policies in the Keynesian-Fordist model facilitated the incorporation of broad sectors of the poor, especially the urban poor, into the political and economic system. Latin America during this period was characterized by widespread social mobility, stimulated—within certain limits—by the state. Together these varied elements helped constitute what was known as the 'nation-popular state', or the 'national-developmentalist state'—the Latin American proxy of the western European 'welfare state'.

Social policies contributed to capitalist development, were reformist by nature, and fed social mobility. As a result, they gave broad legitimacy to the political system. Citizen rights were thus imbued with socioeconomic rights. Citizen rights were also expanded into the political realm, as women and indigenous people were granted the right to vote. The implicit paradigm of social policy—and of state policies in general—was integration" ("Neoliberal" 17).

12   In *Hybrid Cultures* García Canclini frames the emergence of a new capitalist configuration, new power relations, and the erosion of dependency theory's monumental and geographically defined center-periphery positionalities, with the following important insights on transnationalization: "In Brazil, the advance of massification and industrialization of culture did not imply—contrary to what tended to be said—a greater dependency on foreign production. Statistics reveal that in the last several years its cinematography and the proportion of national films on the screens grew: from 13.9 percent in 1971 to 35 percent in 1982. Books by Brazilian authors, which accounted for 54 percent of publishing production in 1973, rose to 70 percent in 1981. Also, more national records and cassettes are listened to, while imported music declines. In 1972, 60 percent of television programming was foreign; in 1983 it fell to 30 percent. At the same time that this trend toward nationalization and autonomy is occurring in cultural production, Brazil is becoming a very active agent in the Latin American market of symbolic goods by exporting soap operas. As it also succeeds in broadly penetrating the central countries, it became the seventh world producer of television and advertising, and the sixth in records. Renato Ortiz, from whom I take this data, concludes that they went 'from defense of the national popular to the exportation of the international popular' " (230).

13   García Canclini's notion of the democratization of culture is somewhat problematic here. In her evaluation of García Canclini's work, Jean Franco notes that "postmodernists contend that television, mass marketing and new technologies have democratized culture, breaking down the barriers between 'high' and 'low', and making possible hybrid combinations (salsa, for example) that enrich Latin American culture. Latin American culture, they argue, has always been heterogeneous and has always drawn on all kinds of repertoires, and can thus claim to be postmodern *avant la lettre*. Far from implying the death of local cultures, García Canclini argues, the market has stimulated the invention of new artisan designs, allowed culture to reach new publics, and forced people to invent a new political symbolism and new forms of social action. As an example of the latter, he cites the masked Superbarrio in Mexico City who dresses in a costume reminiscent both of Superman and the kitsch outfits of wrestlers, and negotiates on behalf of the marginalized sectors of the population" ("What's Left" 17–18). García Canclini has also suggested that the market in contemporary Latin America has undermined historically constituted hierarchies: "The patrimonies of different cultures and epochs are mixed in a replete present which, at the same time that it suggests a fantastic abundance, abolishes the hierarchies among historical periods. All these styles and ways of

life collected under discontinual forms, in the middle of the fragmentation of heterogenous societies, seem not even in the present to possess order or hierarchy ("Memory" 438). In response, however, George Yúdice has maintained that "García Canclini tends to overstate the case of hybridization in abolishing 'the hierarchies among historical periods' " ("Postmodernism" 551). However, García Canclini also points out in *Hybrid Cultures* that new and more mobile networks of social control (now masked by, and precisely as, the democratization of cultural production) have emerged in recent times as the marketplace increasingly takes on the role of the ideological state apparatus: "The corporations' simultaneous ownership of large exposition halls, advertising and critical spaces afforded by TV and radio chains, magazines, and other institutions allows them to program cultural activities that have an enormous impact and are very expensive, to control the networks over which they will be broadcast, the critiques, and even to a certain extent the decodification that different audiences will make" (61). This is hardly a democratization of culture.

14 Within this context it is almost inevitable, then, that postmodern resistances should transpire increasingly within the regime of market forces. Identity politics' insistence on empowerment and self-worth, for example, is always a plea for institutional recognition, and perhaps even an attempt to naturalize what Jameson has called postmodernity's "hysterical euphoria in [its] visions of some delirious pluralism of late capitalism with its alleged authorizations of social difference" ("Actually" 173).

15 Indeed, the politics of subaltern micro-identity is one of the few areas in which political mobilization has been effective in Latin America in recent years. In Ecuador the indigenous movement has called attention to the cultural, ecological, economic, and political dangers of agribusiness's promotion of nontraditional production, the transformation of traditional labor practices, and the linking of local labor to international consumer markets (Pacari 26–28). In Chile the Mapuches organize in an attempt to protest the consequences of the country's possible absorption into NAFTA (Millaman, 30–31). In Brazil the alliance of the Nongovernmental Organizations and grassroots organizations actively promoting local and/or regional multiculturalist agendas counters (though not always progressively) the state's neo-Republican attempts to reunite the nation through the reinculcation and rearticulation of national patrimony, together with popular respect for national symbols such as the flag and the national anthem (Santiago 50–53).

16 A similar communiqué, published in *La Jornada* on February 16, 1994, underlines the category of collective subaltern identity as a state of injury in the EZLN: "The word of truth that comes from the depths of our history, from our pain, from our dead who yet live with us, will fight for dignity in the lips of our leaders. The mouths of our rifles will be silent so that our truth may speak with words for all, for those who fight with honor and speak with honor. . . . For us, the smallest of these lands, the faceless, without history, armed with truth and fire, coming from the night and the mountain, the true men and women, the

dead of yesterday, today and forever, for us, nothing, for everyone, everything"
(quoted in Clarke and Ross 78–79). Also note the following communiqué from
February 1, 1994: "There was so much pain in our heart, such was our death
and pain, that it could no longer fit, brothers, in this world which our grand-
parents had handed down to us in order to continue living and struggling. So
great was the pain and hurt that it no longer fitted in the hearts of many, and
it overflowed and filled other hearts with pain and hurt, and the hearts of the
oldest and wisest of our peoples were filled, and the hearts of young men and
women were filled . . . of children . . . and the hearts of animals and plants were
filled . . . and the wind and the sun were pained and injured, and the earth was
pained and injured. Everything was just pain and hurt, everything was silence.
And then that pain that united us made us speak" (EZLN 119; translation mine).

17 While these comments ring true for identity politics as a generalized practice, perhaps we could suggest that the EZLN is more complex in its codifica-
tions. The liberal order invariably strives to convert political identity into private interest. If this is the case, refusal to fix an identity, a set of identity claims,
or a whole social movement within a singular line of thought or strategy of
struggle would prevent that identity/movement from being institutionalized,
controlled, and fully integrated or subsumed by the state. For example, in a
communiqué from March 1994 the EZLN presented a list of thirty-four demands ranging from "free and democratic elections" and "access to accurate
information about events" to "[an] end to illiteracy of indigenous people" and
"the complete cancellation of all the debts" (Clarke and Ross 81–84). When
placed alongside the older national identity paradigms that the EZLN constantly
upholds (their undying faith in the Mexican flag, in the revolutionary national
heroes, etc., and in the national mythology that gave rise to the state that they
now seek to challenge), such an accumulation of varied and perhaps disparate
demands takes on the guise of a deliberate artifice designed to elude definition by the state and, presumably, their own integration. In other words, one is
left wondering what it is exactly that the EZLN desires from the state. Perhaps
we could suggest that what the EZLN desires in this communiqué is to maintain a creative and open-ended tension between the immediately recognizable
demands of national and minority identity formation, and an ever-elusive language of wanting without end. This allows them to "exploit politically a recovery of the more expansive moments in the genealogy of identity formation,
a recovery of the moment prior to its own foreclosure against its want, prior to
the point at which its sovereign subjectivity is established through such foreclosure and through eternal repetition of its pain" (Brown 76). What it wants,
in other words, is to straddle the border between the necessary recognition of
the historical formation of the state, the upholding of contemporary injury, and
the possibility of forging an alternative and transformative political language of
desire that remains, as yet, unnameable and undefined in the institutional terms
laid down by the historical formation of the state. What such a flexible and
open-ended strategy of identity-claim formation (itself a "whatever" strategy

of identitarian contingency) has won the EZLN, of course, is sustained survival in the face of a state apparatus that is not particularly renowned for its tolerance of protest and insurgency.

18 Later, in *Utopia Unarmed*, Castañeda quotes Benjamin J. Barber ("Jihad vs McWorld", *Atlantic Monthly,* March 1992, p. 63) and expresses what could be the utopic horizon of regional federalism: "Thanks to this kind of economic integration, the regional-federalist impulse that Latin America needs can become a reality: as the level of decision-making rises supranationally, it also makes state or local decision-making more plausible and effective. This view also converges with a broader trend, formulated elsewhere and for other areas, perhaps still far off for Latin America, yet relevant for its future: 'a confederal union of semi-autonomous states, tied together into regional economic associations and markets larger than nation-states—participatory and self-determining in local matters at the bottom, representative and accountable at the top'" (319-20). Apart from the question of representation and accountability at the top, such a model is perhaps already a little too close to neoliberalism for comfort.

19 Yúdice points to what he considers to be a fundamental difference in U.S. and Latin American forms of consumption: "The politics of consumption in Latin America does not refer, in the first place, to actions wielded in the activity of purchasing (or boycotting) consumer commodities. Rather, Latin American cultural politics points to a collaboration of diverse actors working in different scales of social space: from the local group to transnational businesses, financial institutions, media, and NGO's. In the US we tend to wage our cultural politics within narrowly circumscribed fields, often with little interaction across the spectrum of social space" ("Civil" 21). Having said this, however, hemispheric differences in the modes and modalities of consumption are perhaps not as clear-cut as Yúdice appears to suggest. For example, as we will see in our discussion of García Canclini's rethinking of "civil society in an age of globalization and regional integration" (20), García Canclini subscribes quite markedly to what Yúdice takes as being the U.S. notion of consumption: that is, to the activity of defining and positioning oneself in light of consumer commodities. However, he understands this form of consumption as a social practice capable of creating new affective identifications (commonalities or groupings) from which to formulate an institutional infrastructure for political and social mediation. In other words, rather than following Yúdice's vision of structural and practical differences between northern models of consumption and those of the South (22), García Canclini's position tends toward the reproduction of the notion of Americanization that Yúdice identifies as a major problem for, and potential obstacle to, the effective organization of a Latin American politics of citizenship and consumption.

20 All translations of *Consumidores y ciudadanos* are mine.

21 In contrast, Carlos Vilas provides us with the following sobering information: "In 1980, 118 million Latin Americans—about a third of the region's total

population—were poor. By 1990, that number had increased to 196 million, or nearly half the total population" ("Neoliberal" 16).

22 Elsewhere Vilas compares current processes of marginalization with those of the past: "There is a clear difference in the identity of those being pushed into poverty from those of the past. They do not hold much in common with the recently urbanized, predominantly illiterate Latin American masses that were active participants in the populist and developmentalist experiences of the 1940s and 1950s. Today's marginalized population holds citizenship rights and, up to a decade ago, was integrated into the formal labor market, participated in unions and other social organizations, entered the educational and health systems, and benefited from welfare and pension systems. Many of them joined the democratic mobilizations that forced the military dictatorships out of power and also participated in certain cases, as in Central America, in revolutionary attempts at social change. . . . This marginalized population poses social as well as political challenges to states and political organizations. The loss of collective allegiances usually leads to what Geertz . . . has called a retreat to 'primordial attachments', or what Bourdieu . . . has termed the 'retreat to the habitus' (i.e., the household, kinship, or ethnic group). Such retreats, or regressions, lead to increased social fragmentation as particularistic emotional ties substitute for collective identities based on notions of class and citizenship. This phenomenon may be understood as a transitional stage in the development of new social arrangements; it involves under any circumstances instability and uncertainty" ("Economic" 156–57).

23 Enrique Dussel's words are paramount in this regard: "Capital that defeats all barriers requires incrementally more absolute time for work; when it cannot supersede this limit, then it augments productivity through technology; but this increase decreases the importance of human labor. It is thus that there is *superfluous* (displaced) *humanity*. . . . The result is poverty, poverty as the absolute limit of capital" (20).

24 As Ernesto Laclau puts it, hegemony is the suturing of potential dislocations in the name of the possible constitution of new spaces of representation (*New* 61). The achievement of hegemony is, in other words, the covering-up of dislocation and disjuncture in the name of the resurrection of social objectivity, translatability, homogeneity, and coherence.

4 Hear Say Yes in Piglia: *La ciudad ausente*, Posthegemony, and the "Fin-negans" of Historicity

1 The emergence of exhaustion—of a certain ending—has not just dawned on us like the sudden revelation of a postmodern truth. It is the limit that modernity has been living with, and within, for decades, without really wanting to heed it in its fullness, never mind to think it through in its consequences. Derrida, on the other hand, has known it all along: "Many young people today . . . probably no longer sufficiently realize it: the eschatological themes of the 'end of his-

tory', of 'the end of Marxism', of the 'end of philosophy', of the 'ends of man', of the 'last man' and so forth were, in the '50s, that is, forty years ago, our daily bread. We had this bread of apocalypse in our mouths naturally, already, just as naturally as that which I nicknamed after the fact, in 1980, the 'apocalyptic tone in philosophy'. What was its consistency? What did it taste like? It was, *on the one hand,* the reading or analysis of those whom we could nickname the *classics of the end.* They formed the canon of the modern apocalypse (end of History, end of Man, end of Philosophy, Hegel, Marx, Nietzsche, Heidegger, with their Kojèvian codicil and the codicils of Kojève himself). It was, *on the other hand and indissociably,* what we had known or what some of us for quite some time no longer hid from concerning totalitarian terror in all the Eastern countries, all the socio-economic disasters of Soviet bureaucracy, the Stalinism of the past and the neo-Stalinism in process (roughly speaking, from the Moscow trials to the repression in Hungary, to take only these minimal indices). . . . Thus . . . for us, I venture to say, the media parade of current discourse on the end of history and the last man looks most often like a tiresome anachronism" (*Specters* 14–15).

2   This is hardly reason for pessimism, as Laclau notes: "Far from perceiving in the 'crisis of reason' a nihilism which leads to the abandonment of any emancipatory project, we see the former as opening unprecedented opportunities for a radical critique of all kinds of domination, as well as for the formulation of liberation projects hitherto restrained by the rationalist 'dictatorship' of the Enlightenment" (*New* 3–4). Indeed, Laclau had already announced the terms of the debate with Chantal Mouffe in *Hegemony and Socialist Strategy:* "Inasmuch as the field of 'society in general' has disappeared as a valid framework of political analysis, there has also disappeared the possibility of establishing a *general* theory of politics on the basis of topographic categories — that is to say, of categories which fix in a permanent manner the meaning of certain contents as differences which can be located within a relational complex. . . . The original forms of democratic thought were linked to a *positive* and *unified* conception of human nature, and, to that extent, they tended to constitute a single space within which that nature would have to manifest the effects of its radical liberty and equality: it was thus that there was constituted a public space linked to the idea of citizenship. . . . What we are witnessing is a politicization far more radical than any we have known in the past, because it tends to dissolve the distinction between the public and the private, not in terms of the encroachment on the private by a unified public space, but in terms of a proliferation of radically new and different political spaces. We are confronted with the emergence of a *plurality of subjects,* whose forms of constitution and diversity it is only possible to think if we relinquish the category of 'subject' as a unified and unifying essence" (180–81).

3   As already stated, the end of history is not the end of thought nor of historicity. After all, Laclau's notion of exhaustion cannot be placed on the side of what Derrida has called (in his critique of Francis Fukuyama) "the vulgate of the

capitalist paradise as end of history" (*Specters* 74). As I advance in this chapter, Laclau's rendering of exhaustion as the (dis)unifying image of our time marks not just the limits of contemporary reflection, but also the affirmation of the possibility of thinking another law of historicity: the limit at which the impossible might open up to alternative pathways. In *New Reflections on the Revolution of Our Time* Laclau evokes this affirmation in the following terms: "If the 'end of history' is understood as the end of a conceptually graspable object encompassing the whole of the real in its diachronic spatiality, we are clearly at the end of 'history'. But from that perspective, 'history' is a quasi-transcendental category, an attempt to inscribe the totality of events and dislocations in conceptual forms transcending them. In another sense, however, we can say that we are at the *beginning* of history, at the point where historicity finally achieves full recognition. . . . In this sense history's ultimate unrepresentability is the condition for the recognition of our radical historicity. It is in our pure condition of event, which is shown at the edges of representation and in the traces of temporality corrupting all space, where we find our most essential being, which is our contingency and the intrinsic dignity of our transitory nature" (83–84). In *Specters of Marx* Derrida seconds Laclau's affirmation, while always having preceded him: "In the same place, on the same limit, where history is finished, there where a certain determined concept of history comes to an end, precisely there the historicity of history begins, there finally it has the chance of heralding itself—of promising itself. There where man, a certain determined concept of man, is finished, there the pure humanity of man, of the *other man* and of man *as other* begins or has finally the chance of heralding itself—of promising itself. . . . Not only must one not renounce the emancipatory desire, it is necessary to insist on it more than ever, it seems, and insist on it, moreover, as the very indestructibility of the 'it is necessary'. This is the condition of a re-politicization, perhaps of another concept of the political" (74–75). Meanwhile for Jean-Luc Nancy this *other* concept of the political "defines at least a limit, at which all politics stops and begins. The communication that takes place on this limit, and that, in truth, constitutes it, demands that way of destining ourselves in common that we call a politics, that way of opening community to itself, rather than to a destiny or to a future" (*Inoperative* 80).

4 In *Phenomenology of Spirit* Hegel transfigured "the individual into 'consciousness' and the world into 'object'. Life and history are thus transfigured, in their very diversity, into *relations of consciousness to the object*. It is still a matter of truth and it is a phenomenologization of the truth as truth of *consciousness*. . . . The phenomenology (of spirit) describes (1) the relation of consciousness to the object *as truth* or as relation *to the truth* as mere object; (2) the relation of consciousness, insofar as it is *the true*, to the object; (3) the *true relation* of consciousness with truth" (Derrida, *Specters* 123). Needless to say, it is the dialectical mediation between truth and consciousness, objectivity and intelligibility, and their relation to the fabrication of a general theory of politics constructed on the basis of topographic categories (nation, nation-state, region,

center-periphery, etc.) that are under question in Laclau's intervention. In the final pages of *Hegemony and Socialist Strategy* Laclau and Mouffe call attention to the ineffectiveness, now, of an organic link between the Left and the internal unfolding of the Hegelian dialectic and its determinations: "The classic discourse of socialism . . . was a discourse of the universal, which transformed certain social categories into depositories of political and epistemological privileges; it was an a priori discourse concerning differential levels of effectiveness within the social—and as such it reduced the field of discursive surfaces on which it considered that it was possible and legitimate to operate; it was, finally, a discourse concerning the privileged points from which historical changes were set in motion—the Revolution, the General Strike, or 'evolution' as a unifying category of the cumulative and irreversible character of partial advances" (192). In contrast to Laclau's formulations, Norbert Lechner, who has posited that "politics is held hostage by contingency" ("Politics" 183), uncovers the complacency of a socialist mourning that appears to be more invested in self-recovery than in the possibility of thinking about the terms of future political interventions.

5   In Argentina, for example, the "Mothers of the Plaza de Mayo" and the "Children of the Disappeared" (*desaparecidos*) bear direct witness to the haunting of the structure of every hegemony. If, as Laclau puts it, every act of institution entails a sedimented concealment, then the symbolic value of the *desaparecidos* resides in the fact that their sustained absence calls attention to the ill-established power base upon which neoliberal hegemony has been constructed since the end of the military regimes in 1983. The *desaparecidos* are an allegorical site that bears witness to the exclusions on which liberal democracy and the culture ideology of consumerism have been constructed in postdictatorial Argentina. In this sense, they are the spectral embodiment of an unrecuperable negativity within neoliberalism's hegemonic repertoires: the symbolic site for the incompletion of the social, and, therefore, also the point at which postdictatorial politics (and political reflection) both stops and begins.

6   "The speculative dialectic is not only a gigantic paranoid machine but, due to the internal nature of its operation, also a marked mechanism of resistance to the paranoid machine. Negativity in the dialectic is the expression of the terror that decenters. It is the death of thought, the process of its corruption. By thinking its own negativity the speculative dialectic resists itself incessantly. It is, then, a paranoid resistance: a paranoid resistance against the paranoid machine. The mechanism is explained by the dialectic itself and by its mode of operation, the function of which is to avoid 'true madness'; paralysis, the apocalyptic disaster of thought" (Moreiras, *Tercer* 164; translation mine).

7   As noted in the previous chapter, George Yúdice uses the term "posthegemonic" to describe current articulations between state and civil processes: "Flexible accumulation, consumer culture, and the 'new world information order' are produced or distributed (made to flow) globally, to occupy the space of the nation, but are no longer 'motivated' by any essential connections to a

state, as embodied, for example, in a 'national-popular' formation. Their motivations are both infra- and supranational. We might say that, from the purview of the national proscenium, a *posthegemonic* situation holds. That is, the 'compromise solution' that culture provided for Gramsci is not now one that pertains to the national level but to the local and transnational. Instead, the 'culture-ideology of consumerism' serves to naturalize global capitalism everywhere" ("Civil" 4; italics mine). Although I am indebted to Yúdice's formulations, my own use of posthegemonic is slightly different. While Yúdice uses the term to give a name to the positive grounds of the contemporary order—to the postnational hegemony of capital (in opposition to the boundaries of the nation-state)—my appropriation of the term, together with Laclau's notion of recalcitrant negativity, permits us to give a name to hegemony's subaltern residues, negative languages, fragmentary responses, cultural leftovers, and fissured experiences. Posthegemony, in this sense, is no longer a name for the hegemony of transnational capital, but the name of those "places in which hegemony ceases to make sense" (Franco, "Latin" 270).

8 "Guaranteed translatability, given homogeneity, systematic coherence in their *absolute forms,* this is surely (certainly, *a priori* and not probably) what renders the injunction, the inheritance, and the future—in a word the other—*impossible. There must be* disjunction, interruption, the heterogeneous if at least *there must be, if there must be* a chance given to any 'there must be' whatsoever, be it beyond duty" (Derrida, *Specters* 35). This, of course, is quite a radical departure from classical marxism. As Laclau puts it: "The main difference is that dislocations have an objective meaning for classical Marxism and are part of a process whose direction is predetermined. The *subject* of change is therefore internal to that process and is determined by it. The subject is completely absorbed by the structure. In our analysis, on the other hand, the location of the subject is that of dislocation. Thus, far from being a moment of the structure, the subject is the result of the impossibility of constituting the structure as such—that is as a self-sufficient object. . . . For classical Marxism, the possibility of transcending capitalist society depended on the simplification of social structure and the emergence of a privileged agent of social change, while for us, the possibility of democratic transformation of society depends on a proliferation of new subjects of change. This is only possible if there is something in contemporary capitalism which really tends to multiply dislocations and thus create a plurality of new antagonisms" (*New* 41). Laclau, of course, is quick to point out his sustained debt to marxism, because "reflection on dislocation and its possible political fruitfulness does have a tradition within Marxism: it is a feature of the group of phenomena linked to 'permanent revolution' and 'uneven and combined development'" (45). Indeed, for Blanchot, Marx himself is the site for sustained reflection on the thought and potentiality of dislocation: "The communist voice is always at once tacit and violent, political and scholarly, direct, indirect, total and fragmentary, lengthy and almost instantaneous. Marx does not live comfortably with this plurality of languages

that are always colliding and disjoining with each other in him. Even if these languages seem to converge toward the same end, they could not be retranslated into each other, and their heterogeneity, the divergence or gap, the distance that decenters them, renders them non-contemporaneous" (quoted in Derrida, *Specters* 35).

9   In Argentine liberal democracy, for example, democratic politics gives the disappearing logics of hegemony a positive force and value. Democracy has become the art of suppressing democratic politics. As Beatriz Sarlo has pointed out, the growing omniscience of market forces (together with the cultural imprints of hyperinflation in the late 1980s and early 1990s) allowed President Menem to present Argentina with a fundamental dilemma in which democratic processes had to be upheld in order for them to be systematically undermined for the common good: "Menem and his cabinet presented Argentine society with a dilemma: to overcome inflation, it was necessary to concentrate power in the executive branch and not in the legislature . . . and it was necessary to avoid a debate in Congress . . . to preserve the parliamentary forms of discussions of laws, the time required for the deliberation would be time miserably lost from establishing economic order. In short, the dilemma presented the institutional role of parliament in the political process as an obstacle to the common good" ("Argentina" 34). In this sense, it is through the systemic logic of the fatal—the simultaneous evocation of parliamentary processes in order to install the demise of the same sign from within its own workings—that neoliberal democracy ultimately affirms and consolidates itself as the success story of the dictatorial projects of the late 1970s and early 1980s.

10 One could easily say that Latin America has always been subversive in its relations to metropolis. But this is to position Latin America (now, as always) as the fissured effect *of* metropolitan master narratives. Here, however, we are dealing with a new phenomenon: the fissure *in* metropolitan *and* peripheral master narratives (progress, industrialization, the nation-state, development, etc.) themselves. We are confronting, in other words, the effects of a shift in intensities that leaves neither metropolis nor periphery untouched, and, indeed, that unworks such categories as discreet places from which to think.

11 Many contemporary narratives lend themselves to such an injunction. Perhaps we could read, for example, Ricardo Piglia's notion of a *relato futuro* (a future story) as an integral part of this process of cultural, political, and philosophical redefinition. As Piglia reveals in his dialogues with Juan José Saer, what he calls *el relato futuro* marks the promise not only of new creative and critical languages, but also of writing beyond the constraints of hegemonic language itself. Within this process Macedonio Fernández becomes, for Piglia, a privileged specter of difference, for Macedonio marks a site of singular outsidedness to the constitution of Argentina's social and cultural hegemonies throughout the twentieth century: "I consider Macedonio to be the only avant-garde writer in the history of Argentine literature. He was the only one who was able to distance himself from existing traditions in order to formulate not only a strategy

for his own fiction (refusing to publish and withdrawing from the marketplace) but also a strategy of breaking with the dominant tradition of the novel itself in Argentina. In this sense, perhaps we can think of the question of the future story, understanding this as the story-to-come that one can infer or imagine as possible, as a kind of writing that exceeds the circumscriptions of the political and linguistic traditions. One could conceive of a utopia in which the kind of language that literature has generated is a language almost unto itself, in excess of local or national registers. Along these lines I think that Joyce's *Finnegans Wake* pointed toward the use of a language that exceeded both the local and the national, even though Joyce was a rancorously Irish writer who was always extremely attentive to what those kinds of traditions could be. But one could also think of the future story as a story constituted in another kind of language" (Piglia and Saer 19–28; translation mine).

12   The notion of Critical regionalism has also been taken up by Fredric Jameson in *The Seeds of Time*, as well as by Alberto Moreiras in *Tercer espacio* and *The Exhaustion of Difference*.

13   As such this narrative, which, as previously noted, is grounded in the rupture in narrative itself, seeks to "mobilize a pluralism of 'regional' styles (a term selected . . . in order to forestall the unwanted connotations of the terms *national* and *international* alike), with a view toward resisting the standardizations of a henceforth global late capitalism and corporatism, whose 'vernacular' is as omnipresent as its power over local decisions (and indeed, after the end of the Cold War, over local governments and individual nation states as well)" (Jameson, *Seeds* 202). Needless to say, such an enterprise requires countless critical interventions (of which my own would be but a tiny fragment), ranging from politics — as currently understood — to economics, and from aesthetics to philosophy. Critical regionalism, in other words, demands the collective construction of a linguistic context — posthegemonic critique — that is capable of opening up the exhaustion and denarrativization of discourses of identity and difference to their as yet unnameable and unthinkable excess.

14   As Alberto Moreiras states: "The Latin American literary space, a between-space that is neither subaltern nor residual, wholly metropolitan nor hegemonic, fashions a space for a critical regionalism the force and epistemic positivity of which remains to be understood. Within this space the emergent sense of metropolitan postmodernity encounters the residual sense of peripheral postmodernity, and both enter into precarious and reciprocal determinations" (*Tercer* 119; translation mine). Needless to say, critics such as Angel Rama, Antonio Cornejo Polar, Silviano Santiago, and Roberto Schwarz all bear witness to the modern ambiguities of Latin America's hybrid sites and forms of articulation. However, the conceptual systems from which they have all produced their critiques (the nation, the nation-state, center, periphery, identity, difference) appear to be increasingly unviable as places of affirmation or as notions lending themselves immediately to sense production in increasingly transnational conditions.

15 For an excellent reading of these narratives, see Avelar (107–35).

16 All translations of *La ciudad ausente* are mine.

17 In the relation between inheritance, transmission, deferral, the production of difference, and the exhaustion of the paradigms of national progress/development, it is hardly by chance that Junior's "proper" name (Miguel Mac Kensey) should conjure up not just the name of Macedonio or the British empire's outer (Argentine/Irish) limits (Miguel/Mac). It also indicates (admittedly, at a stretch) the displaced name of (the foundational) John Maynard Keynes. Indeed, (at even more of a stretch) this is also a name whose sound-sense promises a certain field of knowledge (ken) and of articulation (quite literally, a "ken-say"). But surely this is too much.

18 Note, of course, that *La ciudad ausente* is constantly making reference to its/the machine's narratives as the latest or final narrative. In other words, the end of the machine's history is never complete. Yet it always appears on the verge of inauguration.

5 The Dispersal of the Nation and the Neoliberal Habitus: Tracing Insurrection from Central America to South Central Los Angeles

1 As such, Pandey's investigation into the Bhagalpur riots of October 1989 are far from conclusive: "Possibly as many as a thousand people were killed in the course of the violence, most of them Muslims, but estimates of the casualties still vary enormously. . . . No one can say for certain how many were killed. . . . There is widespread *feeling* that women were abducted and raped on a large scale, but none of the surviving victims will talk about rape; the specific cases recorded . . . were incidents that Muslim women informants *had themselves heard about.* . . . In Bhagalpur, the state's 'archives', those official sources that generations of historians and social scientists have treated as 'core accounts', more 'comprehensive' than any other source, are largely missing . . . the view from the center has largely been destroyed in this instance, at any rate for the first few absolutely crucial days of the 'riots' " (9–20; italics mine).

2 Here I take the notion of part-narrative—and, indeed, Pandey's defense of the fragment in general—as indicative of the foundational character within subaltern studies of the Benjaminian debris that remains for reflection after the storm from Paradise (progress, in other words) has passed by (Benjamin "Theses" 258).

3 It should be noted in advance that because this chapter is an explicit and intentional accumulation of fragments, fissures, and discontinuities I have decided not to separate them from each other explicitly within the corpus of the text itself. Such divisions would merely lend the accumulation of subaltern fragments a false structure and a particular sense of unity, development, and closure that they do not have in reality and cannot have in subaltern studies. My intention in preserving the continuity of textual discontinuities, then, is to avoid what Pandey calls "the temptations of totalizing discourses" (29), and to

highlight the notion of the border, and of fissure, as constitutive of subaltern studies and of cultural and political reflection in neoliberal/postnational times. This is, of course, unsatisfactory—and might provoke a certain sense of unease with the development of the chapter itself—but fragments and borderlands are always characterized by the unease of heterogeneity, fissure, and inconclusive passage.

4   According to DeCesare, this means that "with a population of 5.8 million people and a per capita homicide rate of 150 per 100,000, there are approximately 8,700 murders in El Salvador each year. Salvadoran police statistics place the homicide figure even higher than the PAHO-derived figure at roughly 11,000 per year. It is estimated that about 75,000 lost their lives in the 12-year long Salvadoran civil war—approximately 6,250 per year" ("Children" 42). Of course, the presentation of such statistics is not impartial. Although it is true that the estimated number of dead due to political violence in the twelve years between 1980 and 1992 is 75,000, it is a stretch of the imagination to think that deaths due to political violence and repression in, say, 1980 and 1981 are comparable to the number of deaths in, say, 1989 and 1990. Having said this, however, the Pan-American Health Organization statistics still indicate the extent to which the advent of democracy has perpetuated the rule and role of social violence and of neomilitarized control throughout the Salvadoran social sphere.

5   Salvadoran democracy still upholds the foundational character of death squad logics. However, the telecommunications industries now take it upon themselves to mediate people's fears as if they were the bases for a public culture. As in the United States (and other Latin American nations such as Peru and Argentina) endless public opinion polls fill in the gap left behind in the public sphere by the advent of low-intensity party politics and the generalized public disengagement with official political life that this entails. As DeCesare notes, in the case of El Salvador "most callers who responded to a call-in poll conducted by YSU, one of El Salvador's most popular radio stations, supported The Black Shadow [the antigang death squad], and some even invited the group to come clean up their neighborhoods. Several Salvadoran newspapers have published poll results in which nearly half of respondents support the social cleansing activities of the death squads that target those perceived as criminals" ("Children" 23). The problem with this dissemination of such public opinion is that, given the socioeconomic realities of the nation, increasing numbers of individuals can be identified as street kids, gang members, or just criminals. After all, "nearly half the country's population is under 18 and three quarters of Salvadoran children live in poverty" (24). Thus, as DeCesare continues, "even if impoverished Salvadoran youths could aspire to a *maquila* factory job—the fastest growing sector of the Salvadoran economy—they would earn the Salvadoran minimum wage of $4 a day. With the price of a pound of beans—the Salvadoran staple food—the same as it is in the United States, such wages barely ensure subsistence. At the same time, slick television advertising and the

aggressive marketing of American youth culture have whetted the consumer desires of a generation that will largely be unable to satisfy those desires or even their most basic needs through work. Of the 800,000 adolescents between the ages of 13 and 18 who comprise 14% of the total population of El Salvador, UNICEF estimates that only 40% attend school and 29% work. How the remaining 31%, roughly 249,000 youths, occupy their time is unknown. But youth gang membership is growing at an alarming pace and some studies suggest that as many as 30,000 youths may belong to street gangs nationwide" (24–25). DeCesare notes elsewhere that "the emergence of youth gangs beyond U.S. borders and rising rates of violent crime in countries as culturally distinct as El Salvador and Haiti are routinely blamed on the burgeoning numbers of convicted criminals and gang members who are being sent back from the United States each year. El Salvador has responded to increased crime by suspending rights of habeas corpus and reinstating the death penalty" ("Deported" 7). If this is the case, then we are witnessing the emergence within neoliberal democratic forms of a recalcitrant trans- or postnational (un)popular.

6   These are not the only stories in the novel. There are also two significant sections dedicated to the state and to the intensification of its war of position. In these sections one nameless conscript attempts to explain the logics of National Security Doctrine to a silenced second-person (non)interlocutor. In these episodes the narrator merely ends up affirming the radical end to any possible discourse of national fraternity: "If I forgive you it's because of your ignorance. But I can send you away from here all tied up, don't have any doubts about it; that's what I'm being trained to do by the Special Forces. Even my mom and dad, even you, brother. The thing is, all civilians are shit, brother; you're no exception. They envy our uniforms, the fact that we've gotten ahead in life. That's why when it's time for us to take action, we don't spare anyone. Did you hear me, brother?" (98). Later in the narrative the same conscript provides us with National Security Doctrine's militarized version of cold war sexual politics: "Well, look, all these women are whores; to be a woman is to have been born a whore, while men are separated into two types: the faggots and we the machos, who dress in this uniform. And among the machos one could even select the most macho: those of the Special Forces, those of us who have gone to school with Chinese karate experts and gringo psychologists. Those of us who eat mashed potatoes to be strong" (128).

7   It should be noted that the episode preceding Chepe's death is a death-warning tale (181–89). In this episode the future corpse—Chepe—narrates his late-night encounter (when still a young man) with the beautiful ghost of a rural man-eater (the *siguanaba*). The historical frame of the story is one of genocide, as Chepe himself indicates: "I was almost grown up, nearly eighteen years old. I'd gotten off work at four and gone straight home. There was danger, the slaughter of '32 had just occurred. But I went to the river. What a fool! Can you believe, riding around in the dark" (182). Aroused and overcome with desire for the *siguanaba*, Chepe is attacked by the evil spirit of the countryside and

returns home to retell his traumatic story only after a month of silence (189). The next section of the novel opens with "Right then we saw a cloud of dust over the fences. 'Here comes the jeep with the man,' Private Martínez says" (190). The *siguanaba* story is, in this sense, the narrativization of an oral history organized around, and as, the allegory of (past and present) genocide. Thus, the "community marks itself with the cartography of death events—the spaces of the dead. Local history, biography, and topography intertwine through the network of genealogy. In the recitation of the dead, the sense of collective defilement is deposited into historical narrative. The dead are placed at the origin of collective defilement and local history and in their narration continue to bear the burden of this qualification for the entire community" (Feldman 65–66).

8   The fundamental ground of Christian community is the consciousness of the radical and foundational loss of (the Christian "fall" from) community. Within liberation theology this consciousness initiates the Christian drive for restitution through man's suturing faith in the metaphysical restoration of himself and of the divine to a common immanence. Liberation theology is community structured exclusively around an ideally seamless nostalgia for communion, on the one hand, and for immanent union on the other, even though the immanence of man to God—the relation that founds this notion of communal life— can never, and will never, be restituted in life.

9   The name of the Atlacatl Battalion is by no means insignificant, for it denotes the magical logic of reversal by which the militarized state exhalts an image of past Indian bravery in order to recolonize, resubalternize, or, in this case, merely eradicate the rural peasant's identification with a history of insurrection. The state's work of image/imaginary reversal, however, is not without its twists and turns. In *The El Mozote Massacre* Leigh Binford reveals the national(ist) investments to be found in the use of Indian nomenclatures: "What better instrument of destruction than the Atlacatl Battalion, the first immediate-reaction infantry battalion armed and trained by the United States and named, ironically, after a heroic Pipil chieftain who died resisting the Spanish during the conquest?" (16). Ironic, indeed, that the state should incorporate the name of a colonial subaltern hero for one of its most systematic eradications of subaltern aspirations. But the irony does not end there. As William Fowler Jr. explains, this valorous sixteenth-century Pipil chieftain, who resisted Spanish colonization to the bitter end, never existed. Rather, he is the direct product of a French translator's slip of the hand (and of the intellect) in the years following independence: "In the *Annals* [of the Cakchiquels] there is a significant mention of Alvarado's expedition to the Pipil center of Cuscatlán, El Salvador, and his siege of Panatacat, near Escuintla.... A transcription error committed by Etienne Brasseur de Bourbourg in his study and French translation of the *Annals*, made in 1856..., resulted in the invention of a Salvadoran national folk hero, the Pipil chieftain Atlacatl. According to Recinos, Panatacat or Atacat (rendered by Brasseur as 'Atlacatl') was a Cakchiquel designation for the town of Escuintla. The document states that 'twenty-five days after his arrival in the

city [Iximche], Tonatiuh [Alvarado] departed for Cuzcatan, destroying Atacat on the way. On the day of 2 Queh [May 9, 1524] the Spaniards killed those of Atacat.' . . . The *Título de Alotenango* . . . , a sixteenth century legal document, holds the key to resolving this problem. This document arose from a land dispute between the Cakchiquel of Alotenango and the Pipil of Escuintla. The Cakchiquel testimony confirms that there was indeed a locality referred to in the document as Panacal or Panacaltepeque located one league to the north of Escuintla" (16). Ironic, indeed, that the foundations of state violence be grounded and organized around the inheritance of Indian names designed to keep the subaltern image of anticolonial valor and heroism alive. But even more ironic is the fact that these names are created by European misreadings of local signifiers.

10 Ronald Reagan, of course, took a different view of things. In March 1983, in a speech given to the National Association of Manufacturers, he affirmed the following: "Make no mistake. We want the same thing the people of Central America want—an end to the killing. We want to see freedom preserved where it now exists and its rebirth where it does not. The Communist agenda, on the other hand, is to exploit human suffering in Central America to strike at the heart of the Western Hemisphere. By preventing reform and instilling their own brand of totalitarianism, they can threaten freedom and peace and weaken our national security" ("Strategic" 1).

11 El Salvador's insertion into postnational economic and security configurations has been actively promoted by the so-called global economic community. In *The Limits of Economic Reform in El Salvador* Wim Pelupessy evaluates this process in the following terms: "In the mid-1990s Salvadoran Finance Minister and former high-ranking official of the World Bank, Manuel Enrique Hinds, . . . suggested an integration into the North American economy to overcome the then still existing dysfunctional structural constraints. The exchange rate to the dollar should be fixed, and the economy then integrated into the dollar area. Import duties should be eliminated, and the country converted into a free-trade zone for foreign (mainly US) investment. Fiscal and financial systems should be reformed, state intervention reduced, and competition stimulated by law. The integration of the Salvadoran economy into the chain of production and trade of strong US multinationals was seen as the only viable road to development with sufficient trickle-down effects for the population" (181). This proposal, Pelupessy continues, was a "consistent extension of the trend shown by the 1986 change in Christian Democratic economic strategy and the adjustment policies of the ARENA government after 1989" (183). However, the author warns, the "internationalization of the Salvadoran economy does not automatically mean that its dysfunctional constraints will disappear" (183).

12 The effects of such massive demographic flows from Central America to South Central Los Angeles are taken up by Mike Davis in *City of Quartz,* in which he discusses a *Los Angeles Times* article from March 30, 1990, examining the astounding transformations in the cultural, ethnic, and linguistic composition of

the city's ghettoed poor since the beginning of the Reagan era and the intensification of low-intensity conflict in Central America: "The Black population of
Southcentral has fallen by 30% since 1980 as families flee crime and economic
decay for Inglewood, the Inland Empire or even back to the South. The Latino
population, on the other hand, has increased at least 200% (Mayan Indians
now live in the Jordan Downs projects) and Black youth are suddenly minorities in the four major high schools. The old Slauson turf of Fremont High, for
example, was 96% Black in 1980; it is now 71% Latino" (322).

13 The remittances and the impact they have on everyday life in El Salvador (both
for the subaltern classes and the elites) carry the notion of the nation (and
perhaps even the notion of a territorially bounded nation-state) to a point of
aporia. They highlight the need for a more complex debate on contemporary North/South interactions than those still anchored in the boundaries of
national identity or in ideas of national cultural specificity (understood as a binary opposition to so-called homogeneity). Wim Pelupessy does not put the
value of the remittances as high as $1.4 billion per year, but he does uphold
evidence of the enormous capital flows from the United States to El Salvador
that have been sustained since the late 1980s: "In 1990 at least 30 per cent of
the working population and their dependents in the cities derived their support from the informal sector, international aid organizations, the government,
and family remittances from abroad. The flow of dollars sent by Salvadorans
in the United States to relatives in El Salvador was estimated at $300–400 mil-
lion a year for the late 1980s. This was equivalent to over half the total export
earnings in 1988, and clearly of great importance to El Salvador's balance of
payments. Almost a quarter of all families in the country received money from
the United States, and for many this was their only source of income" (102).

14 I take the term low-intensity democracy from William Robinson's *Promoting
Polyarchy*. What Robinson calls low-intensity democracy has also been called
guardian democracy (McSherry). Both terms refer to the same phenomenon:
the maintenance of superficial democratic processes grounded in the formalities of the electoral process, the hegemony of the discourse of the marketplace,
the enlargement of the military presence in civilian institutions, the use of authoritarian practices by civilian democratic governments, new internal security and domestic intelligence doctrines and missions for the military such as
the war against drug trafficking, terrorism, insurgency, and immigration and
refugee flows; the use of political intelligence organizations, impunity for viola-
tors of human rights, and acts by paramilitary groups and unregulated private
security organizations (McSherry 18). The goal of this post–cold war security agenda is to guarantee that "military power endures as a check against
and counterweight to popular majorities, and the political space for opposition
is circumscribed. The security apparatus, ever alert to potential 'threats from
below', remains a political actor that monitors and contains civil society. The
latent threat of military reaction has the power to shape government decision
making and inhibit political participation by social groups" (16).

15   This information from the California Street Terrorism Enforcement and Prevention Act is taken from a document (titled "Gang Evidence: Selected Stat-
utes and Cases") prepared by Russell Griffith, Andrew Thorpe, and Clayton
Hallopeter, which was presented to the Los Angeles County Public Defenders'
Office on March 19, 1997. My thanks to Jimmy Cho for affording me this information.

16   Mike Davis continues his discussion of the redistribution of public space and
the militarization of urban life in Los Angeles in the following terms: "The
totalitarian semiotics of ramparts and battlements, reflective glass and elevated
pedways, rebukes any affinity or sympathy between different architectural or
human orders. As in Otis's fortress *Times* building, this is the archisemiotics of
class war" (*City* 231). In *Ecology of Fear* Davis refers to what I call "the architecture of the present as war without ends or end" as a "low-intensity race war"
that has produced dramatic shifts in California's prison population in recent
years: "In 1988, new prison admissions were 35 percent black and 30 percent
Latino; by 1993, however, the proportions were 41 percent Latino and 25 percent black" (414). Obviously the state's infamous "three strikes" legislature is
playing a pivotal role in liberal democracy's continued low-intensity race war
in California.

17   Carol Nagengast frames the discussion in the following terms: "These arrests
accounted for 10% of all arrests made during the disturbances. More than
700 of the 1,000 individuals detained were immediately deported, without any
charges brought against them. These events were widely publicized and presumably approved by the general public, which was led to believe that 'illegals'
were heavily implicated in looting and burning" (41).

18   Meanwhile, the education system provides a scientific discourse of social management. The State of California proposes that social problems be challenged
by waging war against the excesses of the self and its conduct. In 1990 the California Task Force to Promote Self-Esteem and Personal and Social Responsibility, first established by the state in 1983 (coinciding, of course, with mass
subaltern migration from Central America to Los Angeles), announced in its
final report that "self-esteem is the likeliest candidate for a *social vaccine*, something that empowers us to live responsibly and that inoculates us against the
lures of crime, violence, substance abuse, teen pregnancy, child abuse, chronic
welfare dependency, and educational failure. The lack of self-esteem is central
to most personal and social ills plaguing our state and nation as we approach
the end of the twentieth century" (quoted in Cruikshank 232). In medieval
and renaissance times management of the nameless multitude, and protection
against the penetration power of mass migration consisted, to a large extent,
on the policing of city gates and ramparts as well as on the placing of duties on
individual and collective movements. In postmodern Los Angeles the policing
of the ethnic multitude rides on a combination of neomedieval forms of protection against the penetration power of migratory packs and the expansion of
pedagogical low-intensity tactics that are designed to win over the minds of the

people by making them feel good about themselves in spite of the structured realities of their world.

19   Although the term part-narrative, or fragment, denotes the existence of a wider field of subaltern expression to which the part belongs, it must be understood that we are dealing here with the fragment of a wider narrative whose contours escape us. As such, we read Solórzano's words as if they should belong to a more extensive subaltern reflection on postnational experience. History, however, only rarely allows us such privileges.

20   It might be tempting to read this statement as an expression of absolute continuity (something like "before we were fighting in El Salvador and now we're on the streets of L.A.; the struggle continues") and have done with it. But such a reading would be an oversimplification. The slippage within the narrative between clusters of signifiers such as FMLN/hard core/country and gangsta/hard core/neighborhood denotes a qualitative shift in the notion of struggle that upholds a certain specter of continuity on the one hand, while on the other interrupting the notion of continuity. The question raised here, of course, is how to articulate thought through this internally fissured ground of migratory continuity/discontinuity.

21   Indeed, continuing his reflection on practical agency Bourdieu notes that "it is because agents never know completely what they are doing that what they do has more sense than they know" (*Logic* 69), for "the body believes in what it plays at . . . it does not represent what it performs, it does not memorize the past, it *enacts* the past, bringing it back to life — the body is thus mingled with all the knowledge it reproduces" (73).

22   As such, this is not transculturation handed over to the fabrication of common interests and collective hegemonies. If we understand hegemony to be the state's ability to universalize particularities, and thereby to integrate social actors into the construction of a civil society grounded in the positive articulation of differences and equivalences, then we must understand Solórzano's position to be not even the subordinate position within the hegemonic articulation. Rather, it is the limit of any theory of hegemony generated from within state/civil society circuits. It is through her and her fellow gang members, in other words, that we can begin to see the present order as predicated on the production and dissemination of nonhegemonic particularities: on the expansion of posthegemonic "hard cores" of irreducible violence that bear witness to the violent effects of the state's failed universalization of particularities, but also to the subaltern's integration into transnational consumer flows. This can be seen, for example, in the intimate relationship between gang culture, the Central American conflicts of the 1980s, and the emergence of the crack cocaine business in South Central Los Angeles over the last twenty years. The definitive work in this regard is Gary Webb's *Dark Alliance*.

23   For discussion of El Salvador's repopulated communities, see Thompson as well as Lungo Uclés ("Building").

24   There is, of course, no such thing as a gratuitous "perhaps": "What is going to

come, *perhaps,* is not only this or that; it is at last the thought of the *perhaps,* the *perhaps* itself. . . . Now, the thought of the 'perhaps' engages the only possible thought of the event—of friendship to come and friendship for the future. . . . And there is no more just category for the future than that of the 'perhaps'. Such a thought conjoins friendship, the future, and the *perhaps* to open on to the coming of what comes—that is to say, necessarily in the regime of a possible whose possibilization must prevail over the impossible" (Derrida, *Politics* 29).

25 Following Homi Bhabha's extended discussion of hybridity in "DissemiNation," Alberto Moreiras proposes "savage hybridity" in the following terms: "Hybrid subjectivity, through its very undecidability qua hybrid, preempts the closure of any discursive position around either identity or difference. Hybrid subjectivity, at its limit, does not some times allow for identity and some times for difference, but rather simultaneously undermines both identitarian and differential positions, which are driven into aporia. More than the site for ambivalence, hybridity, as diasporic ground or abyssal foundation for subjective constitution, is a nonsite or it is ambivalence itself. It is therefore not a place for subjective conciliation. On the contrary, it points to the conditions of possibility for the constitution of the sociopolitical subject as at the same time conditions of impossibility because the subject, through its constitutive, hybrid undecidability, is always already split. This is savage or nomadic hybridity: not what grounds a subject in an antagonistic relation to the state or capitalist domination, but precisely what ungrounds it, or the very principle of its ungrounding vis-à-vis any conceivable operation of state or social regime constitution. . . . Savage hybridity is *not,* to be sure, the subaltern. But, as the "other side" of the hegemonic relationship, savage hybridity preserves, or holds in reserve, the site of the subaltern, just as it preserves the site of a subalternist politics. It is not so much a locus of enunciation as it is an atopic site, not a place for ontopologies but a place for the destabilization of all ontopologies, for a critique of totality— *and* a place for the possibility of an *other* history" (*Exhaustion* 291–94).

26 For Homi Bhabha the people-to-come are grounded in the "relatively unspoken tradition of the people of the pagus—colonials, postcolonials, migrants, minorities—wandering peoples who will not be contained within the *Heim* of the national culture and its unisonant discourse, but are themselves the marks of a shifting boundary that alienates the frontiers of the modern nation. They are Marx's reserve army of migrant labour who by speaking the foreignness of language split the patriotic voice of unisonance and become Nietzsche's mobile army of metaphors, metonyms and anthropomorphisms. They articulate the death-in-life of the idea of the 'imagined community' of the nation; the worn-out metaphors of the resplendent national life now circulate in another narrative of entry-permits and passports and work-permits that at once preserve and proliferate, bind and breach the human rights of the nation. Across the accumulation of the history of the West there are those people who speak the encrypted discourse of the melancholic and the migrant" (164). Needless to say, Solórzano and her fellow gang members bespeak the encrypted foreignness of

both national and postnational languages. And they do this by constantly opening up a void in the history of the *Heim,* while simultaneously reaffirming the
Heim as permanently *unheimlich.* The reality of their postnational languages,
in other words, opens up a semiotic break in the orders of hegemony, translatability, and immediate intelligibility.

6 Of *Pishtacos* and Eye-Snatchers: Neoliberalism and
Neoindigenism in Contemporary Peru

1 Elsewhere in *The Long Twentieth Century* Arrighi speculates that "the un-
containability of violence in the contemporary world is closely associated with
the withering away of the modern system of territorial states as the primary
locus of world power. . . . The granting of rights of self-determination to the
peoples of Asia and Africa has been accompanied by the imposition of unprecedented restrictions on the actual sovereignty rights of nation-states and
by the formation of equally unprecedented expectations about the domestic
and foreign duties attached to sovereignty. Combined with the internalization of world-scale processes of production and exchange within the organizational domains of transnational corporations and with the resurgence of
suprastatal world financial markets, these unprecedented restrictions and expectations have translated into strong pressures to relocate the authority of
nation-states both upward and downward" (331). As I noted toward the end
of the last chapter, the ideological singularity and enclosure of the imagined
community, the *Heim* of the nation-state, in other words, has been displaced
and reterritorialized in the contemporary dissemination of the *unheimlich.* The
result is that the global is local and the local is global (thereby giving rise to
the new term "glocal"); the private is public; the inside is outside; the national
is postnational; subsumption is freedom; peace is war; democracy is authoritarian; free trade is unfree; the subject is dead yet proliferates; scandal is banal;
war is entertainment; truth is credibility; "the future is in information." The
list goes on and on.

2 The intensification, in recent years, of capitalist dematerialization can be seen
through the Dow Jones Industrial Index itself. After its inception in 1896 the
Dow took seventy-six years to reach the benchmark of 1,000, which it finally
achieved on November 14, 1972. It took another fifteen years to reach the mark
of 2,000, which it surpassed for the first time on January 8, 1987. However,
since the fall of the Berlin Wall, the collapse of actually existing socialism, and
the inauguration of the new world order, the index's rate of acceleration—the
intensification in the rate of world capital dematerialization and deterritorialization—has been astounding. The Dow hit 3,000 on April 17, 1991; passed
5,000 in 1995; 6,000 in 1996; and 8,000 in 1997. It broke 9,000 in 1998 and
surpassed 11,000 on May 3, 1999, just a month after breaking the 10,000 mark.

3 For the neoliberal appraisal of such notions as culture or history, see Lawrence
Harrison's *The Pan-American Dream* (a profoundly flawed book advocating the

end of "traditional Ibero-Catholic culture," increased Protestantism, and, of course, global capitalism and liberal democracy as keys to the end of backwardness in Latin America [269]). In a publicity blurb for the book, Samuel Huntington expresses what is at stake for neoliberal globalization in the field of contemporary Latin American culture: "The Pan-American dream will remain just that until Latin American culture converges with North American culture." Culture, and, presumably, the underdeveloped people who practice it, are portrayed as a potentially thorny obstacle to market transnationalization, as well as to neoliberal notions of development and governability. Indeed, for Huntington the problem of culture lies at the heart of the ability of the United States to police the new world order in general. He concludes his *The Clash of Civilizations and the Remaking of the World Order* with an apparent reworking of Sarmiento's civilization versus barbarism paradigm, which uncovers the underlying gang logic of contemporary foreign and economic policy: "In the clash of civilizations, Europe and America will hang together or hang separately. In the greater clash, the global *'real* clash', between Civilization and barbarism, the world's great civilizations, with their rich accomplishments in religion, art, literature, philosophy, science, technology, morality, and compassion, will also hang together or hang separately. In the emerging era, clashes of civilizations are the greatest threat to world peace, and an international order based on civilizations is the surest safeguard against world war" (321). In Harrison's book Chile is highlighted as a showcase of economic and cultural convergence between North and South and, presumably, of "Civilization." Peru (for reasons that lie at the heart of this chapter) is not.

4 Here the term "police" should be understood not only in its present-day usage as the maintenance of order and the prevention of danger by the state, but also as a body of knowledge dating from the inception of the bourgeois ideology of the nation-state that is designed to formulate the promotion of an enterprise culture. In this sense, the term "police" was "known in the eighteenth century as both the 'science of happiness' and 'the science of government', which constitutes society as the object of knowledge and at the same time as the target of political intervention . . . a great effort of formation of the social body, or more precisely an undertaking whose principal result will be something which we today call society or the social body, and which the eighteenth century called 'the good order of a population' . . . . Obrecht enumerates three tasks of police. First, information, conceived as a sort of statistical table bearing on all the capacities and resources of population and territory; second, a set of measures to augment the wealth of the population and enrich the coffers of the state; third, public happiness" (Pasquino 108–13). Recently in Latin America the discourse of governability has taken center stage within public policy circles as a response to increasing economic and social disorder. In the pages that follow I will use the terms "police" and "governability" interchangeably, since the latter is a contemporary version of the European enlightenment understand-

ing of the good order of public matters as the means toward the construction of a state of "wealth and prosperity" (111).

5   It appears that little is safe within this process. In Fujimori's Peru even the naming of a child became subject to the demand to exorcise society of its potentially destabilizing elements: "A new law backed by Fujimori . . . forbids the use of names deemed 'extravagant, irreverant, contrary to public order, or foreign'. The new law . . . will allow employees of the National Register of Identification and Marital Status to censor children's names based on whether they fit in with a vaguely defined social and cultural framework of Peru. Names such as 'Lenin', 'Carlos Marx', and 'Fidel Castro' will be banned because, says one official, 'they have political connotations opposed to the social order'. Also prohibited are names of English origin, such as 'Johnny', and Quechua Indian names" (Kowalski 24).

6   I am drawing on important discussions of Chakrabarty's work to be found in John Kraniauskas ("Hybridity") as well as in Alberto Moreiras's *The Exhaustion of Difference*. The development of my argument in this chapter owes much to (and offers dialogues alongside) Kraniauskas's evaluation of Homi Bhabha and Néstor García Canclini, and Moreiras's analysis of García Canclini and Stuart Hall.

7   In *Grundrisse* Marx states: "Bourgeois society is the most developed and the most complex historic organization of production. The categories which express its relations, the comprehension of its structure, thereby also allows insights into the structure and the relations of production of all the vanished social formations out of whose ruins and elements it built itself up, whose partly still uncovered remnants are carried along with it, whose mere nuances have developed explicit significance within it, etc. Human anatomy contains a key to the anatomy of the ape. The intimations of higher development among the subordinate animal species, however, can be understood only after the higher development is already known. The bourgeois economy thus supplies the key to the ancient, etc. But not at all in the manner of those economists who smudge over all historical differences and see bourgeois relations in all forms of society. . . . Further, since bourgeois society is itself only a contradictory form of development, relations derived from earlier forms will often be found within it only in an entirely stunted form, or even travestied. For example, communal property. Although it is true, therefore, that the categories of bourgeois economics possess a truth for all other forms of society, this is to be taken only with a grain of salt. They can contain them in a developed, or stunted, or caricatured form etc., but always with an essential difference" (105–6).

8   As Kraniauskas ("Hybridity" 112) indicates, the emergence of incommensurability within capitalism's structures and hegemonic narratives produces a subaltern "semiotic break" (Guha, *Elementary* 36) within the order of development's history and its processes of representation.

9   The dematerialized order of finance capital has produced its own other side.

As Aníbal Quijano notes: "Economic 'informalization' is the other side to the domination of the speculative [banking, financial, and business] sector's activities within the 'formal' structure of the economy" (*El Fujimorismo* 13; translation mine). The neoliberal production of informality—a production which has been fully coincident with the emergence of new populations and of new political identities created by mass migration—has produced a predominantly urban populace that is largely subsumed by market forces. Yet this same population is always marked by its significant potential for ungovernability and for real labor. This is literally an outlaw populace that is obliged to exist, work, and organize almost exclusively on the margins of state and economic legality. In this sense it is not just finance capital's constitutive outside but also the embodiment of the threat of the outsider within, reminiscent of the relation between real and abstract labor. Thus, through the informal sectors finance capital and the neoliberal state confront their threshold of workability. They need to promote a continued and sustainable flexibility in labor practices and interregional market accessibility, yet they must constantly manage and/or incorporate informal labor and its insurrectional potential into the realms of state lawfulness and control. The informal economy, then, is what gives neoliberal globalization its energy and force. But it is also the terrain that can bring an end to its governmental forms. Thus questions of culture, of governability, and of potential ungovernability appear to be intimately linked to questions of state security and labor control, to governmental knowledge of population behavior and cultural specificity, and to the interplay between labor/consumer behavior, regional difference, local conceptualizations of territory and region, and the ways in which these notions penetrate urban centers and modify the workings of primary markets and of political and cultural discourse and interaction.

10 This is not to say, of course, that Vargas Llosa is mistaken in his evaluation of the place or relevance of literary indigenism under current conditions. In fact, my intuition is that he is right. The question, however, is how to read the apparent eclipse of its relevance in relation to history, rather than merely taking it to be a symptom of history's end. Meanwhile, it should be noted that the social processes that Vargas Llosa interprets as the end of the history of indigenist representation and of its broad-based sociopolitical articulations were already being assessed (in rather more balanced fashion) in the late 1980s— that is, at the height of Peru's economic crisis—by intellectuals such as Alberto Flores Galindo (see *Tiempo de plagas* 27). See also Matos Mar; Cornejo Polar (*Escribir*); and Quijano (*Dominación* and *El Fujimorismo*) as critical responses to Peru's structural and cultural transformations of the 1970s and 1980s, as well as to the traditional oligarchy's apparent displacement in the years following the reforms of the Velasco regime (1968–1975).

11 *Cholo*, of course, is the heterogeneous effect of the transcultural contact zone. In recent years it is the main agent behind the "Andeanization" and informalization of urban coastal Peru. It is therefore an inside-outside site; the ambiva-

lence of a between that undoes the ground of the dialectic between identity and difference. In other words, I do not read it as a placeholder of an individual or collective identitarian truth or essence of cultural or ethnic hybridity, but rather as the dislocating effect of a social structure—Peruvian capitalist modernity—that has not been able to constitute itself seamlessly.

12 *Cholaje* refers to the process by which hybrid (*cholo*) identity is produced in historical, institutional, and cultural terms.

13 For a detailed discussion of de Soto's ties to international organizations such as, for example, the Republican Party in the United States, see Bromley.

14 Needless to say, we should not get carried away here. It is obvious, in spite of its astounding corruption, that the vision of the Peruvian New Right has won out in the battle for the new order and for the terms of contemporary economic and social organization. This is thanks to Alberto Fujimori's ability to sustain the neoliberal economic model after a successful stabilization program in the early 1990s, together with his regime's weakening of insurgency. For a discussion of the consolidation and development of the New Right in Peru, and of their sustained relation to "Fujimorismo," see Durand (173).

15 A similar though somewhat less sophisticated process of active Mariátegui displacement is reproduced in Vargas Llosa's *La utopía arcaica*. In a book on indigenism that comprises over three hundred pages of analysis, Vargas Llosa dedicates only two pages to Mariátegui and to the link between indigenism and marxism. The relatively obscure liberal thinker Uriel García, however, is discussed in far greater detail. This is hardly surprising, because García's thesis in *El nuevo indio* (1929) is grounded in the emptying out of all possible links between indigenism, ethnicity, and collectivism in favor of a kind of pan-American process of *mestizaje* that is capable of upholding flexible individuality and of negotiating conflictive social levels, languages, and practices in such a way as to foment an entrepreneur culture that is anchored in shared morality and the labors of the individual. García's "new Indian," in this sense, can be read almost as a blueprint for a perfectly individualized, de-Indianized/indigenized, and tamed form of *cholaje*. As Uriel García puts it: "The Indian of today is not merely the historical Indian. The latter is no longer the sole occupier of the land. Nor is it his spirit that values and cultivates it, or his blood that sustains its physiological wealth and material force. The Indian of today is every man who lives in America. Today the ancient Indian is more blood than spirit, while the New Indian should be more spirit than blood. For indigenous is he who creates on the land, and not merely he who works it. The New Indian, then, is not so much an ethnic group as a moral entity. New Indians are the guides of our peoples. They are those who give form to the Continent. Only from this perspective can the past be of any use. We are searching for the man, not the race" (6–9; translation mine). It is hardly surprising, then, that Vargas Llosa should characterize *El nuevo indio* as "the most suggestive of the essays produced by this intellectual movement" (*La utopía arcaica*, 80; trans-

lation mine), for it provides the Peruvian (neo)liberal tradition with a model for reflecting on the emergence and de-Indianization of the *cholo*—Peru's new and informal *homo economicus*—in global times.

16 In his discussion of Bhabha's essay John Kraniauskas adds the following insight: "We are dealing here with something like transculturation in psychoanalytic mode. For example, the very articulation or performance of colonial stereotypification is marked by the cultural difference (the 'other') it negotiates. And it is this constitutive non-identity of the subject of/within enunciation— this splitting and this 'gap'—that provides Bhabha with his most important interpretative and critical resource: it makes the postcolonial perspective, its time and space, possible" ("Hybridity" 119).

17 Obviously the terms "Andes" and "coast" are now far more complex than they are being given credit for here. My maintenance of these homogenizing terms remains faithful, however, to the ways in which these notions have been articulated within the tradition of nation-state and of national culture formation. At the same time, the notion of interface promises the unworking of the tradition's homogenizing drives. Moreover, it should be noted that by "coast" I refer predominantly to Lima and to the Creole cultural and institutional paradigms associated traditionally with metropolis.

18 The road is an obvious symbol of modern national integration, progress, and interregional communication that is reminiscent of the Leguía regime of the 1920s. Without doubt it is taken here from the foundational texts of *indigenismo* such as Arguedas's *Yawar fiesta* (1941), in which the Indian's construction of a road announces indigenous collectivism as a dominant and constructive force within the nation. In *Death in the Andes,* however, the road is the central symbol of a failed national project and of perpetual underdevelopment: "Were they making any progress on that highway? Lituma had the impression it was moving backward instead. In the months he had been here, there had been three work stoppages, and in all of them the same process was repeated like a broken record. . . . The engineers left and the camp remained in the hands of the foremen and the paymaster, who socialized with the strikers and shared the communal meal prepared at dusk in the empty field surrounded by barracks. . . . The work stoppages would end mysteriously, without defining the future of the highway. . . . Work was resumed in slow motion. But Lituma always thought that instead of picking up where they had left off, the labourers retraced their steps" (78). In Naccos, then, notions such as progress and development enter into contact with forms of collective labor that actively unwork them from within.

19 The underlying question of Lituma's investigation is what are these people capable of? And this is a question that lies at the heart of neoliberal governmentality. "What are these people capable of?" denotes a governmental calculation of risk—a paranoid fantasy scenario of potential threat—resulting from the intensification of coastal contact with serrano culture. As Colin Gordon states in *The Foucault Effect:* "In modern liberal societies the social is, *charac-*

teristically, the field of government security considered in its widest sense. . . . The rationality of security is . . . an inherently open-ended one: it deals not just in closed circuits of control, but *in calculations of the possible and the probable.* The relation of government with which it corresponds is not solely a functional one, but also is transactional: it structures government as a practice of problematization, a zone of (partially) open interplay between the exercise of power and everything that escapes its grip" (35–36; italics mine). It is the problematization of notions such as the possible and the probable in their relationship to Andean population, territory, and migration—and in coordination with the cultural logics that challenge state (coastal) lawfulness and reason—that structures Lituma's policing of the social in *Death in the Andes* as well as the internal dynamics of the novel itself.

20 *Pishtaco:* "A stranger. Half gringo. At first glance you didn't know what he was because he looked just like everybody else in this world. He lived in caves and committed crimes at night. Lurking along the roads, behind boulders, hiding among haystacks or under bridges, waiting for solitary travelers. He would approach with cunning, pretending to be a friend. His powder made from the bones of the dead was all ready, and at the first careless moment he threw it in his victim's faces. Then he could suck out their fat. Afterward he let them go, emptied, nothing but skin and bone, doomed to waste away in a few hours or days. These were the benign ones. They needed human fat to make church bells sing more sweetly and tractors run more smoothly, and now, lately, to give to the government to help pay off the foreign debt. The evil ones were worse. They not only slit their victim's throats but butchered them like cattle, or sheep, or hogs, and ate them. Bled them drop by drop and got drunk on the blood. Son of a bitch, the serruchos believed this stuff" (*Death in the Andes* 53–54).

21 As Ranajit Guha notes in *Elementary Aspects of Peasant Insurgency,* rumor forms part of a generalized semiotic of insurgency in which anonymity and creative improvisation enable subaltern agency (260–61): "Rumour . . . is not sealed off by any 'final signified' emanating from a primal source, but remains open as a receptacle of new inputs of meaning . . . [;] rumour functions as a free form liable to a considerable degree of improvisation as it leaps from tongue to tongue. The aperture which it has built into it by virtue of anonymity permits its message to be contaminated by the subjectivity of each of its speakers and modified as often as any one of them would want to embellish or amend it in the course of transmission" (261).

22 I am particularly grateful to John Kraniauskas for bringing these events to my attention in his excellent essay "*Cronos* and the Political Economy of Vampirism."

23 Eudosio Sifuentes suggests that the emergence of the *sacaojos* brought the authorities to an epistemological impasse, the systemic cover-up of which was thought to be fundamental for maintaining state hegemony, as well as for upholding the value and cultural authority of the notion of truth: "In the final days of 1988 the media threw down the following challenge: if there was no official

accusation, no one single case of an eyeless child presented to the police, then it was nothing more than a rumor. In this way the official world considered the truth to be linked exclusively to police evidence, thus highlighting once more the divorce between the country's politico-juridical mechanisms and its popular culture" (149; translation mine). This *chola* uprising produced a moment of dislocation that could not be grasped in the language of capitalist governmentality. Through *chola* performativity, then, we can glimpse the ways in which possibilities of multiple and indeterminate rearticulations of Andean culture open up spaces that fracture (from within) the hegemonic discourses of coastal development and police.

24 The ethnographic bibliography on the *ñacaq*, the *pishtaco*, or the *kharisiri* (as they are called in Bolivia) is extensive (see in particular the bibliography offered by Weismantel 40–43). For analysis of the interregional and transcultural appropriations of the Andean *pishtaco* and, in particular, of its translation into the Peruvian Amazon, see Michael F. Brown and Eduardo Fernández's *War of Shadows* (143). Much has been written on the possible origins of the *ñacaq* and *pishtaco*. Michael Taussig (*Shamanism*) has drawn on the ethnographic work of Efraín Morote Best, as Anthony Oliver-Smith had done before him, and points to a common practice on the battlegrounds of the Spanish conquest that, it is thought, may account for the emergence of the *pishtaco* in times of traumatic upheaval. Hernando de Soto, the Spanish conquistador, was "reported to have used the fat of Indians slain in combat, as in his expedition against one of the Inca's captains holding out in the Sierra de Vilcaza in the Peruvian Andes" (237). As early as the sixteenth century, continues Taussig in reference to Cristobal de Molina's *Relación de las fábulas y ritos de los incas* dating from 1574, Peru's Indians feared that Spaniards wanted their body fat for medicinal purposes: "It had been put about, wrote Father Molina, that Spain had commanded that Indian body fat be amassed and exported for the curing of a certain illness there, and though nobody could say with certainty, it was probably the sorcerers of the Inca . . . who were responsible for this tale designed to sow enmity between Indian and Spaniard. Now the Indians were loath to serve the Spanish, fearing that they would be killed and their body fat extracted as a remedy for the people of Spain" (238). Indeed, the documented colonial practice of treating wounds with body fat is not exclusive to the Andean region. In his *Historia verdadera de la conquista de la Nueva España* Bernal Díaz del Castillo recounts the opening up of a dead Indian in order to use his body fat to cure the wounds of injured Spanish soldiers: "And with the fat of a fat Indian whom we killed and opened up there, we salved our wounds, since we had no oil" (quoted in Szeminski 171). If these are the violent colonial scenes that account for the presence of the *pishtaco*, then perhaps it could be said that the violence of the *sacaojos* resignifies colonialism's situated narratives and corporeal exploitations. But why the eyes rather than some other part of the body? Many have wondered about the significance of eye extraction (see Rojas Rimachi; Sifuentes; Wachtel; and Zapata). Juan Ansión (who draws on Rodrigo Mon-

toya) has provided perhaps the most convincing suggestion: "In Quechua, 'to be able to have eyes' means to go to school and to learn to read and write. Access to school education is the product of a generalized strategy to appropriate White knowledge. Therefore it requires total exposure to the outside, to such an extent that it is often accompanied by the loss of one's own knowledge" (13; translation mine). If this is the case, the *sacaojos* exposes and performs the extreme violence and exploitation of migration, reproducing "the simultaneity of the two movements of deterritorialization and reterritorialization" (Deleuze and Guattari, *Anti-Oedipus* 260) that underlie the expansion of the capitalist social axiomatic in Peru.

25 July 28, 1987, is a fundamental date for understanding this shift in the social experience of the body, as well as its perceived invasion by new institutions and regimes in Lima. As already indicated, the counteroffensive against inflation and the national welfare state came to fruition in the industrialized countries under the influence of Ronald Reagan and Margaret Thatcher. Furthermore, "during the course of the 1980s an increasingly complex network of foundations, universities, think tanks, governmental agencies, and international financial organizations crafted the conditions for multidimensional (political, cultural, economic) support for neoconservative movements worldwide" (Durand 161). Thanks to the leadership of Mario Vargas Llosa and Hernando de Soto, who by the mid-1980s had already been waging a war of ideas against Peruvian populism and socialism for quite some time, the expansion of the Euro/North American Right "coincided with the emergence of a domestic [Peruvian] Right, and both forces mutually reinforced the changes sponsored by their respective agendas" (161; parenthesis mine). On July 28, 1987, President Alán García announced his intentions to nationalize the Peruvian financial system. His announcement "unleashed an unprecedented barrage of opposition from liberal forces, which ultimately killed his proposal and helped mire his government in a near-continuous political crisis for the next two years" (160). It also had the effect of galvanizing the Peruvian New Right, forcing it "to emerge out of the shadows and openly defend its position in the political arena" (160). Mario Vargas Llosa, who would become one of the leaders of the antinationalization front, organized a meeting in Lima's Plaza San Martín that was attended by a crowd of forty thousand people, mainly from Lima's middle classes. As he describes it in his memoirs, this meeting and the antinationalization response that preceded it transformed the political terrain of the nation forever: "It opened up the doors of Peruvian political life to liberal thought that up until then had lacked a public presence, since all of our modern history had been, practically speaking, a monopoly of the ideological populism of conservatives and socialists of various tendencies. It gave the initiative back to the opposition parties, Popular Action and the Christian Popular Party, which, following their defeat in 1985, had appeared to be invisible, and laid the foundations for what would become the Frente Democrático (Democratic Front) and, as Patricia feared, for my candidacy for the presidency" (*Fish* 39). The

political emergence of neoliberalism following García's attempt to nationalize the financial system coincided with a period of economic resistance to the possibility of further interventions into the economy by populist/socialist sectors. The almost immediate decapitalization of the economy after July 1987 produced a period of hyperinflation and of mass unemployment that completely delegitimized the existing party system; intensified informalization; permitted the increasing legitimization of neoliberal discourse; and naturalized the insertion of the IMF and the World Bank into the restructuring of capital in Peru. It is this process that accounts for the initiation of IMF austerity measures and provides us with the background to the Lima *sacaojos* episode. The process of capital restructuration first inaugurated as a response to the events of July 28, 1987, was then consolidated, of course, by the antidemocratic Fujimori/Armed Forces/New Right alliance of the 1990s.

26 At one point Captain Corso finds himself demanding that his prime suspect, the archaeologist Professor Pinto, shed light on his motivations: "How can a person like you end up doing something like this? What's needed? Explain it to me! Did it just happen suddenly or was it like an impulse that had always been there, like a bomb that just had to go off one day? Tell me, Professor! Did you feel you were like everybody else? Or did you know that . . . ?" (translation mine). Pinto, however, refuses to fill in the gap in the Captain's question. As in Vargas Llosa's *Death in the Andes,* Corso's questions point to the ambivalent frontier between colonial and postcolonial history, collective libidinal economy, and contemporary governmentality. As an added note, in spite of its apparent localism *Bajo la piel* remains firmly integrated into the globalized cultural economy, including Peruvian, German, and Spanish participation, collaboration, and capital.

27 All quotations from the film are my translated transcriptions. The film's opening and final scenes stand in stark contrast to Palle's desert topography. Thus the film's reenactment of the road to happiness explicitly traces the passage from a geography of death, sacrifice, and disorder—the desert and the decapitated heads that seem to emerge from within its cultural history—to the lush and tranquil greenery of the captain's private Garden of Eden (his *locus amoenus*) that opens and ends the film.

28 Captain Percy Corso is the Peruvian reenactment of Nietzsche's antiquarian man: "History . . . belongs . . . to him who preserves and reveres—to him who looks back to whence he has come, to where he came into being, with love and loyalty; with this piety he as it were gives thanks for his existence. By tending with care that which has existed from of old, he wants to preserve for those who shall come into existence after him the conditions under which he himself came into existence—and thus he serves life. . . . The history of his city becomes for him the history of himself; he reads its walls, its towered gate, its rules and regulations, its holidays, like an illuminated diary of his youth and in all this he finds again himself, his force, his industry, his joy, his judgment, his folly and vices. Here we lived, he says to himself, for here we are living; and

here we shall live, for we are tough and not to be ruined overnight. Thus with the aid of this 'we' he looks beyond his own individual transitory existence and feels himself to be the spirit of his house, his race, his city. Sometimes he even greets the soul of his nation across the long dark centuries of confusion as his own soul . . . this antiquarian sense of veneration of the past is of the greatest value when it spreads a simple feeling of pleasure and contentment over the modest, rude, even wretched conditions in which a man or a nation lives" (*Untimely* 73).

29 In its evocation and subsumption of "Indianness" *Bajo la piel* assimilates and empties out the apocalyptic sundering of *pachacuti* (the rupture of Incan time leading to a new era). The passage from the fourth decapitation (with which the film begins) to the fifth (the crime of individual passion) produces a new social order—that of individual mestizo happiness. Within this passage from four decapitations to five perhaps the film is making reference to the overcoming, once and for all, of Tawantinsuyo (the Incan "land of the four quarters"). The fifth decapitation eclipses the other four, together with their indigenous connotations. Through the fifth decapitation the history of the other four is silenced, and this in turn grounds Captain Corso's discourse of happiness, the very genesis of the movie, in a moment of cultural and historical transcendence.

30 Once again, the parallels with Nietzsche's thesis on "the uses and advantages of history for life" are uncanny. Percy is the embodiment of what Nietzsche calls the "plastic power" of a man, or of a particular culture, to overcome the inherited burden of history: "I mean by plastic power the capacity to develop out of oneself in one's own way, to transform and incorporate into oneself in one's own way, to transform and incorporate into oneself what is past and foreign, to heal wounds, to replace what has been lost, to recreate broken moulds" (Nietzsche, *Untimely* 62). Percy's path to happiness traces the route from an Indian past that threatens to become the gravedigger of the present, to this past's displacement in, and by, the immediate needs of the present.

31 "It's him. It has to be him," Percy announces after a brief initial conversation with Professor Pinto. For Corso these are indigenist crimes designed to bury the present under the weight of the past. As such, it is hardly by chance that the archaeologist should hail originally from the University of Cajamarca, for this is the origin of Peru's colonial and postcolonial history (the capture of Atahualpa and the final undoing of Tawantinsuyo at the hands of Francisco Pizarro and Hernando de Soto occurred in Cajamarca on November 16, 1532). It is also noteworthy that the fact that Pinto was in Cajamarca between 1979 and 1982, in the years spanning the emergence of democracy and the Shining Path's declaration of war against the state, immediately qualifies the archaeologist as a potential Senderista and enemy of the state.

32 It is suggested in the movie that this indigenist conjuring trick emerges at a time in which indigenist knowledge is no longer hegemonic. Thus Professor Pinto is represented as the guardian and embodiment of a knowledge and of a histori-

cal memory that is no longer of value in Palle. As he tells Captain Corso shortly before his arrest: "Do you think those students are interested in what I know? Most of them don't value knowledge, captain. Many of them are just useless and mediocre. They would make do with a cartoon. But I have to allow them into the museum and repeat the same things to them as if they actually cared."

33 From this point on, Percy becomes one of those men who "make their own history, but they do not make it as they please; they do not make it under circumstances chosen by themselves, but under circumstances directly encountered, given and transmitted from the past. The tradition of all the dead generations weighs like a nightmare on the brain of the living. And just when they seem engaged in revolutionizing themselves and things, in creating something that has never yet existed, precisely in such periods of revolutionary crisis they anxiously conjure up the spirits of the past to their service and borrow from them names, battle cries and costumes in order to present the new scene of world history in this time-honoured disguise and this borrowed language" (Marx, *Eighteenth* 15).

34 Once again, and in the words of Laclau, "insofar as an act of institution has been successful, a 'forgetting of the origins' tends to occur; the system of possible alternatives tends to vanish and the traces of the original contingency to fade. In this way, the instituted tends to assume the form of a mere objective presence. This is the moment of sedimentation. It is important to realize that this fading entails a concealment. If objectivity is based on exclusion, the traces of sedimentation can be so complete, the influence of one of the dichotomous relationships' poles so strong, that the contingent nature of that influence, its *original* dimension of power, do not prove immediately visible. Objectivity is thus constituted merely as presence" (*New* 34).

35 For further discussion of Deleuze and Guattari's notion of neoterritoriality, see Kraniauskas ("Hybridity" 130–32).

7   Operational Whitewash and the Negative Community

1 All translations of Moulian are mine. In her outstanding discussion of the Chilean transition to democracy Nelly Richard interprets what I call operational whitewash as the systematic "*denarrativization of memory*, orchestrated by both consensus and the market as the emptying out of all historical citations" (164; translation mine).

2 For Nelly Richard, "Chile's promotional narrative in Seville highlighted the discourse of ostentation. It was a question of 'showing one's best side', 'projecting an image', 'seducing the other', 'calling attention', 'creating a mirror', 'provoking a kind of reflection' in which the country could once again recognize itself and be recognized as an image. The 'imagined community' (Anderson) represented by the sign 'Chile' in Seville was the result of a combination of entrepreneurs and publicists who coincided in the design of an *efficient* country (performativity), an *attractive* country (visual seduction, scenic display, repre-

sentation) whose screen-like spectacle was designed to set the scene for new times, without the bothersome background of an experiential depth wounded by memories in black and white. After the historical trauma of dictatorship, which generated such a loss in speech, the communicative order had to be 're-consensualized' with references freed of all vagueness and imprecision, in such a way that the dangers of ambiguity and of discursive conflict could not creep up once again through the semantic fissures. It was a question of banishing, at all cost, the image of underdevelopment: the pitiful, distant, dusty, infectious, revolutionary, counter-revolutionary, and confused 'sudaca' image that screams 'periphery' in all its unhappiness, revolt, disorder, and insurrection. The natural, unpolluted whiteness of the Antarctic's millenarian ice was designed to *cleanse* the image of Chile of all its Third World-ish ideological vestiges, and to cancel out the contestatory posture of the 'peripheral enclave' that radicalizes distance by converting it into the inequality of power relations" (165–76; translation mine).

3   "Myth communicates the common, the *being-common* of what it reveals or what it recites. Consequently, at the same time as each one of its revelations, it also reveals the community to itself and founds it. Myth is always the myth of community, that is to say, it is always the myth of a communion—the unique voice of the many—capable of inventing and sharing the myth. There is no myth that does not at least presuppose (when it does not in fact state it) the myth of the communitarian (or popular) revelation of myths" (Nancy, *Inoperative* 50–51). The iceberg, in this sense, is a neoliberal fabrication designed to make myth communicate Chile's market-based commonality. This relation between publicity and the neoliberal production of Latin American myth is taken up in quite fascinating terms by Nelly Richard: "Exhibiting the iceberg in Seville re-edited the gesture (though inverting the geographical coordinates) that *One Hundred Years of Solitude* describes when José Arcadio Buendía pays to touch what he believes to be 'the biggest diamond in the world'. In full hyperreality, Chile's iceberg was designed to offer up premodern reminiscences of that moment in which the 'heart [is] filled with fear and jubilation at the contact with mystery'. It had to surprise the international public with its postmodern mix of mythical residues, high technology, magical realism, hyperconceptualism, virginal nature, and 'special effects'. Perhaps the most determining factor in the iceberg's symbolic arsenal was its characterization as a 'virginal, white, natural, and unprecedented object', as one of the project's creators defined it" (174–75; translation mine).

4   Needless to say, Pinochet's brush with Spanish, British, and Chilean authorities between 1998 and 2001 uncovers the problematic character of such neoliberal iconography. For an excellent evaluation of these juridical processes, see Jon Beasley-Murray's "The Constitution of Society." It should also be noted that the announcement in 2001 that Pinochet is medically unfit to stand trial for crimes committed during his tenure in power can be read as a reminder of the power of operational whitewash in contemporary Chile.

5 Jean-Luc Nancy formulates the discussion in the following fashion: "Finitude . . . is what makes community. That is, community is made or is formed
by the retreat or by the subtraction of something: this something, which would
be the fulfilled infinite identity of community, is . . . its 'work'. All our political
programs imply this work: either as the product of the working community,
or else the community as work. But in fact it is the work that the community
does *not* do and that it *is* not that forms community. In the work, the properly
'common' character of community disappears, giving way to a unicity and a
substantiality. . . . The community that becomes a *single* thing (body, mind,
fatherland, Leader . . .) necessarily loses the *in* of being-*in*-common. Or, it loses
the *with* or the *together* that defines it. It yields its being-together to a being *of*
togetherness. The truth of community, on the contrary, resides in the retreat
of such a being. Community is made of what retreats from it: the hypostasis of
the 'common', and its work. The retreat opens, and continues to keep open,
this strange being-the-one-with-the-other to which we are exposed. . . . By inverting the 'principle' stated a moment ago, we get totalitarianism. By ignoring
it, we condemn the political to management and to power (and to the management of power, and to the power of management). By taking it as a rule
of analysis and thought, we raise the question: how can the community without essence (the community that is neither 'people' nor 'nation', neither 'destiny' nor 'generic humanity', etc.) be presented as such? That is, what might a
politics be that does not stem from the will to realize an essence?" (*Inoperative*
xxxix–xl).

6 All translations of *El infarto del alma* are mine. In her impressive analysis of
this text Nelly Richard locates the medieval poetic tradition, mysticism, and
romanticism as its main literary/cultural models (258–59). While *El infarto del
alma* could be read as a peculiar commemoration of, for example, Ariosto, or
perhaps even of Ovid, I think that we need to evaluate the text in its relation
to Breton's *L'amour fou* and the importance of French surrealism in the book's
recuperation and representation of the Other.

7 As such, Errázuriz's portraits invert and displace the technical prowess and
complexity that characterized much surrealist photography. Quite simply,
there is no room in Putaendo for photomontage, multiple exposure, negative
printing, photo collage, and so forth. There is no working toward the avant-
garde aperture of the Other, only toward the experience of confronting the
Other's immediate exposure and presence. For the analysis of the historical
relationship between photography and surrealism, see Krauss.

8 What is the cause, the reason, or the affective law of commonality that lends
structure and signification to Putaendo's "community of those who have no
community"? Eltit moves toward these questions in the following passage:
"Further on from corridor to corridor, from stairway to stairway, in the middle
of courtyards I greet the second, the third, the tenth couple. There are so many
lovers I lose count. 'He gives me tea with bread and butter'. 'I take care of her'.
They feed each other, take care of each other. They feed each other a little and

take care of each other as best they can, and, as in an X-ray, I see the great metaphor that confirms every couple; life annexed to an other for a cup of tea and a piece of bread and butter. They are living an extraordinary love story confined in the hospital; chronic, indigent, slovenly, crippled, mutilated, staring, walking through all their dependencies with their belongings on their backs. Chileans forsaken by the hands of God and handed over to the rigid charity of the State" (n.p.; translation mine).

WORKS CITED

Achugar, Hugo. "Leones, cazadores e historiadores: A propósito de las políticas de la memoria y del conocimiento." *Revista iberoamericana* 180 (julio-setiembre 1997): 379–87.

Adorno, Theodor. "Culture and Administration." *The Culture Industry: Selected Essays on Mass Culture*. Ed. J. M. Bernstein. London: Routledge, 1991. 93–113.

———. *Negative Dialectics*. Trans. E. B. Ashton. New York: Continuum, 1973.

Aguilera Malta, Demetrio, Enrique Gil Gilbert, and Joaquín Gallegos Lara. *Los que se van: Cuentos del cholo y del montuvio*. Guayaquil: Editorial Claridad, 1970.

Ahmad, Aijaz. *In Theory: Classes, Nations, Literatures*. New York: Verso, 1992.

Alegría, Ciro. *El mundo es ancho y ajeno*. Santiago de Chile: Ediciones Ercilla, 1941.

Althusser, Louis. "Ideology and Ideological State Apparatuses (Notes towards an Investigation)." *Mapping Ideology*. Ed. Slavoj Žižek. New York: Verso, 1994.

Ansión, Juan. "Presentación." *Pishtacos de verdugos a sacaojos*. Ed. Juan Ansión. Lima: Tarea, 1989. 9–15.

Antezana, Luis H. "Sistema y proceso ideológicos en Bolivia (1935–1979)." *Bolivia, hoy*. Ed. René Zavaleta Mercado. Mexico City: Siglo XXI Editores, 1983. 60–84.

Arguedas, Alcides. *Pueblo enfermo*. Barcelona: Viuda de Luis Tasso, 1910.

Arguedas, José María. *Canto kechwa; con un ensayo sobre la capacidad de creación artística del pueblo indio y mestizo*. Lima: Ediciones Club del Libro Peruano, 1938.

———. *Formación de una cultura nacional indoamericana*. Mexico City: Siglo XXI Editores, 1989.

———. *Los ríos profundos*. Buenos Aires: Losada, 1958.

———. *Todas las sangres*. Buenos Aires: Losada, 1964.

———. *Yawar fiesta*. Lima: CIP, 1941.

———. *El zorro de arriba y el zorro de abajo*. Buenos Aires: Losada, 1971.

Argueta, Manlio. *One Day of Life*. Trans. Bill Brow. New York: Vintage International, 1991.

Arrighi, Giovanni. *The Long Twentieth Century: Money, Power, and the Origins of Our Times*. New York: Verso, 1994.

Avelar, Idelber. *The Untimely Present: Postdictatorial Latin American Fiction and the Task of Mourning*. Durham: Duke University Press, 1999.

Bajo la piel. Dir. Francisco Lombardi. Inca Films, 1996.

Balibar, Etienne. "Ambiguous Universality." *Differences: A Journal of Feminist Cultural Studies* 7.1 (1995): 48–74.

——. "From Class Struggle to Classless Struggle?" *Race, Nation, Class: Ambiguous Identities*. Etienne Balibar and Immanuel Wallerstein, trans. Chris Turner. New York: Verso, 1991. 153–84.

——. "The Nation Form: History and Ideology." *Race, Nation, Class: Ambiguous Identities*. Etienne Balibar and Immanuel Wallerstein, trans. Chris Turner. New York: Verso, 1991. 86–106.

Barrios de Chungara, Domitila. *"Si me permiten hablar . . .": Testimonio de Domitila, una mujer de las minas de Bolivia*. Ed. Moema Viezzer. Mexico City: Siglo XXI Editores, 1977.

Barry, Andrew, Thomas Osborne, and Nikolas Rose, eds. *Foucault and Political Reason: Liberalism, Neo-Liberalism, and Rationalities of Government*. Chicago: University of Chicago Press, 1996.

Bartra, Roger. *The Imaginary Networks of Political Power*. Trans. Claire Joysmith. New Brunswick: Rutgers University Press, 1992.

Bataille, Georges. *The Accursed Share, Volume 1*. Trans. Robert Hurley. New York: Zone Books, 1991.

Baudrillard, Jean. *The Illusion of the End*. Trans. Chris Turner. Stanford: Stanford University Press, 1994.

——. *The Transparency of Evil: Essays on Extreme Phenomena*. Trans. James Benedict. New York: Verso, 1993.

Beardsworth, Richard. *Derrida and the Political*. New York: Routledge, 1996.

Beasley-Murray, Jon. "The Constitution of Society: Pinochet, Postdictatorship, and the Multitude." Unpublished manuscript, 2000.

——. "Thinking Solidarity: Latinamericanist Intellectuals and *Testimonio*." *Journal of Latin American Cultural Studies* 7.1 (1998): 121–29.

Behar, Ruth. *Translated Woman: Crossing the Border with Esperanza's Story*. Boston: Beacon Press, 1993.

Belaúnde, Víctor Andrés. *Peruanidad, elementos esenciales*. Lima: Editorial Lumen, 1942.

Benjamin, Walter. "Critique of Violence." *Selected Writings: Volume 1, 1913–1926*. Ed. Marcus Bullock and Michael W. Jennings. Cambridge: Harvard University Press, 1996. 236–52.

——. "The Storyteller." *Illuminations*. Ed. Hannah Arendt, trans. Harry Zohn. New York: Schocken Books, 1969. 83–109.

——. "Theses on the Philosophy of History." *Illuminations*. Ed. Hannah Arendt, trans. Harry Zohn. New York: Schocken Books, 1969. 253–64.

Berger, Mark T. *Under Northern Eyes: Latin American Studies and U.S. Hegemony in the Americas, 1898–1990*. Bloomington: Indiana University Press, 1995.

Beverley, John. *Against Literature*. Minneapolis: University of Minnesota Press, 1993.

——. "The Real Thing." *The Real Thing: Testimonial Discourse and Latin America*. Ed. Georg Gugelberger. Durham: Duke University Press, 1996. 266–86.

———. *Subalternity and Representation: Arguments in Cultural Theory*. Durham: Duke University Press, 1999.

———. "Theses on Subalternity, Representation, and Politics." *Postcolonial Studies* 1.3 (1998): 305–19.

Beverley, John, and Hugo Achúgar, eds. "La voz del otro: Testimonio, subalternidad y verdad narrativa." *Revista de crítica literaria latinoamericana*. 18.36: 1992.

Beverley, John, and Marc Zimmerman. *Literature and Politics in the Central American Revolutions*. Austin: University of Texas Press, 1990.

Bhabha, Homi. *The Location of Culture*. New York: Routledge, 1994.

Binford, Leigh. *The El Mozote Massacre: Anthropology and Human Rights*. Tucson: University of Arizona Press, 1996.

Blanchot, Maurice. *The Infinite Conversation*. Trans. Susan Hanson. Minneapolis: University of Minnesota Press, 1993.

———. *The Unavowable Community*. Trans. Pierre Joris. Barrytown, NY: Station Hill Press, 1988.

Bonasso, Miguel. *Recuerdo de la muerte*. Mexico City: Ediciones Era, 1984.

Bourdieu, Pierre. *The Logic of Practice*. Trans. Richard Nice. Stanford: Stanford University Press, 1990.

———. "Rethinking the State: Genesis and Structure of the Bureaucratic Field." *Sociological Theory* 12.1 (1994): 1–18.

Breton, André. *L'amour fou*. Paris: Gallimard, 1975.

Britto García, Luis. *El poder sin la máscara: De la concertación populista a la explosión social*. Caracas: Alfadil Editores, 1989.

Bromley, Ray. "A New Path to Development? The Significance and Impact of Hernando de Soto's Ideas on Underdevelopment, Production, and Reproduction." *Economic Geography* 66 (October 1990): 328–48.

Brown, Michael F., and Eduardo Fernández. *War of Shadows: The Struggle for Utopia in the Peruvian Amazon*. Berkeley: University of California Press, 1991.

Brown, Wendy. *States of Injury: Power and Freedom in Late Modernity*. Princeton: Princeton University Press, 1995.

Burgos Debray, Elizabeth. "Prólogo." *Me llamo Rigoberta Menchú y así me nació la conciencia*. Havana: Casa de las Américas, 1983. 7–22.

———. "Rigoberta Menchú: La india rebelde." "Mujeres de fin de siglo" *El Mundo. La Revista*. April 14 (1996): 57–65.

Cardoso, Fernando Henrique, and Enzo Faletto. *Dependency and Development in Latin America*. Trans. Marjory Mattingly Urquidi. Berkeley: University of California Press, 1979.

Carpentier, Alejo. *Los pasos perdidos*. Madrid: Bruguera, 1979.

Castañeda, Jorge. *Utopia Unarmed: The Latin American Left after the Cold War*. New York: Knopf, 1993.

Catoira, Ricardo. *El sindicalismo boliviano: Testimonio de un dirigente gremial*. La Paz: Ediciones del Tigre de Papel, 1987.

Cattáneo, Atilio. *Entre rejas (memorias)*. Buenos Aires: Editorial El Chango, 1939.

Céspedes, Augusto. *Sangre de mestizos: Relatos de la guerra del Chaco*. Santiago de Chile: Nascimento, 1936.

Chakrabarty, Dipesh. *Rethinking Working-Class History: Bengal 1890–1940.* Princeton: Princeton University Press, 1989.

———. "Marx after Marxism: Subaltern Histories and the Question of Difference." *Polygraph* 6.7 (1993): 10–16.

Chirveches, Armando. *Casa solariega: Novela de costumbres latino americanas.* La Paz: Talleres Gráficos Marinoni, 1916.

Ciria, Alberto. *Política y cultura popular: La Argentina peronista 1946–1955.* Buenos Aires: Ediciones de la Flor, 1983.

Clarke, Ben, and Clifton Ross, eds. *Voice of Fire: Communiqués and Interviews from the Zapatista National Liberation Army.* Berkeley: New Earth Publications, 1994.

Collier, Ruth Berins, and David Collier. *Shaping the Political Arena.* Princeton: Princeton University Press, 1991.

Collins, Joseph, and John Lear. *Chile's Free-Market Miracle: A Second Look.* Oakland, Calif.: The Institute for Food and Development Policy, 1995.

Conley, Tom. "From Multiplicities to Folds: On Style and Form in Deleuze." *South Atlantic Quarterly* 96.3 (1997): 629–46.

Cornejo Polar, Antonio. *Escribir en el aire: Ensayo sobre la heterogeneidad socio-cultural en las literaturas andinas.* Lima: Editorial horizonte, 1994.

———. *La formación de la tradición literaria en el Perú.* Lima: Centro de Estudios y Publicaciones, 1989.

Coronil, Fernando. "Transculturation and the Politics of Theory: Countering the Center, Cuban Counterpoint." Introduction to *Cuban Counterpoint: Tobacco and Sugar* by Fernando Ortiz. Durham: Duke University Press, 1995. ix–lvi.

Corrigan, Philip, and Derek Sayer. *The Great Arch: English State Formation as Cultural Revolution.* Oxford: Basil Blackwell, 1985.

Cresap, Steven. "Nietzsche as Social Engineer: *The Birth of Tragedy*'s Critique of Action." *Rethinking Marxism* 6.3 (1993): 102–16.

Cruikshank, Barbara. "Revolutions Within: Self-Government and Self-Esteem." *Foucault and Political Reason: Liberalism, Neo-Liberalism, and Rationalities of Government.* Ed. Andrew Barry, Thomas Osborne, and Nikolas Rose. Chicago: University of Chicago Press, 1996. 231–51.

Cuadra, José de la. *Los sangurimas: Novela montuvia.* Guayaquil: Editorial Noticia, 1939.

da Cunha, Euclides. *Rebellion in the Backlands.* Trans. Samuel Putnam. Chicago: University of Chicago Press, 1984.

Dalton, Roque. "All." *Poems.* Trans. Richard Schoaf. Willimantic: Curbstone Press, 1984: 42–43.

Dámaso Martínez, Carlos. *Hay cenizas en el viento.* Buenos Aires: Centro Editor de América Latina, 1982.

Danner, Mark. *The Massacre at El Mozote: A Parable of the Cold War.* New York: Vintage Books, 1994.

Davis, Mike. *City of Quartz.* New York: Random House, 1990.

———. *Ecology of Fear: Los Angeles and the Imagination of Disaster.* New York: Metropolitan Books, 1998.

DeCesare, Donna. "The Children of War: Street Gangs in El Salvador." *NACLA Report on the Americas* 32.1 (July/August 1998): 21–29.

———. "Deported 'Home' to Haiti." *NACLA Report on the Americas* 32.3 (November/December 1998): 6–10.

de Certeau, Michel. *The Practice of Everyday Life.* Trans. Steven F. Rendall. Berkeley: University of California Press, 1984.

Deleuze, Gilles. "Postscript on the Societies of Control." *October* 59 (1992): 3–7.

Deleuze, Gilles, and Félix Guattari. *Anti-Oedipus: Capitalism and Schizophrenia.* Trans. Robert Hurley, Mark Seem, and Helen Lane. Minneapolis: University of Minnesota Press, 1983.

———. *A Thousand Plateaus: Capitalism and Schizophrenia.* Trans. Brian Massumi. Minneapolis: University of Minnesota Press, 1987.

Derrida, Jacques. "Cogito and the History of Madness." *Writing and Difference.* Trans. Alan Bass. Chicago: University of Chicago Press, 1978. 31–63.

———. "From Restricted to General Economy: A Hegelianism without Reserve." *Writing and Difference.* Trans. Alan Bass. Chicago: University of Chicago Press, 1978. 251–77.

———. *Politics of Friendship.* Trans. George Collins. New York: Verso, 1997.

———. *Specters of Marx: The State of the Debt, the Work of Mourning, and the New International.* Trans. Peggy Kamuf. New York: Routledge, 1994.

———. "Ulysses Gramophone: Hear Say Yes in Joyce." *A Derrida Reader: Between the Blinds.* Ed. and trans. Peggy Kamuf. New York: Columbia University Press, 1991. 569–98.

de Soto, Hernando. *The Other Path: The Invisible Revolution in the Third World.* Trans. June Abbott. New York: Harper and Row, 1990.

Dirlik, Arif. "The Postcolonial Aura: Third World Criticism in the Age of Global Capitalism." *Critical Inquiry* 20 (winter 1994): 328–56.

D'Souza, Dinesh. *Illiberal Education: The Politics of Race and Sex on Campus.* New York: Free Press, 1991.

Dunn, Timothy J. *The Militarization of the U.S.-Mexico Border, 1978–1992: Low-Intensity Conflict Doctrine Comes Home.* Austin: Center for Mexican American Studies, 1996.

Durand, Francisco. "The Growth and Limitations of the Peruvian Right." *The Peruvian Labyrinth: Polity, Society, Economy.* Ed. Maxwell A. Cameron and Philip Mauceri. University Park: Pennsylvania State University Press, 1997. 152–75.

Dussel, Inés, and Pablo Pineau. "De cuando la clase obrera entró al paraíso: La educación técnica estatal en el primer peronismo." *Discursos pedagógicos e imaginario social en el peronismo (1945-1955).* Ed. Adriana Puiggrós. Buenos Aires: Editorial Galerna, 1995. 107–73.

Dussell, Enrique. "Beyond Eurocentrism: The World-System and the Limits of Modernity." *The Cultures of Globalization.* Ed. Fredric Jameson and Masao Miyoshi. Durham: Duke University Press, 1998. 3–31.

Eagleton, Terry. *Ideology: An Introduction.* New York: Verso, 1992.

Eltit, Diamela. *Sacred Cow.* Trans. Amanda Hopkinson. New York: Serpent's Tail, 1995.

Eltit, Diamela, and Paz Errázuriz, eds. *El infarto del alma*. Santiago de Chile: Francisco Zegers Editor, 1994.

Encinas, Enrique, Fernando Mayorga, and Enrique Birhuet, eds. *Jinapuni: Testimonio de un dirigente campesino*. La Paz: Hisbol, 1989.

EZLN. *Documentos y comunicados: 1 de enero–8 de agosto de 1994*. Mexico City: Ediciones Era, 1994.

Fanon, Frantz. *The Wretched of the Earth*. Trans. Constance Farrington. New York: Grove Press, 1963.

Feldman, Allen. *Formations of Violence: The Narrative of the Body and Political Terror in Northern Ireland*. Chicago: University of Chicago Press, 1991.

Flores Galindo, Alberto. *Tiempo de plagas*. Lima: El Caballo Rojo Ediciones, 1988.

Fowler, William R. Jr. *The Cultural Evolution of Ancient Nahua Civilization: The Pipil-Nicarao of Central America*. Norman: University of Oklahoma Press, 1989.

Frampton, Kenneth. "Towards a Critical Regionalism: Six Points for an Architecture of Resistance." *The Anti-Aesthetic: Essays on Postmodern Culture*. Ed. Hal Foster. Seattle: Bay Press, 1983. 16–30.

Franco, Jean. "Latin American Intellectuals and Collective Identity." *Social Identities* 3.2 (1997): 265–74.

——. "What's Left of the Intelligentsia? The Uncertain Future of the Printed Word." *NACLA Report on the Americas* 28.2 (September/October 1994): 16–21.

Fynsk, Christopher. "Experiences of Finitude." Foreword to *The Inoperative Community* by Jean-Luc Nancy. Minneapolis: University of Minnesota Press, 1991. vii–xxxv.

Gallegos, Rómulo. *Doña Bárbara*. Barcelona: Araluce, 1929.

Gálvez, José. *Posibilidad de una genuina literatura nacional: El peruanismo literario*. Lima: Casa Editora M. Moral-Pando, 1915.

García, J. Uriel. *El nuevo indio: Ensayos indianistas sobre la sierra surperuana*. Cuzco: H. G. Rozas Sucesores, 1937.

García Canclini, Néstor. *Consumidores y ciudadanos: Conflictos multiculturales de la globalización*. Mexico City: Grijalbo, 1995.

——. *Hybrid Cultures: Strategies for Entering and Leaving Modernity*. Trans. Christopher L. Chiappari and Silvia L. López. Minneapolis: University of Minnesota Press, 1995.

——. "Memory and Innovation in the Theory of Art." *South Atlantic Quarterly* 92.3 (1993): 423–43.

Gil Gilbert, Enrique. *Yunga: Cuentos*. Guayaquil: Trópico, 1933.

Gilly, Adolfo. "Las transfiguraciones del nacionalismo mexicano." *Nexos* 207 (1995): 61–64.

González Prada, Manuel. "Discurso en el Politeama." *Obras*. Vol. 1 Ed. Luis Alberto Sánchez. Lima: Ediciones COPE, 1985: 86–92.

——. "Nuestros indios." *Conciencia intelectual de América*. Ed. Carlos Ripoll. New York: Eliseo Torres, 1974. 193–205.

Gordon, Colin. "Governmental Rationality: An Introduction." *The Foucault*

Effect: Studies in Governmentality. Ed. Graham Burchell, Colin Gordon, and
  Peter Miller. Chicago: University of Chicago Press, 1991. 1–51.

Gramsci, Antonio. *Selection from the Prison Notebooks*. Ed. and trans. Quintin
  Hoare and Geoffrey Nowell Smith. New York: International Publishers, 1971.

Greca, Alcides. *Tras el alambrado de Martín García*. Buenos Aires: Editorial Tor,
  1934.

Guattari, Félix. *Chaosmosis: An Ethico-Aesthetic Paradigm*. Trans. Paul Bains and
  Julian Pefanis. Bloomington: Indiana University Press, 1995.

——. "Machinic Heterogenesis." *Rethinking Technologies*. Ed. Verena Andermatt
  Conley. Minneapolis: University of Minnesota Press, 1993. 13–27.

Gugelberger, Georg, ed. *The Real Thing: Testimonial Discourse and Latin America*.
  Durham: Duke University Press, 1996.

Gugelberger, Georg, and Michael Kerney, eds. "Voices of the Voiceless in
  Testimonial Literature." Special issue of *Latin American Perspectives* 70–71
  (summer/fall 1991).

Guha, Ranajit. *Elementary Aspects of Peasant Insurgency in Colonial India*. New
  Delhi: Oxford University Press, 1983.

——. "On Some Aspects of the Historiography of Colonial India." *Selected
  Subaltern Studies*. Ed. Ranajit Guha and Gayatri Chakravorty Spivak. New
  York: Oxford University Press, 1988. 37–43.

——. "Preface." *Selected Subaltern Studies*. Ed. Ranajit Guha and Gayatri
  Chakravorty Spivak. New York: Oxford University Press, 1988. 35–36.

Hall, Stuart. "Old and New Identities: Old and New Ethnicities." *Cultures,
  Globalization, and the World System*. Ed. Anthony King. Minneapolis:
  University of Minnesota Press, 1997. 41–68.

Halperín Donghi, Tulio. *The Contemporary History of Latin America*. Ed. and
  trans. John Charles Chasteen. Durham: Duke University Press, 1993.

Hardt, Michael. "The Withering of Civil Society." *Social Text*. 45 (winter 1995):
  27–44.

Hardt, Michael, and Antonio Negri. *Labor of Dionysus: A Critique of the State-
  Form*. Minneapolis: University of Minnesota Press, 1994.

Harrison, Lawrence E. *The Pan-American Dream: Do Latin America's Cultural
  Values Discourage True Partnership with the United States and Canada?* New
  York: Basic Books, 1997.

Harvey, David. *Justice, Nature, and the Geography of Difference*. Oxford: Blackwell
  Publishers, 1996.

Heidegger, Martin. *Nietzsche, Volumes 1 and 2*. Ed. David Farrell Krell, trans.
  Joan Stambaugh, David Farrell Krell, and Frank A. Capuzzi. San Francisco:
  Harper Collins, 1987.

Hellinger, Daniel. "Populism and Nationalism in Venezuela: New Perspectives on
  Acción Democrática." *Latin American Perspectives*. 11.4 (1984): 33–59.

Hitchcock, Peter. "The Othering of Cultural Studies." *Third Text* 25 (1993–94):
  11–20.

Huntington, Samuel P. *The Clash of Civilizations and the Remaking of World
  Order*. New York: Simon and Schuster, 1996.

Ianni, Octavio. *Formación del Estado populista en América Latina*. Mexico City: Ediciones Era, 1975.

Icaza, Jorge. *Huasipungo*. Buenos Aires: Editorial Sol, 1936.

James, Daniel. *Resistance and Integration: Peronism and the Argentine Working Class, 1946–1976*. Cambridge: Cambridge University Press, 1988.

Jameson, Fredric. "Actually Existing Marxism." *Polygraph* 6/7 (1993): 170–95.

———. "Culture and Finance Capital." *The Cultural Turn: Selected Writings on the Postmodern 1983–1998*. New York: Verso, 1998. 136–61.

———. "On *Cultural Studies*." *The Identity in Question*. Ed. John Rajchman. New York: Routledge, 1995. 251–95.

———. *The Political Unconscious: Narrative as a Socially Symbolic Act*. Ithaca: Cornell University Press, 1981.

———. *The Seeds of Time*. New York: Columbia University Press, 1994.

———. "Transformations of the Image in Postmodernity." *The Cultural Turn: Selected Writings on the Postmodern, 1983–1998*. New York: Verso, 1998. 93–135.

Jaramillo Alvarado, Pío. *El indio ecuatoriano: Contribución al estudio de la sociología indo-americana*. Quito: Talleres Gráficos del Estado, 1936.

Klein, Herbert. *Bolivia: The Evolution of a Multi-Ethnic Society*. New York: Oxford University Press, 1992.

Kowalski, B. J. "Name Game." *World Press Review* 45.7 (July 1988): 24.

Kraniauskas, John. "*Cronos* and the Political Economy of Vampirism: Notes on a Historical Constellation." *Cannibalism and the Colonial World*. Ed. Francis Barker, Peter Hulme, and Margaret Iversen. Cambridge: Cambridge University Press, 1998. 142–57.

———. "Globalization Is Ordinary: The Transnationalization of Cultural Studies." *Radical Philosophy* 90 (1998): 9–19.

———. "Hybridity in a Transnational Frame: Latin-Americanist and Postcolonial Perspectives on Cultural Studies." *Nepantla: Views from South* 1.1 (2000): 111–37.

Krauss, Rosalind. "Photography in the Service of Surrealism." *L'amour fou: Photography and Surrealism*. Rosalind Krauss and Jane Livingston. New York: Abbeville Press, 1985. 15–42.

Laclau, Ernesto. *New Reflections on the Revolution of Our Time*. New York: Verso, 1990.

———. " 'The Time Is Out of Joint.' " *Emancipation(s)*. New York: Verso, 1996. 66–83.

———. "Towards a Theory of Populism." *Politics and Ideology in Marxist Theory: Capitalism, Fascism, Populism*. London: Verso, 1977. 143–98.

———. "Universalism, Particularism, and the Question of Identity." *Emancipation(s)*. New York: Verso, 1996. 20–35.

Laclau, Ernesto, and Chantal Mouffe. *Hegemony and Socialist Strategy: Towards a Radical Democratic Politics*. New York: Verso, 1985.

Lamborghini, Osvaldo. "El fiord." *Novelas y cuentos*. Barcelona: Ediciones del Serbal, 1988. 17–34.

Lara, Jesús. *Repete: Diario de un hombre que fue a la guerra del Chaco.* Cochabamba: Los Amigos del Libro, 1972.

——. *Yawarninchij=nuestra sangre: Novela quechua.* Cochabamba: Los Amigos del Libro, 1974.

Larsen, Neil. *Reading North by South: On Latin American Literature, Culture, and Politics.* Minneapolis: University of Minnesota Press, 1995.

Latin American Subaltern Studies Group. "Founding Statement." *boundary 2* 20.3 (1993): 110–21.

Lechner, Norbert. "Politics in Retreat: Redrawing Our Political Maps." *The End of Politics? Explorations into Modern Antipolitics.* Ed. Andreas Schedler. New York: St. Martin's Press, 1997. 168–84.

——. "¿Por qué la política ya no es lo que fue?" *Nexos* 216 (1995): 63–69.

Legrás, Horacio. "Subalternity and Negativity" *Dispositio/n* 22.49 (2000): 83–102.

Levinson, Brett. "The Death of the Critique of Eurocentrism: Latinamericanism as a Global Praxis/Poiesis." *Revista de estudios hispánicos* 31 (winter 1997): 169–201.

——. "The Latin Americanist BPL, or, The Market, the Jewish Question, Postcolonial Studies." *Dispositio/n* 22.49 (2000): 63–82.

Lloyd, David, and Paul Thomas. *Culture and the State.* New York: Routledge, 1998.

Lomnitz Adler, Claudio. *Exits from the Labyrinth: Culture and Ideology in the Mexican National Space.* Berkeley: University of California Press, 1992.

Lungo Uclés, Mario. "Building an Alternative: The Formation of a Popular Project" *The New Politics of Survival: Grassroots Movements in Central America.* Ed. Minor Sinclair. New York: New York Monthly Review Press, 1995. 153–79.

——. *El Salvador in the Eighties: Counterinsurgency and Revolution.* Ed. Arthur Schmidt, trans. Amelia F. Shogan. Philadelphia: Temple University Press, 1996.

Madsen, Douglas, and Peter G. Snow. *The Charismatic Bond: Political Behavior in Time of Crisis.* Cambridge: Harvard University Press, 1991.

Mangone, Carlos, and Jorge A. Warley. *Universidad y peronismo (1946–1955).* Buenos Aires: Centro Editor de América Latina, 1984.

Marcus, Bruce. *Nicaragua: The Sandinista People's Revolution.* New York: Pathfinder Press, 1985.

Marechal, Leopoldo. *Adán Buenosayres.* Buenos Aires: Editorial Sudamerica, 1966.

Mariátegui, José Carlos. *The Heroic and Creative Meaning of Socialism: Selected Essays of José Carlos Mariátegui.* Ed. and trans. Michael Pearlman. Atlantic Highlands, NJ: Humanities Press International, 1996.

——. "Prólogo." In *Tempestad en los Andes* by Luis E. Valcárcel. Lima: Editorial Universo, 1972.

——. *Seven Interpretive Essays on Peruvian Reality.* Trans. Marjory Urquidi. Austin: University of Texas Press, 1971.

Marichal, Carlos. "The Vicious Cycles of Mexican Debt." *NACLA Report on the Americas* 31.3 (November/December 1997): 25–31.

Marof, Tristán. *La justicia del inca*. Brussels: La Edición Latino Americana Librería Falk Fils, 1926.

———. *La verdad socialista en Bolivia*. La Paz: Talleres Gráficos de el Trabajo, 1938.

Martín Barbero, Jesús. "La comunicación plural: Paradojas y desafios." *Nueva sociedad* 140 (1996): 60–69.

Martínez, Rubén. *The Other Side: Fault Lines, Guerrilla Saints, and the True Heart of Rock 'n' Roll*. New York: Verso, 1992.

Martínez Estrada, Ezequiel. *Muerte y transfiguración de Martín Fierro*. Mexico City: Fondo de Cultura Económica, 1948.

———. *¿Qué es esto? Catilinaria*. Buenos Aires: Editorial Lautaro, 1956.

Martini, Juan Carlos. *La vida entera*. Barcelona: Bruguera, 1981.

Marx, Karl. *Capital: A Critique of Political Economy; The Process of Capitalist Production*. Ed. Frederick Engels, trans. Samuel Moore and Edward Aveling. New York: Random House, 1906.

———. *Capital, Volume 2*. Trans. David Fernbach. London: Penguin/New Left Review, 1978.

———. *The Eighteenth Brumaire of Louis Bonaparte*. New York: International Publishers, 1994.

———. *Grundrisse: Foundations of the Critique of Political Economy*. Trans. Martin Nicolaus. New York: Random House, 1973.

Marx, Karl, and Friedrich Engels. *The German Ideology, Part 1*. Ed. C. J. Arthur. New York: International Publishers, 1970.

———. *The Manifesto of the Communist Party*. Trans. Paul M. Sweezy. New York: Monthly Review Press, 1964.

Matos Mar, José. *Desborde popular y crisis del Estado: El nuevo rostro del Perú en la década de 1980*. Lima: Instituto de Estudios Peruanos, 1984.

Matto de Turner, Clorinda. *Aves sin nido*. Lima: Ediciones PEISA, 1973.

McSherry, J. Patrice. "The Emergence of 'Guardian Democracy.'" *NACLA Report on the Americas* 32.3 (November/December 1998): 16–24.

Menchú, Rigoberta. *Me llamo Rigoberta Menchú y así me nació la conciencia*. Ed. Elizabeth Burgos Debray. Havana: Casa de las Américas, 1983.

Mignolo, Walter. *The Darker Side of the Renaissance: Literacy, Territoriality, and Colonization*. Ann Arbor: University of Michigan Press, 1995.

Millaman, Rosamel. "Chile's Mapuches Organize against NAFTA." *NACLA Report on the Americas* 29.5 (March/April 1996): 30–31.

Moraña, Mabel. "El boom del subalterno." *Revista de crítica cultural* 15 (1997): 48–53.

———. *Literatura y cultura nacional en Hispanoamérica (1910–1940)*. Minneapolis: Institute for the Study of Ideologies and Literatures, 1984.

Moreiras, Alberto. "The Aura of Testimonio." *The Real Thing: Testimonial Discourse and Latin America*. Ed. Georg Gugelberger. Durham: Duke University Press, 1996. 192–224.

———. *The Exhaustion of Difference: The Politics of Latin American Cultural Studies.* Durham, N.C.: Duke University Press, 2001.

———. *Tercer espacio: Literatura y duelo en América Latina.* Santiago de Chile: LOM Ediciones, 1999.

Morote Best, Efraín. "El degollador (ñakaq)." *Tradición: Revista peruana de cultura.* 2.4 (1952): 67–91.

Monsiváis, Carlos. " 'Just Over that Hill': Notes on Centralism and Regional Cultures." *Mexico's Regions: Comparative History and Development.* Ed. Eric Van Young. San Diego: Center for U.S.-Mexican Studies, 1992. 247–57.

———. *Mexican Postcards.* Trans. John Kraniauskas. New York: Verso, 1997.

Moulian, Tomás. *Chile actual: Anatomía de un mito.* Santiago de Chile: LOM Ediciones, 1997.

Nagengast, Carol. "Militarizing the Border Patrol." *NACLA Report on the Americas* 32.3 (November/December 1998): 37–41.

Nancy, Jean-Luc. "The Deleuzian Fold of Thought." *Deleuze: A Critical Reader.* Ed. Paul Patton. Cambridge: Blackwell Publishers, 1996. 107–13.

———. *The Inoperative Community.* Ed. Peter Connor, trans. Peter Connor, Lisa Garbus, Michael Holland, and Simona Sawhney. Minneapolis: University of Minnesota Press, 1991.

———. *The Sense of the World.* Trans. Jeffrey S. Librett. Minneapolis: University of Minnesota Press, 1997.

———. "War, Law, Sovereignty—*Techné.*" *Rethinking Technologies.* Ed. Verena Andermatt Conley. Minneapolis: University of Minnesota Press, 1993. 28–58.

Negri, Antonio. "What Can the State Still Do?" *Polygraph* 10 (1998): 9–20.

Nietzsche, Friedrich. *The Birth of Tragedy.* Ed. Michael Tanner, trans. Shaun Whiteside. London: Penguin, 1993.

———. *Untimely Meditations.* Ed. Daniel Breazeale, trans. R. J. Hollingdale. Cambridge: Cambridge University Press, 1997.

O'Hanlon, Rosalind, and David Washbrook. "After Orientalism: Culture, Criticism, and Politics in the Third World." *Society for Comparative Study of Society and History* 34 (1992): 141–67.

Oliver-Smith, Anthony. "The Pishtaco: Institutionalized Fear in Highland Peru." *Journal of American Folklore* 82 (1969): 363–68.

Ortiz, Adalberto. *Yuyungo, historia de un negro, una isla y otros negros.* Buenos Aires: Editorial Americalee, 1943.

Ortiz, Fernando. *Cuban Counterpoint: Tobacco and Sugar.* Trans. Harriet de Onís. 1940; Durham: Duke University Press, 1995.

Ortiz, Renato. "Cultura, modernidad e identidades." *Nueva sociedad* 137 (1995): 17–23.

———. *Mundialização e cultura.* Sao Paolo: Brasiliense, 1994.

Pacari, Nina. "Taking on the Neoliberal Agenda." *NACLA Report on the Americas* 29.5 (March/April 1996): 23–32.

Paige, Jeffrey. *Coffee and Power: Revolution and the Rise of Democracy in Central America.* Cambridge: Harvard University Press, 1997.

Pandey, Gyanendra. "In Defense of the Fragment: Writing about Hindu-Muslim

Works Cited

Riots in India Today." *A Subaltern Studies Reader, 1986–1995.* Ed. Ranajit
Guha. Minneapolis: University of Minnesota Press, 1997. 1–33.

Pasquino, Pasquale. "Theatricum Politicum: The Genealogy of Capital—Police
and the State of Prosperity." *The Foucault Effect: Studies in Governmentality.*
Ed. Graham Burchell, Colin Gordon, and Peter Miller. Chicago: University of
Chicago Press, 1991. 105–18.

Pelupessy, Wim. *The Limits of Economic Reform in El Salvador.* New York: St.
Martin's Press, 1997.

Pérez Firmat, Gustavo. *The Cuban Condition: Translation and Identity in Modern
Cuban Literature.* Cambridge: Cambridge University Press, 1989.

Perón, Juan Domingo. *Filosofía peronista.* Freeland: Buenos Aires, 1974.

Piglia, Ricardo. *La ciudad ausente.* Buenos Aires: Editorial Sudamericana, 1992.

———. *Crítica y ficción.* Buenos Aires: Ediciones Siglo Veinte, 1990.

———. *Respiración artificial.* Buenos Aires: Editorial Pomaire, 1980.

Piglia, Ricardo, and Juan José Saer. *Diálogo.* Santa Fe: Universidad Nacional del
Litoral, 1995.

Poppe, René. *Narrativa minera boliviana.* La Paz: Ediciones Populares
Camarlinghi, 1983.

Porras Barrenechea, Raúl. *El cronista, Felipe Huamán Poma de Ayala.* Lima: Sine
nomine, 1971.

Portocarrero Maisch, Gonzalo, Isidro Valentín, and Soraya Irigoyen. *Sacaojos:
Crisis social y fantasmas coloniales.* Lima: Tarea, 1991.

Prakash, Gyan. "The Impossibility of Subaltern History." *Nepantla: Views from
South* 1.2 (2000): 287–94.

Puig, Manuel. *El beso de la mujer araña.* Barcelona: Seix Barral, 1976.

Quijano, Aníbal. *Dominación y cultura: Lo cholo y el conflicto cultural en el Perú.*
Lima: Mosca Azul Editores, 1980.

———. *El Fujimorismo y el Perú.* Lima: Seminario de estudios y debates
socialistas, 1995.

Rabaté, Jean-Michel. "Lapsus ex machina." *Post-Structuralist Joyce: Essays from
the French.* Ed. Derek Attridge and Daniel Ferrer. New York: Cambridge
University Press, 1984. 79–101.

———. "Narratology and the Subject of *Finnegans Wake*." *James Joyce: The
Centennial Symposium.* Ed. Morris Beja, Phillip Herring, Maurice Harmon,
and David Norris. Urbana: University of Illinois Press, 1986. 137–46.

Rama, Angel. "José María Arguedas transculturador." *Señores e indios.*
Montevideo: Arca, 1976. 7–40.

———. *Transculturación narrativa en América Latina.* México, Siglo XXI: 1982.

———. *La novela en América Latina: Panoramas 1920–1980.* Veracruz:
Universidad Veracruzana/Fundación Angel Rama, 1986.

Reagan, Ronald. "Central America: Defending Our Vital Interests." Washington,
D.C.: United States Department of State, Bureau of Public Affairs, April 27,
1983.

———. "Saving Freedom in Central America." Washington, D.C.: United States
Department of State, Bureau of Public Affairs, July 18, 1983.

———. "Strategic Importance of El Salvador and Central America." Washington,

D.C.: United States Department of State, Bureau of Public Affairs, March 10, 1983.

Richard, Nelly. *Residuos y metáforas: Ensayos de crítica cultural sobre el Chile de la Transición*. Santiago de Chile: Editorial Cuarto Propio, 1998.

Riva Agüero, José de la. *Carácter de la literatura del Perú independiente*. Lima: Editorial Rosay, 1905.

――. *El Perú, histórico y artístico: Influencia y descendencia de los montañeses en él*. Santander: Sociedad de Menéndez y Pelayo, 1921.

Roach, Joseph. *Cities of the Dead: Circum-Atlantic Performance*. New York: Columbia University Press, 1996.

Robinson, William I. *Promoting Polyarchy: Globalization, U.S. Intervention, and Hegemony*. Cambridge: Cambridge University Press, 1996.

Rojas Rimachi, Emilio. "Los 'sacaojos': El miedo y la cólera." *Pishtacos de verdugos a sacaojos*. Ed. Juan Ansión. Lima: Tarea, 1989. 141–48.

Rowe, William, and Vivian Schelling. *Memory and Modernity: Popular Culture in Latin America*. Verso: London, 1993.

Rubin, Jeffrey. "Decentering the Regime: Culture and Regional Politics in Mexico." *Latin American Research Review*. 31.3 (1996): 85–126.

Saer, Juan José. *El entenado*. Mexico City: Folios Ediciones, 1983.

――. *Nadie nada nunca*. Mexico City: Siglo XXI, 1980.

Saldívar, José David. *Border Matters: Remapping American Cultural Studies*. Berkeley: University of California Press, 1997.

Sánchez, Luis Alberto. *Indianismo e indigenismo en la literatura peruana*. Lima: Mosca Azul Editores, 1981.

Santí, Enrico Mario. "Latinamericanism and Restitution." *Latin American Literary Review* 20.40 (1992): 88–96.

Santiago, Silviano. "Atração do Mundo: Políticas de Identidade e de Globalização na Moderna Cultura Brasileira." *Gragoatá* 1.2 (1996): 31–53.

Sarlo, Beatriz. "Argentina under Menem: The Aesthetics of Domination." *NACLA Report on the Americas*. 28.2 (September/October 1994): 33–37.

――. *La imaginación técnica: Sueños modernos de la cultura argentina*. Buenos Aires: Ediciones Nueva Visión, 1992.

Scheper-Hughes, Nancy. *Death without Weeping: The Violence of Everyday Life in Brazil*. Berkeley: University of California Press, 1993.

Schultz, George. "Struggle for Democracy in Central America." Washington D.C.: United States Department of State, Bureau of Public Affairs, April 15, 1983.

Schutte, Ofelia. *Cultural Identity and Social Liberation in Latin American Thought*. Albany: State University of New York Press, 1993.

Schwarz, Roberto. *Misplaced Ideas: Essays on Brazilian Culture*. Ed. John Gledson. New York: Verso, 1992.

Sebreli, Juan José. *El asedio a la modernidad: Crítica del relativismo cultural*. Buenos Aires: Editorial Sudamericana, 1991.

Sifuentes, Eudosio. "La continuidad de la historia de los pishtacos en los 'Robaojos' de hoy." *Pishtacos de verdugos a sacaojos*. Ed. Juan Ansión. Lima: Tarea, 1989. 149–54.

Works Cited

Sigal, Silvia. *Intelectuales y poder en la década del sesenta*. Buenos Aires: Puntosur Editores, 1991.

Sinclair, Minor, ed. *The New Politics of Survival: Grassroots Movements in Central America*. New York: Monthly Review Press, 1995.

Sklair, Leslie. *Sociology of the Global System*. New York: Harvester Wheatsheaf, 1991.

Sklodowska, Elzbieta. *Testimonio hispanoamericano*. New York: Peter Lang, 1992.

Sommer, Doris. "No Secrets." *The Real Thing: Testimonial Discourse and Latin America*. Ed. Georg Gugelberger. Durham: Duke University Press, 1996. 130–57.

——. "Resisting the Heat: Menchú, Morrison, and Incompetent Readers." *Cultures of United States Imperialism*. Ed. Amy Kaplan and Donald E. Pease. Durham: Duke University Press, 1993. 407–32.

Soriano, Osvaldo. *Cuarteles de invierno*. Barcelona: Bruguera, 1982.

——. *No habrá más penas ni olvido*. Barcelona: Bruguera, 1982.

Spivak, Gayatri Chakravorty. "Can the Subaltern Speak?" *Marxism and the Interpretation of Culture*. Ed. Lawrence Grossberg and Cary Nelson. Urbana: University of Illinois Press, 1988. 271–313.

——. "Subaltern Studies: Deconstructing Historiography." *Selected Subaltern Studies*. Ed. Ranajit Guha and Gayatri Chakravorty Spivak. New York: Oxford University Press, 1988. 3–32.

Stein, Steve. *Populism in Peru: The Emergence of the Masses and the Politics of Social Control*. Madison: University of Wisconsin Press, 1980.

Stoll, David. *Rigoberta Ménchu and the Story of All Poor Guatemalans*. Boulder: Westview Press, 1999.

Surin, Kenneth. "On Producing the Concept of a Global Culture." *South Atlantic Quarterly* 94.4 (1995): 1179–99.

Szeminsky, Jan. "Why Kill the Spaniard? New Perspectives on Andean Insurrectionary Ideology in the Eighteenth Century." *Resistance, Rebellion, and Consciousness in the Andean Peasant World, Eighteenth to Twentieth Centuries*. Ed. Steve J. Stern. Madison: University of Wisconsin Press, 1987.

Tamayo, Franz. *Creación de la pedagogía nacional*. La Paz: Ministerio de Educación, Bellas Artes y Asuntos Indígenas de Bolivia, 1944.

Taussig, Michael. *The Magic of the State*. New York: Routledge, 1997.

——. *Shamanism, Colonialism, and the Wild Man: A Study in Terror and Healing*. Chicago: University of Chicago Press, 1987.

Thompson, Martha. "Repopulated Communities in El Salvador" *The New Politics of Survival: Grassroots Movements in Central America*. Ed. Minor Sinclair. New York: Monthly Review Press, 1995. 109–51.

Thurner, Mark. *From Two Republics to One Divided: Contradictions of Postcolonial Nationmaking in Andean Peru*. Durham: Duke University Press, 1997.

Valcárcel, Luis E. *Tempestad en los Andes*. Lima: Editorial Universo, 1972.

Valenzuela, Luisa. *Cambio de armas*. Hanover, N.H.: Ediciones del Norte, 1982.

Vallejo, César. *El tungsteno*. Lima: Hora del Hombre, 1948.

Van Young, Eric. "Introduction: Are Regions Good to Think?" *Mexico's Regions:*

Comparative History and Development. Ed. Eric Van Young. San Diego: Center for U.S.-Mexican Studies, 1992. 1–36.

Vargas Llosa, Mario. *Death in the Andes*. Trans. Edith Grossman. New York: Penguin, 1996.

———. *A Fish in Water: A Memoir*. Trans. Helen Lane. New York: Farrar, Straus, and Giroux, 1994.

———. *La utopía arcaica: José María Arguedas y las ficciones del indigenismo*. Mexico City: Fondo de Cultura Económica, 1996.

Vega, Garcilaso de la. *Los comentarios reales de los incas*. Lima: Sanmartín, 1918–20.

Vidal, Hernán, and René Jara, eds. *Testimonio y literatura*. Minneapolis: Institute for the Study of Ideologies and Literature, 1986.

Vilas, Carlos. "Economic Restructuring, Neoliberal Reforms, and the Working Class in Latin America." *Capital, Power, and Inequality in Latin America*. Ed. Sandor Halebsky and Richard L. Harris. Boulder: Westview Press, 1995. 137–63.

———. "Neoliberal Social Policy: Managing Poverty (Somehow)." *NACLA Report on the Americas*. 29.6 (May/June 1996): 16–25.

Viñas, David. *Cuerpo a cuerpo*. Mexico City: Siglo XXI, 1979.

———. *Literatura argentina y política II: De Lugones a Walsh*. Buenos Aires: Editorial Sudamericana, 1996.

Wachtel, Nathan. *Gods and Vampires: Return to Chipaya*. Trans. Carol Volk. Chicago: University of Chicago Press, 1994.

Walsh, Rodolfo. *Operación masacre y el expediente Livraga*. Buenos Aires: Continental Service, 1964.

Webb, Gary. *Dark Alliance: The CIA, the Contras, and the Crack Cocaine Explosion*. New York: Seven Stories Press, 1998.

Weismantel, Mary. "White Cannibals: Fantasies of Racial Violence in the Andes." *Identities: Global Studies in Culture and Power*. Ed. Nina Glick Schiller. 4.1 (1997): 9–43.

Williams, Gareth. "The Fantasies of Cultural Exchange in Latin American Subaltern Studies." *The Real Thing: Testimonial Discourse and Latin America*. Ed. Georg Gugelberger. Durham: Duke University Press, 1996. 225–53.

Williams, Philip J., and Knut Walter. *Militarization and Demilitarization in El Salvador's Transition to Democracy*. Pittsburgh: University of Pittsburgh Press, 1997.

Williamson, John. "The Progress of Policy Reform in Latin America." *Latin American Adjustment: How Much Has Happened*. Ed. John Williamson. Washington, D.C.: Institute for International Economics, 1990. 358–78.

Wright, Winthrop. *Café con leche: Race, Class, and National Image in Venezuela*. Austin: University of Texas Press, 1990.

Yúdice, George. "Civil Society, Consumption, and Governmentality in an Age of Global Restructuring: An Introduction." *Social Text* 45 (Winter 1995): 1–25.

———. "The Expediency of Culture." Unpublished manuscript, 1999.

———. "Postmodernism in the Periphery." *South Atlantic Quarterly* 92.3 (1993): 543–56.

Works Cited

———. "We Are *Not* the World." *Social Text* 31–32 (1992): 202–16.

Zapata, Gastón Antonio. "Sobre ojos y pishtacos." *Pishtacos de verdugos a sacaojos.* Ed. Juan Ansión. Lima: Tarea, 1989. 137–40.

Zimmerman, Marc. *Literature and Resistance in Guatemala: Textual Modes and Cultural Politics from El Señor Presidente to Rigoberta Menchú.* 2 vols. Athens: Ohio University Center for International Studies, 1995.

Žižek, Slavoj. *Tarrying with the Negative: Kant, Hegel, and the Critique of Ideology.* Durham: Duke University Press, 1993.

231–72. *See also Cholaje;* García
Canclini, Néstor; Savage/nomadic
hybridity

Center-periphery; Disciplinarity; Representation; *Testimonio*

South Asian Subaltern Studies Group, 3

Spivak, Gayatri C., 10, 15, 19, 70, 90, 95, 100, 149, 174, 275, 287, 312–13 n.13

Stein, Steve, 48–49, 59

Surin, Kenneth, 74–75, 80, 100

Taussig, Michael, 188, 191, 194, 346–47 n.24

Testimonio, 2, 13, 46, 72, 77–78, 83–84, 88–92, 203–13, 216, 310–11 n.6, 311 n.7, 311–12 n.10. *See also* Disciplinarity; Populism; Representation

Transculturation, 13, 23–70, 253–55, 337 n.22. *See also* Fictive ethnicity;

Indigenism; Modernity; National-popular, the; People, the; Region

University, 48–51, 63–64. *See also* Cold War; Critical reason; Disciplinarity; Hegemony: post-hegemony

Vargas Llosa, Mario, 16, 227–32, 236–48, 266, 343–45 n.15

Vilas, Carlos, 129, 132–33, 318–19 n.11, 322 n.21, 323 n.22

Viñas, David, 52, 307 n.15

Yúdice, George, 25, 109, 112, 119, 124–25, 130, 133, 279, 320 n.13, 322 n.19, 326–27 n.7

Zapatistas, 121–23, 320–21 n.16, 321–22 n.17. *See also* Micro-identity

Gareth Williams is Assistant Professor of Romance
Languages and Literatures and Latin American Studies
at Wesleyan University.

Library of Congress Cataloging-in-Publication Data
Williams, Gareth
The other side of the popular : neoliberalism and
subalternity in Latin America / Gareth Williams.
p. cm.
Includes bibliographical references and index.
ISBN 0-8223-2925-5 (cloth : alk. paper) —
ISBN 0-8223-2941-7 (pbk. : alk. paper)
1. Latin America—Civilization—20th century.   2. Latin
America—History—1948–1980.   3. Latin America—
History—1980–   4. Social change—Latin America.
5. Capitalism—Social aspects.   6. Liberalism—Social
aspects.   7. Latin American literature—History and
criticism.   I. Title.
F1414.2 .W55   2002
980.03'3—dc21   2001007556